Biomedical Entanglements

Person, Space and Memory in the Contemporary Pacific

Series editors: Prof. Jürg Wassmann (University of Heidelberg, Institute of Anthropology), Dr. Verena Keck (Goethe University Frankfurt, Institute of Anthropology)

Advisory board:
Prof. Pierre R. Dasen (University of Geneva, Department of Anthropology of Education and Cross-Cultural Psychology), Prof. Donald H. Rubinstein (University of Guam), Prof. Robert Tonkinson (The University of Western Australia, Department of Anthropology), Prof. Peter Meusburger (University of Heidelberg, Department of Economic and Social Geography), Prof. Joachim Funke (University of Heidelberg, Department of Psychology)

Volume 1
Experiencing New Worlds
Jürg Wassmann and Katharina Stockhaus

Volume 2
Person and Place: Ideas, Ideals and Practice of Sociality on Vanua Lava, Vanuatu
Sabine C. Hess

Volume 3
Landscapes of Relations and Belonging: Body, Place and Politics in Wogeo, Papua New Guinea
Astrid Anderson

Volume 4
Foodways and Empathy: Relatedness in a Ramu River Society, Papua New Guinea
Anita von Poser

Volume 5
Biomedical Entanglements: Conceptions of Personhood in a Papua New Guinea Society
Franziska A. Herbst

Biomedical Entanglements
Conceptions of Personhood in a Papua New Guinea Society

Franziska A. Herbst

berghahn
NEW YORK • OXFORD
www.berghahnbooks.com

First published in 2017 by
Berghahn Books
www.berghahnbooks.com

©2017, 2020 Franziska A. Herbst
First paperback edition published in 2020

All rights reserved. Except for the quotation of short passages
for the purposes of criticism and review, no part of this book
may be reproduced in any form or by any means, electronic or
mechanical, including photocopying, recording, or any information
storage and retrieval system now known or to be invented,
without written permission of the publisher.

Library of Congress Cataloging-in-Publication Data

Names: Herbst, Franziska A., author.
Title: Biomedical entanglements : conceptions of personhood in a Papua New Guinea society / Franziska A. Herbst.
Other titles: Person, space and memory in the contemporary Pacific ; v. 5.
Description: New York : Berghahn Books, 2016. | Series: Person, space and memory in the contemporary Pacific ; volume 5 | Includes bibliographical references and index.
Identifiers: LCCN 2016025398| ISBN 9781785332340 (hardback) | ISBN 9781785332357 (ebook)
Subjects: | MESH: Health Knowledge, Attitudes, Practice | Sociological Factors | Personhood | Health Services | Papua New Guinea
Classification: LCC R683.P26 | NLM W 85 | DDC 610.9953--dc23
LC record available at https://lccn.loc.gov/2016025398

British Library Cataloguing in Publication Data

A catalogue record for this book is available from the British Library

ISBN: 978-1-78533-234-0 (hardback)
ISBN 978-1-78920-822-1 (paperback)
ISBN: 978-1-78533-235-7 (ebook)

Dedicated to the memory of my brother Kueni Semi,
who passed away all too young

Contents

List of Maps, Figures, and Illustrations	viii
Acknowledgments	x
Language Notes and Conventions	xiii
List of Abbreviations	xvi
Introduction	1
Chapter One. Ethnography and the Fieldwork Setting	13
Chapter Two. Bunapas Health Center	27
Chapter Three. Technologies of Disenchantment: Medical Pluralism through a Series of Lenses	48
Chapter Four. The Web of Care Relationships	99
Chapter Five. Ingenious Women: Making Biomedical Reproductive Health Care Meaningful	134
Conclusion	191
Glossary	207
References	211
Index	231

Maps, Figures, and Illustrations

Maps
1.1. Lower Ramu region. 19
2.1. Bunapas Health Center catchment area. 28

Figures
3.1. Phase model of Rita's perspective on her illness, the biomedical perspective, and the employed treatment. This figure correlates information on the illness phases as described by Rita herself, the biomedical perspective (as outlined in her clinic card), and treatment employed from 1987 to 2010. 69
4.1. First dish moving in each direction between two inpatients and a health worker. The numbers (1) to (3) indicate the chronological sequence. 111

Illustrations
2.1. Giri nurse attends to patients at Bunapas Health Center outpatient clinic (2009). 29
2.2. Bunapas Health Center ward (2009). The sticks fixed to the sides of the beds are substitutes for drip stands. 32
2.3. Mothers at Unkanan Outreach Clinic (2009). Mothers turn in their children's clinic cards. The village health aid arranges the cards in piles. 36
2.4. Family gathers around a young male patient in the Bunapas Health Center ward (2009). The man was in a fight at Base Camp and was attacked with a bush knife. He has been admitted with a severe laceration of the buttocks. 45
3.1. Malaria rapid diagnostic test (2009). A health extension officer pricks a girl's finger to obtain a drop of blood for a malaria rapid diagnostic test. 54
3.2. Spirit platform (2007). Relatives stand in front of the platform on which offerings to the bush spirits have been made. Note the ladder for the spirits to climb up onto the platform. 86

4.1.	Sandra goes to Bunapas Health Center to bring Benjamin sago pudding (2009). She carries a netbag with empty containers to fetch water from one of the health center's tanks. She balances the sago dish on her head, smokes a hand-rolled cigarette, and has a baby carrier strapped on with her son inside.	102
4.2.	Diana's mother dishing out sago pudding in the health center's makeshift kitchen (2009). The sago will be accompanied by coconut cream soup with cane grass inflorescences, native spinach (*Amaranthus gangeticus*), and the paired edible leaves of the *Gnetum gnemon* tree (tulip).	112
5.1.	Drai Kaikai serves *fav bigbigi mbah* to Brian (2007). Drai Kaikai is balancing Brian's dish of sago pudding, bamboo shoots, and a very few wild fig leaf buds on her head.	141
5.2.	Virtuous Giri dancers (2007). The dancers' skin gleams in the sun. Their movements are fast and weightless.	144
5.3.	Menarcheal woman washing her body with wild cordyline leaves (2007).	147
5.4.	Woman combing out the fiber from a pandanus aerial root with a knife to make thread (2007).	173
5.5.	My brother and sister-in-law's five-month-old son Mboruni nestling inside a netbag (2011). Note the cloth between the infant and the netbag protecting the baby's skin from being "eaten" (kaikai) by the rough plastic fabric from which this netbag is made.	174
6.1.	National Department of Health poster: "Pasin sanguma i no save kamapim sik TB" (2010).	199

Acknowledgments

Most of all I am indebted to the people of Giri—who include Giri patients and medical staff—in particular, Regene, who generously shared their time, knowledge, and hospitality with me and who are largely disguised through pseudonyms in the results portion of this book. I remain immensely grateful for the insights they gave me into their perspectives on health, illness, and personhood and into their experiences with the body and biomedicine.

I further offer sincere acknowledgment to all other patients of Bunapas Health Center and to the non-Giri Bunapas Health Center and Modilon General Hospital staff. Special thanks go to the Lower Ramu–based medical personnel who greatly helped me in my work. From Modilon General Hospital, I thank Ilalon Daing of the clinic for sexually transmitted diseases, Bernard Belari of the general medical ward, and Susan Baniau, Terence Kuaru, and Martina Tolane of the psychiatric unit, for insightful conversations.

I am profoundly indebted to Jürg Wassmann and Verena Keck for their constant support and encouragement. I thank them for sharing their knowledge and experiences prior to my departure and for visiting me in Giri. I am deeply grateful for Andrew Strathern's and Pamela Stewart's interest in my work. I would also like to express my appreciation to Andrew for reading through an earlier version of this book.

My research was carried out as part of the Person, Space and Memory in the Contemporary Pacific (Wassmann & Stockhaus 2007) project at the University of Heidelberg, which was initiated by Jürg Wassmann and funded by the VolkswagenStiftung. Research for this book was made possible by a two-year grant from the VolkswagenStiftung. Return research visits to Papua New Guinea were enabled by the German Academic Exchange Service (DAAD), in the project Subject-Related Partnerships with Institutions of Higher Education and Developing Countries, which gave me the opportunity to guest lecture in the Faculty of Arts at Madang's Divine Word University in 2009 and 2011.

It was only because of the goodwill of the National Research Institute of Papua New Guinea that I was granted permission to come to Papua New Guinea. I am especially grateful to Jim Robins for giving me his support throughout the years. I thank the Madang provincial administrator, the late Joseph Dorpar, for permitting research activities in Bogia District. Vigamba Gingin ("Peter Dare"), then Giri ward member and vice-president of the Yawar Local Level Government Council, is thanked for supporting my research from the outset and inviting me to return to Giri for follow-up research visits.

I owe many thanks to the Modilon General Hospital attending staff and the Madang Provincial Health Office and, in particular to Markus Kachau, the Madang provincial health advisor, for approval to conduct research at Bunapas Health Center, access medical information from the Bunapas area, and interview Giri patients being treated at Modilon General Hospital. Furthermore, I wish to express my gratitude to Paul Mabong, Deputy Director of Health of the Madang Provincial Administration, for providing me with an excellent overview of the biomedical facilities throughout the province.

There are other people and institutions to acknowledge: Nicolas Hamny of the Madang Planning Office, himself from Giri, provided census data for the Lower Ramu area. The staff of the Papua New Guinea National Archives in Port Moresby made accessible patrol reports of the Lower Ramu region from the 1940s through the 1970s. Franz Göttlicher of the German Federal Archives in Berlin kindly forwarded correspondence between the Imperial Colonial Office and the governor of German New Guinea from 1912 and 1913. Jan and the late Eunice Messersmith of the Pioneer Bible Translators office in Madang Town made available material in the Kire language. Val Zerna granted me access to the Churches of Christ archives in Adelaide in 2009. I am especially grateful to her and her team for scanning and sending me countless articles from their journal, The Australian Christian, on the mission's activities in the Lower Ramu area.

I owe a particularly huge debt of gratitude to Frank Beale, Lou Beresford, and Janet Hunting of the Australian Churches of Christ mission for their willingness to share their experiences as missionary and mission nurses in the Lower Ramu region, respectively, and for the valuable information they provided about the introduction of biomedicine to Giri. In 2009, Frank and his wife, Ros, and Lou and Burnett Beresford welcomed me to their homes in Maryborough and Gympie with great hospitality, and they sat down with me for interview sessions that lasted several days.

During my stays in Madang Town and Port Moresby, I met several people who supported me in the most diverse ways: in 2006, Sam Mbamak from Bosmun village facilitated my first contact with Giri villagers. Catherine Levy provided comment on linguistic data and draft interview guides. Meri and Monty Armstrong accommodated me for several weeks at their Madang home in 2007. Besides, Meri assisted me in locating various publications in Divine Word University's Archbishop A. Noser Memorial Library, a reference library dedicated to Papua New Guinea studies. Trevor Hattersley kept two large cardboard boxes with my belongings for more than a year and was always there to give me a lift. Just like Diane and Mike Cassell, he made me feel at home in Madang Town.

I was extremely fortunate to meet Tracy Danielle Winfrey at Divine Word University. Over the years, she and her parents, Anastasia and Jim Winfrey, became close friends. Thanks are due to them for their warmth and hospitality. In Germany, Anastasia and Jim kept me updated on Madang happenings and Giri affairs and were my communication link to the Giri people. In 2012, I gladly seized the opportunity to reciprocate some of the hospitality I had received when Tracy's sister Priscilla visited me in Heidelberg. In Port Moresby, Michelle Carumba and Frieda Popen were the most amazing hosts, and they were also some of my most entertaining guests in Madang Town. Upon my first arrival in Madang Town, Patrick Gesch promptly created an occasion for me to practice my Tok Pisin with his Sepik friends. Mark Solon provided extensive, insightful conversations about my fieldwork situation and organized transportation from Giri to Madang Town in 2007. Both Mark and Pat invited me to their homes on numerous occasions and always had a sympathetic ear.

Several people read and commented on my texts during the various stages of work leading up to this book and should be thanked: Julia Thiesbonenkamp-Maag, Almut Schneider, and Anthony Pickles. To Julia also go my cordial thanks for readily discussing many aspects of this book, from the early stages of writing onward; her input contributed significantly to the development of this book. Additionally, I wish to acknowledge Anthony's help in language revision of two draft chapters. In regard to proofreading, mention must further be made of Michael Cofrin and Paul Fletcher of the Heidelberg University Graduate Academy. I gratefully acknowledge Valerie Appleby and Kelly Burch's excellent scrutiny of the language and fine copyediting.

The anonymous Berghahn reviewers contributed valuable time and helpful suggestions to improve the book, though the surviving shortcomings are my own. I thank Molly Mosher, Duncan Ranslam, Jessica Murphy, and Alina Zihharev of Berghahn Books for their hard work and continuous support.

Pamela Swadling provided kind assistance in making sense of the few available bits of archaeological information I had on the Giri region. Anita von Poser was always happy to discuss my observations and insights; over the many years, she was very helpful and supportive, offering encouraging suggestions. Moreover, Anita and her husband Alexis drew my attention to a number of important historical sources, and thanks are due to them for lending me some difficult to access literature.

I thank my friends Frauke Meeuw and Charlotte von Schuckmann for their listening ears and for the innumerable discussions leading to new reflections on topics. Danilo D'Andrea came into my life near the end of writing this book. His love and companionship nurtured my spirit through the final steps. Finally, I want to thank my family for believing that this book was possible. Thanks go to my twin sister, Bernadette Herbst, for her encouragement throughout the book process. For their unfailing support and interest in my work, I thank my parents, Barbara Puschmann-Herbst and Volkhard Herbst. Mum and Dad, I owe everything to you.

Language Notes and Conventions

During my fieldwork, I communicated with people in the major lingua franca of Papua New Guinea, Tok Pisin (Melanesian Pidgin). Virtually everyone in Giri understands and speaks the language, though the degree of fluency with which people speak the language varies. In my fieldwork, people of the oldest generation had learned Kire, the vernacular language of Giri, as their first language.

Like their ancestors before them, people of the oldest generation have been exposed to Tok Pisin in various situations, both inside and outside of Giri, throughout their lives. In the years before the Pacific War (1941–45), Giri contract workers learned Tok Pisin on plantations along the north coast and brought it back to the Giri villages. Some men were trained as catechists in the Catholic mission headquarters at Alexishafen (near Madang Town) or learned carpentry from the missionaries and worked for years, or even decades, in Madang Town, the provincial capital. Then the first (Catholic) mission station and school was established in Giri in the early 1950s.

The current generation's command of Tok Pisin depends much on their outside experience, involvement with missionaries in Giri, and visits to mission schools. In daily interactions with their peers, they usually speak Kire. To their children and grandchildren, they speak Kire and, to varying degrees, Tok Pisin. However, even if spoken to in Kire, their children and grandchildren may reply in Tok Pisin. Frequently, elderly people slip Kire words or phrases into a conversation occurring predominantly in Tok Pisin. People also adopted this style when speaking to me, in their attempts to teach me the vernacular language. My elderly mother Thiap (who is introduced below) would often summon me, "*Sim bisane* i kam" (Give me the small knife), or ask me, while patting down my netbag, "*Puk* i stap insait long *mbathar* bilong yu?" (Do you have areca nuts in your netbag?).

Currently, most children in Giri acquire Tok Pisin as their first language. Yet many children continue to learn Kire alongside Tok Pisin. Particularly in the Giri villages of Kimning and Birap, I noticed that many adults in their thirties and forties often spoke Kire to their children, whereas Tok Pisin appeared to be significantly more prominent in Giri 1 and 2. (The numbering of several Giri villages stems from the Australian colonial era.) To some children, Kire functions as a second mother tongue, with Tok Pisin being the first; others learn their local language as a second language, with Tok Pisin again being the first. Most children develop proficiency in understanding Kire, but not all speak it with any degree of fluency. It is also not uncommon for children to develop an active command of their vernacular language only through vernacular (tok ples) language instruction in the two years of elementary school.

In sum, it appears that Giri children grow up with an increasingly passive understanding of Kire and do not often use the language actively. Giri villages are currently shifting from the vernacular to Tok Pisin in a very similar manner to that described by Kulick (1992) for Gapun (a sociolinguistic group inhabiting a region between the Lower Ramu and Lower Sepik rivers). Moreover, many in the younger generations have achieved English language literacy through public school education.

In different phases of my research project, I received vernacular language training from various interlocutors. But my command of Kire was limited to making village small talk, exchanging compliments, answering people's questions on my comings and goings, and asking these very questions of them. I was usually able to discern the topic of a Kire conversation, but I could not follow every argument. Yet, collection of indigenous terms and discussion of their meanings was an integral part of my research. I paid particular attention to vernacular words that centered on conceptions of health, illness, medicine, and the body (i.e., my research focus).

Apart from English interviews with the former Australian personnel of the Churches of Christ mission, which I conducted in Queensland, I carried out all of my interviews in Tok Pisin. In group interviews involving elderly persons, elderly interlocutors would sometimes speak Kire, and younger participants would directly translate during the interview. Often, fruitful discussions arose between the elderly and their "interpreters," with the latter asking the former a series of intriguing questions.

The Pioneer Bible Translators, an evangelical, nondenominational mission, fixed the vernacular language of the Giri in writing. Pioneer Bible Translators (Anonymous [1992] 1997) introduced a Kire alphabet, which I use in this book to represent Kire words. The alphabet has sixteen consonants (*b, d, f, g, h, k, m, n, ŋ, p, r, s, t, v, w, z*) and six vowels (*a, e, i, ɨ, o, u*), but the English letters *c, j, l, q, x,* and *y* are not found. A single letter indicates short vowels, and long vowels are written with double letters.

For the most part, I follow these spelling conventions here, as the Giri widely accept, use, and teach them at Giri elementary schools. Yet, I have made two changes. First, I do not use the letter *w,* because it is interchangeable with the letter *v,* and very few Giri appear to use it. Second, I include another phonetic symbol; the inverted *e* sound (or schwa [ə]) is not properly represented in the alphabet proposed by the Pioneer Bible Translators. Here, I follow the conventions of Stanhope (1972: 51), a medical missionary who lived in Giri from the early to mid-1960s and penned an introductory article on the Kire language in which he made use of the schwa symbol.

Consonants are pronounced as they are in English, with the exception of the interchangeable utilization of *v* and *w*, which I just mentioned. A symbol that may be unfamiliar to some readers is the *ŋ*. This is how it is pronounced:
ŋ—as in to*ng*ue; e.g., *fiaŋ* (dog).

Vowel pronunciation, including the symbols *ə* and *ɨ*, is as follows:
a—as in c*a*r; e.g., *dam* (pig).
ə—as in *a*bout, or the French p*eu*; e.g., *mbəgam* (fish).
e—as in m*e*t; e.g., *vove* (white cockatoo).
i—as in mach*i*ne; e.g., *pi* (to eat).
ɨ—as in the French r*ue*, or the German f*ür*; e.g., *nimsɨk* (bandicoot).
o—as in p*o*t; e.g., *ndo* (bush fowl).
u—as in B*u*ddha; e.g., *sum* (wound).

Hyphens represent glottal stops in vowel clusters, as, for instance, in *mba-atik* (bad, dangerous, malevolent, evil). However, all graphizations are to be taken with caution, as they are no more than mere approximations of an oral language. Furthermore, within the Giri, there are differences in the rendition of phonemes and some vocabulary items.

In this text, words in Kire are italicized and are listed in the glossary. Tok Pisin words are presented in a sans-serif font. Words from other vernacular languages appear in quotation marks. Tok Pisin words and words from other vernacular languages do not appear in the glossary. My Tok Pisin orthography is based on the conventions outlined in Mihalic's ([1971] 1986) *The Jacaranda Dictionary and Grammar of Melanesian Pidgin* and the *Papua New Guinea Tok Pisin English Dictionary* published by Oxford University Press (Baing et al. 2008). If my spelling of a word differs from that given in the two dictionaries, I have reflected the pronunciation my Giri interlocutors used. Kire and Tok Pisin words are not anglicized; they appear without the English plural marker -*s*. My interlocutors' speech was translated into English. I performed all translations myself.

Abbreviations

BBA	birth before arrival
BHC	Bunapas Health Center
DOTS	Directly Observed Treatment, Short-Course
GoPNG	Government of Papua New Guinea
MGH	Modilon General Hospital
PMV	public / passenger motor vehicle
TB	tuberculosis
WHO	World Health Organization

Introduction

At the time of our first conversation about her illness, Rita was thirty-eight years old and married with five children. On that day in April 2007, she described her illness with the following words: "I have difficulties breathing in... When I am ridden by shortness of breath, I am not able to sleep... My throat rattles... I will faint from shortness of breath." Her health status had deteriorated over many years and finally reached its nadir. In the same colloquy, Rita dated the onset of her respiratory illness (*bibi tivi*; literally: "short breath") to "some time after 1996."

When I later studied her clinic card, I discovered that Rita had employed biomedical care for respiratory problems at a much earlier point than the point she had marked as the onset of her illness. Her clinic card showed that she had complained about a cough in twelve of her twenty-one visits to biomedical institutions in 1987 and 1988. Another twenty visits in which she described symptoms ranging from a cough to a productive cough (including a cough that produced white sputum and blood and a cough associated with restlessness at night), shortness of breath, and chest pain followed until the end of 1995. Altogether, between 3 July 1987 and 20 May 2009, Rita made 162 visits to biomedical institutions; in sixty-seven of these visits, she addressed her respiratory problems.

Throughout the years of 1987 to 1995, Rita took a variety of biomedical drugs—cough linctuses, Procillin (procaine penicillin), chloramphenicol, and amoxicillin. Apart from the medications prescribed by health workers, Rita drew on a local herbal remedy to treat her cough. She drank the extraction of a thick leaf called *kamfarkhem*. She also bought a liquid made from tree bark from two Giri women (at least that is what she thought was the ingredient). Rita assumed that her illness was a physical disorder that would respond to biomedical drugs and herbal remedies.

What happened in 1996 that changed Rita's view of her complaints and made her determine that year as the starting point of her respiratory illness? Norma, an older woman from Giri 1 who was related to Rita through her husband, told Rita's husband, Tim, that Rita had been ensorcelled in 1996. Norma elucidated that a man had followed Rita on her way to a pond in the swamps and stolen her underpants while Rita bathed and did her laundry. Norma even named the man. Tim passed on the information to his wife, and Rita reminisced about the respective day. She had noted that her underpants were missing when she got dressed after the bath. Rita was alarmed because she knew that her *fava ŋan* was absorbed into the fabric of her underwear.

The concept of *fava ŋan*—body substance adhering to one's skin—refers to female sexual secretions; but other bodily substances, such as sweat (*zoruk*), urine (*sik*), sperm (*nzip*), and saliva (*hui-in*), are also designated as *fava ŋan*. The Giri believe that their *fava ŋan* is attached to items that have been in contact with their body and thus absorbed their bodily fluids; for example, areca nut husks, cigarette butts, or clothes. The same applies to excretable parts of the body; for instance, fingernails or hair. From anthropological literature, we are familiar with the sorcerer's utilization of personal leavings, such as food remains, excreta, or hair clippings (Eves 1995: 218; Fortune [1932] 1989: 150; Hogbin 1935/36: 20; Lindenbaum 1979: 65; Patterson 1974: 141; Stephen 1996: 87, 93).

That Rita's underpants were nowhere to be found was one of the two reasons Rita accorded credibility to Norma's story. Second, Norma's kinship ties to Rita and her husband rendered her believable. Having heard Norma's report, Rita perceived her health status to be deteriorating, and she began to categorize her illness as local in nature—caused by poison sorcery and thus not receptive to biomedical cures.

I consulted Rita's clinic card again. Would the data support Norma's claim of ensorcellment? Did Rita's health status worsen in 1996 or later? On Rita's clinic card, no data were available for 1996, and only five visits—just two of them for her respiratory illness—were registered in 1997. But if we look at the three-year period from 1995 to 1998, it stands out that this was a phase in which the health care personnel shifted her treatment from cough to asthma medication. In 1995, Rita was given, for the first time, amoxicillin and Septrine (antibiotics)—not exclusively to treat her respiratory complaints but also for urinary tract infections.

In the same year, she began taking salbutamol tablets—medication given to treat bronchospasms (a symptom of, for example asthma or obstructive pulmonary disease). In 1998, she received her first inhaler for asthma treatment. The first entry of the word "asthma" on her clinic card was also made in 1998. She was diagnosed with "chronic asthma," though a question mark was placed after the diagnosis. It appears from Rita's clinic card that her visits to the health center in 1998 were almost exclusively for respiratory problems—thirteen out of fourteen visits.

The same entry from 1998, which mentions chronic asthma, is accompanied by a remark: "[She] went to see an herbal officer at Nubia in 1996; ever since then she kept on going on and off." Her encounter with the herbal specialist—surprisingly referred to as the "herbal officer," here, a term I had never heard that gives it an oddly formal touch—took place before she had received Norma's information. Rita later explained to me that herbalists would not be able to help her if she had been ensorcelled, as they do not have any power against sorcery. At the time of her journey to Nubia, Rita was in search of an alternative to the health center's cough medication and the *kamfarkhem* extraction.

This section of a vignette that is more thoroughly presented in chapter 3 illustrates how biomedicine is embraced in a local Giri context and how the version of biomedicine practiced in the area and local concepts, relationships, and practices are entangled in a single medical system. In chapter 3, we see that Rita felt it necessary to find out whether she suffered from a local or a foreign illness. Moreover, we learn that Rita utilized a biomedical technology (the X-ray) as a means to disclose whether she was suffering from a local or foreign illness.

Other case studies in the book reveal similarly complex entanglements of Giri ways of being, personhood, and social relationships with biomedicine. The fundamental question that guided my work was How do the Giri reinterpret and construct biomedicine against the backdrop of local conceptualizations of the person in health and illness? The structure of the introduction is derived from the two major themes inherent in this question; I start with a review of anthropological inquiry into biomedicine and then turn to anthropological investigations of (particularly Melanesian) personhood.

Anthropological Inquiry into Biomedicine

Recently, biomedicine in its cultural contexts has come under wide anthropological gaze. In the preface to their *Encyclopedia of Medical Anthropology*, Ember and Ember provide a succinct definition of the term:

> The professional medicine of Western cultures has been called "biomedicine," because it mostly deals with the biology of the human body. But biomedicine, like the medicine of other cultures, is also influenced by conditions and beliefs in the culture, and therefore reflects the value and norms of its creators. So, if biomedicine is socially constructed and not just based on science, its beliefs and practices may partly derive from assumptions and biases in the culture. (2004b: xiii)

However, at the outset, it was not biomedicine that attracted anthropologists' attention but indigenous medical systems. Even after medical anthropology evolved into a specialized field in the 1970s, inquiry remained focused on indigenous medicine. Van der Geest surmised that the lack of anthropological research interest in biomedicine at that time was related to "too little exotic attraction for the ethnographer" (1984: 60). What is more, it seems that the self-perceived scientific objectivity of biomedicine kept anthropologists from turning their attention to the examination of biomedicine as a sociocultural system for quite a long time. In Western societies, participants commonly think of biomedicine as factual knowledge (Amarasingham Rhodes 1996: 166–67) and illness as a natural occurrence (Hahn & Kleinman 1983: 313).

Western biomedicine is founded on the philosopher/mathematician René Descartes's (1596–1650) argument that mind, "a pure thinking entity" (Risse 1993: 14–15), and body, "ruled by universal laws of matter and motion" (14), can be separated. Descartes's conceptual framework, culminating in the Enlightenment, has promoted a mechanical approach to the human body: "The body was conceived of as a vast hydraulic network of hollow pipes, moving blood and nervous fluid in the circulatory and nervous systems under the influences of the mind" (15). The Cartesian mind-body dichotomy holds that "diseases . . . are physical entities occurring in specific locations within the body" (Amarasingham Rhodes 1996: 167); as part of the natural realm, the body is "knowable and treatable in isolation" (Hahn & Kleinman 1983: 313). Hence, in Western societies, biomedicine and the body have been conceived of as independent entities, not sociocultural artifacts.

Eventually, anthropological investigation into biomedicine was ignited in the early 1980s by two seminal articles (Hahn & Kleinman 1983; Young 1982) and a special issue of *Culture, Medicine and Psychiatry*, edited by Gaines and Hahn (1982). These works called researchers to treat and explore (European and North American) biomedicine as a sociocultural system and, as such, one medical tradition[1]—one ethnomedicine—among others.[2] This approach has strongly stimulated comparative studies of biomedicine and other medical systems (Gaines & Davis-Floyd 2004: 96). Biomedicine, rooted in Western industrialized countries, is not practiced and consumed uniformly throughout the world.

It is multiple: *"not one, but many medicines"* (Hahn & Kleinman 1983: 315). When transplanted, it takes new forms (see, e.g., Gaines & Davis-Floyd 2004: 104; Kleinman 1995: 24–25; Lock & Nguyen 2010: 5–6; Saillant & Genest 2007: xxii–xxiii). A quote from DelVecchio Good aptly captures this view: "Although biomedicine is fostered through an international political economy of biotechnology and by an international community of medical educators and bioscientists, it is taught, practiced, organized and consumed in local contexts" (1995: 461). Furthermore, we must add another dimension: today, biomedical knowledge is produced and technologically innovated not only in Western countries but also elsewhere (Kleinman 1995: 25).

My major objective was to study biomedicine in its local entanglements. This book explores how Giri consume biomedicine, both inside and outside of biomedical institutions. A substantial amount of research was carried out at the local health center (Bunapas Health Center) and the provincial hospital (Modilon General Hospital). Therewith, this work forms part of a growing body of anthropological research that studies the domain of biomedicine by way of investigating biomedical institutions. What is more, this book is at once the ethnography of a rural health center in Papua New Guinea (Bunapas Health Center) and a medical ethnography of contemporary Giri. Anthropologists have only recently begun to carry out ethnographic studies in Papua New Guinea biomedical settings, and academic literature in this field is just beginning to emerge (Keck 2005; Street 2009, 2011, 2012, 2014; van Amstel & van der Geest 2004).

The paucity of ethnographic studies in medical settings is characteristic of not only the Papua New Guinea context but also the non-Western world more generally (van der Geest & Finkler 2004). Even anthropologists working in Western countries have only recently turned toward description and interpretation of hospital cultures, having only gained greater access to Western clinical settings since the mid-1970s (Young 1982: 258). Yet, anthropologists and other social scientists have predominantly centered their studies on physician-patient relationships and other microscopic settings (Baer et al. 1997: 223). Hospitals, as such, have not been the focus of much anthropological research; though, as van der Geest and Finkler suggested, hospitals are "premier institution[s] of biomedicine" (2004: 1995).

Highlighting this relative scarcity of ethnographic studies situated in hospitals, van der Geest and Finkler (2004) called for more ethnographic studies in biomedical settings in a "Hospital Ethnography" issue of *Social Science & Medicine*. Perhaps, they surmised, a major reason for the prevailing absence of hospital ethnographies may be related to the fact that hospitals have, for a long time, been regarded as "identical clones of a global biomedical model" (2004: 1996) and "places where established universal principles of biomedicine were practised uniformly" (1995). Their central concern was to show that hospital life reflects the features of its society. Therewith, they turned against the idea that the hospital is a culture set apart from life outside the hospital—a view that was prominent among sociologists, who had begun to scrutinize hospitals in the late 1950s.

Sociological description and analysis of life in hospitals (e.g., Caudill 1958; Fox 1959; Laub Coser 1962; Roth 1963; Stanton & Schwartz 1954) were concerned with exploring what G. Sykes called "a society within a society" (1958: xii). Instead of treating the hospital ward as a "tight little island," a "world unto itself" (Laub Coser 1962: 3), van der Geest and Finkler took the view that the hospital is "an important part . . . of the 'mainland'" (2004: 1998). As such, hospital ethnographies "open . . . a window to the society and culture in which the hospital is situated" (2004: 1998). A particular strength of their edition is that it embeds wards and hospitals in the wider sociocultural context. The authors disclosed how values, rules, and notions of the outside world pervade biomedical institutions.

Four years later, another special issue on hospital ethnography (with van der Geest among the editors) appeared—this time in *Anthropology & Medicine*—though with a different focus. The editors (Long et al. 2008: 73) noted in their introductory article that only scant ethnographic research had been directed toward relationships other than those at patient-clinician interfaces. They advocated the inclusion of a multiplicity of stakeholders, such as nurses, health managers, allied health personnel, relatives, friends, advocates, and support groups. Among the few pieces of work that have dealt with this variety of actors is Zaman's (2005) ethnography of an orthopedic ward in a Bangladeshi hospital that considers—aside from patients and doctors—relatives, ward boys, cleaners, gatekeepers, and nurses. Most recently, ethnographies of two African hospitals, one in Kenya (Mulemi 2008, 2010) and one in Tanzania (Sullivan 2011, 2012), have appeared, adding to the growing body of literature on non-Western hospitals and responding to the calls of the 2004 and 2008 hospital ethnography special issues.

A principal objective of this book is to contribute to the qualitative literature of medical settings in non-Western countries. This work was written with the objective of illuminating how Giri actors give local character to two establishments in which biomedicine is practiced. Yet, my work stands apart from the contemporary hospital ethnographies by Zaman, Mulemi, and Sullivan, in that my point of departure is not so much the medical institution itself as my Giri interlocutors, whom I followed in their quest for diagnosis and medical treatment.

My study was primarily focused on Bunapas Health Center (BHC), which is the sole health center of the Giri region and beyond. Eventually, my interlocutors also led me to the provincial hospital, Modilon General Hospital (MGH). My intention was not to write a comprehensive ethnography of each medical institution—especially MGH, with patients and a workforce that come from across the province and even beyond. Instead, I explored both the local health center and the provincial hospital, with a focus on Giri stakeholders: Giri patients, medical personnel, and caretakers.

Anthropological Inquiry into Conceptions of Personhood

This book analyzes Giri ideas of personhood and details the bearing of these local conceptions of the person on biomedical services. How do Giri people reinterpret and appropriate biomedical services against the backdrop of their conceptualizations of the person? The Giri person is, as theorized by the New Melanesian Ethnographers (most prominently Marilyn Strathern [1988] and Roy Wagner [1991]),[3] essentially a social being, constituted relationally through interactions with others. In the cultural logic of the Giri, social relations have a significant bearing on individual health and illness. I support

Keck's argument that "no adequate investigation of health and illness . . . would be possible without an understanding of the concept of the person" (2005: 53). This book discusses at length the relationship of health and illness with concepts of the person.

Mauss's ([1938] 1985) lecture on the person sparked much debate over personhood in anthropology. His argument that understandings of personhood are culturally and historically produced has been advanced in subsequent literature. Battaglia (1983: 291) demonstrated that Sabarl (Southern Massim) personhood is represented by both Mauss's "personnage" and the autonomous individual, which are, she suggested, in a dialectical relationship. Various anthropologists studying personhood have found it useful to differentiate between the individual, the self, and the person.

Harris (1989) and Morris (1994), for example, considered the concepts of individual, self, and person—when clearly defined—useful analytical tools. However, as A. Strathern and P. Stewart (1998c: 172) argued, to come to a clearer understanding of personhood it is necessary to examine personhood from the perspective of indigenous ontology. By taking the Melpa-speaking Hageners' (Western Highlands Province) concept of "noman" as an example, A. Strathern and P. Stewart (1998c: 175–77, 2000: 64–66) showed the artificiality of the categories of individual, self, and person.

"Noman" can be translated as "mind, intention, will, agency, social conscience, desire, or personality" (A. Strathern & P. Stewart 1998c: 175). It includes individual and social aspects of personhood. One may say, then, in general terms, that "*noman* signals the domain of 'personhood'" (177). Von Poser's (2013: 9) exploration of Bosmun personhood may be cited here as a further, and topical, example. She found that aspects of individual, self, and person (approximating the concepts described by Harris [1989]) are conflated in Bosmun constructions of personhood. Wagner (1991) is a third Melanesianist who gave preference to local ideas.[4] His approach is discussed below. Self and person are not isolated from one another but are interrelated and overlapping.

Giri consider a strict separation of person, self, and individual inapt. Like other cultural groups of Melanesia and beyond, Giri give tremendous importance to the person and not, as seen in Western cultures, to the self (Fajans 1985; Keck & Wassmann 2010: 185–86). In other words, Giri are predominantly "person oriented" (Fajans 1985: 383). But I do not claim that Giri think in analytical categories of person, self, and individual. As Fajans said in her analysis of the Baining (East New Britain) person, "My analysis, while not an indigenous model (the Baining are not explicit about these matters), is in keeping with the Baining emphasis on external behaviors and relationships, and their lack of interior, emotional, subjective explanation" (1985: 371). She supplied numerous examples to support her argument.

According to Fajans (1985: 367, 371, 383), the Baining are reluctant to speak about their own and others' subjective motivations and feelings; instead, they provide descriptions in terms of "aspects of social roles, interpersonal interaction, and the nature of social behavior and action" (371). The idea (widespread in Oceania but also found elsewhere [see Danziger 2006, 2010; Wassmann et al. 2013]) that it is virtually impossible for one to know the thoughts and feelings of others has recently become known as "the doctrine of 'the opacity of other minds'" (Robbins & Rumsey 2008: 408). I shall give a brief example of Giri people's reluctance to speculate about others' inner motives, an instance that Fajans (1985: 383), herself, described.

Early on in my fieldwork, I talked to a young Giri man about the different pathways that Giri schoolchildren habitually take to the schools located in the Giri 1 and 2 main villages. My conversational partner described two commonly used paths—one leading along the gravel road, on which one is exposed to the hot sun, and the other a shorter, shady bush track. He then mentioned a schoolboy who usually took the hot and longer gravel road. When I asked him why this boy did not walk along the apparently more pleasant bush track, he answered, "Mi no inap long save" (I cannot know).[5] When I inquired further, he simply replied, "Em i les" (He does not want to). My repeated inquiry as to why he did not want to take the bush track was answered again with "Em i les tasol" (He just does not want to).

The works of two Melanesian scholars, Marilyn Strathern (1988) and Roy Wagner (1991), were particularly influential in spurring the shift of focus from Western notions of the autonomous individual to the relational person. M. Strathern (1988) made the case that the Melanesian person is—in distinction to Western notions of personhood—primarily constituted by relations with a multiplicity of other persons. In keeping with the example of Melanesian leadership, M. Strathern (1988: 156–59) replaced the idea of the (Hagen) big-man as an autonomous, self-contained, "entrepreneurial" (Rio & Smedal 2008: 240) individual, with the image of a relational person. In the words of Rio and Smedal, "More than being the generator of social relations he is a visible manifestation of the social relationships that he encompasses—he is their outcome, their effect. The big-man is an image that sociality produces" (2008: 240). Theorizing on the person as a set of relations with others led M. Strathern (1988: 13) to formulate the concept of Melanesian persons as composites, or "dividuals," rather than persons marked by individuality.

Wagner reconceptualized the role of Hagen big-manship along the same lines, setting out to "develop . . . Marilyn Strathern's concept of the person who is neither singular nor plural" (1991: 162). According to Wagner, Melanesian individuals are not discrete, self-contained entities. Rather, the individual and group mutually construct and imply one another. He called this "the fractal person," which is "never a unit standing in relation to an aggregate, or an aggregate standing in relation to a unit, but always an entity with relationship integrally implied" (163).

M. Strathern's and Wagner's approaches have been immensely influential, and other Melanesianists have taken up and amplified their claim that Melanesians "do not think about social life in terms of the individual versus the society" (Hess 2009: 42). Their works have been augmented, scrutinized, and challenged by subsequent works and have fostered a perpetual debate about Melanesian personhood.[6,7] LiPuma (1998) and A. Strathern and P. Stewart (2000: chap. 4) have expanded on M. Strathern's theory. They have claimed that both relational (or dividual) *and* individual modalities mark Melanesian personhood, wherefore A. Strathern and P. Stewart spoke of the "relational-individual" (2000: 2, 63).

Critique was leveled at M. Strathern for comparing Melanesian notions of personhood to the ideology of the fully individual Western person, and not to reality (LiPuma 1998). LiPuma (2000: 131) suggested that most aspects of Melanesian personhood can be found in Western societies; Western persons are also "interdependent, defined in relation to others, depend on others for knowledge about themselves, grasp power as the ability to do and act, grow as the beneficiary of others' actions, and so forth" (LiPuma 1998: 60).

If we follow A. Strathern and P. Stewart, and LiPuma, aspects of individuality have always been present, at least to some extent, in Melanesian conceptions of personhood. However, concepts of personhood are not static. LiPuma (1998: 64, 2000: 128–29) suggested that individual aspects of Melanesian personhood have gained importance with modernity.[8] Counterexamples exist, however. Lipset, for example, demonstrated, by means of courtship stories told by young men from the Murik Lakes (East Sepik Province) region, that precolonial courtship and marriage practices have "remained somewhat enclaved" (2004: 211) from encompassment by modernity and individualism.

Giri people act, for the most part, relationally, but they also strive for individuality. The medical context provides evidence of this duality. For example, Giri staff at BHC expressed that they sometimes felt overwhelmed by their kin's requests for medical treatment outside of regular consultation hours and for accommodation in staff housing during phases of health center closure (see chaps. 2 and 4 on closures). Health workers complained that their kin did not respect the fact that they acted in their roles as health professionals. In the health workers' opinion, they should be enabled to "transcend their relational identities" (Wardlow 2006: 20) in the professional context, and relatives should refrain from approaching them with extra requests. However, there is also evidence of health workers giving special attention to their kin, seizing the opportunity that unfolds in such situations to strengthen their bonds with kin by aiding them (see chap. 4 for extensive discussion).

The Chapters

This book is organized into five chapters. Chapters 1 and 2 give the relevant background information for chapters 3 to 5. I open chapter 1 by situating myself in the ethnographic setting of the study, placing myself in the web of social relations within which I became embedded in the research site, thus providing an introduction to key interlocutors. The second section of the chapter provides an ethnographic sketch of the Giri focused on village settlement and social organization. The latter portion of the chapter describes this book as ethnography in terms of the doing and writing up of fieldwork. Particular emphasis is laid upon fieldwork as a process of mutual knowledge production between researcher and interlocutors.

Chapter 2 starts with a historical glimpse of biomedical services in Giri. The main thrust of the chapter is the delineation of various perspectives on the local health center, BHC, as it is today. Beginning with an overview of the different health center services, I then look at understandings of BHC from the viewpoints of those who administer and receive health care. Through this, I offer first impressions of local manifestations of biomedicine and, thus, lay the foundation for the issues addressed in the subsequent three chapters. The objective of these chapters is to explore the appropriation of biomedical practices, technologies, and knowledge. All three chapters address the question of how Giri, who have their own medical traditions, respond to incoming medical ideas and aid. Furthermore, chapters 3 to 5 show that Giri people's encounters with biomedicine are not limited to the services offered in the Giri area, as Giri patients actively seek biomedical care at other biomedical institutions, particularly at the provincial hospital in Madang.

In chapter 3, I elaborate on terminological and technological innovations. To be precise, I demonstrate, through two case studies, how these novelties have impacted the established medical system. By inflection, I elucidate how the introduced theories and diagnostic and therapeutic strategies have become localized—bearing in mind that biomedicine is not a homogenous entity but instead shaped by the local setting and its actors. In regards to biomedical technologies, I argue that they are recontextualized according to indigenous knowledge of the body, health, and illness. My basic argument is that the Giri notion of the person as a predominantly relational being governs the appropriation of biomedicine, through which biomedical artifacts and procedures become invested with social meaning. This argument is pursued through the following two chapters.

Chapter 4 exposes the strategies through which biomedical space is transformed into Giri place. Focusing on the social relations of therapy management, the chapter explores how the complex webs of relationships in which patients and health workers are suspended pervade the local health center and the provincial hospital. Among other topics, I detail the significance of giving and sharing local food as a strategy employed by caring family members to comfort and strengthen patients and to actualize social relationships. Moreover, I outline the important roles that Giri medical and paramedical personnel play as part of Giri patients' support groups at MGH, particularly as mediators between patients and hospital services but also as food providers and hosts to patients and their family members. I suggest that provision of care and support is grounded on the principle of reciprocity. The chapter concludes with a discussion highlighting my understanding of reciprocity as a principle that Giri people have applied to the health center and hospital.

In chapter 5, I turn to reproductive health and deliver insights into Giri women's employment of the biomedical reproductive health services offered at the local health center and provincial hospital. I argue that Giri women are highly creative agents who dovetail biomedical health care (such as pharmaceuticals they receive throughout pregnancy, birth, and the postpartum period) with traditional practices connected with birth (such as postpartum seclusion). Women's ingenious strategies to reinterpret biomedical care allow them to draw on the former without having to counterpose the latter. However, a transformation of traditional practices comes with biomedicine gaining a foothold in the Giri medical system. Biomedicine, for example, challenges the relevance of placental burial—a practice that was, in the past, of utmost importance because it was said to anchor the Giri child in its web of social relations. At this point, I advance the argument that the Giri person is primarily relational. It will be made evident that, from conception onward, the child becomes through the contributions of others.

The conclusion picks up threads from the different chapters of the book and summarizes these into a discussion of the local entanglements of biomedicine and how Giri conceptions of the person bear on the form that biomedicine takes in Giri. Biomedical practices, technologies, and services are appropriated and imbued with social meaning. In Giri thought, social relations affect individual bodies and the way in which individuals experience their bodies in health and in illness. Giri decisions to draw on or dismiss certain biomedical services are informed by their relational understandings of the person. Eventually, the conclusion discusses implications for public health interventions in Giri, suggesting ways to bridge medical anthropology and public health. Also, I look at possibilities for further research.

Notes

1. I use the term "tradition(al)" throughout this work to encompass all that is customary and conventional, referring to historically contingent values and practices of Giri culture. I do so with the knowledge that tradition is not static or rigid but characterized

by fluidity. Innovation is part of tradition. Importantly, tradition is contingent upon human agency, as recently emphasized by Otto: "Traditions appear highly changeable and their maintenance or adaptation involves the active involvement of human actors" (2007: 36).
2. Fabrega (1975) advocated the view that biomedicine is as much a cultural product as are other medical systems.
3. Josephides (1991) coined the term "New Melanesian Ethnography."
4. This was noted by A. Strathern and P. Stewart (1998c: 174).
5. It must be noted that Giri also often used this phrase to indicate that I had asked an inappropriate question—for example, a question touching upon knowledge that I or other people present must not know (cf. Goldman 1993: 283–84). In the latter case, interlocutors often got back to my unanswered questions in dialogue, pointing out that a particular person, who had been present during the initial conversation, must not know certain information.
6. Besides relationality, other central notions by which Oceanic personhood has been explored are partibility and permeability (see, e.g., Hess 2009; Mosko 2010; P. Stewart & A. Strathern 2000: 17–20; A. Strathern & P. Stewart 2000: 64).
7. Anthropologists working in various locations have picked up M. Strathern's work. One might remember that M. Strathern took the term "dividual" from Marriott's (1976: 111) reading of South Asian personhood and applied it to Melanesian notions of sociality. Not surprisingly, contemporary works for South Asian dealings with notions of dividual personhood often reintroduce M. Strathern's concept to the South Asian context (e.g., Aura 2008; Osella & Osella 2006).
8. Modernity is not a singular phenomenon but is plural; it is not solely a Western product but has complex and multiple origins; not only does it unfold within Western countries, but its processes and dynamics can be found outside the geography of the West. Countering Eurocentric accounts of modernity, cultural theorists have thus come to embrace the notion of alternative, multiple, or plural modernities that accommodate this very diverse and culturally specific manifestation of modernity (T. Mitchell 2000: xii). As for Papua New Guinea and anywhere else, local, regional, and global forces shape particular versions of modernity (Foster 2002). The works of Gewertz and Errington (2004; Errington & Gewertz 1996) examine the realization of Papua New Guinea modernity (also see Hirsch 2001).

Chapter One
Ethnography and the Fieldwork Setting

This first chapter sets out to explicate the trajectory of my research activities with the Giri, to discuss the ethnographic approach to research and writing, and to provide some ethnographic background on the field site. I focus a significant part of the chapter on anchoring myself in the web of social relations at the field site. Furthermore, I use the arrival story as a means to introduce some key interlocutors in my research.

In keeping with anthropological convention and with what I believe to be an ethical protection of people's privacy, I disguise, to some extent, the identities of the people I write about. I use pseudonyms for individuals, except when presenting public or historical figures. Real names are used throughout much of the following section and in the introductory notes to chapter 2 when I sketch the history of biomedical services in Giri. Although the use of pseudonyms ensures confidentiality by veiling the identity of my interlocutors from those who do not have intimate knowledge of the people and village happenings, Giri villagers, and others who are familiar with the people and events in the village, might be able to determine the true identity of the people appearing in this work. In order to protect individuals within the community, I refrain from divulging certain information, such as comprehensive transcripts of medical records and clinic cards; culturally sensitive knowledge, particularly threatening information; and, of course, information that I have been explicitly told not to publish.

The Field

This book is based on twenty-two months of ethnographic research carried out in northeast Papua New Guinea during four fieldwork phases between September 2006 and August 2011, of which twelve months were spent in the Lower Ramu River area and ten months in the provincial capital, Madang Town. During my first and longest research period, from September 2006 to October 2007, I spent the bulk of research time in Giri and approximately three months in Madang Town. In June 2009, I returned to Papua New Guinea to teach at Madang's Divine Word University. After work and on the weekends, I met with Giri people. During the semester break, I made a short trip to Giri, and after the end of the semester I stayed in the village for one and a half months. In 2010, I visited Giri again for a few weeks. My most recent visit to Giri was in July 2011, following two months in Madang Town that had, again, involved a guest lectureship at the local university.

In September 2006, I arrived in Madang Town, the provincial capital on Papua New Guinea's north coast. A few weeks later I found myself, accompanied by a group of Giri villagers, on the North Coast Road heading toward Giri. We passed through Bogia Town some two hundred kilometers north of Madang Town. By that time, a dirt road had replaced the tarmac. Darkness had us covered when we turned inland at Hansa Bay, opposite to offshore Manam Island. We drove on and off of rugged side roads to drop off passengers. When we abruptly stopped in the middle of the bush, I had no idea where I was.

The PMV (public/passenger motor vehicle) driver told me that I had arrived. He honked the horn to inform the Regene people about the arrival of their "child," as the Giri people began to call me, perhaps in allusion to my still fragmentary personhood. Together with a few Regene villagers who had been on the PMV, I made the twenty-minute walk through sago swamps to the village. A short time later, I was sitting on a low stool next to a fireplace and eating my first yam meal under the gaze of the ward councilor and his extended family. I sat, staring into the darkness, trying to picture what the village would look like in the daytime.

Giri 1 villagers had determined that I would live in the village of Regene. They considered the village a safe place, as it is set back from the road and thus from the dangers of the outside world—strangers, drunkards, and so forth. I was given generous hospitality by the Regene villagers and felt instantly at home. An advantage was the closeness to the local health center. I could easily walk back and forth within thirty minutes. Nevertheless, I soon began to follow Regene villagers on their journeys to see relatives in other Giri villages. The people of Kɨmnɨng village (the largest of the Giri villages) turned out to be enthusiastic and extremely knowledgeable interlocutors, and I frequently stayed for a few days, or even a week, in Kɨmnɨng. I was also in regular contact with people of other Giri 1 communities and of Giri 2, Tung, Varanɨng, and Birap villages.

My Regene home for the first four months was a tiny trade store opposite ward member Vigamba's house. Although I was never formally adopted, I received the Giri name Rɨgɨna by Vigamba's family, and he and his wife Mosari treated me as one of their daughters. In February 2006, I moved to a two-room house with a veranda that Regene villagers had begun building soon after my arrival. My relocation caused mild trouble and petty jealousy between my old and new "hosts," as the new house was located in the midst of houses that were inhabited by members of a family from another clan group.

The most senior resident member of this family was Thiap, a recently widowed woman. She lived in one of the four already established houses in the hamlet. Three of her sons and their wives and children occupied the remaining houses. Throughout the first few months of my research, Thiap was confined to her house, completing a year in seclusion following her husband's burial. As she could be visited by other women and was always at home (in distinction to other interlocutors, who often spent the day in their gardens), I became a frequent visitor to her house. I well remember the many conversations we had at her door, her leaning from inside the house against the woven bamboo wall and me sitting on the veranda, leaning against the wall from the outside.

Thiap seemed to enjoy our conversations, as she said they made a welcome change from her rather uniform days in seclusion, and I soon embosomed this blunt woman with her sharp sense of humor. Our conversations continued after she left the enclosure, though it became much harder to track her down, because she turned out to be very physically active. When I speak of "my mother" in this book, I refer to her. She is also the point of reference when I talk about my sisters, brothers, or other relatives.

At most times, other Regene women and children lived with me in the house. Throughout much of my first research period, my youngest sister Ngamok and her one-year-old daughter occupied one of the two rooms. At a later stage, Thiap lived with us because her house (the oldest in the village) threatened to collapse. At different times, she had several of her grandchildren stay with us. In 2009, Regene and other Giri 1 and Giri 2 communities were affected by several deaths. In great fear of malicious sorcery, people moved closer together. All of my four brothers were, at the time, imprisoned,[1] which meant that there were no men present to protect the hamlet. Therefore, all but one of my sisters-in-law, Kanaiva, who was from a non-Giri village, moved to other hamlets. Kanaiva, her two daughters, Thiap, and another of Thiap's granddaughters moved in with me. Although the little house was quite crowded, I much valued the companionship. Besides, I had had an attempted break-in during the night soon after I had moved to my new house and felt more comfortable with housemates.

When I arrived in Regene in 2010, I found Ngamok, who was then newly married, inhabiting the house with her daughter and husband. I left the house to her and instead occupied a room in the house of Romu, a woman who had become one of my key interlocutors throughout the years. Romu and her husband Dimam would again offer me a room in 2011, when my house lay in ruins after a tropical storm hit the village.

Despite the fact that I shared my house with several women, we had separate households. At sunrise they woke and retreated from my house to cook at their own hearths and to give me privacy for writing up fieldnotes, a task that I usually completed in the mornings. Thiap and Ngamok mostly cooked beside

Thiap's ramshackle house, and Kanaiva at her own house. I soon learned that cooking and sharing meals on a regular basis is absolutely crucial for initiating and sustaining positive social relations. On a daily basis, women would send plates of food to my house. Particularly in the beginning, I had difficulty figuring out who had sent which dish. Often women had one of their daughters or classificatory daughters carry the dish to my house and, if I was absent, they would just leave the covered plate on my veranda.

Over the months I learned to identify the sender by the kinds and tastes of food and, most importantly, the color and shape of the plates. Thiap, for instance, would usually serve my food on a plain, dented aluminum plate, and Romu had allotted me a small white enameled plate with a blue rim and flowers painted onto the inner surface. Kaina's meals, with thick coconut cream and fresh spices, tasted best; Mosari and Mbənam cooked with little or no salt. I usually cooked only once a day, in the evening, because it was quite time consuming. Yet, I tried to reciprocate meals as best I could. This was not always an easy task, because women would come to collect their empty plates after a few days, if their meal had not been reciprocated. I also carried dishes to my interlocutors' homes in acknowledgment of their assistance. I cooked on several ceremonial occasions in Regene and other Giri villages, welcomed guests to Regene village and to my house with meals, and emphasized my unburdened relationships with the sick by bringing them food.

To the Giri people, I became socially visible through these acts of food giving. It was through the medium of food that I gained personhood and gradually became recognized as a person. Not only did I gain much of the knowledge I have of Giri life through participation, but I firmly believe that the sharing of food also infused relations of trust between my interlocutors and me. Furthermore, food preparation in Giri is a highly gendered activity, through which I positioned myself as a woman. Anderson (2011: 24–25), for example, described how she gained more thorough access to women's domains during her third period of fieldwork on Wogeo Island only when she headed her own household and engaged in much of the same activities as the other women in her village. I had some of the most intimate conversations with Regene women at the oxbow lake while fishing, doing laundry, washing dishes, and taking baths.

Aside from my close personal relations with Thiap, my four brothers, my sister Ngamok, and my sisters-in-law Kanaiva and Kaina, I perceived what I would call friendship between Romu and me and with two other women—Ndenbɨr and Mutang. With Ndenbɨr I entered into a close relationship at the very beginning of my research in Giri. She taught me how to light a fire and cook local food, she savored the meals that I prepared, she supplied me over the years with a myriad of her own dishes, and she took me to her garden, where she placed vegetables in my netbag for me to take home.

I became her companion on her trips to other Giri villages and to various markets in the region. Although it is difficult to say if Ndenbir perceived our relationship similarly to how I did,[2] Regene villagers soon began to call us *kurkum,* or poro (comrade, mate), and would expect that we, as consociates, knew the whereabouts of each other. In the strict sense of the term, *kurkum* refers to a friend with inherited ties. These friendship ties are said to come into existence with one's clan and be handed down over the generations. The relationship between *kurkum* is for life and is characterized by mutual respect, affection, and reciprocity. The typical couples that one sees at Giri dancing feasts are usually formed by two *kurkum.*

I entered the relationship with Mutang, a medical worker at Bunapas Health Center, at a much later stage. I owe much of the knowledge I have of the health center's treatment regimens and use of biomedical technologies to her. Mutang accompanied me on my visits to various places, among them the aid post in Giri 1, Rumogo (a Tung hamlet and historic site of the first aid post in the Giri area), and the Ramu camp of a former mission medical assistant. Conversely, I joined Mutang on a couple of the health center's outreach clinics.

Then there was a large group of Giri people, predominantly Regene villagers, with whom I associated more irregularly, depending on the topics I was working on at the time. A middle-aged woman with whom I predominantly discussed aspects of pregnancy and childbirth was Mberik. Mberik much enjoyed our conversations; she was an enthusiastic respondent and, in this role, turned out to be a master of semistructured and unstructured interviews. During my stays in Kimning, Thiap's older sister Kororap's family hosted me. Kororap's son Peter and his wife Agatha offered me a room in their house. Right at the outset, I was invited at night to one of the large men's houses in Kimning for an incipient discussion of growing up, reproductive health, and male identity. Kimning men became my key tutors on these subjects, and our discussions continued during my time in Madang Town. Alongside this group of men, another circle of women of different ages soon formed around my hostess Agatha, with whom I would discuss issues of womanhood.

The majority of my research was carried out in Giri village communities. However, I soon became aware of Giri people's usage of, in particular, two biomedical institutions: Bunapas Health Center (BHC) and Modilon General Hospital (MGH). BHC is one of the district's eight health centers and covers most of the Lower Ramu villages. It is located at the Ramu River's edge, a fifteen-minute walking distance from Regene village via a narrow path leading through grasslands. Hardly a day would pass without at least one or two Giri patients coming through the health center. Even though Regene patients often outnumbered patients from the more distant Giri villages, the health center turned out to be an excellent locale for making contact with a substantial number of non-Regene Giri patients. In February 2007, having received approval from the Provincial Health Office in Madang, I expanded my field site to BHC. I established relations with health center personnel and accompanied them on a few mobile clinic visits to non-Giri Lower Ramu villages.

MGH is one of Papua New Guinea's eighteen government-run provincial general hospitals and serves as a referral point for BHC. I went to MGH for the first time in May 2007 with Rita, one of my interlocutors, whom I followed in her quest for medical diagnosis and treatment. I approached hospital authorities and was kindly granted permission to follow up Rita's case, to see other patients from the Giri area who were both inpatients and outpatients, and to interview health personnel. In order to further my research at MGH, I stayed behind for an extra two months when Rita returned to Regene. I also went back to the hospital at later stages of my research.

Ethnographic Orientations

Administratively, the Giri villages belong to the district of Bogia in Madang Province and come under four wards in the Yawar Local Level Government area. Giri people occupy ten villages (Giri 1 and 2, Kimning, Varaning, Tung, Birap, Minung, Temning, Puir 1, and Puir 2) and numerous smaller hamlets and seasonal camps. A survey that was carried out between March and September 2006 by the local village recorder for a global fund program to fight malaria in order to determine the number of bed nets needed suggests a population size of 3,314. I conducted a complete census of Regene, the community in which I lived, as my first fieldwork activity. I found that 155 people, whose average age was 19.2 years, inhabited Regene.

Villages, scattered hamlets, and seasonal camps of the Giri people are located in an area between 144°38' and 144°44' east longitude, and 4°13' and 4°20' south latitude (see map 1.1). They are located at the middle reaches of the Lower Ramu area, between thirty and sixty kilometers inland from Hansa Bay. On the west, Giri territory is bounded by the Ramu River—Papua New Guinea's fifth largest river by volume of flow (Rannells 1995: 152). To the southeast, it extends over undulating hills up to three hundred meters above sea level (Stanhope 1972: 49). Tropical rain forest and grassy downs covering crests and slopes dominate the landscape. There are large sago swamps and smaller bamboo groves in the valleys and along the Ramu. During the wet season (lasting from about November to May), heavy rainfall can cause flooding of low-lying areas and roads. The dirt road that leads to the coast may become impassable, cutting off Giri people's access to the North Coast Road and thus to Madang Town.

Giri people who live in the village are largely dependent on subsistence agriculture based on descent tenure and ownership of land. Sago is the main

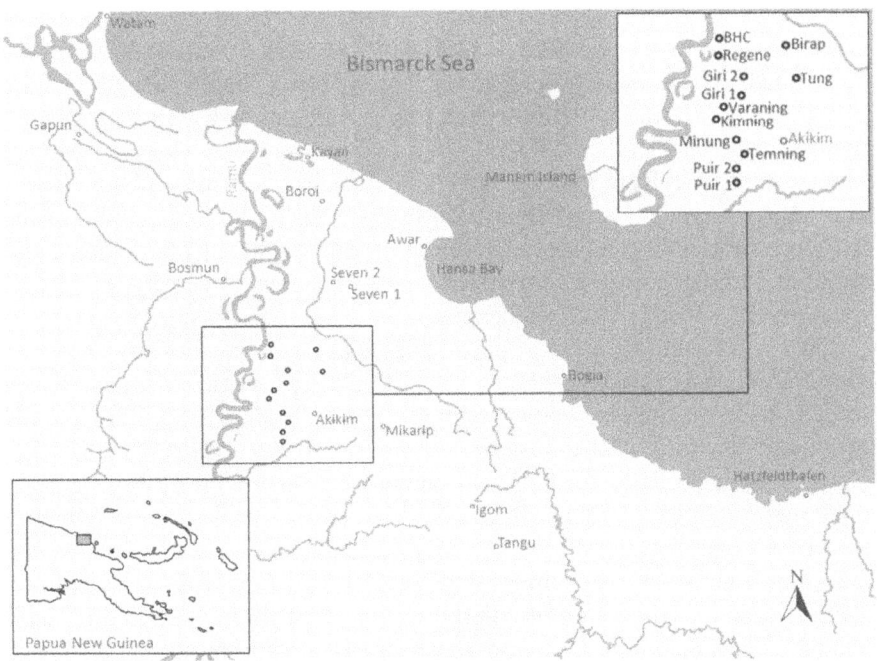

Map 1.1. Lower Ramu region.

staple food of the Giri people. Aside from sago processing, subsistence food production entails swidden horticulture, game hunting and trapping (particularly of wild pigs, bandicoots, lizards, and birds), fishing, small-scale pig and poultry husbandry, and gathering of wild fruits, nuts, seeds, mushrooms, bamboo shoots, green leafy vegetables, and grubs. The main crop that Giri people cultivate in their gardens is yam. Other crops include taro, sweet potato, cassava, a great variety of banana and plantain species, and pumpkin. Cash cropping, with the chief crop being cocoa, is on the rise. Some of the land previously used for subsistence is now dedicated to cash crop production. Women have access to small amounts of cash through the sale of local produce in Giri markets. The local markets also provide a source of income for Giri men, with kinswomen selling the men's catch of fish and game or parts of these.

Social organization is patrilineal, and marital residence is typically patri-virilocal. Yet it sometimes happens that men reside on their wives' paternal clan land. Often, Giri people marry within their own language group. In recent years, marriage outside the ethnic group has become more common. Following their relocation at marriage, women begin to cultivate gardens at their husband's place. They do, however, continue to harvest the sago that was planted for them by their kin on their own paternal clan land.

A typical Giri village accommodates members of several clans (*ka-a;*[3] [bikpela] bet) and subclans (*ka-a bisane;* liklik bet [also called *rai bavira;* literally: "one line"]). Suku and his sister Hade were said to be the two progenitors of the Ndiaki clan association (which they had founded with their respective marriage partners). Ndiaki split into two further clans, Rom and Mange. Members of both Rom and Mange clans and their subclans inhabit Giri 1. The village Regene is a settlement of Rom peoples (including peoples of the two Rom subclans—Mbinge and Saminger): Rom men with their women and children. Among the women married to Regene men, a majority are also of the Rom clan or of one of its subclans.

Large rectangular wooden platforms (*ka-a,* bet) covered by thatched roofs mark the place of residency of particular clans and subclans. These roofed platforms are also known as men's houses (hausboi). They are usually positioned centrally in the cluster of respective homes and serve as meeting places and the focus of much of ceremonial life. The village of Regene hosts three men's houses, one for each clan/subclan (Rom, Saminger, and Mbinge). Regene village is divided into four major hamlets (Regene, Tuguge, Forge, and Daun Camp) and three minor hamlets (Krikip, Regene Kir, and Mambu Camp). Regene is the largest hamlet. It was the first hamlet to be established, and the village then expanded from there. The clan platform of Rom is located in Regene. The second men's house—that of the Saminger people—is found in Tuguge. The Mbinge platform is in Daun Camp.

Associations between clans and land are strong; aside from common mythical ancestry and oral history, members of the same clan share land (bush, grassland, and swamps) and bodies of water. Clan membership defines a person's rights to use garden land, to fell large trees for canoes in bushland, and to access hunting and fishing grounds. For a variety of reasons, including population growth and unresolved conflicts, family lines have left the ten main villages and established new hamlets. Sometimes larger villages have formed from these hamlets, as is the case with Regene and Garati. Garati was formed when Tung people followed the Churches of Christ mission, which moved its station down to the Ramu River. Regene was established in the mid-1960s, when inhabitants of the larger Giri 1 village relocated to the fertile garden land and sago swamps near the Ramu River and its oxbow lake. For Kimning people who live farther away from their sago swamps and the Ramu, it is not uncommon to entertain simple houses in so-called bush camps, where they temporarily reside for sago work and fishing.

Doing and Writing Ethnography

Famously, the term "ethnography" has a double meaning, referring to both a set of data collection methods and the written record. I understand my book to be ethnographic in both senses of the term: it is built upon data collected using an array of qualitative methods, and it is the written product of ethnographic research. Let me first consider ethnography as a data collection method. As Schensul et al.'s text tells us, "Ethnography is a scientific approach to discovering and investigating social and cultural patterns and meaning in communities, institutions, and other social settings" (1999: 1). Fieldwork is a particular kind of ethnography. It is "a spatial practice of intensive, interactive research organized around the serious fiction of a 'field.' The field is not so much a discrete, single place as it is a set of institutionalized practices, a professional habitus [i.e., the *habitus* of anthropologists]" (Clifford 2003: 18).

Clifford's definition calls attention to the fact that there is no such thing as a preexisting field that is discovered by the ethnographer. The ethnographer constructs the field as a consequence of a specific research project; ethnographers, thus, are "place-makers" (Madden 2010: 38), and ethnographic fields are "the synthesis of concrete space and investigative space" (39). My medical anthropological interest constructed my field. Another ethnographer in Giri with a different topic of interest would certainly have constructed a field different from mine. She or he would have selected contexts specifically relevant to her or his own research project.

The field of my ethnographic study included multiple sites. The Giri people whom I followed in their medical quests both opened up and, at the same time, delimited my field, and I continually reconstructed my field throughout the research process. In "multi-sited ethnography" (Marcus 1995), the researcher may follow diverse phenomena—things, metaphors, stories, lives, conflict, or, as in my case, people—through different settings (106–10). It is through this "mobile ethnography" (96) that I hoped to trace Giri villagers' employment of biomedicine.

Also, I wanted to show how conditions of medical settings shape patients' experiences with biomedicine. Following Giri patients and conducting research at different sites, I engaged with a heterogeneous group of actors that involved patients, their caregivers, and BHC and MGH personnel. As Marcus (1995: 100) argued, it is not necessary to treat all sites with the same set of fieldwork methods or the same intensity. In the village context, participant observation and qualitative interviews were heavily used. In the hospital, I participated in groups of caregivers and heavily drew on semistructured interviews. In addition, at the health center I referred to hospital records.

In terms of fieldwork and data collection, "being there" refers to the idea that the ethnographer is the central tool of data collection and recording

(LeCompte & Schensul 1999: 1; Madden 2010: 18–19, 82–83; Murchison 2010: 13). Not only does the ethnographer become intellectually immersed in the field, but the "subjective experience of being in the field" (Madden 2010: 82) becomes inscribed in his or her body and, more generally, in ethnography. The ethnographer's body is an "organic recording device" (ibid.), because ethnographers use their five senses in data collection. They collect data by way of observing behavior, listening to what their interlocutors say, touching pieces of material culture (such as cooking utensils, textiles, or personal ornaments), tasting local food, and paying attention to smells (Murchison 2010: 14).

In short, fieldwork is an embodied activity (Coffey 1999: 59; Madden 2010: 19). One of the bodily experiences I recorded during my fieldwork in Giri was the sharp smell of chemical disinfectants inside BHC. Giri patients commonly perceived this "smell of medications" (smel bilong marasin) as nauseating, wherefore they often avoided entering the premises of the health center. Similarly, I noted the stifling heat of the children's medical unit of MGH. Sarah, for example, tried to ease her daughter's condition by constantly fanning her and dabbing her body with a damp cloth. I felt so dizzy on several of my visits that I lingered underneath the ward's sole fan or stepped outside to cool off. On another occasion, I took a medicinal plant to treat a stomachache.

After this, I was bitten by a centipede on the face and lay on a veranda in Giri while women rubbed the thick gel of an aloe leaf on the bite wound and fanned me. (This thoroughly disquieted me since, until then, I had only observed Giri people fanning the bodies of the deadly sick or corpses to keep away flies.) Following a conversation on the usage of aromatic ginger as a perfuming agent, my interlocutor suggested that I try it. Hence, I picked a few leaves and, in my next bath, substituted my soap with the aromatic leaves. One day, while peeling plantains for my dinner, I received news of the death of a Regene woman. Even though I was hungry, I interrupted food preparation and waited until the next morning to resume my cooking, as fires in the hearths must, out of respect, not be lit until the corpse is buried.

My primary fieldwork role was that of the participant observer who participates in the daily and nondaily activities of one of the social groups in the research setting. This was, for example, as a member of patients' therapy managing groups at the provincial hospital when I provided Giri patients with food, or as a family member in a mourning ceremony in the village when I found myself sitting and crying along with the mourners. More specifically, I was a participating observer—an outsider participating in some parts of the life around me (Bernard 2006: 347). My role oscillated along a continuum of participant observer and observer, yet I only rarely acted as a complete observer. An example of the latter would be my time spent observing patients' and health care personnel's interaction and discourse at BHC. What is more, participant observation in its strict, traditional, Malinowskian sense was not always open to me in the two clinical settings of my study—BHC and MGH.

Wind (2008) posed the question of which roles are usually available to ethnographers who work in clinical settings. For Danish hospital settings, she defined three common roles: patient, health worker, and relative/visitor (82). To participate over an extended period as a patient was not possible. I underwent only a few diagnostic procedures, including a blood count, at the hospital and received only minor treatments, including the treatment of diarrhea and a surgical dressing. For ethical reasons, and because my research was primarily based in a village community, it was not an option to admit as a pseudopatient to either of the medical institutions, as, for example, was practiced by van der Geest's coresearcher in a Ghanaian hospital (see van der Geest & Sarkodie 1998). Also, I have no medical training and thus could not participate as a health worker.

At times, my role was that of a visitor/caregiver, though it involved only a few of the various caring tasks generally performed by caregivers (mainly as a food provider and a conversational partner). My ethnographic fieldwork in the two clinical settings can more appropriately be described as "negotiated interactive observation" (Wind 2008). This concept explains a way of doing fieldwork in clinical settings when none of the roles that have a precedent in the setting are available to the ethnographer but the ethnographer is more than a mere observer, interacting with the people studied: "The concept of negotiated interactive observation captures what happens when you are doing fieldwork without at the same time assuming that you become one of 'them'" (87).

I shall now address the second issue—writing ethnography. The authority of ethnographic texts has been critically and widely discussed since the 1980s in the postmodern "writing culture" debate (Clifford 1983; Geertz 1988; Marcus & Cushman 1982). Ethnographic texts of other societies have been revealed to be, at best, partial accounts influenced by subjective factors such as the ethnographer's theoretical stance, ideological biases, cultural background, personal values, and interests. Since then, many authors have met the postmodern challenge by way of making themselves visible in their texts and being reflectively aware of their active role in knowledge construction/production. Knibbe and Versteeg neatly summarized the mutual aspect of knowledge production: "The general consensus in anthropology nowadays is that a fieldworker creates knowledge in interaction with the people in the field: not objectivity, nor pure subjectivity, but intersubjectivity is what an anthropologist should strive for" (2008: 52).

The problem of authorial voice and how it should be accounted for leads me to the symbolic anthropologist Wagner and his sense of culture. Allow me an excursus to his and Ingold's understanding of culture, which underlies my own work. Wagner (1975: 2) argued that absolute objectivity is impossible, because the anthropologist is influenced by his or her own culture. Famously, Wagner suggested that culture, including the anthropologist's own, is an invention: "We might actually say that an anthropologist 'invents' the culture he believes himself to be studying, that the relation is more 'real' for being his particular acts and experiences than the things it 'relates'" (4).

Wagner's argument was informed by his dynamic processual view of culture. He claimed that culture is not a fixed entity but is constantly created and recreated (1975: 50). His work denotes a shift away from the conception of culture as simply the result of tradition (Ingold 1994: 329). Instead, his approach regards culture as grounded in human practices, as "situated in the relational context of people's mutual involvement in a social world" (ibid.). So, too, for Ingold—according to Bourdieu's theory of practice ([1972] 2002)—cultural knowledge is not theoretical. It is not "a corpus of intergenerationally transmissible knowledge" (Ingold 1996: 104; see Ingold 1993) but lived through practice in everyday life. Cultural knowledge is not "imported by the mind into contexts of experience" but, rather, formed in human interaction "in the practical business of life" (Ingold 1996: 105).

Through practical involvement, people acquire tacit dispositions (Bourdieu calls this "habitus"), which operate, in turn, as a resource, leading people to behave in certain ways (Ingold 1996: 105). Hence, taking as a frame Bourdieu's view of culture as practice "embedded in local contexts and in the multiple realities of everyday life" (Griffiths 2001: 102), we may acknowledge heterogeneity in the practices and views of members of a society. As Ingold said:

> What we do *not* find are neatly bounded and mutually exclusive bodies of thought and custom, perfectly shared by all who subscribe to them, and in which their lives and works are fully encapsulated ... The isolated culture has been revealed as a figment of the Western anthropological imagination. It might be more realistic, then, to say that people *live culturally* rather than that they *live in cultures.* (1994: 330)

In recent years, scholars in medical anthropology have also emphasized that the use of culture as an explanatory concept and analytic tool for understanding health and illness is fraught with substantial limitations (Lock & Nguyen 2010: 6). Lock and Nguyen said, "The assumption, held formerly by the majority of anthropologists and others, that in a named culture everyone participates equally in local socioeconomic arrangements, exhibits similar behavioral patterns, and adheres to shared values is no longer tenable" (ibid.). Cultures are not essentialist and monolithic but, rather, hybrid, fluid, and constantly evolving, acted out through individuals and changed by them.

As I move through the chapters, it will become fairly obvious that what I have called "construction" in the introduction to this book (as in "Giri construction of biomedicine") is not a process that is "determined" by culture. It would be wrong to reduce Giri people's dealings with biomedicine to some cultural logic that Giri people blindly follow. Instead, I found Giri people to actively engage with biomedical knowledge, practice, and technology or, in other words, to actively shape the biomedical realities in which they live.

My understanding of culture complies with these approaches that see culture as grounded and dynamically enfolding in practice and situated in particular contexts. Giri people proved themselves pragmatists in each situation; we may view their actions "largely in terms of pragmatic choice and decision making" (Ortner 1984: 150). Sometimes, though, as is demonstrated later in the book, it can also be pragmatic to dismiss biomedical interventions in relation to kastom[4] (custom, tradition; cf. Ortner 1984: 150). And yet, in their attempts to act according to kastom, Giri people changed kastom. This occurred, for example, when, in a healing practice, a white chicken was employed to indicate whether bush spirits had accepted gifts of food and money. The chicken, the food, and the money were innovations to the worship practice.

Much emphasis has also been placed on sound ethnographic fieldwork and data processing as the authoritative basis for written ethnography (see contemporary anthropological method and methodology books, such as Bernard 2006; Madden 2010). However, "good" data are not necessarily "hard" data. Knibbe and Versteeg (2008), who adopted a phenomenological research approach for their projects, understood themselves to be apprentices in new life-worlds. Apprenticeship meant, in their research, that participation (e.g., praying for someone) could be more worthwhile in understanding what was happening, than could collection of "hard" data (e.g., recording the words said in a prayer; ibid., 52–53).

Knibbe and Versteeg saw the anthropologist as "someone who has knowledge of different worlds, whose bodily being has been shaped by different habitats and as such will always be 'different'" (2008: 57). To them, this quality of understanding differently than the other participants of the life-word has its own value (58). I can only agree with their argument that the ethnographer's body is "a productive starting point for analysing culture" (Csordas 1990: 39). This brings us back to the above notion of the ethnographer's body as an "organic recording device" (Madden 2010: 82).

Synopsis

Beginning with my arrival in the field, the present chapter has provided the ethnographic background for this book. I established my field site as one of multiple locations rather than a fixed place. The field emerged as I followed my interlocutors on their medical quests. Some of the interlocutors with whom I maintained particularly close relationships were introduced. I discussed the issue of doing and writing ethnography. Some of the key points that were made included the understanding of fieldwork as an embodied activity, the mutual aspect of knowledge production in ethnography, and the dynamic view of culture. Concerning the fieldwork role, I functioned primarily as a participant observer in the wide range of health-related activities in which the Giri people engaged. However, in the local health center and the provincial hospital, I used "negotiated interactive observation" (Wind 2008) as the main approach. I also offered an ethnographic sketch of the field site. In the next chapter, I illuminate the institutional background for what follows. The second chapter, thus, provides a bridge to the empirical chapters 3 to 5.

Notes

1. In 2008 and 2009, a significant number of Regene men spent time in Beon Prison outside Madang owing to a local land dispute.
2. Wagner (1975: 6) noted that the anthropologist's idea of friendship may be markedly different from views that the people she or he has come to work among hold about friendship and the commitments and obligations that it entails.
3. Literally, the term *ka-a* means the physical platform.
4. Kastom is a concept that encompasses a broad spectrum of meanings. Lindstrom and White noted that the term may refer to both "custom" and "tradition" in English. They use the term "custom" to mean "all conspicuous cultural forms and practices that people talk about and incorporate into their sense of identity"; they define "tradition" as "the large subset of custom that is tagged explicitly as handed down form the past, from one's ancestors" (Lindstrom & White 1994: 5). However, there are many varying, individual connotations of the term kastom (Keck 1993a; Lindstrom & White 1994). Keck (1993a), for example, found that young Yupno men, who have more outside experience, define kastom differently from those without any significant outside experience. The first group regards contemporary village lifestyle as kastom. To the latter group, kastom, in contrast, means the way of the ancestors (pasin bilong tumbuna), which they perceive their own village lifestyle to be distinct from. It will become apparent throughout this work that Giri people generally use the term kastom to refer to the ways of their ancestors, that is, ways that may or may not have been carried into contemporary society. Kastom describes the ideal way of behaving or doing something and is, as such, usually viewed in positive terms. It goes without saying that kastom is subject to change. Contemporary practices that Giri people describe as kastom may have been quite different in the past. The Giri use the terms kastam and kastom interchangeably but use the latter term with greater frequency. Hence, unless it is otherwise used in a direct quote, I use the spelling kastom.

Chapter Two
Bunapas Health Center

The development of biomedicine in Giri has been intimately tied to colonization and proselytization, as it has been in much of Papua New Guinea and Oceania. For many decades of colonial governance, New Guinea's indigenous population was, at best, marginally aided by—and at other times completely left out of—public health measures; Giri was no exception to this. Biomedicine in Giri has a history of roughly seventy years (see Herbst 2013: section 1, chap. 2 for a comprehensive account of the history of biomedical services in Giri), having entered the Giri area after the Pacific War. Giri encounters with biomedicine were at first sporadic, occurring a few times a year during Australian government patrols. Health care services only really developed with the arrival of the Australian Churches of Christ mission,[1] which settled in Tung, one of the Giri villages, in 1958.

Giri villagers played an active role in bringing biomedical health services to their area. In the early 1950s, the Roman Catholic mission had already established a mission station and school in Giri 1 village, and the Tung villagers were eager to have their own school in which to learn Tok Pisin, reading, and writing. When Tung villagers got word that the Australian Churches of Christ were looking for a site to start missionary work, Birime, the first Tung luluai,[2] assisted by the Tung tultul, summoned a gathering, and the Tung discussed whether they wanted the Churches of Christ mission to settle there. Despite discrepant arguments, the need for a teacher emerged more strongly than the opposition, so Birime, with a large group of other Tung men, walked to Bogia to see the kiap (administrative field officer) and express the community's approval of the Churches of Christ's settlement and to ask for the consent of the Australian administration (Frank Beale, pers. comm. 2009; Roi Ndun 16 November 2009; Shabre Sinam 1 November 2009; Yabru Zueri 1 November 2009).

The mission opened an aid post in the same year, began to train its own medical assistants, and rapidly expanded its medical work. In 1966, it inaugurated the area's first hospital, Paternoster Memorial Hospital, which serviced virtually the entire Lower Ramu population, even extending into the Middle Ramu region. The hospital was built in the Bunapas area at the Ramu River. The main reason for the shift from Tung to the Ramu River was that the medical officer of the Madang district had recommended resettlement to an area that could be accessed more easily via waterway and would thus attract more patients.

Map 2.1. Bunapas Health Center catchment area.

Medical mission personnel regularly visited the villages of the catchment area with their outreach clinics. The mission undertook medical patrols on three different routes, covering the entire Lower Ramu region and reaching as far south as Chungrebu (see map 2.1). After independence, Giri people opened, with government support, a new aid post in Giri 1 village (in 1976). The actual government takeover of the hospital facilities happened quite late (i.e., in the mid-1980s). This resulted in the hospital's downgrade to a health center and eventually entailed relocation of the facilities a few hundred meters from Paternoster Memorial Hospital. The new facilities were opened as "Bunapas Health Center" (BHC) in 2000.

These days, BHC covers a smaller area than the Paternoster Memorial Hospital once did. It supervises the aid posts in Akurai, Bivi (a hamlet of Temning people), Bosmun, Bulivar, Giri, and Seven (though not all aid posts are continuously staffed), and the Kayoma Health Sub-Center (see map 2.1). BHC services villages of the Lower Ramu Constituency (from Bulivar to Wokam, reaching as far inland as Korak), but other aid posts and health centers now care for the coastal villages (from Marangis to Awar) and the villages of the Middle Ramu Constituency (starting past Wokam and reaching to Tsumba) (pers. comm. Paul Mabong 2009).

Giri villagers deplore that the new buildings are of a lower standard and less numerous than the Paternoster Memorial Hospital's facilities. The Paternoster Memorial Hospital buildings comprised a general ward, a pediatric ward, a maternity ward, a labor room, an emergency room, an operating room (for minor surgery), a first aid room, a consultation room, a dispensary, a storage room, and office space. In fact, the health center was rebuilt as a single building with only two wards (of which one is utilized as office space), a storage room for medications, and a tiny emergency/examination room. The office space is also used for the storage of medications and medical equipment and as a consultation room if sensitive matters, such as birth control, are discussed. Generally, though, the health workers see patients on the building's veranda. Two, sometimes three, chairs are arranged around a table, and the patient (and accompanying relative) sits facing the health worker. Sometimes, though, the patient remains seated on the bench that is provided for other waiting patients. A counter in the foyer is used for dispensing medications.

BHC suffers from underfunding, which limits outreach activities. Further, lack of medications (including vaccines) poses a constant problem. Giri villagers generally find today's health services to be less compelling than those of mission times. Some of their criticisms of present-day facilities and how they are run are further addressed below.

This chapter gives a topical account of BHC through the summary of patient figures and the words of the residential population. I also explore the active role that local health workers play in shaping the face of health

Illustration 2.1. Giri nurse attends to patients at Bunapas Health Center outpatient clinic (2009).

services in Giri. This chapter is divided into three parts. The first part lays out the medical services currently available at BHC. This section is devoted to the presentation of figures that health center staff collected. Despite their sketchiness, the figures give a general idea of the scale of services provided. The second and third parts are dedicated to the two central groups of actors at BHC: those performing and those receiving health services. I discuss the roles of the three categories of health professionals employed at BHC and provide an overview of BHC's employees throughout the years in which I conducted my research. I conclude this chapter with Giri accounts of the health center, its staff, and the services offered. Here, I extensively deploy quotations from interviews, because they excellently capture Giri people's experiences with and thoughts about BHC.

Through the Lens of Numbers

BHC is one of eight health centers in Madang's Bogia District,[3] and it caters to the medical needs of more than 11,500 people. It supervises six aid posts and one health subcenter (see above) and is responsible for patient referral to Bogia Health Center and MGH, Madang's provincial hospital. The district health center in Bogia serves as an intermediary referral point between the other health centers in the district and MGH. BHC provides essential ambulatory curative services and basic inpatient services to the population within its catchment area. Apart from its diagnostic and treatment services, a range of prevention-oriented activities are carried out, such as child immunization, family planning, and prenatal, natal, and postnatal (including neonatal) care. Health workers serve patients at the health center and conduct outreach patrols to the more distant villages; outreach is often conducted for maternal and child health services and immunizations.

Outreach clinics are also conducted to inspect aid posts and villages that have been struck by outbreaks of epidemics and to curb epidemics. Outreach clinics are meant to visit every village at least once every three months for immunization activities (Madang Provincial Administration 2008: 1). In reality, however, patrols occur infrequently. Awareness campaigns are another part of BHC's work. Occasional health education and hygiene promotion programs, with reference to present health hazards (such as cholera in 2009), are conducted. In cooperation with schools and churches (Churches of Christ, Seventh-Day Adventists, and Foursquare), the health center delivers awareness of sexually transmitted diseases, including HIV/AIDS.

Outpatients

The vast majority of clients are outpatients. Figures produced by BHC staff reveal that the health center had a total of 6,501 outpatient visits in 2006. This means that, on average, more than every second person residing in the health center's catchment area made one outpatient visit to BHC that year. The majority (71.5 percent) of these visits related to new cases; the remaining 28.5 percent were follow-up visits relating to a previous case. The leading causes for outpatients' medical visits (only pertaining to new cases) in descending order and as diagnosed by the attending health professional were malaria, respiratory diseases, skin diseases, diarrhea, and accidents and injuries.

The large intra- (as well as inter-) annual variation in recorded outpatient numbers is striking. In May 2006, for example, 627 outpatient visits were registered, whereas only 271 were recorded in October of the same year. Records for January to July 2007 reveal 2,531 outpatient visits, whereas, by comparison, figures show 4,720 visits for the same period in 2006. The limited data presented here do not allow the identification of a trend or any other kind of statistical claim to be made.

It can at least be noted that the significant variations in the patient census, on the one hand, reflect actual fluctuations in the number of patients who visited BHC's outpatient clinics. These fluctuations may have been due to a multitude of factors, among them villagers' tiredness of walking to the health center on the muddy path during the rainy season, seasonal variations in the occurrence of some diseases, conflict between communities serviced by BHC, and the impact of public health awareness and prevention projects conducted by health center staff. (These programs have doubtlessly had some measure of impact, though there is still plenty of room for improvement.) On the other hand, variations could also have been due to underrecording, periodic closures of the health center, and the number of mobile clinics that were conducted.

Inpatients

On most days, the health center also accommodated a number of inpatients on its single general medical ward. The ward is equipped with six bedsteads. There are no mattresses, and patients roll out woven sleeping mats, cover the wooden beds with bed sheets, or just sleep on the bare wood.

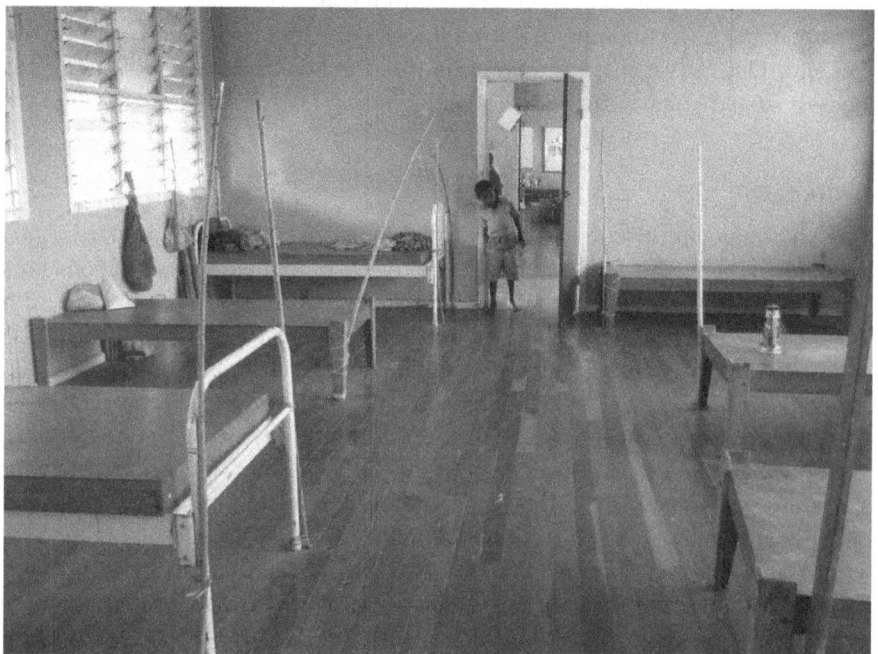

Illustration 2.2. Bunapas Health Center ward (2009). The sticks fixed to the sides of the beds are substitutes for drip stands.

The total number of patients who were admitted to BHC's ward over periods of thirteen months from 2006 to 2007 and ten months in 2009, remained virtually constant, with a monthly average of 18.2 inpatients between 2006 and 2007 and 19.6 admissions in 2009. During both periods, pneumonia was the leading medical condition followed in 2006 to 2007 by malaria and then accidents and injuries. In 2009, accidents and injuries ranked second and malaria third. BHC personnel labeled a significant proportion of cases as "other," because they did not fit into any of the predefined categories in the nationally standardized annual health center record. The health center's (partly available) admission and discharge logbooks show that a substantial proportion of cases labeled "other" were gynecological and obstetric in nature. Common conditions were uterine fibroids, retained placentas, self-induced abortions, miscarriages and threatened miscarriages, and confinements. Other diagnoses included food poisoning, gastroenteritis, peptic ulcers, arthritis, septicemia, and tuberculosis.

At BHC, admissions that result in self-discharges, referrals, and deaths are reported in a separate record. In practice, referral cases are sent to the district health center in Bogia or to MGH, depending on the medical care required. However, as medical options at Bogia Health Center do not differ much from those at BHC, most patients are directly sent to MGH, where medical doctors are present.

For example, all cases that require X-ray diagnosis or major surgery are referred to MGH. Forty-six patients were referred to MGH during the periods of 2006 to 2007 and 2009. When a patient is transferred, she or he must bear the transfer costs. Ambulance rides are expensive (about sixty kina[4] from BHC to Bogia Health Center and about two hundred kina from BHC to MGH) and, although BHC has its own ambulance that is mainly crewed by BHC's officer in charge, it is often unavailable (for example because it sits in the repair shop). A PMV ride from Bunapas to Madang (approximately 250 kilometers) costs twenty-five kina per person and usually takes half a day, though this journey is dependent on the lackluster availability and condition of the PMVs.

Sixteen deaths, of which ten were among children, occurred during the 2006 to 2007 and 2009 periods at BHC. Four deaths were attributed to pneumonia, two to neonatal sepsis, two to malaria, and another two to snakebites. There was one death each associated with liver failure, anemia, diarrhea, meningitis, an unspecified respiratory disease, and an unknown cause. The number of self-discharges (or "abscondences," as they are officially called) was relatively small, with ten cases. Patients' principal reasons for terminating health center stays were hunger and food insecurity (see chap. 4 for patients' food provision). Further common motives for self-discharges were conflict with members of the local population, isolation from one's ethnic group, and mistrust of health workers' diagnosis and the treatment success.

Maternal Health

In addition to general inpatient and outpatient services, special emphasis at BHC (as in Papua New Guinea, more generally) is given to maternal health. The most recent statistics of the World Health Organization ([WHO] 2011: 324, 495) and the Government of Papua New Guinea ([GoPNG] 2010a) delineate a decline in Papua New Guinea women's reproductive health. Improving during the 1980s, women's health status has begun to decrease again since the 1990s. Levels of maternal mortality, which were still high in the 1990s, have risen sharply (especially in rural areas). The reported maternal mortality ratio nearly doubled between 1996 and 2006 and is now high in comparison with other Oceanic countries (9–11, 26).[5] This has led the GoPNG (2010a) to explicitly define the improvement of maternal health as one of the priority issues in its current national health plan. Key objectives on the road to lowering the high levels of maternal mortality are specified as doubling the number of women giving birth in "well-functioning" (2) health facilities and promoting the advantages of birth control (26).

BHC runs prenatal clinics on Tuesdays, and Thursday is "family planning day" (involving birth control services and biomedical education regarding the reproductive system and sexuality). Maternal outreach clinics are conducted—though, due to funding difficulties, on an irregular basis. BHC workers generally encourage women—particularly if they are nulliparous (having never given birth) or of parity five or more—to deliver in a biomedical institution. They may give birth at BHC, though the health center is not well set up for births.

Health center obstetric records reveal that, between 2004 and October 2009, 135 babies (seven of which were stillbirths and neonatal deaths and one an incomplete abortion) were delivered at BHC, and more mothers proceeded to the health center, with a total of eighteen newborns, after having given birth before arrival (BBA). In the case of maternal deaths, health center staff is called upon to fill in individual "Maternal Death Investigation Reports" and forward them to the provincial health information officer. This includes deaths that do not happen at the facility but about which health workers hear. However, the available annual health center reports are somewhat unclear about the number of maternal deaths, despite the report explicitly containing spaces reserved for maternal deaths.

BHC provides for four prenatal visits, in line with the national policy and WHO recommendations (WHO 2005: 168). The health center keeps records of the number of both prenatal clinic visits and tetanus toxoid doses (to prevent tetanus infection) given to pregnant women during their visits. However, the number of tetanus toxin injections administered to expectant women does not accurately mirror the demand BHC receives. It is not unusual for BHC to run out of vaccines. Especially after maternal health outreach clinics in which it is common for a large number of pregnant women to be vaccinated, BHC may be without vaccines for several weeks, awaiting resupply. It has also happened that BHC's vaccine refrigerator has broken down, and health workers have been forced to discontinue vaccination services because they have not been able to store vaccines within the proper temperature range.

Family Planning

In the mid-1960s, the Churches of Christ mission began family planning services in the Giri area, with the aim of controlling the population growth that their own medical work had set off—in particular their stationary and outreach maternal and child health care (Frank Beale, pers. comm. 2008). In about 1969 or 1970, the mission introduced a Western form of family planning, the intrauterine device, to the villages (Frank & Ros Beale, pers. comm. 2012). The intrauterine device became popular among local women as a long-term birth control method, but, from the early 1990s, no more insertions were performed at BHC due to a lack of qualified personnel.

These days, BHC personnel almost exclusively give hormonal contraceptives to women seeking birth control. Women pay a fee of one kina per clinic visit, including hormonal contraceptives, for three months. The most widely administered Western birth control method is Depo-Provera,[6] an injectable hormonal contraceptive. The combined oral contraceptive pill was the second most commonly given contraceptive. The minipill, which, compared to the combined pill, has the advantage that it can be used while breastfeeding, came third. Only 0.4 percent of all acceptors received other, nonhormonal options for birth control: one new acceptor and one reacceptor were advised to use the ovulation method (a fertility awareness method based on mucosal symptomology and the calendar), and one reacceptor was given condoms. Condom acceptors were only registered if they relied exclusively on condoms for family planning, and not if condoms were used in addition to a hormonal contraceptive or the ovulation method.

Health center staff explained that they generally advise women to select either Depo-Provera or a contraceptive pill, and they rarely suggest condom use as a single regular method for contraception because of the difficulty of ensuring a continuous supply of condoms. Also, health workers found that the ovulation method is ineffective in most cases; the method requires several days of abstinence and is difficult to follow, because women have to count days and differentiate between "wet" and "dry" days.[7] Tubal ligation is not done at BHC, but BHC workers routinely suggest that women with five or more children have a tubal ligation performed at the provincial hospital. Men can also sign up for vasectomy procedures. When a minimum of ten men have registered for vasectomies, BHC may ask for a visiting team of physicians to come to the health center to administer the procedure. A vasectomy is minimally invasive, whereas tubal ligation is considered major surgery. A consent form for tubal ligation and vasectomy, which both partners must sign, is printed on the last page of the maternal clinic card.

Whether women receive contraceptives (and which contraceptives they receive) depends on BHC's availability of supplies. Since 2006, it has happened several times that the health center has run out of different contraceptives. For instance, in May 2010, BHC ran out of combined pills, so acceptors of the combined pill were forced to take the minipill or put up with a Depo-Provera injection instead. A consignment of female condoms arrived in 2006, but even before women could become confident using them, BHC ran out of its supply; there have been no female condoms since.

Child Health and Outreach Clinics

Since the days of the mission, child health has been one of the health center's areas of focus, alongside maternal health. Immunization activities have been intensified for diphtheria, tetanus, pertussis (whooping cough), measles, and

Illustration 2.3. Mothers at Unkanan Outreach Clinic (2009). Mothers turn in their children's clinic cards. The village health aid arranges the cards in piles.

poliomyelitis. Furthermore, a vaccine against *Haemophilus influenzae* type b (a bacterium that may cause pneumonia and meningitis in children) was introduced into the childhood vaccination schedule in 2008. The hepatitis B vaccine and the Bacille Calmette-Guérin vaccine that is given to protect against childhood tuberculosis are also part of the regular child vaccination program.

Immunization services are free of charge. Mothers may bring in their infants for immunization on Wednesdays and Fridays. Maternal and child health outreach clinics are only conducted on an irregular basis due to funding difficulties and a shortage of vaccines. Nonetheless, outreach clinics are indispensable for raising the immunization coverage rate. Apart from the elevation of immunization activities, the current national health plan provides control of neonatal deaths through basic prenatal care and reduction of malnutrition and pneumonia mortality rates. All interventions, including immunization activities, target children below the age of five (GoPNG 2010a: 25).

In 2009, the health center had no funds for outreach clinics. Nevertheless, BHC personnel ran outreach clinics whenever villagers organized and paid the costs of the journey. In the villages, health workers relied on residents' hospitality for food and, if necessary, overnight lodging.

Bunapas Health Workers: Taking on and Shedding Positions

I wish to reiterate that the aim of this work is to explore Giri people's employment of biomedicine. BHC is certainly the most important institution when it comes to Giri villagers' usage of biomedical treatments. The health workers give a unique local veneer to biomedicine as it is enacted at BHC. They are at the interface between the patient and the health care system; Giri people experience biomedicine in their encounters with Bunapas health workers, some of whom are Giri and some of whom are from other Papua New Guinea localities. I begin this section with a concise overview of health workers' roles, which are definitionally dependent on the cadre they belong to. Then, I sketch BHC's employment situation.

Between 2006 and 2011, BHC was staffed by four to eight health workers belonging to three cadres of primary health workers: community health workers, nursing officers, and health extension officers. Community health workers are on the front line of primary health care. Since 1987, they have replaced what was known under Australian rule as "aid post orderlies" (Mallett 2002: 156). Community health workers attend a two-year course and deliver first aid treatment and basic obstetric care, dispense basic drugs, give injections, assist in health center clinic activities, and engage in health promotion and education. Throughout the training, particular emphasis is placed on maternal and child health (ibid.). Community health workers make up the largest proportion of health center staff.

Nurses, together with community health workers, form the "backbone of primary health care services in rural areas" (WHO 2011: 326). General nurses for rural health services undergo a three-year training program (Dawson et al. 2011: 14; Miles 1984: 135). They provide autonomous and collaborative care and supervise births. The community health workers and nursing officers support the health extension officer, who heads the health center. Health extension officers have higher clinical and diagnostic skills than do nurses (Thomason & Kolehmainen-Aitken 1991: 159). They receive four years of training and are responsible for patient care, coordination of community health services, and health center administration. Aside from these permanent staff members, trainees are also accommodated. Virtually every year, BHC hosts health extension officer and community health worker trainees.

In practice, health workers' roles are less distinct and constantly overlap and intertwine (also see Davy 2007: 234). Rosters show that shifts are often inadequately covered—partially due to staff shortages. Also, employees' preferences for scheduled days off impede adequate coverage of work requirements. It sometimes happens that a single community health worker works a shift without any supervision. Also, as it emanates from BHC's obstetric register, it is not uncommon for community health workers to take over responsibilities for the supervision of births.

Beyond the health center, biomedical care in the area is very limited. A few villages have an aid post staffed with one community health worker each. A village health volunteer sometimes aids villages without aid posts. There are about fifteen village health volunteers in the Lower Ramu area. These are unpaid lay health workers who have received a couple of weeks' training in health promotion and the provision of simple health care.

Most communities within BHC's catchment area have village midwives (so-called village birth attendants) who have received very basic Western-style midwifery training. The majority of these village birth attendants were trained in week-long courses held by World Vision (a global Christian aid, development, and advocacy organization founded in the United States in 1950) in the 1990s. More recently, the Australian Agency for International Development-funded Women and Child Health Project has offered training. Village birth attendants also work on an honorary basis, a fact much criticized by many of them, who feel inequitably treated relative to salaried aid post and health center staff.

A high staff turnover at BHC characterizes the years between my initial visit to Giri in 2006 and my most recent visit in 2011. In 2006, BHC was staffed with eight health workers: one health extension officer, who was in charge of the facility; two nursing officers; and five community health workers. Among them were two long-term Giri staff members: a nursing officer (who had been at BHC since 1991) and a community health worker who also held the position of disease control officer. (He had been brought over from the mission, and, aside from a couple of years in the 1990s, had continuously worked at BHC since that time.)

The other employees were from other villages across Madang Province, and one employee was from the bordering East Sepik Province. By the end of 2009, all non-Giri staff members, apart from the health extension officer, had left BHC. This was primarily due to conflict between residential youths and the health workers and their families. Two health workers had been verbally assaulted (a female community health worker resigned from her position after she was subjected to sexually offensive language by local youths), and the house of a health worker couple had been broken into. The other health worker left because a co-worker had slapped her in the face. The assault on staff led to temporary closures of the health center.

In 2009, newly posted personnel arrived: a non-Giri community health worker couple and a female Giri health extension officer who then worked side by side with the acting officer in charge. The two community health workers hastily left Bunapas less than a year later, after residential youths attacked the husband. BHC staff again went on strike and entirely closed its gates for a couple of days. However, the reasons for closures of the health center are manifold and mostly rest on villagers' disinclination to maintain the health center facilities and surroundings. The communities that are serviced by BHC are responsible for the upkeep of the outdoor kitchen area, pit toilet, and waste pit. Furthermore, they must cut grass at the health center grounds and clear the trails that lead to the clinic. In the majority of cases, only those services that are directly affected by villagers' nonperformance are shut down. For example, if BHC is without a toilet or waste pit, no inpatients (including confinements) are accepted.

Aside from conflict situations, many staff members felt drained from the long shifts[8] and hoped to find work at a facility with three eight-hour shifts. A community health worker in her late thirties who worked at BHC from 2001 to 2008 before she and her husband took positions at Bogia Health Center emphasized the improved working conditions there:

> [We were] not many and we saw that if we worked one day—there were only one . . . or two of us—we were possibly working until in the afternoon and again working until in the night, huh?! But when we came here . . . we saw that we are very many, and when we are many we feel that we share the workload, and when we work in the morning and come home we don't go back again and work during the night. At Bunapas we went back again for the night because there were no other staff members who could go . . . see the patients. Thus, we would go back again and see them. And here this is not the case, if we come [home], then we surely come [home].

Throughout 2010, BHC was left without replacement staff and operated with only four members of staff. Serious staffing problems arose in May of that year, when two of the remaining four staff members were granted three months' vacation from work, as they had not been on leave for three years. The health center was left with the officer in charge and one other health extension officer, who took on the role of a nurse. The officer in charge was only marginally involved in routine treatment, and the other health worker could not possibly attend to all patients alone. Some services had to be closed due to the lack of nursing staff.

Bunapas became infamous as a place where community members were hostile toward health workers and harassed them. The remaining employees were concerned that the health center would be unable to recruit any personnel and would remain understaffed. To my surprise, BHC was almost fully staffed again in mid-2011.

Beyond the Numbers:
Recipients' Ways of Looking at the Health Center

As outlined in detail above, Giri people have been living with biomedical facilities in their midst for more than fifty years and, for that same period of time, have experienced services at the front line. Also, they have observed hospital services and staff performance more closely than has anyone else. This section is aimed at understanding the institution from Giri viewpoints.

In a series of in-depth, semistructured interviews, I spoke with thirty-five Giri women and twenty-one Giri men about their opinions of the workings of the health center, BHC's physical and social environment, and the people who work at the health center. Questions such as, "Could you talk about what kind of place Bunapas Health Center is?" "What health workers do you like?" "Why do you like that particular health worker?" and "Which improvements to the health center would you suggest?" were typically asked. Interviewees illustrated the scenery, thematized gains from and problems with the health center and its staff, and expressed wishes for its development. In more personal accounts, they immersed me in their feelings. Many respondents addressed issues that are widely identified as flaws in Papua New Guinea's health delivery system: chronic underresourcing, insufficient supply of medications, ill-equipage, and poor maintenance of buildings (Bauze et al. 2009: 3; Buchanan-Aruwafu & Amos 2010; Izard & Dugue 2003; Pendene 2009). A Giri man captured the atmosphere:

> Okay, Bunapas hospital[9] . . . is nice. It is located in a . . . good spot. Nice view from it . . . So, if you are at the hospital and feel that the building with its corrugated iron roof is too hot, you, the patient, may go sit down in this spot under

the big shady [trees] along the Ramu River and . . . catch the cool breeze. At the same time, you see the motorized canoes go up and come down. The Highlanders with their areca nut filled bags come down again to go to town or so . . . The staff houses are also located along the Ramu . . . The staff can live there enjoying the nice view. They look all the way down to Base Camp. At the same time, they look the way up again.

Although it was not untypical for my interlocutors to begin their responses as above, most of them soon reverted to more critical positions. The subsequent voice critically emphasizes the need to erect further ward buildings:

It would be good if the government would look more after this hospital, and it must complete the works of this hospital. All things must come [here] . . . like wards and everything—delivery and maternal wards and . . . [wards] for the sick to stay in [i.e., special wards]. I think this would be alright. Because now yet everything is combined—the mothers give birth in the same house in which the other inpatients stay, [in] *this* room. And this is not good.

As did many other interlocutors, this woman complained of the confined premises that force women to give birth in a tiny emergency/examination room and force new mothers to share a room—the general medical ward— with all other patients if they are not in the physical condition to walk home promptly after delivery. The fact that inpatient and outpatient services are delivered in the same building was also criticized.

Many interviewees emphasized the convenience of their relative spatial proximity to the health center: "It is alright because we only pay a kina . . . [W]e stay at our own house, and we go to get medications and come back again. That is how it is and it is absolutely fine." This woman lived just a fifteen-minute walk away from BHC, but Giri people from the upper villages of Puir, Minung, and Temning were hardly able to cover the distance to and from the health center in a day's walk. These patients would rather go to the smaller, but closer Igos Health Sub-Center in the Mikarip area, located east of Giri (see map 2.1).

The comparatively low service fee was also noted as a plus factor. In the 1990s, after the government had taken over Giri health services, a nominal medical fee of twenty toea per clinic visit was introduced at BHC. The cost rose in 2002 to fifty toea and, since 2008, to one kina.[10] This amount covers a visit's consultation, examination, and treatment, a three-day supply of medications, and other medical materials, such as dressings. However, not all essential medications are available at all times. The bulk of rural health facilities in the country are affected by shortages of drug supplies, due to inefficiency and corruption in procurement and distribution processes

(Anonymous 2011; Buchanan-Aruwafu & Amos 2010: 34; GoPNG 2010a: 14–15; Noho 2011).

At health centers and aid posts throughout Madang Province, only 56 percent of required monthly key supplies of drugs were available in 2008 (in 2006 it was 56 percent, and in 2007 it was 60 percent; GoPNG 2010b: 75). The situation intensified when, after an inspection by town authorities in December 2010, the deteriorating Madang area medical store was closed, and government-run health facilities were left without supplies (Evara 2011b, 2011c; Umau 2011). BHC personnel usually solved such problems by giving similar, instead of the exact same, medication. One woman said, "Sometimes there won't be any medication—the right medication for this sickness. Then, they will give another medication . . . for this sickness."

Respondents also voiced dissatisfaction with diagnostic consultation and the quality of communication between health professionals and patients. A pregnant woman spoke about her visit to the health center:

> I told her to examine me. But she didn't check me. And she also gave me medication, but didn't tell me the following, 'You must take the tablets in the following way: two in the morning, two at midday, two in the evening.' She didn't tell me. I came up [to the village] and I did as I pleased. I took one by one [i.e., one in the morning, one at midday, and one in the evening].

Another woman contrasted the consultation practices of BHC and MGH personnel:

> When . . . I am sick and I go to Madang's hospital they will ask me all sorts of questions of detail, huh?! . . . They will ask me the following: 'Does your stomach ache or not? Does your head ache?' They feel obliged to ask you about everything . . . I am happy about this because they question me and they want to find out about my body—if my body has a sickness or has no sickness. And [at] Bunapas Health Center, sometimes we go down and we say we are sick, and when we say that we are sick, they will just give us medications for the sickness. They won't ask questions like, 'You are sick and do you suffer from headaches or do you feel nauseous or does your stomach ache or . . . ?' They won't ask this kind of questions of detail.

Some of BHC's health workers were considered to be better listeners than others. One woman said, "[Nurse's name deleted] is a good woman . . . She gives time to listen to the story of the sickness. But [nurse's name deleted] does not listen to the story of the sickness."

Many respondents advocated the employment of local health workers, who were thought to make communication between patient and health professional easier. Respondents indicated that they would feel more comfortable talking to a local health worker. A man from Kimning village stated, "It is easy for us to come talk if many local women [and] men are employed [at BHC]. And they know us and . . . we know each other. Easy! And when . . . another person from another village moves here, it will be a bit difficult. He doesn't know me well." A Regene woman said about a Giri nurse, "She is a local woman. Whatever worries I may have, I can go and directly tell her in the vernacular. She will understand well." Another woman said:

> Once I was sick and went down [to BHC]. At that time she [i.e., a community health worker] was not particularly clear about who I was . . . So, I went down and she asked me, 'Where are you from?' And [I said], 'I am from Regene.' Okay, this was the first time and she did not speak much with me . . . Okay, when I returned the next day she knew [that], oh, I am from Regene. And then she began to behave well toward me.

Above, I related complaints about workload and staff shortage from Bunapas health workers. Community responses, in contrast, have found fault with staff performance, claiming that health workers are lazy and sometimes absent during clinic hours. One man said:

> Oftentimes, I notice that they don't think about the patients . . . They don't have in mind to quickly help the patients. Oftentimes, when the patients come down [to BHC], they wait, wait, and wait . . . So, they don't help them quickly . . . Sometimes, he or she [i.e., the health worker on duty] will go out, go to do his or her gardening . . . When we come and ask, they say that it is this woman's or this man's duty . . . This is one of our problems here at the hospital.

It appears from this quotation that health workers do not necessarily fill in for others who are scheduled for work but absent. There are exemptions, but patients are often forced to go to health workers' homes to ask for medical attention. As one woman stated, "And if we wait at the hospital but no[body comes], then we will directly go to their houses."

Probably the most serious critique that Giri villagers levied was not directed toward the health center and its staff but toward members of the community. Giri people deplored the fact that many crimes occur at and around the health center, making the area widely known as the "worst place" in Giri. Aside from assaults on health center staff and burglaries and vandalism of staff houses and the health center, it sometimes happened that patients and their carers were harassed by drunken residential youths and driven off the health center grounds. Hence, people within the catchment area of BHC frequently expressed discomfort and fear about going to the area, which they increasingly perceived as a "bad and dangerous place" (ples nogut). A typical response that pictures the environment in which the health center operates in negative terms was that of a Regene woman:

> Bunapas hospital is alright, but . . . [it would be good if] they would set it up in a good environment where the cooperation of ehm . . . the adolescents [is secured], huh?! . . . I mean, our adolescents have to cooperate with the doctors [i.e., medical staff] . . . It would be good if no damage would happen. And Bunapas hospital is located . . . in a place that is not good. The name is besmirched . . . It's not a good place. I mean, the adolescents vandalize, do all sorts [of mischief], steal, et cetera.

Emily, from Kɨmnɨng village, revealed how fear of going to the area in which the health center is located has affected women's health-seeking behavior. Although Emily takes her children to the outpatient clinic, she anxiously avoids admission to the ward:

> We have noted that the people in the area commit many crimes. Thus, I am frightened . . . So, if I take my child down on my own, I won't stay [overnight]. I am nothing but frightened. I will take him [i.e., her son] back to the village. If my husband goes with me, the two of us will stay [overnight].

The proximity to Base Camp, which is just a few kilometers downstream and within sight of BHC, additionally discomfited patients. Until 2011, Base Camp had been the main reloading point for areca nuts on the Lower Ramu, and the place was notorious for violent crimes, drinking, and gambling. On more than one occasion throughout my stay in Giri, a patient came to BHC to seek medical aid after being injured in a fight at Base Camp.

Nonetheless, respondents from various Giri villages emphasized that BHC is "their local hospital" (asples haus sik bilong mipela), for which all communities must bear responsibility. A thirty-four-year-old Regene woman stated:

> We do not look after Bunapas Health Center properly. It is overgrown and many crimes occur at Bunapas Health Center . . . So, I myself am not particularly happy about Bunapas Health Center because there are many crimes. The patients come and stay on the ward, the villagers—outside villages. They [i.e., residential adolescents] come and harass the carers of the inpatients at Bunapas. So it is . . . I am not too happy about . . . the hospital because Bunapas is not properly looked after, there is no proper respect for the Bunapas staff. Therefore, I am not particularly happy. Regarding the hospital being there to help us, I am happy about this. But about . . . us the communities taking care of the hospital . . . we do not take proper care how it should be taken care of. So, this makes me not happy.

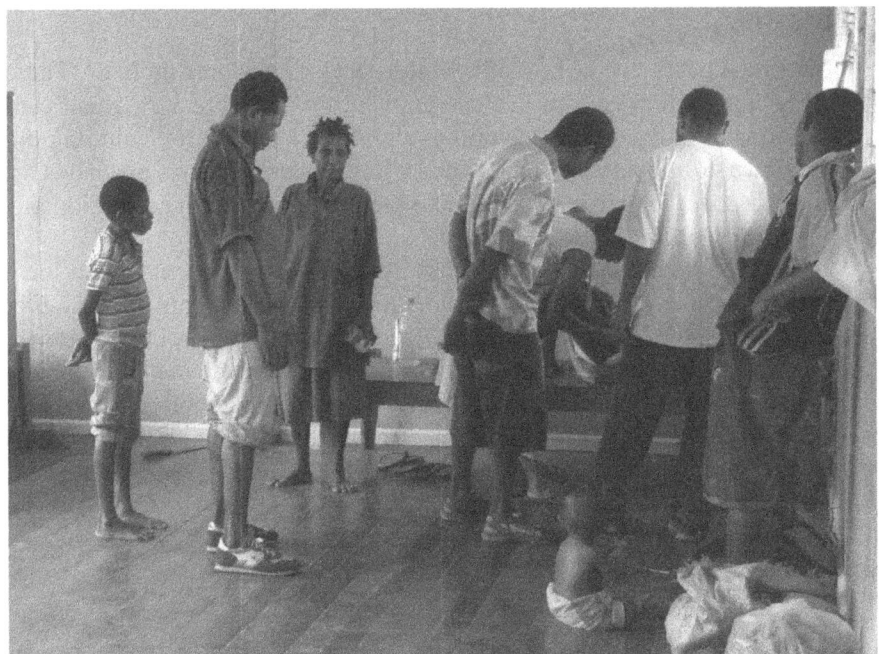

Illustration 2.4. Family gathers around a young male patient in the Bunapas Health Center ward (2009). The man was in a fight at Base Camp and was attacked with a bush knife. He has been admitted with a severe laceration of the buttocks.

This woman touched upon the issue of the maintenance on the part of the community. At the time of the interview, the pathway leading from her village, Regene, to the health center was overgrown with sword grass.

Above, I presented some thoughts and concerns that Giri people have about BHC. Several of the statements speak to the patient-health worker interaction. As one woman said, health workers might treat patients they are unfamiliar with gruffly; but this changes as soon as the health worker relates to the patient. The importance of interpersonal relationships to accessing health care and the ways Giri patients establish and foster relations with health care personnel receive special attention in chapter 4. As will become apparent, these manners are culturally embedded. Also, in that chapter, I show that the social networks patients build and maintain at biomedical institutions (BHC and MGH) are larger than just themselves and the health workers. Other patients, carers, and paramedical personnel become part of patients' networks.

Synopsis

I provided an overview of the public health services rendered by BHC. These services can be divided into five categories: inpatient care, outpatient care, maternal health care, family planning, and child health care, including outreach clinics. Numbers were intertwined with personal accounts given by Giri villagers in order to gain a more detailed picture of the health center, its staff, and its inner workings.

Villager perspectives also provided us with first glimpses of the local nature that biomedical practice takes in Giri. Their statements are, however, far from telling the whole story of biomedicine's local manifestations. Hence, in keeping with my aim to portray a Giri version of biomedicine, I turn, in the next chapter, to the Giri's current utilization and interpretation of biomedical services. Even though BHC is the biomedical facility that many area residents depend on for their care needs, we will see that Giri people also visit biomedical institutions outside the Giri area. I further analyze how the Giri navigate their way through a myriad of treatment options, of which biomedical therapy is only one.

Notes

1. The Australian Churches of Christ is an association of independent churches active in community service and overseas mission work. It grew out of an early nineteenth-century movement, with origins in the United Kingdom and the United States.
2. Luluai were government-appointed interpreters for the patrol officers, local representatives of the administration to their communities, and thus the link between the administration and the village. Each luluai had an assistant in his village, the tultul. The system of luluai and tultul stemmed from German colonial times and was continued by Australia after the takeover of the territory (see Banks 1993: 13–15; Downs 1980: xv).
3. The other health centers are the district health center in Bogia, Daigul/Hatzfeldthafen Health Center, Igos Health Sub-Center, Kayoma Health Sub-Center, and three mission-run health sub-centers in Ariangon, Malala, and Bieng.
4. One Papua New Guinea kina is equivalent to ca. 36 US cents. One hundred toea is equal to one kina.
5. In 2006, 733 maternal deaths per 100,000 live births were registered in Papua New Guinea, compared to 210 deaths in Fiji and 4 in Australia (GoPNG 2010a: 10).
6. Depo-Provera is a disputed contraceptive that was only approved in the United States in 1992, after a long debate (Russell 1999; see Strathern 1989: 146). Aside from the arguments that revolved around the contraceptive's medical side effects, the Depo-Provera debate was underpinned by ideological contradictions of the drug supporters and its opponents. The supporters—of whom the WHO and the U.S. Agency for International Development were two—hoped to use Depo-Provera to control population growth. The opponents, feminist and consumer organizations, saw women's control of their reproduction jeopardized, because Depo-Provera is largely not in

the control of the female receptors. It is injected by a health worker (and not administered by the woman herself) and once it has been injected, it cannot be removed or reversed. The woman has to wait for the hormone to wear off. The same applies to the intrauterine device, whose insertion and removal requires intervention by specifically trained medical personnel (Hartmann 1997: 301; Russell 1999: 69–72). During family planning clinics that I attended at BHC, health center workers emphasized to women the convenience of only one injection in three months with Depo-Provera. Among its Giri receptors, Depo-Provera enjoys popularity as a highly effective contraceptive providing long-term protection. Furthermore, women (and patients in general) often show reluctance to use oral medications because they experience swallowing tablets as extremely unpleasant. (Women who are on oral contraceptives occasionally skip a pill.) Conversely, an injection every three months is, in their opinion, "one-time pain." Furthermore, most women see one of the injectable's side effects—that Depo-Provera can stop their menstrual periods altogether—as a benefit (see Russell 1999: 75). Giri women also use indigenous techniques to induce amenorrhea (see chap. 5 on the ambiguity of menstrual blood).

7. The method is ineffective for women with irregular menstrual cycles. Sexually transmitted diseases pose a further problem, because they can lead to an increase in vaginal discharge, which makes distinguishing "wet" versus "dry" days difficult.
8. BHC has only two shifts—one from 8:00 AM until 4:00 PM and the other from 4:00 PM until midnight. If emergency patients happen to arrive between midnight and the morning shift, accompanying relatives go to health workers' homes to wake them up.
9. Giri villagers and health workers variably use the terms "hospital" (haus sik) and "health center" (helt senta) when referring to BHC.
10. In contrast, fees at MGH apparently rose to exorbitant levels in 2012. As Albaniel-Evara (2012b) wrote, pregnant women are charged with an enormous forty-kina fee upon their first prenatal visit. Patients coming in to be treated for domestic violence have to pay one hundred kina. The formerly free children's outpatient services now cost four kina, and admission to the children's ward is twenty kina. In her article, Albaniel-Evara quoted a Giri man who was troubled by the increased fees.

Chapter Three
Technologies of Disenchantment
Medical Pluralism through a Series of Lenses

This chapter is the first of three to address the question of how Giri people, who have their own medical traditions, respond to new theories of illness causation and novel treatments. I focus, in this chapter, on terminological and technological innovations. To be precise, I demonstrate, through the investigation of two case studies, how these novelties have impacted the established medical system. Through an examination of inflection, I elucidate how the introduced theories and treatment strategies have become localized. In doing so, I bear in mind that biomedicine is not a homogenous entity but instead is shaped by the local setting and its actors. I show how, in a global and networked world, an instance of biomedical technology, an instance of entertainment technology, a parlor game, and a drug have come to play a central role in Giri theories of illness causation and local treatment strategies.

I deal with traditional beliefs about illness causation and therapeutic care as well as glocalized (Robertson 1992, 1995) aspects of biomedicine. It is important to comprehend how ancestral spirits, who are very much present in Giri life, are believed to cause illness in order to understand why Giri people think that marijuana can have an illness-causing "spirit." My analysis revolves around the Giri patient, who is, as Keck eloquently described, "the (sick) node in a constantly reconfigured web of relationships" (Verena Keck, pers. comm. 2011; my own translation[1]). As in the other chapters, special emphasis is placed on the utilization of BHC and MGH services. Information from the biomedical perspective is combined with ethnographic data.

Excursus: Illness, Disease, and Sickness

Given that much of this book deals with ill health, it seems useful to clarify what anthropologists usually mean when they speak of "illness," "disease," and "sickness." A subdivision of the generic "sickness" into "illness" and "disease" was defined by Kleinman, who introduced illness and disease as two different explanatory concepts: "*Disease* refers to a malfunctioning of biological and/or psychological processes, while the term *illness* refers to the psychological experience and meaning of perceived disease" (1980: 72). Before long, Kleinman (1982: 169–70) reformulated his classification to make clear that "disease" does not refer to an actual "malfunctioning" but instead to the medical professional's interpretation. However, soon after this, Hahn leveled the criticism that the illness/disease dichotomy merely reiterates the old mind/body dichotomy in a new way (1984).

Sobo recently summarized the problem: "While 'disease,' as the dichotomy defines it, is anchored in the body, 'illness' is conversely anchored in the mind: disease is thus attributed (whether it has it or not) a real, concrete, scientific factuality or objectivity that illness, as a subjective category, may be denied" (2011: 15–16). Other medical anthropologists, among them Keck (1992) and A. Strathern and P. Stewart (1999), have also uncovered weaknesses in Kleinman's initial division. Not only have they criticized the idea that disease is not a physical given, but they have conveyed the point that the concept of disease comes from a Euro-American biomedical tradition and may be lacking in other cultures.

However, A. Strathern and P. Stewart also suggested that notions comparable to the concept of disease in biomedical terms may exist: "Analogous ideas may be present that enable us to see how people distinguish narrowly between a particular condition and the wider experience of suffering from it and showing its symptoms" (1999: 6–7). They advocated the perpetuation of the terms, with an awareness of their limitations: "At the widest level, though, the distinction is useful in terms of the difference between a narrow definition of a condition (disease) and its broader experiential setting (illness), a distinction that may coincide with a difference of perspective between the 'doctor' and the 'patient' in a given case" (7). Throughout this work, the terms "illness" and "disease" are used in the manner suggested by A. Strathern and P. Stewart (1999).

Criticism was also made by Mol (2002) from a perspectivalist viewpoint. Perspectivalism shakes off the concept of disease as "biological malfunction," treating "disease" and "illness" as two differing perspectives: "In perspectivalism, the words 'disease' and 'illness' are no longer used to contrast physical facts with personal meaning. Instead, they differentiate between the perspectives of doctors on the one hand and those of patients on the other" (10–11). Medical anthropologists generally tend to focus on the study of illness, and not disease. However, some social scientists, such as Mol, have refused to limit themselves to the exploration of illness and leave the study of disease to physicians. Mol set out to investigate atherosclerosis of the leg arteries as disease.

Her aim was to study "disease 'itself'" (Mol 2002: 12). Mol studied atherosclerosis as a multiple, and investigated how this multiple is coordinated, in practice, into singularity. She turned against the view of disease as a singular and fixed object and thus opened a new field of research for the social sciences: "If we no longer presume 'disease' to be a universal object hidden under *the* body's skin, but make the praxiographic shift to studying bodies and diseases while they are being enacted in daily hospital practices, multiplication follows. In practice a disease, atherosclerosis, is no longer *one*. Followed while being enacted atherosclerosis multiplies—for practices are many" (83).

Medical Pluralism and Conceptual Innovation

Frankel and Lewis's anthology *A Continuing Trial of Treatment* (1989) was a landmark publication for studies of medical pluralism in Papua New Guinea. The contributors to this volume impressively argued that medical pluralism has become a common pattern in Papua New Guinea societies.[2] Without doubt, the Giri medical system can be described as pluralistic because it incorporates traditional medicine, biomedicine, nonindigenous shamanic (glasman) medicine, Christian healing techniques, and herbal treatments. Giri people view these different medical traditions as anything but irreconcilable.

Throughout an illness episode, Giri patients and their therapy managers usually pragmatically employ multiple diagnostic methods and therapeutic procedures. Sometimes, they draw heavily on biomedical health services; at other times, they resort to traditional practices, to Christian prayers, or to a nonindigenous shaman. Sometimes they draw upon the different diagnostic and therapeutic procedures consecutively; sometimes they use them in parallel. People's choices of diagnostic and treatment procedures depend on a multiplicity of factors, including accessibility and cost (see Macfarlane 2009: 49; Macintyre et al. 2005: 89).[3]

In accordance with other Papua New Guinea cultures, Giri integrate the different medical traditions into one medical system rather than several systems coexisting side by side (see, for instance, LiPuma 1989: 302; Roscoe 1989: 201). A notably visible innovation in the Giri medical system, as a consequence of the population's contact with biomedicine, is the extension of local illness categories, through which biomedicine is integrated in the local medical framework. An excursus on the usage of Kire medical terms reveals that, prior to pre-Western contact, Giri people distinguished between "minor illness" (*rimrim do-ogi*) and "major illness" (*rimrim ba-akeri*). *Rimrim do-ogi* (*rimrim* is the generic term for "illness"; *do-ogi* means "small," "little," or "minor") describes bodily disorders that are nonlethal and can be ascribed to natural causes, such as minor wounds or coughs.

These are normally treated with home remedies. Conversely, *rimrim ba-akeri* (*ba-akeri* means "big," "large," "great," or "major") refers to social illnesses caused by sorcery, bush and ancestral spirits, taboo violation, or social transgression. Illnesses that fall into this category are mostly severe illnesses, often with a fatal outcome. Diminished appetite with subsequent weight loss is regarded as a major illness, if these symptoms endanger a person's life and are attributable to a social cause. However, a nonlethal headache or a sprained ankle as a result of trespassing on a taboo place inhabited by a bush spirit would also fall into this category. Classificatory systems that distinguish bodily disorders from social illnesses are well known from all corners of Papua New Guinea. Keck, for instance, dedicated her *Social Discord and Bodily Disorders* to this topic, as is evident from the book's title (see Keck 2005: 79).

Contemporary Giri people differentiate between "local illness" (*gun rimrim; gun* means "village" or "place") and "ordinary ailments" (*rimrim;* literally just "illness"). This categorization is a more recent phenomenon and was, according to my interlocutors, adopted from terminology employed by health workers at Tung Aid Post, the Paternoster Memorial Hospital (later BHC), and MGH. These medical workers delineated diseases for which they can provide biomedical treatment as "physical disorders" (sik bilong bodi) in contrast to "local illnesses" (sik bilong ples; literally: "illnesses of the village"). The latter are illnesses that remain unaffected by biomedical therapy. The Giri people added a third category: "foreign illness" (sik bilong waitman; literally: "illness of the white people"). This term circumscribes illnesses, such as measles, that Westerners introduced.

Some "foreign illnesses" existed in Giri before Western contact, although they were, in ancient times, understood as only an assemblage of symptoms and—depending on the perceived etiology and severity—identified as either "minor illness" (*rimrim do-ogi*) or "major illness" (*rimrim ba-akeri*). One such illness is malaria, or "maralia"—a word that resulted from mishearing on the part of Giri villagers and which, today, is widely used in the Giri area. The term "foreign illness" is often used interchangeably with "physical disorder," as the Giri assume that all such illnesses respond to biomedicine (waitman marasin; literally: "medicine of the white people"). Nevertheless, physical disorders are also susceptible to local—primarily herbal—remedies. In Kire, Giri people also classify "foreign illness" as *rimrim*.

Similar to the former conception of "major" illnesses, local illnesses are grounded in disrupted social relations[4] with the living, ancestors, and bush spirits (*thor;* masalai);[5] this includes other people's wrongdoings and the knowledge of these and violation of behavioral codes and social norms. Local illnesses are susceptible only to traditional cures, and harmonious social relationships must be reinstated to restore health. In other words, the social self can only be restored by healing the social body (see, e.g., Ayers Counts 1991; Frankel 1986: 124–36).

A typical etiology of a local illness follows: A person is visited by a hungry relative but refuses to give him or her garden produce or a bamboo tube filled with sago. The host not only denies food but closes up, thus also denying the relationship. Some time after the visitor leaves, the host suffers from a headache, and she or he knows that the hungry relative's shadow soul (ŋina) caused it. Giri people understand the person to be "faceted, multiple, and not completely contained within the body" (Lindstrom 1999: 197); they think of this relative's soul entering and affecting the refuser's body.[6] Thus, the shadow soul temporarily transgresses body boundaries.

Other examples of local illness may be found in a man who lies in bed with fever after he has felled a tree on another's land and thus enraged the resident bush spirit; a wasted middle-aged woman who is said to have consumed tabooed foods twenty years ago when she was a *mon mbik* (literally: "new woman"; i.e., a young woman who, following her menarche, stays in seclusion as part of the female life cycle and initiation ritual that marks a woman's entrance into adulthood); or an elderly man who loses his eyesight after he has watched assault/death sorcerers (*fiaŋ guma;* sanguma man) kill another person. The scenario of a man who sickens after he has chopped down a tree on foreign land once more exemplifies Giri conceptions of permeability—the resident bush spirit punishes the offender with a fever. Moreover, this example illustrates that relationality also links individuals to nonhumans.

In relation to permeability, A. Strathern and P. Stewart also took sorcery as an example, asking, "How else to explain the great concern throughout New Guinea and elsewhere with sorcery as a force that breaches body boundaries?" (2000: 64). Whereas, in Giri thought, poison sorcerers extract bodily substance (*fava ŋan*) from the victim and then get the victim to imbibe a poisonous substance, the breach of body boundaries in assault sorcery is more brutal: assault sorcerers are said to attack their victims, cutting them open with bamboo knives and operating on them with tools made from flying fox bones. Assault sorcerers remove a major piece of flank meat—the person's "strength" (strong bilong man)—replacing it with soil and stitching the victim's body up again, lest others notice the intrusion.

The shift from the categories of minor and major illness to ordinary illness and local illness enforces a differentiation between naturally and socially induced illnesses. Recently, a major alteration has occurred, in that the concept of *rimrim* now embraces serious illnesses—in addition to minor complaints—since they respond to biomedical treatment. Several of the contributing authors of *A Continuing Trial of Treatment* (1989) and others have observed changes of illness categories that match those of the Giri.[7] The extension of illness categories is a phenomenon that is also prevalent in non-Melanesian Oceanic cultures.[8]

Technological Innovation

When biomedicine is transplanted to non-Western cultures, it is generally subjected to considerable transformation but also impacts the local medical system, setting changes into motion and often leading to repercussions. The introduction of biomedicine to Giri transformed not only illness terminology but also biomedical technologies. In my discussion of this, I follow Lock, who defined "technology" as "tools, machines, artefacts, prostheses, and other devices that have been created through human effort for the purpose of changing, manipulating, or controlling the natural and human worlds" (2004: 93). The Giri are far from passive receptors of biomedical technologies. Giri interaction with and employment of biomedical technologies has led to innovation in the domain of illness diagnosis; this, in turn, has retroactively impacted their theory of illness causation and—more obviously—treatment choices.

Lock and Nguyen put it this way: "Biomedical technologies are not autonomous entities, the effects of which are essentially uniform whenever they are put into operation" (2010: 5). Further, they suggested: "Biomedical technologies are, of course, designed expressly to facilitate human intervention into the workings of the human body in health and illness; in implementation they change us, and even as they themselves are constantly modified, they change the world in which we live" (20). Below, I focus on a specific diagnostic imaging technology that enjoys a certain popularity among the Giri—the X-ray machine (and the images it produces)—and show how Giri people actively make sense of and incorporate this technology into their system of medical beliefs. As will become apparent, the X-ray has taken on an unexpected life in Giri.

First let me say a few words on the history of biomedical diagnostic technologies in Giri. Churches of Christ mission personnel introduced these technologies. Lou Beresford (pers. comm. 2009) remembered those early times and how the missionary nurses diagnosed filariasis at their clinic, with the help of microscopic examination of a patient's blood sample. Until the governmental takeover of BHC, hemoglobin counts were taken to detect anemia. Today, BHC still has a functioning microscope; it is exclusively utilized, though, by BHC's disease control officer to identify tuberculosis organisms in sputum samples. The microscopic examination of blood samples for malaria diagnostics has been abandoned since the introduction of malaria rapid diagnostic tests.

Other diagnostic technologies include two combined aura-/ophthalmoscopes, a stethoscope, three fetoscopes, and four or five vaginal examination trays (each composed of sponge-holding forceps, a small bowl, a beak speculum, and a Sims's speculum), three hanging scales, a balance scale, and a foot scale. It is clear that only very basic biomedical diagnostic technology

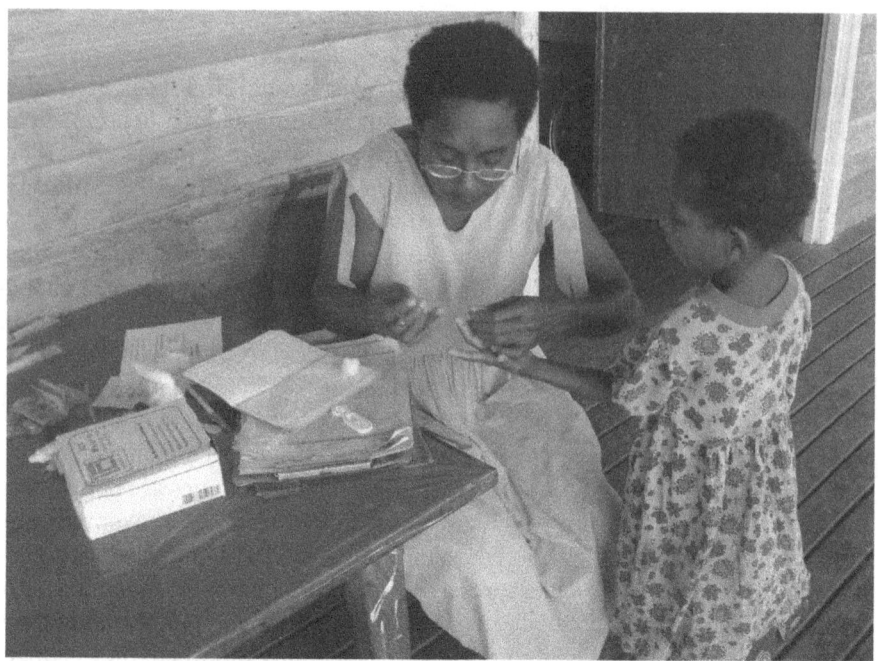

Illustration 3.1. Malaria rapid diagnostic test (2009). A health extension officer pricks a girl's finger to obtain a drop of blood for a malaria rapid diagnostic test.

is available at BHC. If more elaborate technologies, such as X-ray, ultrasound, or further blood tests, are required for an examination, the patient is generally referred to MGH.

Before I delve into the first ethnographic case study, I shall provide background information on the medical tradition from which the X-ray originates. With the Enlightenment, a strong belief in natural science took hold in Europe and North America, and thence, a "truth-to-nature" relationship came to characterize Western medicine. In the late nineteenth and early twentieth centuries, a claim to mechanical objectivity evolved, which "is characterized by a drive to repress any wilful intervention on the part of the observer in the process of representation" (Lock & Nguyen 2010: 37). Although the elimination of subjectivity was illusory, mechanical objectivity was alluring when biomedical technologies advanced (ibid.; see Daston & Galison 1992, 2007 on the notion of objectivity in science).

X-rays, accidentally discovered by the German Wilhelm C. Röntgen in 1895, heralded a new era in biomedicine. Schinzel splendidly phrased this: "The inside of the living human was only accessible via invasive intrusions into the body. The invention of X-ray, later followed by a variety of sophisticated medical imaging technologies opened new alternatives per 'optical invasion' into the living body, overcoming the limitations of the impermeable layers of skin, tissue, organs and bones" (2006: 190).

In the past, the Giri were familiar with postmortem examinations in cases of suspected unnatural death (usually performed to detect traces of sorcery), but not with direct views into the living body (only sorcerers are said to cut open living bodies). Postmortem examinations were common, as only a very small number of deaths in Giri were ascribed to natural causes (cf. Tuzin 1980: 142; von Poser 2013: 206). In theory, older people (or, as the Giri say, "overaged" people [*guma gu mbik vur*]) may die a natural death. In practice, however, I never heard of anyone actually dying because they were "overaged."

In my time with the Giri, I remember only two deaths that were said to have been the consequence of grief and not of assault/death sorcery (*fiaŋ guma*) or of poison sorcery (*kuk*)—one being the suicide of a university student and the other the passing of a middle-aged paralyzed woman. Giri encounters with living body imaging had already begun, though—not with the X-ray but through contact with glasman (Papua New Guinea medical specialists on whose healing techniques the Giri began to draw some time after World War II). Glasman generally claim to have "X-ray vision." Nevertheless, the Giri themselves did not catch a glimpse into the living human body until their experience with X-ray images at MGH began.

In the case study that follows, I untangle what it means to Giri people to look into their bodies underneath the very meaning-laden skin (see chap. 5 for discussion of skin). Biomedical imaging technology enables the Giri to obtain information on the state of their health in a quick and easy way. Those readers who have an X-ray image of a broken bone in mind will be stunned by the creativity and wit of Rita, who made use of the X-ray and its potential. The second purpose of this case study is to show Giri illness categorization in practice. Rita felt it necessary to define her illness in terms of either local illness (*gun rimrim*) or foreign illness (*rimrim*), and her actions depended on the category to which she allocated her illness at different stages of the illness episode.

Rita utilized the X-ray as a means to determine whether she was suffering from a local or foreign illness. Whenever new information became available or she noticed a change in her health status, former assumptions about the nature of the illness were overthrown. As will become apparent, this involved an arduous process of trial and error in treatment. Both this case study and the case study that follows demonstrate that a distinction between diagnosis and treatment is unsustainable. Instead, the identification of the problem is intimately interwoven with attempts toward its resolution (cf. Csordas & Kleinman 1996: 4).

Prelude to Case Study 1: Clinic Cards

Several authors have shown that it is extremely fruitful to include information from the viewpoint of biomedicine in medical anthropological work. Among them are K. Sykes (2007), who talked to a nurse at the local aid post, and Keck (2005: section 2, chap. 2), who reviewed medical files and conducted interviews with multiple health center staff. For the first case study, detailing Rita's illness episode, I dovetail Rita's own interpretations with information from her clinic card (helt buk). Over a period of three years, I conversed with Rita in numerous interviews (sometimes in a triad with her husband, who supplemented information).

Ideally, patients should carry their clinic card to every clinic that they attend—be it an aid post, health center, or hospital—so that medical personnel can get a general idea of the patient's medical history and keep the card up-to-date. In practice, patients often forget to bring along their clinic cards, cannot find the cards because children have played with and misplaced them, or lose them—often when fire destroys houses, because patients mostly keep their clinic cards (with other valuables, such as money, school certificates, and traditional finery) in the sago thatching of the roof of their house.

Gaps in medical history, as recorded on the clinic card, are therefore hardly avoidable. The Papua New Guinea Department of Health distributes clinic cards, and they can be purchased at hospitals, health centers, aid posts, and pharmacies. The price of four kina for an adult clinic card, four kina for a child's clinic card, and five kina for a maternal clinic card (all prices as of 2010 at BHC) is a fair amount of money, given that five kina is the equivalent of two bamboo tubes full of sago (on which a family of four can feed for two days). Hence, the health personnel frequently write their notes on all kinds of paper that they find in their office (such as patient information leaflets or ripped pages from medical records), which they hand to patients (who generally do not keep them).

In Rita's case, I was lucky; she generously granted me access to her clinic cards, which she had kept since mid-1987. Large gaps only appeared from mid-1990 to mid-1992 and in 1996. Although I prepared full transcripts of her clinic cards, I did not include them in this book in order to protect her privacy.

Case Study 1: Medical Pluralism in the Life of Rita

In the introduction of this book, I began telling the story of Rita's illness. I discussed the onset of her illness and presented two major threads in her analysis of the cause of her illness. She initially assumed that her respiratory illness was a physical disorder that would respond to biomedical drugs and herbal remedies. However, from 1996 onward, having heard her relative Norma's report, Rita began to categorize her illness as local in nature—caused by poison sorcery and thus not receptive to biomedical treatment.

In 1998, a year in which she was first diagnosed with asthma and frequently struck by bouts of ill health (according to her clinic card) and a phase in which she believed her illness to be caused by sorcery, Rita consulted two glasman in an attempt to clarify whether the man whom Norma had named had ensorcelled her and in order to find a cure.

The X-ray Vision of a Glasman

Glasman—non-Giri Papua New Guinea shamans—are new to the Giri medical system. The Giri either visit glasman in their respective villages or pay glasman to come to Giri. I shall now explain how glasman medicine is effective in cases of ensorcellment and describe its origin. A Regene man, aged thirty-eight, explained the term glasman as follows: "He assesses a person . . . looks [inside] the person . . . inside the person's entire body. He looks at a person's body—starting with his fingers and moving upwards to his head—[identifying whether] the illness is located in which body part." A man of similar age, from Birap 2, added, "He will look into you and study you. He will find out what had caused the illness or who had ensorcelled you. He will tell you." The glasman sees the cause of the illness inside the body; he identifies traces of sorcery in the victim.

Allan, in his description of glasman medicine in the Dreikikir area (East Sepik Province), highlighted that "'Glassing' involves looking into a person's body in search of sorcery material or other objects . . . which may have been placed there by a sorcerer" (1989: 60–61). Mihalic stated, in his translation of the Tok Pisin word glasman, that the glasman sees things that are not visible to everyone. The glasman is "a seer, anyone who claims the gift of seeing the spirits or communicating with them" (Mihalic [1971] 1986: 88). W. Mitchell spoke of the glasman as "a diagnostician with second sight" (1990: 432).

Lattas (2000: 327–28) surmised that the word glasman originates from shamans' utilization of dreams and visions in a way that is analogous to white people's employment of binoculars or field glasses—in the sense that both enable a direct gaze on what is otherwise hidden (see Lohmann 2003 on the role of dreaming in glasman medicine). The Giri use the Kire term *rii gari guma* (literally: "man who sees the illness")—a translation of the Tok Pisin term glasman—because they do not have an indigenous term for this novel concept. In contradistinction to the Giri, the Sambia[9] of Eastern Highlands Province have traditional shamans who work in a similar way to that of the glasman and have equivalent screening abilities: "Trance provides the characteristic 'X-ray' vision of the shaman, allowing him or her to see inside the patient's body for divination" (Herdt 1989: 100).

Giri villages are among a considerable number in the Madang and Sepik Provinces into which glasman medicine has found its way since the Pacific War. The sociolinguistic groups nearest to Giri that have an account on glasman medicine are the Rao[10] and Breri. Their villages are situated in the Lower Ramu area farther upriver and to the area south of the Kire. In an article from 1968, Stanhope discussed the interaction of traditional and imported medical systems, with an example of the latter being glasman medicine. According to Stanhope, the glasman deals with "disturbed relationships" (1968: 144). Although Stanhope's assumption of a disparity between the different health systems and his perception of "competing" systems rather than interplaying ones need to be reexamined, his description yields valuable data on the introduced glasman medicine. As in Giri, in the Rao-Breri region, the emergence of medical specialists is a recent phenomenon.

Stanhope (1968: 138) pointed out that, up until the antecedent generation, medical knowledge and techniques were shared and diagnostic methods and treatments were applied by virtually all members of the community—with age and experience the only factors of distinction. This complies more or less with Giri's previous system, with the exception that, prior to glasman, only the clan leaders dealt with sorcery accusations in Giri. The Breri depend on Rao practitioners because they do not have their own glasman.

Two individuals brought glasman medicine to Rao: Gramuri and Gregotongi. Gramuri was from the Rao village Urinebu and gained his knowledge between 1940 and 1958 on New Britain. Gregotongi was from Ambai'ati, located farther upriver between Annaberg and Aiome, and was famous for his knowledge of this specialist medicine. Gramuri would examine the patient's body to locate the source of the complaint and listen to the patient's history. Gregotongi would only treat victims of sorcery. Three Rao men went to Ambai'ati to receive training from Gregotongi (Stanhope 1968: 142).

In Maindroin, a Sissano village on the north coast of the West Sepik Province, glasman medicine arose in the mid-1940s and spread from there to many villages along Papua New Guinea's north coast. Biomedical work began much later in Sissano, when a clinic run by five Franciscan nuns from Queensland, Australia was established in 1962. The first glasman in Maindroin was a man who had served the allied troops in the Sepik region and had much outside experience. He discovered his abilities in 1947 when looking after his first child, born with a twisted leg, who was treated at the Aitape hospital. In subsequent years, glasman fanned out to Serra, Matapau, and across the Torricelli Mountains. In 1990, glasman were more powerful in Maindroin than were traditional healers, even though several traditional healers had integrated elements of glasman practice into their own. These days, if traditional treatment is unsuccessful, glasman are usually consulted.

The glasman employ Christian faith healing and exorcism in addition to traditional beliefs and practices (Haiveta 1990: 441–43). Haiveta remarked, "The term *glasman* may have something to do with the examination through a microscope of blood samples on glass slides observed by local people in hospitals" (443). He said further, "In the Maindroin context, he is a person with the ability to see *past* events that point to the cause of sickness and the power to heal in a state of trance" (ibid.).

The examples of the development of glasman medicine in Rao-Breri and Maindroin illustrate how various medical practices—such as Christian faith healing—have been incorporated into glasman medicine and how the latter has been shaped by contemporary streams of thought. Traditional healers have acquired new skills and used them in a biomedical-like way—that is, analogously to a microscope or an X-ray. As mentioned above, the Giri did not traditionally have medical specialists, such as glasman, who could relieve ensorcelled persons. Rita pragmatically remarked about ensorcelled ones prior to glasman: "They were bound to death."

There was only one way to save the afflicted: village leaders would meet and talk about the victim's illness and the conflict that could have brought it on. Throughout the following days and weeks the villagers would watch one another's behavior to determine who behaved suspiciously and must therefore hold the item impregnated with the victim's bodily substance (*fava ŋan*). One villager, who had previously been accused of sorcery, illuminated the identification process:

> All men in the village observe the movement of all men. They will observe the movement of all men [and] say: "He perambulates to what purpose; he goes that way. He made this work on this day." All men in the community observe every man. You will watch me and I will watch you and you and I will watch another man in our village. During this phase the men find out that this man knows sorcery [techniques]. And very importantly, you are not allowed to touch anything in the sorcerer's basket. This is forbidden, strictly forbidden! If you ask for something, he himself will get it and give it to you.

Village leaders from all Giri villages would meet again, unmask the identified sorcerer, and force him to release his victim. Such meetings still take place, but often the presumed sorcery victims, such as Rita, seek the help of a glasman rather than ascribing their illness overhastily to the actions of a specific sorcerer.

The first glasman on whose services Rita drew was from Begesin (Middle Ramu District) and had a history of successfully treating cases of Giri sorcery. A thirty-eight-year-old relative from Regene told me about one of these cases. A girl from Giri lived with her parents in the coastal village of Malala (located twenty kilometers past Hatzfeldthafen [see map 1.1] in the direction of Madang), where her father worked as a school cook. The cook suspected a Giri boy, who attended school in Malala, to have stolen a branch of his areca nut. When the boy went home during the holidays, he told his father about the cook's accusations. When the cook's daughter became ill, the cook remembered that the boy's father had previously come to Malala, where he had attended the Independence Day celebrations and must have appropriated a leftover piece of bread (with the girl's saliva clinging to it).

In anger from the affront to his son, the visitor was believed to have ensorcelled the cook's daughter. It is not unusual for the sorcery victim to not be the actual offender but close kin (cf. Chowning 1987: 164). As a visitor to the cook's house at the time, my interlocutor had witnessed the onset of the girl's illness. She had excruciating stomachaches and her parents brought her to Hatzfeldthafen Health Center. Admitted to the health center, she was treated with biomedical drugs, but the pains persisted, so the health personnel referred her to MGH. The girl's father decided to consult a glasman first—having in mind the incident at Independence Day. He and my consultant carried the girl to the glasman's house in Malala. The glasman requested a tobacco leaf, a red cordyline leaf, and an areca nut from the cook. (To prepare to see inside a patient's body, the glasman chews a piece of a special bark or vine combined with areca nut, mustard, and lime.)

In this case, he worked a magic spell and smoked the tobacco; then he uttered another incantation and chewed the areca nut (see Lohmann 2003 on the role of tobacco in glasman techniques). When the glasman swallowed the juice, the men heard his throat making a clacking sound. My interlocutor explained: this was the moment when the glasman pulled the things causing pain from the girl's stomach and swallowed them. He threw them up again and pieces of broken glass and a razor blade came to light. The glasman spat the items in a coconut shell of water and instructed the cook to throw the shell and its content into a toilet pit. The girl recovered from her illness.

The vomiting up of pain-causing objects was described by Allan: "Treatments usually involve the removal of foreign objects from the body of the patient by sleight-of-hand or mouth. These objects are placed in a coconut shell of cold water to neutralize their power and are shown to the patient and onlookers who are invariably greatly impressed" (1989: 61). In Giri opinion, the diagnostic function (the screening of the body) is the primary concern of the glasman's performance. Yet, the glasman techniques have a second objective: therapy—that is, the removal of harmful objects from the patient's body. I emphasize this as an instance in which the dovetail relationship of diagnosis and therapy becomes apparent.

Rita and her husband met this Begesin glasman in Madang Town. Rita stated that he had "seen" her illness and had confirmed that she had been ensorcelled. Several times the glasman requested twenty kina for his services but did not undertake any such treatment as described above. Rita's health status did not improve, so she and her husband abandoned the "swindler"—as the couple called him. A few months later, Rita heard relatives talking about another glasman from Kayoma (see map 2.1). A man from Regene village had taken his ill father to the man, and another female relative from Giri 2 had told Rita that the same glasman had cured her illness. Rita and her husband decided to give it a second chance and undertook the journey to Kayoma. Accompanied by Rita's mother's brother (*vurfek*) Edgar and her then small children Phyllis and Christian, they traveled up the Ramu in a motor canoe.

The glasman took his customers to an in-law's family house. He split a gorgor[11] stem in the middle, pulled it open, and told Rita to step in the opening and pass through it. Afterward, he gave Rita a fluid to drink, which may have been an extraction from the same gorgor plant. The group returned to the glasman's house, and Tim and Edgar began to question the healer about Rita's illness. They expected him to expose the cause of her illness. Had she been ensorcelled? By whom? And for what reason? But the man did not give a definite answer. That is the "way of the glasman," as Rita formulated it. He would not give any information without extra payment, but Rita and her husband did not have any more money to give to him. Indeed, for the "small work" with the gorgor, he had already charged ninety kina.

Rita meticulously observed her health status during the following weeks, but the expected improvement did not occur. She and her husband sent a letter to the glasman to query his work. The glasman replied and informed them that healing would have taken place had there not been dispute in Rita's family that had inhibited Rita's convalescence. The glasman went on to say that the dispute must have arisen after he had completed his treatment. At that time, Rita and Tim did not take the glasman's letter seriously and got the impression that he wanted to talk his way out of their complaint.

Of Sik Bilong Bodi and "Trial" Tuberculosis Treatment

From 1999 to 2006, Rita exclusively relied on biomedical treatment. No more than ten visits for her respiratory problems are noted in her clinic card during this phase. On 16 November 2004 she was first diagnosed with pulmonary tuberculosis, though a question mark follows the diagnosis in the clinic card. The clinic card does not unequivocally state how the health worker arrived at this diagnosis, especially because Rita was known at BHC as a chronic asthmatic patient. The medical record does not indicate that a sputum test (to identify tuberculosis organisms) was carried out. One reason for the diagnosis may be that the attending community health worker, who had only recently started work at BHC, was not familiar with Rita's case. He noted in the clinic card that Rita complained of "shortness of breath & dry cough since 9 years," but he might not have checked earlier entries properly and may have thus overlooked references to asthma.

That Rita also complained of weight loss and a lack of appetite, was mildly febrile "at times," and had not responded to earlier broad-spectrum antibiotics (all noted by the community health worker) must have informed the health worker's decision to put Rita on "trial" tuberculosis treatment. Furthermore, a general trend in Papua New Guinea to put more energy into fighting tuberculosis may have influenced the health worker's decision. Since the 1997 inception of the DOTS (Directly Observed Treatment, Short-Course) program to combat tuberculosis—a major strategy in the World Health Organization's (WHO's) global tuberculosis eradication program—implementation of the National TB (tuberculosis) Program Unit had begun.

Nevertheless, I was surprised that anyone would have been willing to put Rita on "trial" tuberculosis treatment considering, on the one hand, that it involved a combination of strong drugs (Rita received isonicotinic acid hydrazide, rifampicin, and pyrazinamide) and, on the other, that biomedical diagnostic technologies were available at BHC (such as a sputum test) and MGH that would have allowed clarification of this suspect diagnosis. On her next visit, on 6 December 2004, Rita was put on another course of tuberculosis treatment. Rita increasingly experienced backaches, pains in her coccyx region, and numbness of her extremities. She had developed another serious condition, which appears first on 5 July 2000 in her clinic card as "dysuria/ feeling an organ hanging outside—prolapsed." On 31 August 2004 she was diagnosed with "pelvic inflammatory disease." One and a half years later, a female nursing officer referred her to MGH with suspicion of a prolapsed uterus or a fibroid in the uterus.

A month later she visited the outpatient clinic at MGH and was referred to MGH's medical clinic, where she was diagnosed on 4 April 2006 with osteoarthritis and sacroiliitis and was put on Indocid, which she had already received a couple of times from BHC. To summarize, the phase from 1999 to 2006 was characterized by a number of differing diagnoses, which Rita understood collectively to be bodily disorders or, as in the case of tuberculosis, foreign illnesses. She received a range of powerful biomedical drugs. Still, her health status deteriorated, rather than improved. Rita was torn: Was Norma a reliable source? Had Norma spoken untruth or should her statement be believed? Did she suffer from a local illness or a bodily disorder?

The Meaning of Darkness on the X-ray Image

This question became more pressing in April 2007, when Rita's health status dropped to the worst it had ever been—so poor that she lost consciousness (*ŋama rimgi;* literally: "dead, yet still alive") from time to time due to shortness of breath. She felt so weak and miserable that she would not leave her bed for days. To ease the symptoms, her husband and children prepared *kamfarkhem* extract for her again, but the desired alleviating effect did not occur. Rita and her family feared that she would suffocate. Throughout these difficult days, girls and women from the entire village heavily trafficked the path leading to Rita's house—Forge, Tuguge, and even Regene women and girls carried prepared dishes to her house.

Every day, Regene villagers carried plates of sago pudding, boiled plantains, root and tuber crops, and sometimes rice dishes, all supplemented with fish, leafy vegetables, and occasionally meat to nearby kin (on similar food-shifting routines, see Kulick 1992: 27; L. Stewart 1989: 117; von Poser 2013: 114–18). I had learned that this radius is sometimes extended. The reasons for this are manifold—for instance if kin from another village visit, a group of men has plaited sago leaves for one's rooftop, or a church group from another village has come for a seminar. Seriously ill villagers are also included in this circle, not least to emphasize one's good relationship with and worries about the sick person in order to avoid accusations of sorcery, should death occur.

Another group of people frequented Rita's house—Giri church folk came to pray for her recovery. Tim had asked kin-related members of the Giri Roman Catholic Church (i.e., the Parish Steering Team) from Regene, Kɨmnɨng, Akɨkɨm, and Varanɨng for their support. On an early morning, they approached Rita and Tim's house in Daun Camp. They hit the ground with sago palm leafstalks and made a thunderous noise. Rita and her family shivered when they heard the awful din, though they knew that the noise was made to chase away malevolent spirits.

It was such a racket that two Forge women, who had not known about the Parish Steering Team's scheduled visit, were worried that a fight had been brought to their village. The women aimed to flee to the swamps until other household members who knew what was going on finally stopped them. The church group shouted: "You, you malevolent spirits, we chase you away in the name of Jesus! You go and go altogether; you pack up your entire luggage! You have to pack up and you have to go! Your place is the hell fire!" After they had thus cleared up Rita's residential area, they prayed and recited Bible texts. Rita's health status improved slightly.

Rita and her husband could again take up their major thread in analysis of the cause of her illness: had she been ensorcelled or did she suffer from a *sik bilong bodi*? Although Norma was Rita's relative and Rita had been suspicious when she could not find her underpants, there was a problem with Norma: she was known in Giri for being *ŋanŋan* (mad/crazy), as she was controlled by her dead son's *thum* (embodied or disembodied vital energy; here: "spirit of the dead"). Norma had been so full of grief when her only son died prematurely (of assault sorcery) that she touched the deceased's face with hers and drank the blood that ran out of his nose.[12] A twenty-two-year-old woman from Tuguge told me a slightly different version, saying that the older woman had drunk the saliva from her dead son's mouth.

Both substances retain parts of the person's animating life energy (*thum*). At the moment Norma came into contact with her son's bodily fluids, his *thum* was at the margin of leaving his body, which eventually happens after corporeal death. Through her contact with the fluids, her son's—only for a moment disembodied—*thum* entered her body. She had been controlled by her son's *thum* ever since, with him acting through her body. This is a good example of the partibility of persons in Giri conceptions of personhood. Here, I quote P. Stewart and A. Strathern, who said: "Aspects of personality and knowledge are thus not separated off from the body but are expressed through its fluids . . . The corpse's fluids contain some of the life force or 'soul' of the deceased" (2001a: 14).

A person's *thum* is not inextricably bound to a certain body but, instead, a force that animates one body then turns to another. This is not to say that Norma's son's *thum* was a depersonalized entity. Quite the contrary, Norma had internalized the relation with her son (i.e., one of the relations she was composed of), though this made her *ŋanŋan*. But this quality was also twofold in another sense: Norma had gained an additional ability—an ability that other people do not have; she could predict other people's deaths and see future happenings that were invisible to others. The Giri believe that this ability to see future events is otherwise reserved for the spirits of the dead. But because Norma was *ŋanŋan,* her actions and statements were often unintelligible to other villagers and conceived of as unreliable. Therefore, Tim questioned Norma again. The old woman confirmed the information she had formerly given.

Rita was then in a condition that permitted a visit to BHC; she would even endure a journey to Madang to unfurl the illness' cause. Rita and Tim decided to bring in a new and extremely potent technology—the X-ray. Rita made a visit to BHC, accompanied by Tim, in order to consult the health extension officer, who assured her that she would be referred to MGH for a thorax X-ray. But before he could write a referral letter, he had to carry out a sputum test at BHC. Rita was scared by her recurrent fainting episodes and not willing to wait for any further tests at BHC.

The only thing that she wanted was an X-ray image taken. In May 2007, she and Tim decided to go directly to MGH, without any referral letter, and to consult a medical doctor. I met Rita and her husband in Madang and was stunned by her decisiveness to get the X-ray picture taken—even if it meant undermining the formal referral process. How did Rita succeed? As all Giri villagers do when they are in Madang Town, she and Tim stayed at a relative's house. Arthur, their host (Tim's mother's second cousin), was employed as a porter of the MGH operating theater, and he organized for Rita to have the X-ray taken.

Rita gave him her clinic card and four kina—two kina for the X-ray and two kina for a blood test. Arthur accompanied Rita to both the pathology unit, where a distant relative from Birap 2 carried out the blood test, and the radiology unit. Arthur gave Rita's clinic card to the radiologist and told Rita to wait until her name was called. Rita was very glad to have finally taken her chest X-ray: "I felt happy. I mean, I really wanted to find out about the illness, which illness exactly was inside . . . or what destroyed the lungs and caused shortness of breath. I felt so happy to go and sit down and see this thing [i.e., X-ray machine] work on me." And she was absolutely thrilled by the examination, which she, however, described in rather objective terms:

> When I went inside, the male health worker instructed me to take my T-shirt off and sit down on some kind of chair. When I sat down, he got this paper and placed it behind my back and I was up against the paper. And then he placed this X-ray light—this torch—he placed it right on my chest. And he told me thus, "You have to prop up your chest like this [health worker shows Rita how to do it] and breathe in . . . breathe in heavily and breathe out." And I breathed in and I breathed out and he said, "Okay, enough." That was it. And I got up, he removed the paper from here [i.e., there], went [away and] gave it again to another health worker in another room and I came outside.

Rita's depiction of her X-ray experience is exemplary of many Giri people's views on the machine. The X-ray machine and the slides that it produces are mostly described as beneficial, because they shed light on the nature of one's complaints. Most of the people who told me about their X-ray experiences emphasized their excitement about the procedure and were rather comfortable when the machine worked on their body. However, a young woman suffering from a painful chronic hip dislocation said that her initial excitement turned into disappointment when the doctor told her—after he had looked over her X-ray slides—that there was "no hope" for her. Her bones were somewhat "decayed," he said, while pointing out on the X-ray photographs what he was talking about.

Rita was more content with the doctor's interpretation of her X-ray slide. The X-ray image was passed on to Rita shortly after the examination. Two days later, I met Rita and Tim and accompanied them to MGH, where Arthur had arranged a meeting between Rita and Wendy, an anesthetist and distant relative from Giri 1 who worked in anesthetics and intensive care at MGH. Their conversation took place in front of the operating theater, where Wendy noted "chronic asthmatic" for a diagnosis. The biomedical drugs she prescribed were Septrin, bronchodilators, and a Ventolin inhaler. The specific biomedical diagnosis, whether it was asthma, tuberculosis, or something else, was unimportant to Rita. In our entire conversation about her X-ray experience, she did not mention tuberculosis or asthma once. The only thing that counted for her was that there was a positive biomedical diagnosis, which, to her, meant that biomedical drugs were available to heal her.

For Rita, the X-ray was a technological aid for diagnosing or excluding sorcery. Rita understood the X-ray machine's principle of operation to be similar to the techniques of the glasman: both screen the body in order to identify signs of sorcery. It is not surprising that Rita drew a comparison between the X-ray and the glasman's power—his "X-ray vision." The X-ray image, as Rita said, would be completely dark if she suffered from a local illness (sorcery), and the health personnel would not be able to diagnose any illness. However, if she suffered from a sik bilong bodi, the X-ray would show changes on her lungs.

Rita explained to me that small holes (*thori bisarire*) in—or boils (*mvigvigi*) on—her lungs were visible on the X-ray image. To her, this meant that she suffered from a sik bilong bodi. Rita's view of the power of the X-ray machine includes a component that does not appear in Western biomedical thought: not only does the X-ray relay information on the body, but it may also indicate that an illness is social (if the image blacks out, producing a plain black slide, which is not uncommon in an aged device). Rita's understanding transcends Western biomedical thought, in which the X-ray image has the power only to mirror bodily states. But, besides the space they leave to indigenous inventiveness, the X-ray photographs produced at MGH also leave the hospital's doctors with ample scope for interpretation, because the images are often anything but diagnostically conclusive.

It sometimes happens that MGH's machines run short of their image processing chemicals and produce aberrations in X-ray photographs (Street 2011: 821–22). A doctor explained one such image to Street: "The photo is very hard to see clearly. You might think this is miliary TB because there are white dots covering the lungs, but in fact that is from the chemicals they are using. It is a bad picture" (a medical doctor cited in Street 2011: 822). Hence, the holes or boils that Rita saw on her X-ray image may also have been "additions" produced by the machine.

Eventually, Rita returned to Regene with a supply of prescribed medications, which she intended to take. Yet, she pointed out that if the intake of the biomedical drugs did not result in her recovery within a few years (an unlikely outcome in the case of chronic asthma), she would know that her illness had been caused by sorcery. Thus, the diagnostic power of the X-ray would eventually be challenged again by the ineffectiveness of biomedical drugs.

Social Discord

More than two years later, in August 2009, I visited Giri again. I could not wait to talk to my friends and was curious about Rita's thoughts on her illness and the course it had taken. Since her visit to MGH in May 2007, she had taken the prescribed medication, which gave her relief to the point that she felt only slightly impaired when fulfilling her quotidian tasks. During heavy bodily work, she felt her lungs—her alveoli—swelling; they felt heavy and gummed up, and her heart would throb. In the night she suffered from moderate asthma, which she could overcome by using her salbutamol inhaler. Rita assessed her health status:

> I feel okay. I just feel okay. It does not happen that I am afflicted by very serious short-windedness—only a very moderate one. Therefore I work. I am able to carry pots of water. I am able to cut grass . . . I work in the garden—I hold the [digging] stick, I break up the soil, plant yams, I hold the shovel and cut off tree roots . . . It is alright.

But still, Rita had not been healed, even though she was experiencing far milder symptoms than in 2007. Instead of ascribing the persistency of the symptoms to the ineffectiveness of any of the previously employed methods, she saw the cause as "not being ready" in herself. Rita picked up the thread that the Kayoma *glasman*, who had proclaimed that the healing process was inhibited by disturbed relations with her kin, had brought into play. Rita emphasized that healing would only take place once social relationships were reestablished as balanced and harmonious. Thus, she clearly placed her illness within the framework of local illness.

Rita identified two major disturbing and interconnected negative influences: (1) her husband was not at peace with her, and (2) she and her husband had an unresolved dispute with her siblings. I shall summarize in brief this two-stranded conflict, which began in 2003 when Tim's younger sister Audrey returned to Regene after an argument with her husband (Rita's younger brother Henry, to whom Audrey was a second wife) during which he hit her. At the time, Audrey was pregnant with her son. She left her husband, and the case over her son's custody went to the Bine (Giri) village court. The village court decided on shared custody, but, in reality, the boy exclusively stayed with his mother in Regene. Tim was enraged about Henry's shoddy behavior toward his sister, and Tim deplored the fact that Rita's kin had not respected him and his kin. He affronted Rita and beat her up. Thereupon, Rita's younger brother Albert (who had an income from his work at a tuna cannery north of Madang) bought a pig, which he gave to Tim to ease the situation and wash his hands of the affair.

As a consequence, Albert decided, in 2006, that he would stop paying his brother Ralph's school fees. Ralph was living with Rita and Tim and grew up more as Rita's son than Albert and Rita's brother, because their parents had died when Ralph was a small child. Rita and Tim were heart-struck, because Ralph was an excellent student, and he had already received several awards for his distinguished grades. In a letter, Albert informed his sister and her husband that he would only pay Ralph's school fees if Ralph were to move back to Giri 2 (their father's village and the village in which Albert had been adopted after his parents' death). In order to circumvent this, Tim sent a letter to another of Rita's brothers (who worked at the same tuna cannery as Albert), asking him to meet Ralph's school fees. (Tim and Rita were not able to find that sum of money.) Albert intercepted the letter and replied to Tim that Ralph's school fee money had been "eaten up" by Tim and his family—meaning that they had already eaten the pig that he had bought.

In November 2006, at the morning market, Rita revealed to me that I had appeared to her in her dream. In her dream, my face was dirty, I was wearing a filthy T-shirt, and my waistcloth had ridden up a bit; my skin was black. I had sat down on Rita's pillow and Rita had asked me: "Franziska, you have come. Why don't you dress up neatly and come?" I had replied, "I have sorrows and that's why I don't dress up well." Rita had recognized her mother in me and understood that her mother had come to reveal her worries about Ralph's outstanding school fees. Rita and Tim could not strike an agreement, and, shortly after, Ralph dropped out of school, married a Garati woman, and moved to her village.

Henry suffered from heart pain, listlessness, and pettishness, and his condition gradually worsened. In November 2009, Giri 2 village elders called a meeting to reconcile his disputes. Henry had asked for the meeting, as he thought himself a man with too many troubles. He was incensed by the fact that his son was growing up with Audrey and quarreled about it with Audrey and her siblings. In addition, he had had several disputes with his own siblings about the use of sago, coconut, and cocoa groves. Henry hoped to clear conflict out of the way so that he might recover.

Tim and Rita also hoped to come to an agreement with Henry to enable Rita's own recovery, and the couple sent word to Giri 2 that they were willing to settle the dispute. In consideration of his own health, Henry finally conceded custody to Audrey at the time, accepting that the time would come when his son would stay with him—which would be either if and when Audrey married again or when their son reached adolescence. Rita had continued to take the biomedical drugs, thinking that perhaps healing would finally take place. But her illness was unlikely to come to a swift end. When I left the village in 2010, Rita was pursuing a novel lead. Had she violated norms of spiritual relations and enraged a bush spirit who had taken revenge and caused her illness?

Epilogue to Rita's Case

The bar chart below (figure 3.1) is a simplified illustration of three points on which I have focused in the discussion above and briefly recapitulates the essentials of Rita's case. For Rita, it was fundamental to find out whether she suffered from a local or a foreign illness. The upper bar in the figure shows which explanation Rita held to be more likely at different times of her illness episode (although she was, as I demonstrated, most often torn between the two options). The middle bar shows the disease phases as described in Rita's clinic card. The lower bar, which draws on Rita's statements and her clinic card, pictures the treatment she employed.

Saethre (2007) argued, in his article on medical pluralism among the Warlpiri (Australia), that the diagnosis—the categorization of an illness as belonging to Aboriginal people or belonging to white people—is only one criterion for the treatment sought; other factors are, for instance, social norms

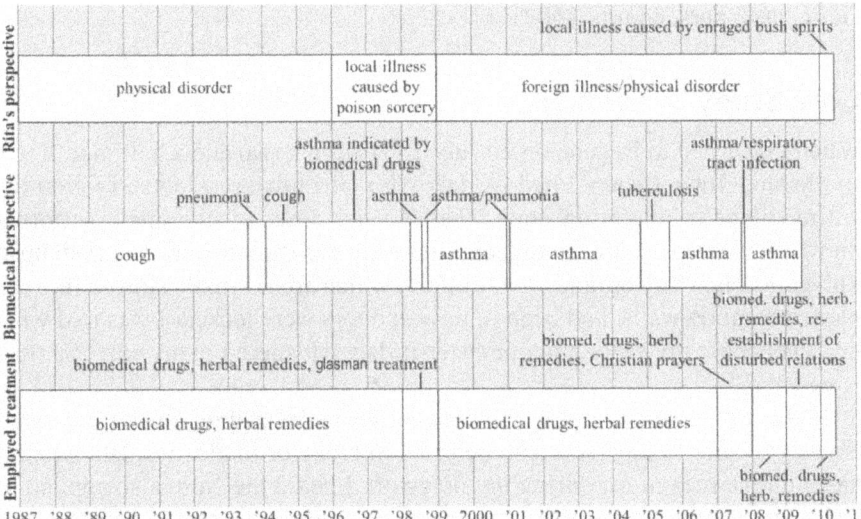

Figure 3.1. Phase model of Rita's perspective on her illness, the biomedical perspective, and the employed treatment. This figure correlates information on the illness phases as described by Rita, the biomedical perspective (as outlined in her clinic card), and treatment employed from 1987 to 2010.

and convenience. A glimpse at the phase model above shows that local etiological beliefs did not fully direct Rita's treatment choices. For instance, Rita took biomedical drugs even at times when she stated that her illness was caused by sorcery. Likewise, she used herbal remedies during periods when she suspected her illness to be caused by enraged bush spirits.

The spatial proximity to the health center and the inexpensive medical fee enabled a large number of biomedical visits, whereas she consulted the expensive and geographically distant glasman only twice. Only with her relatives' support could she realize her desired visits to MGH—of her husband, who accompanied her to town and to the clinics, and her relatives, who harbored her in Madang, introduced her to MGH, and examined and treated her at the hospital.

Before I turn to the next case, I want to express a last line of thought. Although Rita had good reason to believe Norma's standpoint, Rita seemed to feel hesitant about accusing a specific sorcerer. The State of Papua New Guinea condemns sorcery in its Sorcery Act, and sorcery accusations may have far-reaching consequences for the incriminated individual, who may be legally charged (see Independent State of Papua New Guinea 1971).[13] As Rio (2010: 184–85) pointed out, by making it an imprisonable offence, the national judicial system takes the handling of sorcery away from the customary system. That Rita explained her condition as a bodily disorder or foreign illness most of the time may have been a deliberate strategy to avoid conflict (Julie Park, pers. comm. 2007).

Case Study 2: Samuel

When I returned to Regene on 20 July 2007 from a two and a half month trip to Madang Town (where I had worked with Giri town residents), I found the entire village in an unusual state. The place felt deserted: the small platforms, on which women usually store their cookware and dishes, were emptied; bush knives, kitchen knives, and other cutlery, which are normally shoved into the plaited bamboo walls, had been removed; doors were locked. I was told what had happened; my sister and our sister-in-law whispered in my ear: "Samuel is ŋanŋan!"

In this exclamation, and as explored earlier in the chapter, the term ŋanŋan is used to refer to a person who behaves in crazy or mad ways. But ŋanŋan has multiple meanings; during my fieldwork I heard the word also applied to short-term bodily states resulting from the consumption of homebrew and marijuana: being "drunk," "high," or "disoriented." Naughty, unreasonable, or inconsiderate behavior is also ŋanŋan, as is ignorance. If a person is so deep and sound asleep that he does not notice anything that happens around him, he sleeps ŋanŋan. A delirious person is ŋanŋan.

When my sister and sister-in-law said that Samuel was *ŋanŋan,* they meant that he was mad and, as will become evident, even that he was ill. But they did not reckon him to be *mentally* ill. Samuel's madness was categorized as an illness and, as such, perceived as not much different from other illnesses. Giri people know no such indigenous category as "mental illness" that can be contrasted with other illnesses. The concept of "mental illness" that has its roots in Cartesian mind/body dualism does not exist in Giri culture. Giri understandings of the person (involving the component parts of the person and the relations between them) differ dramatically from the Cartesian model. Giri people do not separate the person into purely mental and physical components.

The central elements that make up the Giri person are human body/skin (*fav*) and bodily strength (*ngapngaŋ*), personal spirit/vital energy (*thum;* animals also have *thum*), shadow soul (*ŋina;*[14] visible to babies and dogs but invisible to the eye of adult humans), intellect/knowledge/thought/ability to reason (*vuŋ khom;* literally: "good face or nose"), and name/s (usually a clan name, a Christian name, and often nickname/s[15]). There are a multitude of examples of the mindful causation of bodily states. As Wassmann and Keck noted, "A single element [of the person] can act on the others and thus, for instance a disturbed social relationship can affect the body and manifest itself as illness" (2007: 5). If a person's *vuŋ khom* leaves her or his body, she or he develops bodily symptoms that range from fever to bodily deformities, and even paralysis. The shadow soul (*ŋina*) can cause headaches. Another person's shadow soul may become disembodied and cause illness in someone who has, for example, mistreated him.

Homesickness can also cause bodily illness, which is a mind/body correlation Lutz (1988: 100) touched on in her descriptions of the Ifaluk in the Caroline Islands. If those who are homesick think too much about someone whom they miss sadly (a close relative, a lover, or an intimate friend [see below for *kurkum*]), their shadow soul can cause illness in the latter. Here, one could say on a more abstract level, "Emotion in the self can cause illness in the other" (ibid.). In Giri, deaths are sometimes said to be the consequence of grief (*ndigndigi*). One 2007 death attributed to grief was that of a paralyzed, unmarried woman who had led a pitiful existence, sitting all day in the entrance of her house. I follow A. Strathern's (1996) plea for the use of Scheper-Hughes and Lock's heuristic concept of the "mindful body" (1987), which allows us to understand bodily experiences as those connected to the mind and mental states as those that are experienced and expressed physically.

A. Strathern said, "Once we recognize that there is a mental component in all bodily states and, conversely, a physical component in all mental states, the boundary between mental and other illnesses disappears" (1996: 4). Similarly, to the Giri, the term "mental illness" wrongly curtails the meaning of *ŋanŋan,* which, in Giri thought, does not solely refer to mental states (as discussed above). Goddard (1998, 2011) made a similar point for the Kakoli of the Upper Kaugel Valley (Western Highlands Province). Writing about madness, he argued convincingly that the Kakoli vernacular term "kekelepa" is not synonymous with "mentally ill": "*Kekelepa* refers to social behaviour in both individuals and groups and should not be taken to mean 'mentally ill' or to be an indigenous parallel to psychiatric notions of psychopathology" (Goddard 1998: 63). Instead, Kakoli people understand madness "in social terms, as behaviour estranged from the range of responses appropriate to the social context" (2011: 2); in other words, as behavior that is "socially 'out of place'" (2011: 71).

Within cultures, the perception of conditions may transform over time. Whether a phenomenon is characterized as an illness depends on the cultural meaning it is given. Csordas and Kleinman noted, "Historically, new problems can emerge, recede, be discovered, or even be created" (1996: 5). For Giri, as we will see in Samuel's case, madness can be an illness. Furthermore, as is true of other local illnesses, it can be caused by angered ancestral spirits (*thum*) or enraged bush spirits (*thor*). Ancestral spirits can also cause bodily symptoms of illness. My interlocutors talked about Samuel's madness as an illness (but not as a mental illness!), and I follow them in doing so in order to convey their points of view.

Samuel's case differs significantly from Rita's, in that biomedical services played only a marginal role in Samuel's illness episode and virtually no biomedical information is available for his case. That Samuel only received very limited biomedical treatment was primarily due to the poor options available at the local health center, and not to his and his relatives' general rejection of biomedical services. His case provides important clues for improvement of the biomedical services at BHC and MGH. It shows the Giri dilemma of an illness that is (at least temporarily) perceived to be caused (at least partially) by a foreign agent (marijuana)—and should thus be treated biomedically according to Giri belief—but for which the proper medication "has not arrived yet." Samuel's kin were forced to turn not only to local, customary (and modified) healing techniques but also to Christian prayers. Hence, I consider this study to be exemplary of the medical pluralistic situation found in Giri.

We may again take up Saethre's (2007) line of thought: that treatment choices depend upon a multiplicity of factors and not only on the patient's, carers', and relatives' diagnoses; the unavailability of biomedical services is a preeminent criterion here. This case study is about a man who, instead of receiving medical attention, was taken into custody and locked away in a cell at the town police station. Even though MGH (unlike BHC) has a psychiatric unit staffed with two psychiatric nurses and a health extension officer with additional psychiatric training, Samuel never received hospital treatment. This case study is also about the ways in which his kin, who took him back to the village, sought to ease his condition by engaging in various healing practices. These practices ranged from the appeasement of ancestral and bush spirits to Christian healing prayers and a procession at the opening of a church conference.

The case study was principally conducted in 2007. Follow-up data for the case study was collected in subsequent years. Whereas Rita mainly self-managed her illness and her illness episodes were mostly told from her own perspective, the ethnographic information on which I rely in Samuel's case comes from my own observations and personal encounters with Samuel. Further data were obtained from lengthy semistructured interviews and unstructured conversations (including brief colloquies) with members of Samuel's therapy managing group, comprising close and more distant kin. Samuel's illness is also presented from his relatives' perspectives.

Since, as we will see, Samuel's illness episode was, for the most part, interpreted by Regene villagers as the result of spirit possession, let me say a few words on a subject on which a respectable body of literature exists (for extensive literature reviews see Boddy 1994; Schieffelin 1996). Perspectives on the topic have shifted from investigations of spirit possession as hysterical psychosis and theatrical performance in the 1960s and 1970s (best known are the studies on "wild-man behavior") to a study by Schieffelin (1996) exploring "Evil Spirit Sickness" among the Bosavi (Southern Highlands Province) as a sociohistorical event. Others include Jorgensen (2007), who studied the history of spirit mediumship among the Telefolmin (West Sepik Province), and Lattas (2010: chap. 4), who studied the incorporation of modernity into madness in Kaliai (New Britain). Several of the earlier studies suggested that mad behavior is a mechanism for the release of tensions (e.g., Newman 1964; Salisbury 1968).

The following case study illustrates that neither Samuel's business aspirations nor his choice of bride were supported by his kin. Although it could be construed that, in those difficult times, being *ŋanŋan* served Samuel as a loophole—a valve to express his sorrows and his anger—I reject this as the sole interpretation. As we shall see, Samuel's illness episode lasted, in the Giri's perspective, for more than a year (from July 2007 until December 2008) and was thus more than a sudden emotional release. However, it is not too farfetched to interpret Samuel's behavior as an act of incipient individuality (LiPuma 1998: 72). Yet one must be mindful of Samuel's intense marijuana consumption, which added, no doubt, a new level to this study of madness.

Ŋanŋan—*Village Life Centered upon a Case of Madness*

On the morning after I returned from my journey to Madang, I met Samuel by chance at his parents' house. Samuel's parents had taken me under their wing upon my first arrival in Giri. Although I moved, after a few months, to the center of the village and thus left the vicinity of Samuel's close kin group, I still felt bound and indebted to his parents and would respectfully report back after longer periods of absence. Samuel's father was a key political figure in Regene and, throughout my stay in 2006 and 2007, the councilor of the Giri 1 ward. It was he who drew up a work schedule for community work and he and his wife were considered role models in customary matters. Most importantly, they engaged in expansive acts of sociality on an everyday basis, which contributed significantly to the family's status.

Every morning and evening, Samuel's mother would serve sizeable dishes of sago pudding to any men who sat on the clan platform beside their house. She would instruct villagers who approached her to purchase bamboo tubes filled with sago that it is not Giri kastom to sell food. Then she would bestow a gift of sago-filled bamboo tubes—and possibly other comestibles that she had at her house (such as leafy vegetables or bananas)—upon them and possibly share areca nuts with them. Samuel's parents had five children, of whom Samuel was the eldest. While I talked to Samuel's father, Samuel approached his parents' house and came up to me. He wanted to know where I had been for such a long time (i.e., several weeks), and I replied that I had been in town.

To welcome me back, Samuel called on me to shake hands with him: "Come on, let's shake hands!"[16] I put forth my hand, but Samuel abruptly backed away. I noticed that his hands were wounded and swollen, and I suggested shaking his forearm in order not to hurt him. He agreed, took my arm and squeezed it lightly and then moved backward and forward to repeat the "armshake." Samuel's parents interrupted our encounter brusquely and told Samuel to leave. Samuel's father passed his granddaughter to me, saying that I could take her to a neighbor's house. I understood this to be a request aimed at protecting the baby girl and me from Samuel, and I decided to take off. Samuel approached me and asked me to pass the baby (who had begun to cry) to him. Samuel's father jumped in, chased his son away, and walked me (with the baby in my arms) to the neighboring house. Later I was to learn that Samuel's injuries stemmed from a fight with his father.

I shall now go back in time to the onset of this illness episode in order to make these happenings intelligible. Samuel had just returned from a journey to Madang Town, where he had smoked marijuana throughout his stay of several weeks. On the second night after his return to Regene, his illness began to show. A twenty-eight-year-old distant male relative from Regene village gave an account of the night of 13 July 2007:

> [Samuel] began to become ill last Friday—Friday the week before last . . . In the night . . . he sat together with [Wayne] and [Sean] in their small men's house. They were sitting there and he smoked marijuana. He smoked marijuana. They sat there

talking about anything and everything. Then he became scared. In the dead of night, the two wanted to leave him. He was scared. He was scared of staying back alone. He was scared of staying back alone and thus told the two, "You two must not leave me and sleep; I am scared!" Okay, the two stayed with him. Their eyes were very sleepy and [Sean] took off. [Sean] went to bed. Okay, [Wayne] jumped down [from the platform] . . . He went. He [i.e., Samuel] called out to [Wayne] to come back again, saying, "I am scared, you must not go!" Okay, [Wayne] defied his words and went. And [Wayne] wondered: Why is the man scared? And the . . . two began to suspect that his old illness must have recurred.

Upon returning to his dwelling house, and afraid of being alone, Samuel squeezed himself between his wife and another female relative with whom his wife shared a mattress. After a while he heard a noise—as if someone had jumped down from the veranda of the abandoned house opposite. His wife also caught the sound. Samuel became very scared; he thought that this sound must have been a spirit of the dead. He stayed awake all night. On Saturday morning, Samuel and the other adolescent and middle-aged Regene villagers left for the Giri sports games, which take place every Saturday throughout the dry season on a field in the vicinity of Varaning village. On the pathway, Samuel met three adolescent men from Garati village and asked them for *yaua* (homebrew; named after a short, thick, sweet banana from which it is often made by letting the fruit ferment). Samuel drank the homebrew and smoked marijuana with them. All of a sudden, he asked them where his wife was.

The irritated Garati men pointed in her direction and told him that she was standing right behind him (which she actually was, waiting for him to proceed to the playing field). They resumed their journey to Varaning. After they arrived at the field, Samuel sat together with his in-laws and smoked more marijuana with them. In the evening, Samuel and his wife went to Varaning, where they stayed for a meal at a relative's house, then went to Giri 1 to spend the night. Samuel stayed awake all night and roamed the village shouting out loudly in fear. By this time, the Giri 1 villagers knew that Samuel had gone *ŋanŋan*. Back in Regene, Samuel climbed the roof ridge of a house under construction in Krikip. His wife tried to stop him, but he explained that some little boys—bush spirits—had told him to play tag with them on top of the house. After a while, the spirits came down again and urged Samuel to follow suit: "Run down here and jump, we will catch you!"

Samuel summoned his wife, who was standing by him, to help the spirits catch him. She warned her husband not to jump because she would break under his weight: "You are not a ball rolling down so that I can catch you!" Nevertheless, Samuel jumped and crashed to the floor, hitting his coccyx hard. Samuel was close to passing out from the pain, but a relative who lived in the neighboring house helped him back on his feet. Samuel's wife went to

Regene village and informed the villagers about the accident. My interlocutor explained to me that the bush spirits had tricked Samuel.

Samuel's condition deteriorated rapidly in the days that followed. He was incessantly suffering from anxiety, scared of sleeping, and restless. He disappeared from the village several times, walking to neighboring places. When he disappeared for the first time, Regene men formed three search parties—of three to four men each—to find Samuel and bring him back to the village. When they finally found Samuel in Korak (see map 2.1), they brought him back as far as Mbor (in Giri 1), but Samuel resisted going any farther, and the men left him there. He returned to Regene the next day.

A few days later, Samuel's father used the health center ambulance to search for his son, who was again on the move. He found him about one hundred kilometers from Giri, at the coast. A member of one of the search parties explained why Samuel had been walking endlessly (for hours and hours until stopped by others) without turning back: he was afraid of turning around, as he saw only darkness when doing so. The Regene men began to put a close watch on Samuel. They slept on the platforms and watched over Samuel around the clock.[17] Throughout the nights after my return to the village, six men slept on the Tuguge platform, and they tied Samuel to the main pole of the platform during nighttime.

The impact of Samuel's illness on community life in Regene was vast. The Regene were bound to the village for weeks; garden and sago work was neglected and food became scarce. The range of goods in the local stores shrank remarkably. On the Saturdays following the onset of Samuel's illness, none of the Regene villagers went to play sports games. The fear of being exposed to the sight of Samuel's naked body (as he had repeatedly disrobed in public) and of being verbally harassed by Samuel drove women and children inside their houses. Among many others, one of Samuel's classificatory mothers had been assaulted with coarse language.

At midday of the day on which Samuel and I exchanged "armshakes," one of my sisters-in-law summoned me to eat a meal at her house. After our meal, we relaxed on her veranda and chatted with one of my sisters, who had brought me another plate of food. Samuel walked past the house, cursed at us, and yelled for us to fornicate with him. He proceeded to Forge and shouted abuse at various villagers, not leaving anybody out. His father hurried after him and apologized to me for Samuel's behavior, explaining that Samuel was deranged (tingting paul) because he was possessed by spirits. Another of our sisters-in-law came to join our intimate women's circle, but, soon after, the women jumped up when they heard Samuel returning.

They instructed me to follow them inside the house. (This was the first time in ten months that I had entered my sister-in-law's house; communal life is public in Giri, and it is inappropriate to walk into other people's houses.)

Peering through the small holes in the braided bamboo wall, we watched an argument between Samuel and another villager. Samuel had armed himself with a sago palm leafstalk and challenged the man to a fight. Samuel touched on a precarious theme in the man's life: his ongoing sexual relationship with his first wife, from whom he was divorced. Samuel's opponent, equipped with a tree branch, made a step forward; he showed no fear and emphasized that he was very ready to fight. Before long, Samuel drew back and retreated to Forge.

Some men had suffered injuries (such as bite wounds or bruises) when attacked by Samuel, often when restraining him—holding him down and tying him up. The first time Samuel's male kin began to use violence against him was after Samuel jumped off the rooftop and wandered through the Krikịp bush. Samuel had broken off banana leaves and lay down on the leaves. When he noticed that a relative had gone after him, he got angry and threw a sprouting coconut at his follower to shake him off. Several male kin finally overcame Samuel, tied him up, and carried him to Regene. On the way, Samuel bit off cocoa branches when they passed through the cocoa grove of one of the carriers. My twenty-eight-year-old male interlocutor remembered:

> We began to chase him, beat him . . . he came and took off his trousers right here. He took off his trousers here, in the night, took off his trousers, now naked, we held him, he fought us, we held him, restrained him. When he took off his trousers, mother . . . aunt [Emma—Samuel's father's older sister] . . . she saw this and cried. She knew that he was totally out of his mind. Okay, [Sean—male kin restraining Samuel] . . . cried; [Seth—male kin restraining Samuel] cried.

Samuel bit three men and broke a rake on one of them when they tried to tie him up. Thereupon, his father beat Samuel so hard with a fan belt that Samuel's father's older sister's son jumped on Samuel's father to stop him from whipping Samuel any more. On the Thursday before I returned to Regene, Samuel's father beat his son with a tree branch. The branch broke on Samuel's back, but his father continued his beatings. One of my brothers came running and snatched the branch off him. The wounds that I had noticed on Samuel's hands stemmed from this incident.

As in Rita's case, a stream of plates was sent to Samuel's parents' house. Rita carried a sago dish from Daun Camp all the way up to Regene. In the afternoon of the first day after my return, I baked flat sago bread. As usual, I distributed portions to my mother, sisters, brothers, and their families. Similar to their Bosmun neighbors' notion of a thorough meal (von Poser 2013: 52), Giri believe a proper meal consists of a base of stirred sago porridge garnished with pieces of meat (preferably pork, but also bandicoot, chicken, or other sources of protein such as fish or sago grubs) and leafy vegetables in coconut cream. Although my sago bread was not a thorough meal, I carried some to Samuel's parents' house to show compassion for Samuel's illness.

While I am not at all inclined to fabricate a romanticized image of Giri society as a harmonious, tightly integrated whole, I wish to emphasize that social cohesion was strong in the weeks after Samuel fell ill.

"Ghost Game" and the Evocation of Ancestral Spirits

From the above description of happenings during the first eight days of Samuel's illness episode, it is obvious that the consumption of marijuana and homebrew had something to do with him becoming *ŋanŋan*. Samuel accused the young Garati men of poisoning the homebrew and marijuana he consumed and thus of causing his illness. On the eighth day, Samuel's father gave an account of his son's illness that would be more or less sustained by the community over the following months: Samuel's body had been weakened by a number of things concurrently—marijuana consumption, contact with a charmed ginger plant (*Zingiber* sp.), and mental distress. Two adolescent kinsmen had stored (for later use) a ginger plant commonly utilized in love and war magic in the house they mutually inhabited with Samuel. The plant had come from a village farther up the Ramu in which one of the men's older brothers resided among his wife's kin.

The exposure to the plant had caused Samuel's bodily strength (*ngapngaŋ*) to diminish and thus weakened his body. Smoking marijuana had inhibited the process of blood renewal and thus also sapped his *ngapngaŋ*. Samuel was downcast because his mother's siblings, in particular her sisters residing in Forge (female descendants of Samuel's mother's father and the man's older brother), objected to Samuel's expecting wife, a woman from Birap 2 village whom Samuel had recently chosen for himself and taken to Regene village. They criticized Samuel for being "too young" to marry,[18] and the woman Samuel had chosen was found not to have the sublime qualities of a worthy marriage partner; their main argument was that she was "too short" and less handsome than Samuel. Samuel was sorely struck by his maternal kin's rejection of his wife, and his worries (*ndigndigi;* literally: "think much") furthered his vulnerability. As a result, several spirits were able to take possession of Samuel. I shall now explicate who these spirits were and how they entered Samuel's body.

I had heard from my brothers that Samuel had invoked spirits of his dead kinsmen through the "ghost game." I remember that I had thought to myself, "what a strange term," and wondered if Giri people played games or gambled with their deceased ancestors. My interlocutors put me right: the "ghost game" is employed as a medium to communicate with the dead in a spirit séance. Samuel's first playing experience occurred in 2003. I will go back to illuminate this first encounter with the "ghost game," since it is fundamental to understanding the 2007 happenings. Samuel had played the "ghost game" with his father's older brother's two sons at their father's house in Madang Town. To play the game, a board on which the numbers zero to nine, the letters *a* to *z*, and the fields yes/no (*yes/nogat*) are written needs to be prepared. A circle has to be drawn in the center of the board, and an empty glass, the indicator, placed upside-down on the circle. None of the numerous Regene villagers I consulted had ever seen such a board or played the game.

They considered it an urban thing that had not made its entrance into Regene village. Obviously, I was reminded of what is commonly known as a spirit or Ouija board.[19] These boards are used to communicate with spirits by way of a planchette. The players (usually at least two) place their fingers on this indicator, which moves over the board to the numbers, the yes/no fields, and the letters, thus spelling words. Spitz explained: "On the Ouija board . . . neither partner believes the other is guiding the planchette and consequently they both believe that the movement comes from some external source (unless, of course, they are willing to acknowledge that unconscious processes are at work)" (1997: 74). Although Ouija is a parlor game, it is not uncommon for players to actually claim to be in contact with the dead.

The earliest and probably most famous case is that of the St. Louis, Missouri, housewife Pearl Lenore Curran (1883–1937), who spoke through a spirit board to a woman named Patience Worth. After Curran's father died, her friend Emily Grant Hutchings suggested contacting Curran's late father through Hutching's spirit board. Instead of the father, a long-deceased unmarried Englishwoman named Patience Worth, as the woman spelled out during a séance, got in touch with Curran. The spirit Patience Worth, who allegedly had lived in the seventeenth century, would dictate remarkable poetry to Curran. Both women, Curran as a medium and Patience Worth as an author, soon gained popularity in the United States (Diliberto 2010). Curran appropriated the spirit board from a relatively unimportant leisure pastime to a legitimate tool to communicate with the dead.

Neoshamans have developed a contemporary fascinating modification of the Ouija board and its operation principle. In the United States, a group of "techno-shamans" (Wallis 2003: 71) or "cybershamans" (Brown 1997: 125) has embraced the use of the internet in their practice. Instead of using an actual Ouija board, as Curran did, these cybershamans surf the worldwide web as an electronic Ouija board (ibid.), believing that "surfing of cyber-space compares with shamanic journeys through the spirit world" (Wallis 2003: 71).

To return to Samuel's case, my Regene conversational partners explained that Samuel had summoned the spirits (*thum*) of two of his maternal forefathers until one of them slipped under the glass (which was used as a movable indicator); this was felt by the sudden heaviness of the glass. Samuel put a finger on the glass and asked his ancestors' spirits about their names, which they spelled out by moving the glass to the respective letters. (This verification of the name is essential, since "uninvited" spirits may sometimes slip under the glass.)

After Samuel ascertained the identity, he asked various questions about the deaths of both forefathers but also consulted them on his own future and asked them for their suggestions for mounting a business (see Telban 2001 for Ambonwari [East Sepik] postmortem divination in which spirits are asked questions that they answer with distinctive tapping rhythms for yes and no). For some time, Samuel had been filled with enthusiasm for the idea of starting his own business, and he fantasized about laksori (luxury). Later, in 2004, Samuel told my thirty-five-year-old brother about a fast way to make money (isi bisnis), which he learned from the ancestral spirits in 2003.

Samuel thought formal education was instrumental in starting his own business, and he had wanted to continue school after grade ten. However, his parents had refused to pay his school fees because he had not achieved good marks throughout his school years. Samuel was downcast by his parents' refusal to financially support his aspirations, and, in search of business opportunities, he fled to Madang Town, where he began to smoke marijuana heavily. His grief and the marijuana consumption considerably weakened his body and allowed his forefathers' spirits to transgress his body boundaries (as would happen again in 2007). Directly after Samuel played "ghost game" in Madang Town, he became ŋanŋan for the first time. He roamed through town from one house with Giri inhabitants to the next.[20]

He was totally stubborn and arrogant (bikhet olgeta, as a female relative of Samuel said) and destroyed kitchenware from Giri relatives. The police eventually arrested Samuel and placed him in preventative custody at the town police station. Apparently he was wounded twice with a knife—the "sedative measures" of the policemen, as the same woman explained. The older brother of Samuel's father—with whose sons Samuel had played "ghost game" and who was a police officer—urged Samuel's family to come to Madang Town and take him back to Regene. When his relatives arrived in town, Samuel was raging in the police station. As a result, they were told to come back in another two days. On their return, they found out that Samuel had already been set free.

The responsible police officer explained that there had been no reason to keep Samuel locked up any longer than necessary. Samuel's mother's brother caught a PMV to Regene to persuade Samuel's mother to go to Madang and convince her son to return to the village. She was exceedingly worried and distressed, so her husband arranged for the Bogia police car to drive him to Madang, where he picked up his son. This was about two weeks after Samuel's father's older brother had sent word. Samuel had recovered from his illness episode at that stage. Voices were being raised in the village that Samuel's parents could have prevented his illness by attending to their son's desires. At least they could have supported him by opening a small trade store or a secondhand clothing store to give Samuel a meaningful task in life and an avenue to make money—to give him the feeling of "being alive" (stap laip).

In the séance, Samuel had furthermore asked the ancestral spirits if he would become *ŋanŋan*. We have, in the case of the old woman Norma, already learned of the ancestors' ability to forecast occurrences. The spirits gave Samuel a positive answer. Yes, he would become *ŋanŋan*. The dialogue with my interlocutor took a sudden and absurd twist when he remarked that Samuel and his two siblings had not played the "ghost game" on a flat board but on a television screen. The three men had used a television screen to communicate with their ancestors, much in the same way that techno-shamans use computers as electronic divination devices (see Brown 1997).

My interlocutor added that the screen had turned black when Samuel asked this last question; there was "only darkness" (tudak tasol) on the screen—a clear sign that the spirits answered in the affirmative as to whether he would become *ŋanŋan*, as my conversational partner pointed out to me. My inquiries into how it was possible to play the game on a television screen led to nothing—my interlocutor conceded that he had not been present during the séance and that Samuel's father's brother's sons had not touched on this topic in any depth.

Nevertheless, I learned two important lessons. First, Western visual technology may be used to converse with the dead. The television screen (and possibly its moving images) became a lens through which Samuel obtained entrance to the sphere of the dead. For Rita, the X-ray enabled a view into the living human body, and, for Samuel, the television screen gave a glimpse into the Giri ancestors' universe. Hence, both technologies enhance Giri perspectives on their world. Second, the television screen not only enabled contact with the ancestors but also served as a diagnostic tool for Samuel. The blacking out of the television screen informed Samuel about his illness—as did the X-ray (which may black out and only produce plain black images) in Rita's case. And, although it is highly questionable whether a television screen was utilized in the manner described, my interlocutor's statement is valuable, as it points again toward the "ghost game" as a foreign thing and apparently a powerful technique—though not uniquely and unequivocally understood among Regene villagers.

The appropriation and localization of Western technologies to contact the dead has been studied and analyzed in depth in Kaliai by Lattas (2000, 2006, 2010: chap. 3; see Telban & Vávrová 2014 for Ambonwari). Modern technological artifacts, such as televisions, binoculars, and telephones, were reinvented in multiple ways by various millenarian movements. Behind this lay the objective of coming closer to the dead: "Kaliai cult followers sought to end the isolation of the dead from the living by unearthing, catching, and communicating with their ancestors via modern technology" (Lattas 2000: 326). Lattas (2006: 19) wrote about a Kaliai woman who used a self-made camera and binoculars "to find the hidden presence of the dead in the landscape" (see Lattas 2010: 113–14).

In another sequence, Lattas (2000: 334–42, 2010: 117, 124–35) described the technologization of the Kaliai landscape. Censure, a Kaliai cargo cult leader, talked to the dead through "telephone holes" in the ground and, in turn, the dead "photographed" the cult followers through these holes. In Samuel's case, the television screen and spirit board were further utilized as a means to access secret (Western) knowledge—knowledge on how to start a business and make big money (also see Lattas 2010: 114 on employment of emulated Western technologies to access white people's hidden knowledge and Telban & Vávrová 2014 on mobile phones used to call the dead to ask them for goods and to put money in one's bank account).

In 2007, Samuel played the "ghost game" a second time with his father's brother's sons in Madang Town—using the same method to converse with his dead kinsmen. I want to bring to mind again that Samuel's body was considerably weakened at this stage, and Samuel had smoked marijuana heavily in Madang. And so it happened that the spirits took possession of Samuel's body during the séance, entering his body and making him *ŋanŋan* in the same way that Norma was made *ŋanŋan* by her dead son's spirit. Samuel's wife had accompanied him to Madang and, when she saw his health decline, persuaded him to return to the village. After their arrival, Samuel's health status deteriorated visibly under the continuous consumption of marijuana and homebrew. The Regene also noticed bodily changes in Samuel. His eyes had changed; a boy compared them to marbles, and one of Samuel's classificatory mothers remarked that they were glazed and blue like the eyes of the deceased.

The possibility that bush spirits had contributed to Samuel's illness could not be ruled out. After all, they had played with him in Krikịp and it would have been easy for a bush spirit to take away a central aspect of his personhood—*aŋ vuŋ khom* (literally: "his or her good face or nose")—from his weakened body. *Vuŋ khom* encompasses a person's intellect, knowledge, thoughts, and ability to reason and, in this way, is analogous to the Melpa concept of "noman," as outlined by A. Strathern and P. Stewart (A. Strathern 1996; A. Strathern & P. Stewart 1998b, 1999). A person—adult or child—becomes disabled, *ŋanŋan,* or otherwise ill if *vuŋ khom* leaves the body. This may happen when a person shivers (*ringi*) from fear (for example when encountering an assault sorcerer). The idiom "jumping out of one's skin," referring to someone who gets very frightened, captures very well what happens with the *vuŋ khom* when a person shivers.

When Christian was a small baby, he happened to lose his *vuŋ khom* for nearly two weeks. It was captured by the female bush spirit Sarfaŋ, who occupies the bushland called Mbar. At the time, his mother Rita and her husband had a garden plot in that area. On their way to the garden, Rita almost stepped on a snake that was lounging on the pathway. When she vaulted over the snake, Christian—sleeping in the netbag that Rita carried over her head—shivered and Sarfaŋ trapped the infant's *vuŋ khom*. When the family arrived in their garden, Christian began to cry and would not stop crying throughout the whole day. In the evening he developed a fever, and on the following morning his parents took him to the mission hospital in Bunapas. After twelve days and two courses of biomedical drugs, Christian was still not better. In a dream, Rita learned why her son had not yet recovered. In the dream, she saw her relative Sarfaŋ, who was married to a man from Varaning and had been named after the bush spirit (a considerable number of Giri people are namesakes to bush spirits).

Sarfaŋ carried Christian in her arms and walked along the pathway that leads from Varaning to Regene. Rita was delighted and exclaimed (in her dream), "Ah, you are bringing me my baby!" But the woman abruptly turned her back on Rita and answered in an angry tone: "This is not your child, it is mine. Hence, I take it away with me." Rita understood that the woman was not her relative Sarfaŋ but the bush spirit who had captured her son's *vuŋ khom*. (It is not uncommon that, in dreams, bush spirits appear in the body of living persons [this also applies for ancestral spirits].) Rita and her husband made offerings to the bush spirit woman and thus compelled her to release Christian's *vuŋ khom*. Rita prepared a ceremonial dish of mushy yam and taro mixed with grated coconut (*khos*), which she carried to Mbar. Sarfaŋ was invited by her guardian (i.e., the leader of the clan that owned the land on which Sarfaŋ resides) to a small, decorated platform to consume the repast and was entreated to accept the meal and the further offerings of money and drapery.

A forty-three-year-old woman from Birap 2 told me about another incident that had happened some twenty years ago in Madang. An eleven-year-old girl from Birap had gone with her parents to the bush near Madang's Wagol Community Compound. (A community of Giri people resides in this otherwise mainly Sepik-inhabited settlement.) The girl's father hit her, she shivered, and her *vuŋ khom* separated from her body and was taken away by the resident bush spirit. The girl was severely disabled ever since. Her limbs became deformed, her eyes and nose disfigured; she was paralyzed, unable to talk or feed herself. Her parents brought her back to Birap village, where her mother helped her with her personal hygiene and cared for her over the next sixteen years. The girl passed away at the age of twenty-seven. Her case is particularly tragic because nobody in Giri was able to contribute to her recovery. The

Wagol bush spirit is foreign to the Giri people; they do not know his name and cannot contact him. Only the rightful guardian has the power to do so.

If the same had happened to the girl on Giri land, her family would have apologized to the bush spirits and the guardian would have invited the bush spirit to accept their offerings, as in the case above. Therefore, this is an example not only of *vuŋ khom* loss but also of the ways in which Giri illness causation theory develops further in a world in which the outside experience of Giri people grows. This theme is also prevalent in Samuel's case. Samuel had experienced the effects of marijuana and homebrew, which the Giri view both as foreign substances. (The Giri were taught by outsiders how to ferment bananas, papaya, and other fruit into alcohol.) Traditionally, *vuŋ khom* loss is tightly interwoven with the sudden terrifying moment in which a person shivers. But Samuel's body had already become so weak and vulnerable from the consumption of these foreign things that the bush spirits did not even have to wait until he crashed to the floor to take away his *vuŋ khom*. They could easily steal it during their game on the rooftop. This conceptualization is no doubt an innovation to Giri illness causation theory.

Performing Healing

I now explicate how Giri people dealt with Samuel's illness. Certainly, a multiplicity of causes requires multifarious action. It will also become apparent that diagnoses are rarely considered definitive if symptoms persist. Treatment is by trial and error (cf. Frankel & Lewis 1989), and Samuel's illness was repeatedly cast in a new light.

I begin with a chronological description of treatment. The pacification of the spirits and the strengthening of Samuel's body were conditional to his recovery. The Regene took care to make sure that Samuel did not consume any more marijuana and homebrew, putting much effort into hiding tobacco and areca nuts from him, because they feared that even these mildly stimulating substances could create subsequent negative effects. This fear possibly also had to do with their knowledge of the glasman practices of smoking tobacco and chewing betel in order to contact the spirits. The first action that Samuel's father took was to remove the ginger plant from Samuel's house. He was enraged about the two adolescent men's thoughtlessness and beat them. The men fled to one of the men's older brother's resident village up the Ramu. Samuel's father wrote a letter to this man's affinal kin, and, a few days later, the two adolescents returned with a reply letter. I have not read the two letters, but I know that the men conversed about the ginger plant, the harm it had caused, and compensation claims.

Furthermore, the Regene villagers formed two groups. Samuel's maternal kin had vented their anger since Samuel had brought his wife to Regene; they needed to reconcile their resentment toward her. They met in one part of the village in order to come to an agreement with the married couple. At the same time, Samuel's paternal relatives met in another part of the village to appease the bush spirits. Most villagers have distant (and some even close) family ties to both of Samuel's parents, who are members of the same clan. Roughly, those villagers who were more closely related to Samuel's mother (such as those from her subclan and especially those who had railed at Samuel's wife) went to the first meeting, whereas those with close family ties to Samuel's father attended the second. The villagers who were only distantly related to both of Samuel's parents generally split themselves between the two groups.

A maternal relative who led the first gathering requested that the "gossipers" vocalize their anger and objections to Samuel's wife. Most women stood up and spoke about their resentment. Finally, they decided to apologize for their hostility and for attempting to interfere with the marriage. They shook hands among themselves to show their consensus then approached Samuel's wife to reconcile with her. It was decided that they would apologize to Samuel and prepare a meal for him and his wife, during which each gossiper's household would present the couple with a small token of appreciation for the expected baby, such as a plate or a diaper.

The second, all-male group offered gifts to the bush spirits on a bamboo platform, which they had erected on four sticks and fenced with leaves from the fishtail palm tree (see illustration 3.2). A ladder was built for the spirits to climb up. Three cooked sago meals, two rice plates, two areca nut branches, and one hundred kina were heaped on the platform.[21] The men hit the ground with sago palm leafstalks to awaken the bush spirits who reside in the lands adjacent to Regene village. The spirits were then invited to the platform: "You these spirits, if you badger Samuel, we ask you to leave him alone and come and take the food, and you eat, and you go back again!"

The guardian (i.e., clan leader) led the spirits to the platform, stood next to it for a moment, and then gave space for the spirits to climb up the ladder. A white chicken (an innovation to the worship practice) was employed to indicate whether the spirits had arrived and accepted the gifts. Its head was cut off, and then the chicken was tossed up. It landed on the ground, turned around, scurried to the platform, stumbled backward, and dropped dead beside the ladder. The attendees interpreted this as a sign that the spirits had arrived. The dead chicken was placed on the platform next to the other offerings, and the men retreated to the village to let the spirits have their meal in peace and quiet.

It remained necessary to pay respects to the ancestral spirits. Since Samuel had returned from Madang, he had frequently called the names of two forefathers and sat around the site where the two had been buried. With the information the Regene had about Samuel's "ghost game" séance, it seemed most certain that these two spirits had taken possession of Samuel's

Illustration 3.2. Spirit platform (2007). Relatives stand in front of the platform on which offerings to the bush spirits have been made. Note the ladder for the spirits to climb up onto the platform.

body. Given that, these days, bodies of the deceased are buried in the Regene graveyard and Giri villagers suspect that their spirits roam the burial place, Samuel's kin decided to consult the Catholic priest from Giri 1[22] on how to deal with their spirits. The priest told Samuel's paternal and maternal kin to assemble and instructed the clan leader (who had the closest rapport with the spirits and was, by customary law, the only person with the right to call their secret names, thus, the only one who could persuade the spirits to let go of Samuel) to address the spirits while holding and stroking the neck of a white, living chicken.

Afterward, the chicken was killed and cut into two halves. Samuel's kin ate one half, and the other was offered to the ancestral spirits, who were then asked to release Samuel's body. This healing practice is a prominent example of the integration of indigenous religious and Christian healing. Courtens described, for contemporary Ayawasi (in the Bird's Head of West Papua), how local healing performances have been shaped and reshaped in a Christian context. She concluded, "Changes in the indigenous and missionary religious domains are intertwined with changes in healing performances . . . People, by incorporating Christian idiom and symbols, chose to create new healing rites" (2008: 216). With the abandonment of cremation and the introduction of graveyards, the spirits of the dead have come to dwell in Giri burial grounds. The novel healing rite described above was created to communicate with the spirits at their new domicile. In the aftermath of the ceremony, Samuel ceased to call his forefathers' names.

Several weeks after the ceremony, in the late afternoon of 22 August, Samuel offered hints that his ancestors' spirits had retreated. I was cooking a yam and sweet potato meal on the earthen stove on my veranda when Samuel paid me a visit. He appeared to be distressed and uttered the English sentence, "The game is over." I was unsure whether Samuel was referring to the "ghost game" and wanted to avoid importuning him with questions. Therefore, I carried the conversation on by commenting on the Regene men having finished their vespertine soccer practice—their "game."

Samuel did not respond to my remark; he just stood beside my veranda watching me dish out the food. I invited him to come up on my veranda, sit down, and partake of the food.[23] Regene villagers had warned me about Samuel's aggressiveness and put sustained effort in taking Samuel away whenever he approached me or my house. Only after some ten minutes did Samuel's wife head toward my veranda after catching sight of her husband. She called upon Samuel to accompany her to the evening prayer meeting, and Samuel followed her. This was—if correctly interpreted—the only time Samuel directly talked to me about the "ghost game."

Nevertheless, his health status had not improved. Samuel's kin reasoned that if none of their local spirits (bush spirits or spirits of the dead) were making Samuel ŋanŋan anymore, then another spirit must be troubling him. A thirty-five-year-old relative who had been present during the pacification of the ancestral spirits surmised shortly afterwards that Samuel's illness had been caused by marijuana: "Now, [Samuel] does not call his ancestors' names anymore because these spirits, which have been and worked with him, left him. And now we see it this way: he has drug sense now. The real spirits left him. And he does not call the deceased's names." Samuel's father explained to me that the "marijuana spirit" (spirit bilong mariwana) must be threatening his son. Regene people assume that marijuana has a secret name—a name like that of an ancestor or a bush spirit—which is concealed from everyone but the clan leader.

But who was the leader acquainted with this name? The marijuana that Samuel had smoked had come through Madang; Regene villagers suspected that the secret name of the marijuana was known either only by the person on whose land it had been grown (wherever this had been on the island of New Guinea) or maybe only by the Westerners who had initially introduced the plant to New Guinea.[24] Samuel's kin were stuck at an impasse—they could not communicate with the marijuana spirit because the secret name to address him was unknown to them, and they would not be able to bring it to light. Their way of reasoning shows how a foreign agent, marijuana, is integrated into Giri models of illness causation. Madness—which, according to traditional belief, is caused by either ancestral or bush spirits (or, rarely, by sorcery)—is hence ascribed to a "marijuana spirit."

Throughout these weeks, Samuel's illness was viewed by Regene villagers as a local illness and, hence, unresponsive to biomedical therapies. But, as the Giri classify marijuana as "something from the outside world," they also considered the possibility that biomedical drugs will foster Samuel's recovery—that his illness was a foreign illness. In the very beginning of Samuel's illness episode, his father had dragged him, with the help of other male kin, to BHC, where his older sister, a nursing officer, had given Samuel a chlorpromazine (an antipsychotic) injection.

She remembered that any further attempts to administer chlorpromazine were in vain, because Samuel detested the effected somnolence. Therefore, for a short time, his father irregularly hid chlorpromazine tablets in Samuel's food. Samuel's health status, however, did not improve. Some Regene villagers suspected that there must be another biomedical drug that had just not found its way into Papua New Guinea. Repeatedly, I was asked whether I had some waitman marasin to treat Samuel's illness, as Regene people were well aware of my two sizeable plastic containers from which I produced a plethora of medications. Others eventually cast away the idea that Samuel's illness was a foreign illness susceptible to biomedicine; others, again, still believed that the proper medication was yet to arrive.

At this stage, Christian healing practice comes again to operation. Divine intervention through prayer meetings is another Giri acquisition—as we have become familiar with in Rita's case. Through prayer groups, a new group of healers is established, extending the traditional group of local healers (i.e., clan leaders; cf. Courtens 2008: 216 on the creation of a new group of female healers). Prayers of intercession for healing address mostly the archangel Raphael but also God and Jesus. Prayers are often employed in addition to other treatment strategies, though not everyone gives credence to their effectiveness, and they are, to my knowledge, never used as a singular treatment.

However, since Regene villagers could not appease Samuel's marijuana spirit in customary ways, prayer seemed to be a method worth trying out. Furthermore, Samuel's mother was a devoted adherent to the Roman Catholic Church, and she had regularly prayed for her son's recovery since the onset of his illness. She and her husband believed that evil spirits—be they the marijuana spirit or any other spirit—could be cast out by prayers.

Samuel's illness was directly addressed throughout several prayer meetings and church services. At the end of a Sunday morning church service, Samuel's father announced—after mentioning that they had an "ill person" (sikman) in their midst—the arrival of several Catholic priests who would pray over his son. He cautioned the villagers to attend the prayer meetings. If the spirits would vacate Samuel's body, they would search for other bodies to occupy and could easily enter the body of anyone who had committed sin or scorned church services. In particular, he emphasized the importance of the adults being vigilant and not letting their children mill about. Children's bodies are generally perceived as weak, and thus children are more susceptible to spirits than are adults. The spirits were feared to be able to find a way into children's bodies, but if the children participated in the prayer meetings, they were believed to be safe from spirit occupation. If the spirits entered anyone's body, that person would become ŋanŋan just like Samuel.

A few weeks later, a week-long Catholic Church conference was held in Regene. In the morning of the first day, the congregation marched in a procession through the village. The group made earsplitting noises—rattling the corrugated iron roofs (which are catchment areas for rain water), striking the ground with long sago palm leafstalks, and shouting. As I mentioned in Rita's case, this was meant to chase away malevolent spirits lingering around the village. The procedure is typically performed to clear ground before bigger church events or festivities but was, this time, carried out with exceptional thoroughness, with an eye toward ending Samuel's illness.

The marijuana spirit revolted against the attempts to be driven out, which manifested in Samuel's increasingly aggressive behavior. This had already become apparent on the night of 26 July, when I sat with my friend Sarah on her cooking platform. We bolted upright when Samuel smashed a guitar on the ground. Sarah explained: Samuel had asked a relative (who was the strongest and best-educated Regene church adherent and the son of one of the forefathers whom Samuel had summoned) to borrow a guitar. Convinced that he could free Samuel from the malevolent spirit, he had given him an old guitar, over which he had prayed and sprinkled holy water. To Sarah, it was obvious that the spirit had bridled against the guitar and forced Samuel to destroy it.

Despite all the prayers, Samuel's condition improved only marginally throughout the following weeks. He was still confused, was still in a state of agitation, and frequently wandered around the village. He would utter unintelligible sounds and swear at other villagers. However, Samuel was less aggressive toward Regene villagers, in general, and the men ceased to follow him around. Village life was gradually returning to normal. Tension had grown, though, between Samuel and his close kin. Early in the morning of 20 August, before any women had arrived to sell her produce at the Regene market, Samuel's neighbor (to whom he was distantly related) ran after Samuel's wife, who intended to leave her *ŋamŋan* husband and Regene—at least for the time being—and return to her family in Birap 2. Samuel had beaten up his pregnant wife repeatedly and shamed her in public by forcing her to have sexual intercourse with him.

It seemed that the less he insulted and fought other villagers, the more he tormented his wife. The neighbor managed to persuade Samuel's wife to turn around and return to Samuel's parents' house. On another morning, Samuel's mother walked past me on the trail to Forge. She was crying and talking to herself. I did not understand much of what she said—only single words, like "Satan," got through to me. She seemed to be extremely distressed, her T-shirt was pulled up her back, and she was holding her arm. I learned that her husband had ordered her to get up from bed and becalm Samuel, who had punched his wife. Samuel's mother had refused to do so, because she had been resting—suffering from pain due to an eye sickness. Thereupon, her husband had hit her and hurt her on her back and arm. She was seeking shelter from her husband among her siblings in Forge.

In late August and afterwards, my interlocutors voiced opinions that Samuel would not recover through continuing prayers. Prayers can help, but only if all disputes were settled beforehand. Only the reestablishment of social harmony would enable recovery from his illness (see Keck 2005)—which had been caused, to a great extent, by conflict and had resulted in further disputes. Ancestral and bush spirits had been becalmed, and Samuel's maternal kin group had solved its discord, but his kin group had to be unanimously well disposed toward him. Samuel's father had beaten him up twice throughout the illness episode.

Persuading Samuel's father to reconcile with Samuel and apologize for beating him in order to enable his recovery became the predominant topic of conversation in the Regene community. If any hidden conflicts were to be left hidden and unresolved, then whichever treatment strategy was to be applied, healing would not take place. Samuel's father voiced his doubts over whether his son would ever fully recover. Samuel's health deteriorated again throughout the last days of August and he verbally harassed male and female villagers and threatened them with sexual assault. His female neighbor Melinda put it this way: "The marijuana spirit is with him and [as a result] he wanders in the spirit of promiscuity."

Aftermath

When I returned in 2009, 2010, and 2011 to Regene, Samuel was leading a withdrawn life with his wife and their two small children. Samuel had limited his movements to the very proximate area around his house, his garden, and the sago swamps. Throughout my two-week stay in 2010, I did not run across him a single time in any other part of the village. Instead of chatting to the other men in the men's house, he preferred to stay home with his wife. The community no longer interpreted his behavior as being part of his illness. For the Regene villagers, he had recovered but simply avoided other villagers because he was ashamed of the behavior that he had shown.

In December 2008, the Regene abandoned the idea that Samuel did not recover due to some marijuana spirit with whom they could not communicate. When, in December, Samuel's father, together with five other Regene men, was imprisoned, Samuel fully recovered. The provincial court had convicted the six men of severely wounding a member of another Giri clan in a fight several years prior. This suggested to the Regene community that Samuel had been ensorcelled by a specialist from the hostile clan, who had released Samuel when his father (and the other five villagers) received their punishment of several years' imprisonment. A male villager concluded, "And when the six had been imprisoned, they [i.e., the sorcerer/s of the hostile clan] removed this poison."

It is rather atypical for a person to be let go without the antagonized parties gathering and coming to an agreement or—if no agreement can be reached—without pressurizing the specialists. In Samuel's case, this was only possible through contemporary jurisdiction. The two parties could not come to an agreement on the amount of compensation to be paid to the wounded man and his clan, and then a third party—the judiciary—came into play and made the six men "pay" for their act through imprisonment. This led to Samuel's release, though it does not mean that the dispute between the two clans came to an end (as compensation is vital for conflict closure). The court decision (and the following imprisonment) thus functioned as another diagnostic lens; it brought the hostile clan into play. The view that this clan had made Samuel *ŋanŋan* was furthered by a similar case. The son of a Tung community health worker became ill in 2009. He, a few years younger than Samuel, showed similar symptoms to Samuel's, and his own community (and the Regene) also saw him as *ŋanŋan*.

The only striking difference between the two cases is that Samuel was said to be "on and off," whereas the other young man was said to have been continuously ill from 2009 until I left in May 2010. When the search for the causes began, Regene villagers' opinion was divided: some people said that he had become *ŋanŋan* from marijuana smoking, some said that his illness had been caused by sorcery, as the young man's father was said to have been involved in land disputes with the same clan as was Samuel's father. That another man who was considered the heaviest marijuana smoker in the Regene-Bunapas-Garati area never became *ŋanŋan* was evidence for my interlocutors that marijuana smoking does not necessarily lead to illness. Samuel, whose father's clan was at odds with another clan, was believed likely to have become a sorcery victim. But a person is unlikely to be affected by serious illness if she or he and his or her kin lead a relationally harmonious life; marijuana smoking alone does not greatly affect such a person's health.

On one occasion, Samuel addressed his father-in-law by name—this is an offence, as, out of respect, one never addresses or speaks about affines using their proper names (instead, nicknames, kinship terms, or euphemisms are used). Even worse, Samuel swore at his father-in-law and provoked him: "Why do you come to see me? I am not dead so that you need to come and see me!" Still, Samuel was not held responsible for his actions. The only critique was directed at his continual marijuana smoking, because, after his illness episode in 2003, he ought to have been aware of its destructive effects on his body.

Despite the burden that Samuel obviously was for several months, Samuel remained a highly respected young man in his community. Regene villagers unanimously made clear to me that he was a "good man" (*guma-a vuŋ*) and that he would not verbally insult or become violent to others if he were not ill. Although he violated numerous behavioral codes, he and his family received intense community support, and Regene villagers felt genuinely sorry and showed empathy for his situation. Several times I encountered Regene villagers who wept for Samuel.

Epilogue to Samuel's Case

The technologies inherent in Samuel's illness episode are not biomedical in nature and may seem unorthodox—Western entertainment technology and a parlor game. Still, Samuel used the television screen as a diagnostic tool in an analogous way to Rita's utilization of the X-ray. Furthermore, the television screen and spirit board played a role in Samuel's falling ill. Knowledge of Samuel's experiences with these media led his relatives to reason that his illness must be a local illness.

The idea that streams across both stories is that X-ray images (plus the glasman's "X-ray vision") and the television screen have the power to disclose social illness causes. (Although the television screen does not allow the direct gaze into the body, it may function nonetheless as a diagnostic lens.) A number of anthropologists have shown that a general tendency to ascribe omniscient powers to Western technologies is not uncommon throughout Papua New

Guinea. Lattas noted, "Televisions also can voyage over the horizon and seem to have an omniscient reach; they can display what cannot currently be seen because it occurs in faraway places or in distant times" (2006: 25). And A. Strathern and P. Stewart traced the authority of a biomedical technology, the injection, among the Melpa and Huli peoples, who perceived the "shoot" as a powerful medication for a multiplicity of conditions—including conditions that did not require injections from a biomedical perspective—because they were "introduced by the colonial powers who brought other 'strong' things" (1999: 101).

That biomedical services played only a marginal role in Samuel's illness episode is partially due to the poor options offered at BHC and MGH. In what follows, I expound upon the range of psychiatric services in Madang Province. Aside from supplies of chlorpromazine tablets and ampoules, BHC does not have any psychiatric resources. MGH has, unlike BHC, a psychiatric unit staffed with two psychiatric nurses and a health extension officer with additional psychiatric training. In 2010, the three personnel of the hospital's psychiatric unit estimated that thirty to fifty patients drew on their services monthly; this number includes first-time and revisiting patients. And yet, MGH has no psychiatric ward.

Patients are counseled and stabilized on medications in the psychiatric unit but are admitted to the general medical ward (Terence Kuaru, Martina Tolane, & Susan Baniau, pers. comm. 2010). To put it concisely, psychiatric services throughout the province are very limited, and this is not an exception among the provinces of the country (see Goddard 2011: 33). In a *Post-Courier* article from 2007, Kolo deplored the scarce availability of psychiatrists in Papua New Guinea; only six psychiatrists, all of them based in the national capital, Port Moresby, work in the country (see Goddard 1992, 2011: chap. 1 on the development of psychiatric services from colonial times to the early 1990s). As Kolo (2007) stated, no psychiatrist is employed at Madang's provincial hospital. Samuel received chlorpromazine at BHC, but he never received any hospital treatment. This is despite the fact that he experienced an illness episode in Madang Town.

Police involvement in cases of madness is quite common throughout Papua New Guinea. According to Goddard, "The most common pattern of psychiatric incarceration in PNG [i.e., Papua New Guinea] . . . begins with police intervention after violence and continues with immediate medication at the psychiatric ward" (2011: 50). But transfer of violent patients to MGH is problematic, as patients might pose a threat to other patients on the general medical ward. Pressure to establish regional mental health facilities also comes from the police. In 2011, the Madang Provincial Police commander superintendent Wagambie called on health authorities to deal with "mental health patients who are now roaming the streets freely" (Evara 2011d: 6).[25]

In national newspaper articles, particular emphasis is often placed on the link between marijuana use and mental illness. For example, Kolo (2007) dwelled on this link, stating that mental illness among Papua New Guinea schoolchildren is primarily caused by marijuana consumption. According to Kolo, the Papua New Guinea Department of Health made predictions that mental illness triggered by marijuana smoking would be one of Papua New Guinea's major diseases by 2020. Kolo further denounced Papua New Guinea government bodies, stating that none of them—apart from the police, with its arrests—is addressing this pressing topic of marijuana consumption. The issue was repeatedly raised in subsequent newspaper articles (e.g., Albaniel-Evara 2012c; Evara 2011a, 2011d; Setepano 2011). Superintendent Wagambie further appealed to relatives of the mentally ill to assume responsibility for them (see Evara 2011a, 2011d). Hence, instead of being transferred to MGH, Samuel was brought back to the village by his kin.

Synopsis

In this chapter I have provided insights into the ways in which medical pluralism functions in practice. A particular focus was on the ways that Giri people anchor biomedical practices and technologies in their pluralistic medical system. Patients and their therapy managers usually employ multiple diagnostic methods and therapeutic procedures throughout an illness episode. Not uncommonly, formulated diagnoses and recommended treatment regimens differ significantly from one type of practitioner to another. This brings uncertainty for the patient and may also become a financial and emotional burden, especially for patients who suffer from long-term and chronic conditions. In order to gain clarity over their illnesses, Giri people make use of Western technologies in highly creative ways. To substantiate this, two case studies were examined. The first study exemplified the ways in which Giri people utilize biomedical technologies to determine which therapeutic means will work for them. The second study explored what Giri people do if biomedical health care is inadequate.

This chapter suggests that Giri decisions to use particular diagnostic and therapeutic procedures are, when viewed from their own perspective, pragmatic responses to illness as they perceive it. Treatment, for example, is contingent upon the perceived cause of a condition. Hence, it is absolutely possible for fever and madness to be treated in the same manner (with a pill or with spirit propitiation, as the case requires). When Giri people access biomedical care to treat madness and, for example, receive chlorpromazine (as was administered to Samuel), it does not indicate that they have made recourse to psychiatric notions of madness. It can be said for Giri what Goddard formulated for the Kakoli: "Psychiatric services were employed without a subscription to the medical-scientific understanding of madness (as 'mental illness') which psychiatry represents" (2011: 110).

In order to understand why people select certain diagnostic and therapeutic procedures among others, and which meaning they attribute to them, we must consider Giri relational notions of personhood. Social relations are understood to impact heavily on individual health and illness. It comes as less of a surprise, therefore, to find that the Giri people have their own way of reading the X-ray. For Giri patients, X-ray images can do a lot more than simply show their anatomy. In the words that Nichter used to encapsulate his own case study of an Indian patient who was eager to have diagnostic tests performed: "Diagnostic tests prove to have meaning beyond the physical body" (2002: 83). Nichter went on to show how, by having diagnostic tests done, the patient mobilized a therapy managing group, whose members supported him both socially and morally. This finding led Nichter to propose that "tests are not just instruments of surveillance in the sense of Foucault's . . . notion of biopower. Tests provide space within which social relations and agency may be articulated" (98).

In Rita's case, the X-ray was reinterpreted by her in such a way that it became a powerful medium, revealing whether her illness was a bodily disorder or grounded in disrupted social relations. Here, I embrace Street's concept of "relational technologies" (2009: 210), which goes against a purely mechanical reading of technology. The mechanistic understanding of the body that has characterized Western biomedicine for centuries does not accord with Giri conceptions of the body. Giri people believe that unbalanced or unsettled social relations impose on their bodies by making them sick. Whereas the X-ray emerged and was put to use as a diagnostic tool in a Western tradition that viewed the sick body as an object—as a malfunctioning anatomical/physiological entity—the machine has met, with the Giri people, members of a culture that does not view the body as a purely physical entity but as a composite of relations (see M. Strathern 1988; Wagner 1991).

To Giri people, bodily disturbance is entangled with social disturbance. The patient's choice of therapy depends, to a large extent, on their novel interpretations of X-ray photographs. Despite biomedicine playing only a marginal role in the second case study, other Western-introduced novelties (a Ouija board and a television screen) nevertheless took on central importance. Although not "medical" technologies (at least not in their original context), the parlor game and entertainment technology were virtually effortlessly integrated into the local medical landscape. My attempt to bring together two such different case studies might seem odd. However, despite their differences, I suggest that the two case studies sit well together, in that they both show the creative ways in which Giri people employ and locally reinterpret biomedical practices and Western technologies against the backdrop of indigenous knowledge of the body, health, and illness.

I have shown that, in the cultural logic of the Giri, social relations—be they unbalanced or harmonious—bear on individual health and illness. In the chapter that follows, I enlarge upon the study of the social relations of health and illness by directing my focus to therapy management. In distinction from the present chapter, which evolved around two in-depth case studies of Giri patients, the next chapter is predominantly organized according to the actors that mobilize around the patient.

Notes

1. The original German quote reads, "als (kranker) Knoten in einem immer wieder anders zusammengesetzen Beziehungsnetz" (Verena Keck, pers. comm. 2011).
2. Macfarlane (2009) published a literature review showing that medical pluralism is a prominent feature throughout Papua New Guinea.
3. However, it must be emphasized that the various components receive unequal attention in Papua New Guinea's public health system, which is dominated by biomedicine. The GoPNG emphatically promotes biomedicine and the use of pharmaceutical drugs through its national health policy. Yet, as noted in the current national health plan (2011–2020), the country supports the integration of the "safe practice of traditional medicine" (GoPNG 2010a: 36) into the health delivery system on the community level. Famously, the Declaration of Alma-Ata (WHO 1978) explicitly called for the integration of biomedical and local medical techniques. "Primary health care for all" was defined as a key objective, and to implement this, the WHO advocated the inclusion of indigenous practitioners, including midwives. In Giri and other Papua New Guinea cultures, a midwifery tradition had been absent (see Denoon [1989] 2002: 99, 102; Merrett-Balkos 1998: 220). Newly trained village birth attendants (see chap. 5) have thus been "used" to promote biomedicine in the villages, rather than showcase traditional medical knowledge. At the provincial hospital in Madang, herbalists, shamans, and other village healers are not permitted to treat patients in the wards. Giri people draw heavily on biomedical options where they are readily available. But, in other cases, biomedical care provided by the public health system is very limited, and Giri people resort to traditional or Christian practices.
4. Anthropologists who have done research on the social construction of illness in Papua New Guinea societies include Frankel (1986), Frankel and Lewis (1989), Glick (1998), Goddard (1998, 2011), Keck (2005), Lewis (1975, 2000), Lindenbaum (1979), and Mattingly and Garro (2000).
5. Bush spirits came into being with the land and inhabit trees, bamboo groves, boulders, whirlpools, and other natural formations. Over time, bush spirits have retreated more and more into the dense bush in an attempt to escape from human intruders and noisy village life. They are normally rather indifferent to humans but may be benevolent and helpful (*thor vuŋ*) or—if enraged—may be dangerous and cause illness and disability (*thor mba-atik*).

6. As with the Yupno shadow soul, "wopm" (Keck 2005: 55), *ŋina* can also escape from the body when somebody is dreaming.
7. See Counts and Ayers Counts (1989: 284–85), Hamnett and Connell (1981: 491–92), Koczberski and Curry (1999), LiPuma (1989: 296), Roscoe (1989: 202), and Schwartz (1969); also see Macfarlane's (2009: 45) review of the literature dealing with Papua New Guinea illness classification systems.
8. See, for instance, McGrath (1999: 493–95), Macpherson and Macpherson (1990: 83–84, 151–52), Maher (1999), and Saethre (2007).
9. A pseudonym Herdt created to protect the Anga-speaking people of the Eastern Highlands, among whom he had conducted research.
10. Tsumba and Chungrebu (see map 2.1) are two of the Rao villages along the Ramu in which the Churches of Christ mission established stations and started biomedical work.
11. A ginger relative (*Alpinia* sp.). Its roots may be utilized in sorcery (Mihalic [1971] 1986: 89).
12. Lattas (2010: 200–201) reported a similar case of a Kaliai (New Britain) man who drank his dead father's blood out of sorrow and subsequently became mad.
13. The Parliament of Papua New Guinea voted in May 2013 to repeal the 1971 Sorcery Act after Prime Minister Peter O'Neill sought its revocation in the preceding month (Siegel 2013).
14. The shadow soul can cause illness in others. By some Giri it is then referred to as a "worry spirit" (*riri*).
15. In contradistinction to Giri clan names, which are chosen from a fixed stock of names and stress patterns of responsibility to the social group, nicknames appear to be highly individual. Nicknames are generally related to personal traits, habits, offices, and so forth. The ward member at the time of my fieldwork was referred to as Memba, one man who had a big belly was called Bikbel, and another one was named after a lizard species that people reckoned to have a similarly big belly. Another man had the nickname Tri kilok, because he habitually returned much earlier than other villagers from garden work—that is, around three o'clock in the afternoon. Early in my fieldwork, a woman gave me the name *Phonu* (cassowary) when she saw me jumping over a ditch. She commented that my legs were just as long as a cassowary's legs. Despite the name I had been given from the clan's repertoire upon my arrival, the Giri addressed me as *Phonu* from that moment onward.
16. He used the Tok Pisin word sekhan, which also has the meaning "to make peace."
17. This custom of sleeping on the clans' platforms in order to protect the village from raids by neighboring peoples has been completely abandoned in Regene and other Giri villages. In Varaning, a group of young men have revived this and other customary practices.
18. According to a survey that I conducted in 2010 of two thirds of the married male Regene population, the average marital age is 23.3 years. Samuel was approaching his twenty-seventh birthday, thus marrying quite late.
19. The Ouija board is a registered trademark of Parker Brothers.
20. Giri villagers commonly have strong social support networks in Madang Town, and they know where Giri town dwellers reside. Giri visitors to the town make extensive use of their social support networks. For town dwellers, it is anything but unusual to constantly harbor a handful of Giri villagers in their homes.

21. In former times, a girl (before her menarche) would be dressed in traditional finery and displayed for the spirits to see.
22. Regene villagers are almost exclusively adherents to the Roman Catholic Church, which established a mission station in the early 1950s in Giri 1 village and was the first church to permanently set itself up in the Giri area. I am aware of only one Regene man who converted (in early 2010) to the Pentecostal Foursquare Church, which has a community of followers in Giri 2 and Garati/Bunapas. At the time of my fieldwork, none of the Regene villagers was a member of the Churches of Christ (located in Garati/Bunapas).
23. As a very crucial act of everyday sociality, any visitors who are present at your house when you serve food should be given a plate. This even applies to passersby, to whom one is expected to call out in such a situation (cf. Eves 1998: 38–39; Fajans 1985: 379–80; Kahn 1986: 41–42).
24. Marijuana was introduced to New Guinea by Australians after World War II and became, in the late 1970s to early 1980s, more widespread among the local populations (see Halvaksz & Lipset 2006; Marshall 1987, 2004; McDonald 2004, 2005 for the introduction of marijuana to New Guinea). It is illegal everywhere in Oceania. The cannabis produced in Papua New Guinea is consumed locally but also traded internationally (Marshall 2004: 218).
25. Madang provincial health advisor Markus Kachau voiced his intention to upgrade the psychiatric unit at Modilon General Hospital and establish psychiatric units in the province's six districts (Albaniel-Evara 2012c). Very recently, the Madang branch of Bank South Pacific announced its commitment to donate 20,000 kina to upgrade the run-down facilities of MGH's psychiatric unit (Albaniel-Evara 2012a).

Chapter Four
The Web of Care Relationships

This chapter aims at unfolding the social relations of therapy management. It is arguably a global phenomenon that people rarely manage their illness without support or advice from others (see Coreil et al. 2001: 175). Here, I investigate the social webs of Giri therapy managers, which span BHC (the local health center) and MGH (the provincial hospital). Since the primary objective of this book is to map the local entanglements of biomedicine, I focus on the roles therapy managers play in biomedical environments. The groups of actors investigated in this chapter are medical staff from BHC, medical and paramedical personnel from MGH, and family members, who perform a range of caring tasks for Giri patients. The first half of this chapter is devoted to the health center and then I move on to the spatially extended relational webs that span the provincial hospital.

The Concept of the Therapy Managing Group

In order to grasp and then analyze the role of sufferers' social networks, Janzen introduced the concept of the "therapy managing group" (1978, 1987), which serves a brokerage function between the sufferer and the specialist. He developed this theoretical concept in his BaKongo medical ethnography, *The Quest for Therapy in Lower Zaire* (1978). Janzen characterized the therapy managing group as "a community of persons who take responsibility from the sufferer and enter into brokerage relationships with specialists" (7).

In medical pluralistic situations, such as those found in most contemporary societies, including Giri, the therapy managing group may play a central and active role in choosing a therapy from the multiplicity of available options (Csordas & Kleinman 1996: 10). Moreover, therapy management encompasses the provision of social support. Janzen depicted it for the BaKongo as follows: "An observer notes quickly the ubiquitous 'family' around the sufferer: now they are feeding the patient; later they are chatting or just sitting with him; at another time they are washing his clothes. If his condition deteriorates they may begin to mourn for him. But they are never absent" (1978: 4). Nichter (2002: 82) pointed out even more diverse roles of therapy managers: they may lend emotional and financial support to the afflicted, partake in the construction of illness narratives, and provide a space where therapeutic events and healing can occur.

Janzen's concept of the therapy managing group has influenced scholars writing about Melanesia. Keck (1993b, 2005) explored the involvement of a large group of people—more than twenty family members and people from other clans—in events surrounding a little boy's illness and directed at the restoration of his well-being. Keck's work explicitly contains the idea that the composition of the therapy managing group is highly dynamic and contingent upon the boy's state of health and grows in line with the threat of the boy's condition. As Janzen (1978: 67) argued, members of the therapy managing group may vary from one stage of therapy to the next.

Frankel (1986: 174–75) claimed, for Huli, that much of illness management and care takes place at home, with the therapy managing group consisting of only a small handful of household members. Thus, in general, Huli therapy managing groups are considerably smaller than those of the BaKongo, as depicted by Janzen. Yet, in cases of severe illness, a larger number of people may be involved in therapy management. Lepowsky (1990: 1053) drew a similarly flexible picture of the size of the therapy managing group for Vanatinai in the Coral Sea. For instance, there, if an illness episode is ascribed to sorcery, the therapy managing group often consists of only a very few people, as the patient's condition is concealed from other villagers to disguise the patient's weakness and vulnerability from the sorcerer.

The case studies in chapter 3 demonstrated that the size of Giri therapy managing groups varies from case to case and across different stages of an illness episode. At times, only Rita and her husband managed her therapy, but then her mother's brother accompanied her to meet a shaman (glasman), a Giri church group gave her support, and her husband's mother's second cousin, employed at MGH, opened up access to hospital services. From the beginning, Samuel's illness was managed by large groups of people—search parties, groups of men watching him for several nights, and the maternal and paternal kin groups who met, respectively, to propitiate bush spirits and reconcile with Samuel and his wife. In brief, Giri patients are highly social agents, and they often have their therapy managed by (and share illness experiences with) others to whom they are related by means of kinship or coresidence. The involvement of those with whom one shares inherited friendship ties is also not uncommon.

I suggest that the concept of the therapy managing group is sufficiently elastic so that, aside from those carers who are involved by virtue of their close kin relation or spatial nearness to the sufferer, various Giri medical and paramedical staff at BHC and MGH may also be included. As evidenced by Rita, many Giri draw on a wide circle of kinship relations to gain access to biomedical services and to receive support of many kinds throughout their treatment at biomedical facilities. Most sufferers are, as a matter of fact, related (to different degrees) to the Giri personnel on whose aid they call. As is demonstrated below, in the urban context, the wantok system usually takes effect when the kinship relation between sufferer and Giri MGH personnel is distant.

In other words, and starting from the institutional level, we find that a complex network of kinship ties permeates BHC and MGH. I think of the two biomedical settings as places suffused with multiple sociocultural networks that give them a *couleur locale*. Of course, not all of these networks are formed by Giri actors. In chapter 2, I described the extent of BHC's catchment area and MGH caters to patients from across the entire Madang Province. Here, I take a closer look at the Giri networks. The medical institutions of BHC and MGH are places where Giri sociality comes into view, for example, when relatives cook meals for Giri patients or when medical and paramedical personnel accommodate patients at their homes.

Introducing Giri modes of sociality, I inevitably come across the so-called New Melanesian Ethnography (Josephides 1991), with its crucial assumption that "Melanesians create . . . their lives on the basis of kinds of social thinking" (Robbins 2006: 172; see my introduction for a fuller consideration of Melanesian[-ist] perspectives on the person). It emerges from my discussion below that the Giri patient and the relatives and Giri health workers who care for him or her are constituted relationally through their interactions.

Providing Food, Building Relationships

In this section, I unravel complex webs of Giri relationships that pervade BHC and MGH, explicating different relationship constellations. I begin with a small BHC patient, Benjamin, and the key members of his therapy managing group. My focus is on how caring family members related to Benjamin (and to one another) through food, for a crucial task of the BHC inpatient's therapy management group is food provision, as the health center lacks the funds to purchase food for patients.

When I arrived at Sandra's dwelling house in the morning, she was stirring sago in a large pot. Soon after, she sent dishes of sago pudding to a number of houses within a radius of a few hundred meters of her own house—to her mother-in-law and the family houses of her three brothers-in-law. Yet, another plate was covered with the lid of a pot and set aside until Sandra and her household members had finished their meal. Then, Sandra readied herself to go to BHC. The stored meal was one of the many with which she supported her adopted sister Lillie's nine-year-old son Benjamin, who had been admitted to BHC with pneumonia and acute diarrhea.

Illustration 4.1. Sandra goes to Bunapas Health Center to bring Benjamin sago pudding (2009). She carries a netbag with empty containers to fetch water from one of the health center's tanks. She balances the sago dish on her head, smokes a hand-rolled cigarette, and has a baby carrier strapped on with her son inside.

At BHC, inpatients' relatives are fully responsible for the provision of food. The person who engages in the provision of comestibles and food preparation depends greatly on the particular situation. Still, a few general observations can be made. Inpatients from the spatially adjoining communities of Regene and Garati usually receive meals that either their own household members or other villagers with whom they are already involved in daily food-shifting routines have prepared. This is a feasible arrangement, as the walking distance between the Regene and Garati villages and the health center is short.

Meals are cooked in the village and either brought to the patient by the cook herself,[1] by one of her daughters or classificatory daughters, or sometimes by another female relative. In short, these women extend their regular food-shifting routines to the health center. In addition, villagers who are otherwise not in the patient's food-shifting circle may provide the ill person with food, thus emphasizing the good relations they have with the patient. This situation is quite different for patients coming from the more distant Giri villages and other Lower Ramu villages, for whom dropping by with home-cooked meals is more difficult. If a person expects to be admitted to the ward, they and their relatives likely amass food (mainly sago, yam, and plantains but also taro, sweet potatoes, dry coconuts, smoked fish, leafy vegetables, etc.) in advance and bring the comestibles along to BHC.

If other close kin happen to live in Garati or Regene, the patients and their relatives might bring along only small quantities of edibles and primarily rely on this nearby kin. In emergency situations, such as accidents, snakebites, obstructed labor, sudden sickness, or the sudden worsening of someone's condition, relatives are possibly unable to accumulate food on the spot. Usually, in these situations, they promptly engage in food procurement and take the comestibles to BHC after the patient enters. Long-term inpatients receive follow-up visits from kin, who stock them up. Sometimes these visits are frequent and regular, sometimes only occasional.

Food provision does not always go smoothly, and patients may experience hunger and food insecurity. Since the early days at Tung Aid Post, patients' families have been responsible for food provision and preparation. As reported in *The Australian Christian* (Anonymous 1960: 613–14), this came to be a problem for Lianke, a Minung long-term inpatient. Lianke, paralyzed from his waist down, had been diagnosed with transverse myelitis at the native hospital in Bogia. Subsequently, he was sent back to Tung Aid Post, where he was admitted to the ward. The missionary nurses reasoned that Lianke "will have to remain hospitalised for the remainder of his life. It is very unlikely that he will ever regain the use of any of the leg or other muscles that have become affected" (613). Lianke suffered from being cut off from his village:

> Almost every day Sister Hunting is asked by Lianke (the sick man) if he can go home. Life for these people centres very much in their own village. Away from it they have no one to look after them, no one with whom to sit around and talk. All the familiar things are absent ... Who is to look after a man away from home and unable to fend for himself? His garden is all important. He explains to Sister that his old mother, who looks after him, is too old to make a garden on ground that may be allotted to him. The Mission is able to give him some food, but it is still necessary for people from his village to carry food to him, and this is a big task. (Anonymous 1960: 613)

For Lianke, a principal difficulty lay in food production and transport. The missionaries offered to arrange Lianke a garden patch with local landowners, but his mother was too old and frail to lay out a garden. Furthermore, the above-cited passage illuminates Lianke's longing for home and for his *own* garden—a topic I address in detail further below.

First, I shall return to Sandra's food provision activities, with which she supported Benjamin and the relatives who had accompanied him to BHC—that is, his mother, his father, and his two-year-old brother. Sandra prepared the first meal as soon as she came to know about her relatives' arrival from her sister-in-law:

> [Husband's younger brother's wife's name deleted] informed me. She went down to the hospital [i.e., BHC]—took her child down and she came up [again and] informed me thus, "Your sister's child is sick and she stays at the hospital." So, I heard this. In the evening I have to go . . . see her. Hence I cooked. I stirred sago pudding. I carried [it] down. I went and visited her and her husband. I came back again after the two of them had eaten.

"Putting the pot on the fire" constitutes the most basic idiom of Giri sociality and tradition, which Giri people call, "welcoming visitors to the village." This was one of the first practices I experienced and was explicitly taught by Giri villagers. As I detailed in the introduction, I was lavished throughout my stays with a myriad of meals cooked by women from across Regene village. After I had settled in, I got into the routine of cooking daily evening meals, which I shared with my neighbors, other interlocutors, and, importantly, visitors—be they my own guests, those resting on my subclan's platform, or those happening to pass by my house during food preparation or serving times.

Sandra welcomed her relatives at BHC with the meal that she prepared on the day of their arrival, therewith transferring this fundamental kastom to the locality of the health center. She displayed herself as a "good woman" (*mbik vuŋ*), showing generosity through food sharing and acting in accordance with Giri kastom. This is similar to what Anderson (2011: 47) wrote about the Wogeo, Eves (1998: 38–39) about the Lelet, and A. Strathern and P. Stewart (2000: 26) about the Melpa ideas of a "good person" as someone who conforms to the ethos of food sharing. Beginning with Benjamin's admission on 5 October 2011, and over a period of eight days, Sandra supplied her relatives with twelve meals—at least one per day. Thus, she strengthened social ties with them. This was particularly significant to her, given that her adopted sister, Lillie, only rarely visited Giri:

> One reason is that she lives very far away from us. We do not see her regularly. She also does not show her face to [our] parents . . . to any of us. It is this way, she lives far away and when she comes to the hospital [i.e., BHC] because her child is ill, we have to go and see her—see how she is, check how bad the child's illness is.

With Lillie's marriage to a Kukum man, she moved to his paternal village. Kukum, a village of the Abu language group, is, like Giri, located in the middle reaches of the Lower Ramu but along the western banks of the river (see map 2.1). Lillie had not been to Giri for two years. Above, Sandra describes Kukum as "far away" from Giri. Indeed, it is far not only in spatial distance (Kukum being only a few meanders upstream from Giri) but also in social distance. Mutual respect and reciprocity characterize relationships with one's affinal kin. In terms of food, this means that food ideally flows on a regular basis in both directions. In Sandra's case, this means that food should have flowed from Lillie's husband and his kin to Lillie and her kin and vice versa. However, Lillie's husband had not been to Giri in years, and an empty-handed visit would have been embarrassing for him and could have been regarded as offensive and disrespectful by his affines, as Sandra explicated:

> Her husband may visit [our] parents but one must consider that they are his in-laws, huh?! He is ashamed. He is ashamed. He may take his wife and children to see [her] father and mother if he has a small game animal or [other] small food items. But they do not have a [fishing] net. I mean, they live at the edge of the river. [They] don't have a net. And he . . . he said: "I am ashamed. I cannot visit [my] parents[-in-law] empty-handed. I must take something and go visit." So, for exactly this reason they do not show face to [our] father and mother up [in Giri 1].

Although he lived alongside the Ramu, Lillie's husband did not have a nylon fishing net, which would have enabled him to present his affines with Ramu fish. Lillie and Sandra's parents resided in Giri 1, which is set back from the river, located farther inland. In Giri 1, fish is a delicacy due to its scant availability; Lillie's husband felt obliged to provide the sought-after fish. But food moved in only one direction: from Sandra's family to Lillie, her husband, and their two children. If his son's sudden illness had not forced him to travel to BHC, Sandra's brother-in-law would certainly not have come barehanded to Giri. Under the circumstances, Sandra and her kin felt unoffended by the unilaterality of the food flow. Still, Lillie's husband avoided visiting his parents-in-law.

He only did so for a day after another of Lillie's sisters, who lived in Giri 1 and had heard about his arrival, came down to Regene and summoned him to come for a brief visit to Giri 1. I shall put forward the proposition that Lillie's husband engaged in garden work to reciprocate (with his physical energy) the meals that Sandra had supplied for him and his family. Although it was already November, Sandra had not fully prepared her new garden for planting. Her husband had been imprisoned for almost a year, and Sandra had suffered from her husband's absence—in particular from the reduced workforce. Sandra had cleared her garden from scrub and cut down the undergrowth, but felling large trees is a quintessentially male task. Hence, Sandra appreciated her brother-in-law's extra pair of hands around the garden. Besides, we may argue that Lillie's husband augmented Sandra's garden land with his bodily energy—energy that would pass to the crops and eventually be transferred to the consumers of the garden's produce.

In order to understand why it was so important to Lillie's husband that he give food to his wife's kin, we must take into account that relations (and place) are incorporated through food. In chapter 5, I argue that the Giri child is a composite being, constructed of parts of other persons—in particular the mother, whose maternal substances significantly contribute to the child's growth. Food produces the Giri unborn and newborn and establishes a bond between the child and the child's kin—most notably the mother. Food continues to create and maintain social relationships throughout Giri lives.[2] Giri adolescents become food producers. At the same time, they remain consumers of food produced by others. Fajans (1985: 372) argued that Baining infants are not born as "persons" but only gradually attain this status. Baining people reach full personhood—are "fully social" (ibid.)—at the moment of life when they oscillate between the roles of food taker and food giver.

With the act of eating, the Giri person incorporates parts of the place from which the food originates and parts of the person who has put her or his bodily energy into its production. This has likewise been noted in the literature on Melanesia. Knauft captured this incorporation of person and place in Melanesian societies with the words: "Those whose food you consume are those whose labor, land and essence constitute your own being" (1989: 223). Likewise, Hess said for Vanua Lavans:

> Food is certainly the most obvious medium through which partibility, dividuality and permeability can be demonstrated in the relation between people and place. Through planting and incorporating food, a place becomes part of a person and a person becomes part of a place. By being incorporated food literally becomes part of a person, and can be seen as connected to a person's identity, present and anticipated. (2009: 79; see 80–82; von Poser 2013: 180–81, 141–42, passim)

Drawing on M. Strathern's (1988) oeuvre and, more specifically, on her notion of the "dividual," authors such as Battaglia (1990, 1992) and Foster (1990, 1995b) have argued for the Sabarl (Southern Massim) and the Tanga (New Ireland Province) that gifts (e.g., of food) not only create, maintain, and strengthen social bonds between persons but also facilitate and elicit detachment from parts of persons' own and other persons' bodies. Persons do not simply exchange objects but parts of themselves—or, as Mosko aptly put it in his recent article, "Melanesians typically interact as composite beings constituted of the detached parts/relationships of other persons through prior agentive elicitations and exchanges" (2010: 215; cf. Konrad 2005: 45–46; Mosko 2000).

For the Wogeo, Anderson (2011: 98) spoke of food as inalienable exchange objects with which the food giver passes a part of him- or herself to the food taker. A unity is formed, for example, between the body of a Wogeo woman and the sweet potato that she plants or between a Wogeo man and the fish that he catches. Food in Giri is, in the same way, imbued with aspects of those who produce (and prepare) it; hence, gifts of food are "inalienable possessions" (Weiner 1992). Food that contains parts of its producer permeates the bodily boundaries of its receiver and, therewith, constructs both producer and receiver as dividuals.

Stephen laid out this flow of substance for Mekeo society: "Essentially, the interior of the physical body is understood to consist of an unstable flux of substance passing in and out of the bodily orifices. This substance, indeed the body as a whole, derives from others, originally the parents, and is maintained by food provided by caretakers, later supplemented by gifts of food from others in social exchanges" (1996: 87). Eves stressed the qualitative difference between eating and eating food received from others: "Food or other items that are incorporated into the body are means by which the body is sustained or, when exchanged, social relationships are sustained" (1995: 214).

So what food flowed from Sandra to her relatives? Was it food that had been endowed with a notion of place? Was it food that Sandra's labor had enriched? All twelve meals had been made from local ingredients, aside from the salt. Sandra supplied eleven meals of sago pudding—one preceded by fire-roasted yam—and one yam dish. All repasts were topped with leafy vegetables in coconut cream and some with fish that Sandra and her daughters had caught in the Regene oxbow lake. Sago and yam are the major staple foods in Giri. Sago, the ultimate staple of the Giri diet, enjoys the recognition of being the elemental source of bodily strength and well-being. This is often expressed by the phrase saksak em bun bilong mipela (sago is our bone/strength).

Also, and very importantly, sago itself is genuinely social. Giri do not plant sago palms for themselves but for their progeny. This is reminiscent of the practice in neighboring Bosmun, of which von Poser wrote, "One must not eat the sago one has planted oneself" (2013: 83; see 86).[3] Giri parents plant sago palms for their linear and classificatory children but also for their grandchildren, who then internalize their relationships with the sago planters through eating the sago. In the swamps around Giri 1 village, Sandra had ample sago, which her father and other relatives had planted. Throughout my time in Giri, Sandra regularly left Regene village for several days to work her sago in the Giri 1 swamps.

As a seasonal crop, yam contributes much less to the total annual diet than does sago. Yet the Giri are very fond of their yam gardens, and their Akikim neighbors even refer to the Giri people as "red yam" (*nguar hip*). After a long time of yearning, the Giri are glad when the yam harvest begins. Panti wrote, in his article on growing yam, about the first yam meal at the ceremonial opening of a new season: "They eat until their guts are full for they have long been waiting for yams to come" (1992: 21). Yam "gives us a break from our steady diet of sago" (17; see Tuzin 1992: 104 for similar sentiments among the Ilahita Arapesh).

Yam requires constant horticultural attention and, as such, is highly enriched with bodily energy. Both yam and sago are culturally valued foods and, at the same time, identity markers—symbols of Giriness. Hence, I suggest that Sandra enforced her social relationship with Benjamin and his family by giving them locally grown sago (an inherently social food) and yam (tended with her own hands). Store- and market-bought food cannot mediate relations to the extent that gifts of local food can. The former becomes endowed with aspects of the food provider through the activity of food preparation, but, in distinction to produce grown, tended, and harvested in Giri, it is not genuinely relational in itself.

In the Giri view, in opposition to sago and yam, imported, store-bought foods cannot ultimately assuage one's hunger and do not give strength (*ngapngaŋ*) to the body (see Schneider 2011: 44 for a similar notion among the Gawigl of Kaugel and Marapugul valleys in Western and Southern Highlands Province). If living off them, one becomes weary and sluggish. According to this line of thought, Giri patients' conditions are less likely to improve if they constantly eat rice-based meals. Thus, it is not surprising that Sandra did not prepare any rice, instant noodles, or canned fish meals for the sickened Benjamin.

Yet, I shall mention that nonlocal, store-bought foods have an ambiguous quality in Giri, because they also offer a welcome respite from the local diet. Moreover, some value is attributed to them, because one must pay money for them and they are comparably expensive. Also, imported foods are symbolically linked to a Western lifestyle, which some aspire to (cf. Hess 2009: 81). Sandra emphasized that she would, as a matter of fact, purchase such foods if that was what Benjamin wanted: "I must attend to [him] if he wants me to buy a can of fish or a packet of instant noodles or the like because he is her [i.e., Lillie's] child and also my child, huh?!"

Sandra emphasized the vital role accorded to her as Benjamin's eldest "mother" (*niamu*). The Giri have a classificatory kinship system. Lillie, as Benjamin's linear mother, and Sandra, as Lillie's eldest sister, are both *niamu* to Benjamin. Mutual respect and what Giri commonly call laikim pasin, which can be translated as "loving and care," characterize the relationship between a mother and her linear and classificatory children. As Sandra said, a mother should attend to her child's needs and requests.

To conclude, food giving empowers the food giver socially by showing that the food giver has mastered culturally expected generous behavior and has good intentions. Similarly, receiving food empowers the food receiver socially. A patient who receives many plates of food is evidently a person with a large social network. Moreover, eating food that one has received from others adds substance to the receiver's body. On the one hand, personal parts of the food giver enrich the receiver's body. On the other, and at a very basic level, the plain, nutritious value of the received food grows the receiver's body. Finally, I want to note a relational vision of BHC; the provision of local food by patients' relatives is one of the strategies for turning this biomedical institution into a relational place. To buttress this point, I expand on food-shifting practices as they currently occur at BHC in the next section of this chapter.

A Network of Food Shifters Emerges

I understand BHC to be a place where new food-shifting circles emerge. It is not just that relatives supply meals to inpatients, as I suggested above, but that a series of reciprocal transactions takes place among different patients' caring relatives (throughout Papua New Guinea called wasman; literally: "watchman/ men"). Sometimes these carers are strangers to one another, and sometimes they are related to one another. In any case, they try to create or deepen the bonds with their co-carers and other inpatients. This is primarily done through food-sharing activities. On a macrolevel, Giri (and probably many Melanesian cultures) apply what L. Stewart elaborated on for the Lolo of West New Britain: "Giving and receiving food mean that each person has a place within the social system by virtue of the fact that one gives and receives" (1989: 124). The following discussion describes the transcended specificity of the Giri context, with carers (and the patients they tend to) coming from across the health center's wide catchment area. Furthermore, health center staff members also participate in these emerging food cycles.

Many patients, especially those who come from villages outside Giri, are not as lucky as Benjamin, who had close kin living in one of the two nearby communities who ferried daily meals to BHC. For these patients, the tasks of food procurement and meal preparation lie with their accompanying relatives (wasman). Due to staff shortages, each patient must bring an informal carer to look after them. Carers cook in a makeshift kitchen that was erected by other carers after the health center's outdoor kitchen collapsed in 2007. Besides meal preparation, these carers undertake a range of other tasks, such as helping patients with their medications, bringing them to and from the toilet, assisting them with their bodily hygiene, doing their laundry, and keeping them company.

Some patients are accompanied by more than one family member; yet the bulk of the caring tasks is generally performed by a single person, who hovers over the patient. This correlates with what Zaman observed at a hospital in Bangladesh: "Usually one of the relatives then becomes 'attached' to the patient during the whole period of the patient's hospital stay, and plays an important role in caring for the patient" (2005: 110). Typically, the carer is a female family member. Male carers are usually involved only in spouse relations, or they share childcare tasks with their wife. Nevertheless, a child's mother is generally involved at a greater level of intensity than is the father. Often, patients reciprocate the gift of care that they are given with a gift of care in return, whenever this becomes necessary.

I give a snapshot of food-centered activities that I observed during Benjamin's stay at BHC in order to provide an account of food-shifting practices as they occur at BHC. Benjamin had five fellow patients at BHC. They were all from villages outside Giri. None of them had any close relatives living in the communities neighboring the health center, but they were all accompanied by family members. There was Bertha (aged thirty), accompanied by her sister, her husband, and her youngest son and mainly cared for by her sister; Amy (aged thirty-six), accompanied by her parents and mainly cared for by her mother; Crystal (aged thirty-four), accompanied and cared for by her husband; Diana (aged twenty-four), accompanied by her mother, her husband, and her brother with his wife and their two children and primarily cared for by her mother; and Elaine (aged five), accompanied by her parents and mainly cared for by her mother.

So how was it that food-shifting practices were instigated? Bertha was tired of eating plantains, but that was the only food that she and her relatives had left. They had arrived five days before Benjamin, bringing garden produce (mainly plantains) from Amarong. Over the course of their stay, Bertha's mother's brother came around with dry coconuts to make coconut cream (which is used for cooking plantains). To supplement the plantain dishes, Bertha's sister purchased small quantities of green leafy vegetables and edible cane grass inflorescences at the Regene and Bunapas markets. On the morning of the fifth day, Bertha's sister dished out boiled plantains.

She served Bertha and their other relatives, but she also prepared two extra plates—one for Diana and her mother and another for a health worker from Giri 1 who was employed at BHC. Bertha's sister gave the health worker the dish in return for a rice meal that the health worker's mother (who resided with her daughter in the BHC staff housing) had shared on the previous day. Aware of Bertha's longing for a change of food, the health worker's mother had sent plates to Bertha but also to the other inpatients. In this situation, rice appears to have been a legitimate alternative to locally grown banana, despite its inability to "strengthen" individual bodies. The plate that Bertha's sister gave to Diana and her mother was reciprocated soon after, when Diana's mother stirred sago. Just like Bertha's sister, Diana's mother poured additional plates of sago pudding for Bertha, to reciprocate her plantain dish, and for the health worker, to reciprocate her rice dish (see figure 4.1 for a visual presentation of the moving plates).

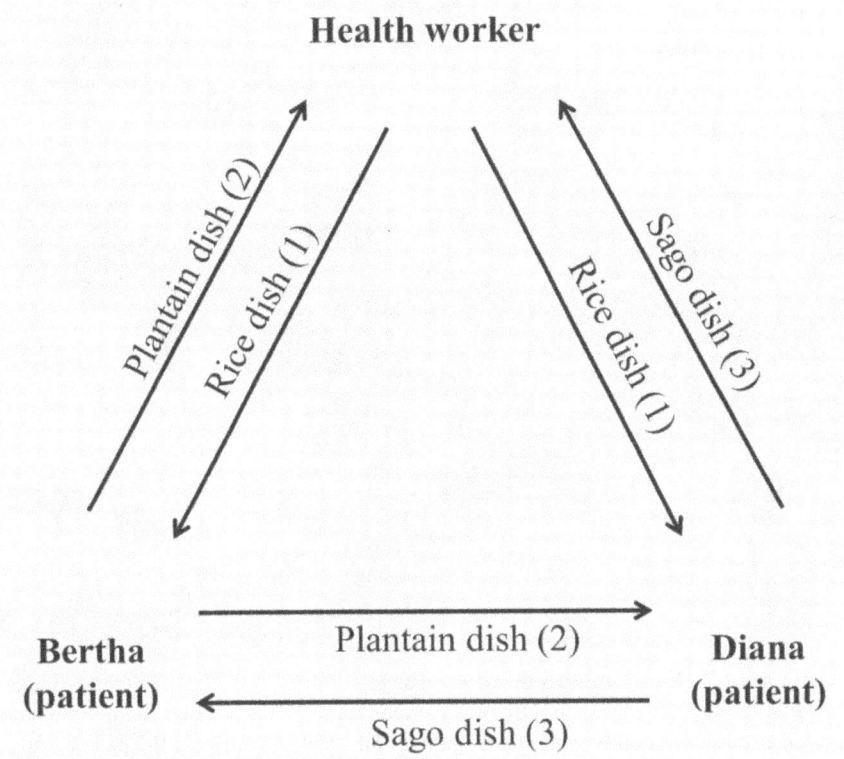

Figure 4.1. First dish moving in each direction between two inpatients and a health worker. The numbers (1) to (3) indicate the chronological sequence.

Often, one shared meal is sufficient for creating a lasting food-shifting relationship. A network of food shifters began to form among the carers and health personnel at BHC. Or, as Diana's mother put it, "I dish out food for them; they dish out food for me." Once such a relationship is established, it continues until the patient is discharged from the health center. Many more plates moved forward and backward between the three parties and between them and other inpatients and their carers. Diana's mother, for example, regularly shared great quantities of cooked food with other patients, their caring relatives, and health workers.

She and her hospitalized daughter had an extensive network of relatives supplying them with ample local produce. On the day of Diana's admission, fourteen family members accompanied them to BHC, bringing along sago, plantains, and dry coconuts. The next day, Diana's sister-in-law arrived with a netbag filled to the brim with plantains, dry coconuts, and cucumbers. The day after, a group of twenty-four relatives brought more supplies. One

Illustration 4.2. Diana's mother dishing out sago pudding in the health center's makeshift kitchen (2009). The sago will be accompanied by coconut cream soup with cane grass inflorescences, native spinach (*Amaranthus gangeticus*), and the paired edible leaves of the *Gnetum gnemon* tree (tulip).

morning, Diana's mother poured sago into thirteen dishes (illustration 4.2), giving a share to every patient and to the abovementioned health worker.

Conversely, and quite remarkably, Amy's parents arrived at BHC without any food supplies. However, they were equally involved in food-sharing activities. Economically better off than the other inpatients and their carers, Amy's father (employed by a logging company) purchased five kilograms of rice, canned fish, and cabin biscuits[4] at one of the Regene stores. His wife bought yams and other vegetables at the Regene market. She cooked two thirds of the rice at once and distributed it on fifteen plates—for her own family members, the other patients and their carers, and the abovementioned health worker's family.

Although in the Giri view store-bought foods are not endowed with aspects of self, they appear to have been valid gifts in reciprocating others' dishes at BHC. Still, all inpatients were from sago-dependent societies, and, according to their views, only sago meals could give strength to their bodies. For instance, when Bertha, after consuming a sago meal prepared by Diana's mother, walked past the woman taking a dirty pot toward the Ramu, Diana's mother made a remark similar to this: "See, she has gained strength and walks down to the Ramu now that she has eaten sago pudding. Eating plantains is simply not enough." Similar to the Giri, Diana's mother was of the opinion that plantains can still one's hunger (pasim bel;[5] literally: "fasten the belly") but not provide the body with any strength.

As noted earlier, in the village, food plates principally circulate between households whose members are closely related through kinship. In addition, other spatially proximate households whose members are more distant relatives, but with whom one is involved in daily interaction, are often included in this circle (cf. von Poser 2013: 114). At BHC, spatial proximity is also a key factor behind the movement of plates. The health worker about whom I wrote above considered herself and her household members to be more deeply involved in food sharing with patients than with other health workers and their families. She believed that this was because her house was the closest to the health center cooking area.

Accepting food from others is, however, also fraught with danger, as sorcerers may place lethal substances in food (see, e.g., Fortune [1932] 1989: 170; Meigs 1984: 101, 106; Lindenbaum 1979: 53–54; LiPuma 2000: 169; P. Stewart & A. Strathern 2004: 6). If Giri people suspect that a meal has been poisoned, they will most likely decline with the phrase, "I am full." But refusing food is tricky, as it means refusing social relations that have been offered. At BHC, patients usually accept the meals offered by other patients' carers and health workers. Meal preparation activities in the health center's outdoor kitchen are visible to the public, which ensures a certain degree of "safety."

Relationships created between people through food sharing transcend the immediate situation. Not uncommonly, former inpatients or carers who happen to be in the Bunapas area visit the homes of health workers with whom they have been formerly involved in food-shifting routines. With these visits, they may bring along garden produce from their village. Guests and their hosts might sit together and share areca nuts, and the health workers or one of their household members will serve a meal.

To come full circle, local food-shifting routines pervade this health center in different ways. I have argued, through the example of food provision for Benjamin, that life at the health center is linked to life outside the health center. Then I have shown that food-shifting routines are established at BHC that closely resemble food-shifting routines observed in Giri village communities, such as Regene, where I lived. Zaman described the Bangladeshi hospital that he researched as "a microcosm of the larger society in which it is situated" (2005: 18). Zaman's depiction is similar to my own observations of food-shifting routines at BHC.

Nevertheless, van der Geest and Finkler's (2004: 1998) description of the hospital as part of the "mainland" appears to be a more accurate image for

BHC, because it allows for the inclusion of already established food-shifting circles that are sometimes extended to inpatients and their carers (as was the case with Benjamin and his relatives) and of food-sharing activities between health workers, inpatients, and carers that newly emerge at the health center and persist even after a patient has been discharged.

Who Cares?

Above, I have described the support that inpatients get through food from their accompanying carers (wasman) and other relatives. These carers have been shown to be mutually supportive. In this discussion, I only marginally touched upon health workers' entanglement in this web of relations. As aforementioned, Papua New Guinea's health system suffers from a lack of workforce, and caring tasks are generally not the responsibility of health workers. The scenario that unfolds at BHC thus differs from that of Western hospitals, where care is, to a large extent, covered by the staff.

Above, we, however, learned about a health worker who interrelated with patients and carers through gifts of food. Under certain circumstances, health workers may become intimately involved in patient care and become key members of the therapy managing group. In the following section I examine one such situation—observed when the health center was closed. The house of the officer in charge was broken into and the health center solar panel with its appendant battery (and the officer's private solar panel and battery) were stolen. It was publicly made known on the bulletin board that BHC would attend only to emergencies and tuberculosis patients and otherwise be closed until the stolen items were returned. In fact, the appropriated items were returned after twenty-two days, and work resumed.

Health Worker Homes—Extensions of the Ward

The example of a woman who was brought to Bunapas when the health center was shut offers an illustration of what it means for health workers to put up patients at their homes. Hannah, a Giri 1 woman in her mid-twenties married to a man from Varaning village, was rushed to Bunapas one night in November 2009 with acute abdominal pain. Upon their arrival, her escorts—her husband and a group of about a dozen family members—learned of the health center closure. As a matter of course, they proceeded to the house of a health center nurse in the staff compound. Emma, the nurse, was closely related to Hannah in a twofold way: she was Hannah's father's younger sister and, at the same time, Hannah's adopted mother's older half sister.

On the following morning, Hannah's affinal kin informed Hannah's own and affinal Regene relatives about her illness. This was also how I found out about Hannah's arrival. A woman who was related to Hannah (as her husband's father's mother's younger sister's daughter) and with whom Hannah was connected through an intimate friendship[6] was the first Regene relative to see Hannah at Bunapas. I followed her. We arrived to find Hannah lying on a small platform in one of Emma's two outdoor kitchens. Hannah was groaning with pain.

The women who had escorted her to Bunapas took turns sitting by her side and massaging her abdomen. Some women were with their small children. Emma sat beside the platform on the wooden seat of a coconut scraper, grating a dry coconut for the meal that she would serve Hannah and her Varaning relatives. In the meantime, Emma's daughter-in-law prepared the sago pudding. Hannah's male escorts were resting on the platform in the other outdoor kitchen, talking, chewing areca nuts, and smoking.[7] More Regene relatives arrived. Emma served the morning meal to her household members and her Varaning visitors.

Upon Hannah's arrival, Emma began to treat her for urinary tract infection and worms. Emma and another Giri health worker held the keys to the health center during the closure period at that time, and it is not uncommon for health workers to take away medications to treat patients at their homes during such periods of closure. Yet, Emma was lacking the equipment and expertise needed to establish a reliable diagnosis. In order to ease Hannah's condition, she injected her with a sedative after Hannah had eaten her morning meal. (Hannah, however, ate only very little, because she was in excruciating pain.)

Hannah fell asleep within a few minutes of the injection, and her Varaning relatives made the one and a half hour walk back to their distant village to pick up some clothes and necessities for Hannah and themselves. Regene visitors also returned to their village, apart from one young Regene woman, who remained by Hannah's side. This woman was related to Hannah, as her father's younger brother's daughter, and took on the responsibility of primary carer in terms of Hannah's bodily hygiene. This gave Emma time to go over to BHC to collect intravenous drip equipment and a glucose solution bag for Hannah and inquire via shortwave radio about transportation to the referral health center in Bogia.

Upon her return, Emma found that new visitors from Varaning had already assembled at her house. Emma had been unsuccessful in dispatching an ambulance from Bogia Health Center, and the Bunapas ambulance was currently unavailable because the officer in charge of BHC had used it to attend a funeral in his home village. Hence, Emma continued her responsibility for Hannah's medical care and for providing meals for Hannah and her relatives. After two more days, with Hannah's health deteriorating, Hannah's affinal relatives eventually managed to organize a private car to Bogia Health Center.

Emma was visibly exhausted upon Hannah's departure. She had already told me, after the first turbulent night, that she was desperate to rest. Yet she stayed up late, accommodating a group of Regene Catholic Church members who had come to pray for Hannah's convalescence. Emma had not had any decent sleep since. Emma suffered from hypertension and regularly needed to see her attending doctor at MGH to get a new prescription for her medications. She had already run out of her medications by the time Hannah arrived but postponed her departure so that she could tend to her. Furthermore, catering to the many visitors had had a significant economic impact on Emma's household expenditures. At the time, her household comprised another five members, who all depended on her income.

In a nutshell, ward closures do not generally lead to workload relief for health workers but instead pose an additional burden on them, particularly those from Giri. Shutting down inpatient care often results in Giri health workers putting up seriously ill patients at their private houses. These workers feel obligated to accommodate patients to whom they are related through kinship, even if only very distantly. Due to BHC's closure, Emma was pushed into accommodating Hannah and her relatives at her own home. But beyond question, Emma would have been highly involved in Hannah's treatment, anyway, and would most likely have supplied meals for Hannah and other Varaning family members had Hannah been admitted to the ward. However, much of the interaction between patient and caring visitors would certainly have occurred in and around the ward. Under the circumstances, not only was medical care moved from the ward to Emma's house, but Varaning and Regene relatives also rested on Emma's kitchen platforms.

Nonetheless, this should not be seen in purely negative terms, since these situations also open up opportunities for health workers to anchor themselves more deeply in the web of social relations. Accommodating Hannah and her companions resulted in a reaffirmation of relationships—most importantly through gifts of meals from Emma's household. Emma's gifts of food were directed to Hannah's affinal kin from Varaning, who were genealogically and spatially distant to Emma and with whom she rarely engaged in food-giving activities. It appears that Emma seized the chance to welcome Hannah's affinal kin at her house and strengthen her bond with them through the food. If she had not embraced this chance, she would have risked a rupture in the relationship. The Lolo have a similar system in place, in which distant kin must at least occasionally be given food (L. Stewart 1989: 124–25). Only those with whom one exchanges gifts of food belong to one's social network.

When her relatives from Regene arrived, Emma apologized to them for not having enough food to share. Refusing to give food to others often indicates that social relations are strained; denying or withholding food from another person means refusing to enter into or continue a social relation with that person.[8] However, when Emma's primary kin from Regene arrived and Emma apologized for not giving them any food, this was not interpreted as rejection. On the basis of genealogical and spatial proximity, Emma engaged in food-giving activities with her Regene relatives on a more frequent basis. Under the unanticipated circumstances of the visit of distant Varaning relatives, Emma's apology served to acknowledge her good relations with her Regene kin.

As L. Stewart wrote: "Gifts of meals are dependent on situation as well. If a number of guests arrive, or in case of sickness, those affected receive gifts of cooked food" (1989: 125). We may add that others, who may normally receive gifts of food, may be left out at this time. Similar to Emma, Hannah's Regene family members were highly engaged in cultivating their relations with Hannah and the Varaning people. They nurtured the relationship with dishes and pots of cooked food, which they brought to Emma's house for sharing. They kept them company, tried to ease Hannah's pain through massages, and prayed for her convalescence. Furthermore, with their contributions, they took the burden off Emma's household as the sole provider of food for the many Varaning visitors.

Excursus: Insisting on Care

When the health center is closed, health workers also assist patients to whom they are not related through kinship and who come from outside Giri. Health personnel do not usually put these patients up but sometimes treat them at their homes. Emma and another female Giri health worker, Dana, both tended various Giri and non-Giri patients when BHC discontinued its services for twenty-two days in November 2009, after the burglary in which solar panels were stolen. Dana, for instance, underwent minor hand surgery on the platform underneath her house and entered the health center to administer the contraceptive Depo-Provera to women who had come from afar to receive their trimonthly injection. Emma and Dana also found a way to help sufferers who were in need of intravenous medications over a span of several days or longer but who did not live close by. Under normal circumstances, these patients would have been admitted to the ward. However, during the period of closure, Emma and Dana discussed with the patients the possibility of medically trained individuals in their village helping out.

They supplied the patients with syringes, cannulas, and their respective medications and asked, in an accompanying letter, those with medical qualifications to administer the drugs. In both women's opinion, it was their medical responsibility to treat arriving patients. They disapproved of the chairman's decision to suspend services. Dana voiced the argument that the continuation of medical services would not jeopardize police investigations and that medical services must only be suspended for reasons of health, if "someone's life is at stake," as she said in English (e.g., in the case of disease outbreaks).

Also, Dana and Emma feared that patients could suffer severe damage or die if they were left untreated and that the aggrieved parties in that situation could take legal action. They decided to continue work until given an official decision from higher authorities—that is, from the district health manager in Bogia or the head of the Provincial Health Office in Madang on whether to continue services or not. On the other hand, they legally trod on thin ice when taking home medications from the health center to treat patients. Also, their acts brought them into conflict with other, male health center staff who endorsed the closure, agreeing that it would pressure the thieves into returning the stolen items.

Thus far, my discussion has been of BHC. BHC becomes local (i.e., a Giri place or, in a broader sense, a Ramu place) through acts of food giving, food receiving, and food sharing. Often, staff embraces health center closures as further opportunities to strengthen social ties with patients. However, in the last section, I demonstrated that closures can lead to conflict between health workers. The next section focuses on MGH, the provincial hospital. MGH is treated in a manner similar to that which I used to depict BHC. After introducing MGH through Giri images of the hospital, I pass over to patients' carers' roles and bring in another group of actors: Giri medical and paramedical hospital workers, who mediate between Giri patients and hospital services. Through this, I show how the hospital is given a "Giri *couleur locale*."

Therapy Managers at Modilon General Hospital

To introduce the hospital, I begin with a presentation of Giri images of this medical institution. It was mentioned above that Giri people value the health services provided by MGH for their diagnostic and therapeutic superiority to those of BHC. But aside from the benefits of hospital services, Giri people also entertain unfavorable notions of the hospital. Commonly, their kin lend them extensive support in this "foreign" environment—both emotional and practical. Giri people rarely go to the hospital without at least one relative with them. This applies to both inpatient and outpatient visits. Kin are integral to hospitalized patients' care, and they even facilitate direct access to certain services, bypassing formal hospital structures.

Let me dwell once more on a point made above about BHC with reference to Zaman (2005). In Bangladesh, relatives' involvement in patient care is more extensive than what is generally seen in Western hospitals. Zaman contrasted the situation in a public Bangladeshi hospital with Laub Coser's (1962) observations of a U.S. hospital, in which responsibility for a patient passed from the patient's relatives to the hospital as soon as the patient was admitted. Family members' access to the hospital was also limited (Zaman 2005: 119–20). But in the Bangladeshi hospital, as Zaman argued, patients' relatives assumed roles that were crucial to the functioning of the ward. With underresourcing and understaffing both chronic issues, relatives not only provided the bulk of patient care but also filled in other tasks, such as serving tea to the doctors and handling paperwork. By doing this, they became essential players in the informal ward organization (Zaman 2005: 110).

At MGH, there are, similar to BHC, two major groups of relatives who aid Giri patients: close family members and Giri who are employed at MGH and either closely or more distantly related to the patient. In the pages that follow, I explore the roles that patients' kin take. Giri outpatients and inpatients-to-be usually stay in Madang Town with their most immediate kin by either decent or marriage ties. However, some villagers have no near kin residing in Madang Town. These villagers are most likely to be harbored by more distant relatives. To begin this discussion, I present Giri views of the hospital. Why is it so important to Giri that they receive support from their kin?

A Place of Reprimand and Death

Critique of the hospital often speaks to one of two negative images. First, MGH is frequently envisioned as a place where people go if they are about to die. Second, it is noted to be a place where patients and carers are reprimanded and treated as inferiors. Giri patients feel subjected to and disciplined by the non-Giri hospital staff (also see Keck 2005: 174–76 for condescending treatment of Yupno people at Teptep Health Center, which results in Yupno refusing to visit the health center).

Beginning with the first image, whereas most Giri patients value the hospital's outpatient care (including laboratory testing and X-ray examination), admittance to certain wards is, for them, tantamount to a death sentence. Lisa, a woman from Varaning village, was the sister in charge of the general medical ward. She explained to me that her ward was known among Giri villagers as the "death ward" (ward bilong dai). Giri people know that patients have already died in perhaps every bed of the ward, and they fear that whoever occupies a bed on the ward will, as a matter of fact, not leave the hospital alive.

A middle-aged Regene woman who had never been to MGH said, "I believe that I will die straight." And a twenty-four-year-old healthy Regene man stated: "I will go if I am terribly sick. But I will remain [in the village] if I feel that I can survive [without receiving inpatient treatment]." A young male community health worker who recently moved back to Regene explained what seemed to be the prevailing line of reasoning: "[If one] stays at Bunapas [and] is referred to the big hospital [Giri] people understand this to mean that one now goes to the place of death. So, this is the last hospital one goes to.

One will either recover or one will die." Giri people's fear of admission also pertains to the pediatric ward—the ward where children die. In contrast, they are less perturbed about admission to the obstetric, gynecological, surgical, and eye wards.

In Lisa and her colleagues' opinion, it is not without reason that patients feel their lives threatened. Lisa disclosed that she and her fellow workers had noticed that one death on their ward would often be rapidly succeeded by another: "If one person dies it appears that tomorrow another one will die. When two have died we know already that it will take a long time [until yet another person dies]. One person dies and drags another one with them to death." In the cultural logic of the Giri, the spirit of a deceased (*thum*) not uncommonly hauls another person into death, because the deceased does not want to be left alone and seeks a companion.

Not only patients but also carers feel threatened by spirits roaming the ward. Alicia once stayed overnight in a ward at MGH while she looked after her mother. She barely slept:

> And the time I stayed with her until the next morning, I felt that I was not happy to stay in the hospital because I was frightened . . . I was afraid of all sorts of sicknesses from the hospital. People use the beds and die there, I fear their spirits. Therefore, I do not like to stay in the hospital.

Alicia also expressed that, apart from the spirits of the dead, she dreaded the many sicknesses that one may get at the hospital. Carers who are healthy when they come to the hospital may catch a sickness in the ward. Wards are perceived to be places where the deathly sick meet.

Villagers who have seen the hospital only from beyond the fence and know of its inside only through stories told by others feel particularly insecure about MGH.[9] They are afraid to embarrass themselves by getting lost, erroneously approaching a person who is not in charge, or being unable to comprehend a doctor's words. MGH is a place where mostly strangers work—people with whom one has not established trustful relations, people who come from and belong to unknown places, and people who might turn against one. This idea shines through the statement of a twenty-five-year-old woman.

Helen knew exactly what steps she had to take in order to talk to the physician in charge. She suffered from an extremely painful chronic hip dislocation and regularly came to MGH for strong painkillers. Yet she dreaded the hospital visits:

> Oh, it is that some [staff] are usually cross. So when I go, I am afraid, huh?! I go with fear. Some will be cross . . . So, I fear that they could scold me. [It is] this way. Because I don't know them well, think about it, huh?! It would be very difficult to

know from which place this one is, from which place that one is. [It is] like this. And so I am a bit anxious when I go to the big hospital.

This fear is enforced through local discourse in which MGH is often envisioned as a place where patients are mistreated. Reports of incidents experienced by Giri villagers at the hospital nourish this image. Sandra, for instance, experienced a laboring woman being slapped and yelled at by a nurse:

> Some doctors . . . I mean they get cross, angry, don't appropriately talk to the patients, to birthing women . . . I went to take [name of her firstborn daughter deleted] there [to have her blood checked because she suffers from frequent severe bouts of malaria]. When I took [her firstborn daughter], I mean [the nurse] did not yell at me, another woman was about to give birth and she cried out, cried out, cried out and, alas, the sister came, beat her badly, reviled her in an inappropriate manner . . . She was not a relative of hers.

With her last sentence Sandra framed her statement: whereas kinspeople would give support and show compassion, strangers' behaviors are often perceived to be linked to negative intentionality.

Lisa, the nurse, observed that Giri patients and carers at the hospital are quiet and shy. She interpreted their withdrawn behavior as a fear of rude doctors and nurses:

> I see it this way: The Giri people who come don't speak much or er . . . demand or whatever. They come and they just stay quiet. They just follow whatever the nurses or doctors say. They don't . . . I mean the others who come and speak much and demand or ask many questions or whatever . . . No, they don't do this . . . They just accept [it]. They just take whatever medication we give to them . . . They must be anxious, or? . . . They must have this kind of thoughts, "What if we speak and the nurse . . . or doctor will get cross with me?" . . . Therefore they don't like to speak.

In this and the above quotations, we find excellent demonstrations of Foucault's (1975) 1995 subjugated, "docile bodies" produced by discipline. However, patients evade nurses' action by drawing on their social support networks. Most patients already feel more comfortable if they are accompanied by one or more relatives, who lend them emotional support—who "give strength" (givim strong) to them. Relatives help patients find their way around in the hospital, thus taking pressure off the patients, who are very mindful of behaving appropriately. Sometimes, if patients feel very emotionally uneasy about being admitted to the ward, related hospital workers take pity on them and put them up at their homes.

Carers underneath the Hospital Beds

As at BHC, at MGH, every patient is accompanied by a carer who is, in most cases, a female relative. Patients' relatives assist hospital patients in much the same ways as they do at BHC. Also, patients reciprocate care. Rita, for example, was accompanied to Madang Town by her sister-in-law, for whom she had cared in 1999 after a gynecological operation. While awaiting a gynecological operation at MGH, Rita told me:

> We will exchange now. A long time ago I came and I watched over her when she came [in] for an operation. And now when I will have the operation behind me [and] come stay [in the ward] she will watch over me. It will now be thus: she will become the carer and I will become the sick patient, and a long time ago she became the sick patient and I came [as a] carer.

Still, there are a couple of significant differences in patient care between BHC and MGH. First, though patients usually depend on one key carer, often a larger group of family members stay in BHC's ward. At MGH, only one carer is permitted to stay overnight. A bed is not provided for the carer, and, even when the ward is not busy, the carer is obliged to sleep on the floor underneath the patient's bed. This circumstance is frowned upon by carers, who see it as a threat to their own health. Alicia endured a night on the floor beside her mother's bed in the hospital's general medical ward. She was afraid of getting sick:

> Okay, there must be beds for the carers to watch over these patients because it is not safe if we sleep on the hospital floor. The hospital's cement [floor] is not . . . particularly safe because it is not myself who is sick so that I came to stay here inside. There are all sorts of sick people who come . . . and use this patch of floor. They are here and walk up and down here and put all kinds of germs on this cement [floor]. So, we generally sleep on this floor. The patient sleeps on the bed and we sleep just next to them—on the floor, on the cement. If we have a blanket or mat we put it [on the cement] and we sleep. If not, then we just sleep on the floor. This is something we do wherefore I do not feel happy to go [as a carer to the hospital]. So, I feel that they must change this hospital. The carer must have his own bed to sleep on.

Exemptions from the one carer rule are sometimes made, as in the case of children, with whom both parents stay, or patients who are nearing death, who are attended by several close family members. Unoccupied beds, though, are not allocated to these carers.

Nonetheless, most patients have visitors from the village, who steadily stream in and out of the ward during daytime and spend the night in Madang Town houses with other relatives. These visitors come to see the patient and carer inside the ward. Visitors who meet in the ward may proceed to a shady spot on the outside lawn, escaping the dreadfully stuffy wards. If the patient is in good enough condition to leave the ward, she or he (with her or his carer) will usually join the other relatives outside. It is common for visitors to come and go from the hospital several times a day. Areca nut consumption is prohibited on the hospital's premises, and visitors go to the bus stop opposite the hospital for chewing. Also, visitors from Giri usually run errands for themselves and relatives from the village. Often, they return from shopping in the town center with snacks for the patient and key carer that have been purchased from a market, a takeaway food bar, or a supermarket.

A second difference is that whereas at BHC one of the carer's main tasks is to prepare meals for the patient, Giri carers do not usually engage in food preparation on MGH premises. At first glance, this appears to be just a matter of course, because the hospital provides meals. But, when taking a closer look, it becomes apparent that hospital meals form only a small proportion of a patient's diet. Collecting hospital food from the central hospital kitchen at mealtimes is one of the carers' major tasks. But the supplied food differs greatly from typical Giri food and consists almost exclusively of snacks of cabin biscuits and meals of plain, cooked, often brown rice with a few, mainly dark, chunks of canned tuna. Giri patients soon grow tired of this unbalanced and untasty diet (see above for the inability of store-bought foods to give energy to the body).

The food "won't fully satisfy your desire" (i no inapim tumas laik bilong yu), as the mother of a girl on the pediatric ward once said. Moreover, brown rice and canned tuna do not carry the same value as white rice, canned mackerel,[10] and other store-bought foods. They are not linked to a Western lifestyle, but instead associated with dearth and misery, because they are also the food that prisoners receive. In addition, the preparation of hospital meals is not a public activity. Patients and their carers do not know who has prepared the meals, and they cannot know the intentions of those who have; thus, the food is potentially harmful. Often, I saw Giri carers setting aside rice and canned fish meals, which were eventually invaded by ants and finally disposed of by carers. Besides, hospital meals are not enough to feed both patient and carer.

Although the medical, surgical, and pediatric wards of MGH are each equipped with an outdoor kitchen area, meal preparation on the hospital grounds is not a viable alternative for Giri carers. In the Giri view, these kitchen areas are unclean and germ-laden. This is in contradistinction to carers' thoughts on BHC's makeshift kitchen, which appears to be considered an acceptable place for food preparation. Perhaps this is related to Giri people's notion of MGH as a foreign place and a place of death, whereas BHC is seen as "their local hospital." Preparing food at MGH would pose a threat to consumers' health. Instead, meals are cooked at relatives' homes in town and ferried to the hospital. The central carer who tends the patient at the hospital usually does not leave the hospital to cook meals; rather, other relatives undertake meal preparation.

Relatives' homes are the first port of call for villagers who come into Madang Town. The brought-along produce is bestowed upon these hosts with whom villagers (other than the one carer, who eventually moves with the patient to the hospital) stay. Giri hosts gladly receive the cherished local produce, and food is cooked by either female hosts or female visitors. Whenever a pot of sago is stirred or a pot of yam or other garden produce boiled, the food is shared among the entire household, including all visitors. Portions for the patient and carer are brought to the hospital. With many mouths to feed and hosts' cravings for locally produced sago and yam, it is often the case that the food that carers bring with them does not last until the patient and carers return to the village.

Although patients feel that local food is most favorable for the body, sharing the brought-along food takes the utmost priority. Subsequently, meals provided by town kinspeople mainly consist of a white rice base topped with leafy vegetables (sometimes cooked in coconut cream) and, occasionally, corned beef or canned mackerel. If possible, the cook tries to respect the patient's food desires, purchasing plantains, yam, taro, sweet potatoes, and so forth. All in all, patients' kin provide a rather well-balanced diet for the patient, although some patients possess a much stronger network of food providers—a much stronger therapy managing group—than do others in Madang Town. Those with a weaker support group rely more heavily on the bland hospital food.

In addition to kinspeople, Giri hospital workers support Giri patients at MGH. In the next section, I discuss the roles they play for Giri patients.

Mediators

For Giri villagers who come to Madang Town for medical treatment, Giri medical and paramedical personnel perform three central tasks: they act as mediators, facilitating the interface between patients and hospital physicians; they serve as hosts to patients and their carers from the village; and they supply inpatients and carers in the hospital ward with meals.

Giri patients and their accompanying carers approach some Giri MGH workers more frequently than others. The most crucial factor influencing their choice of whether to approach certain staff is the kinship and social tie between them. In addition, there are other factors, such as the housing situation of the Giri staff, staff members' readiness to help others, and the size of staff members' professional networks. Regene patients most commonly approached Arthur from Giri 1, porter and aide of the operating theater. Although he had resided in Madang Town since 1989, Arthur maintained close and warm relations with his kin in the village. Hardly a month passed without members of his and his wife's immediate and extended kin from Regene and Giri 1 villages visiting. Visitors included sick villagers who sought treatment at MGH but also family who came to town for various purposes. Concerning the medical cases, Arthur drew support from a long-established and extensive contact network of MGH staff. Arthur described the role he played for Giri patients as follows:

> There are many who come [to town] whom I help to come through . . . to come to go to the outpatient [clinic], with the modalities to go see a doctor, helping them to get medications . . . I generally . . . instruct them to go . . . "You go this way and that way to see this doctor." Because in here . . . it's that I know many doctors, huh?! So that there will be easy access allowing them to go . . . see them and having a medical record written . . . thus speeding up the process. And they can go get medications quickly and go back again [to the village]. Well, nowadays it's . . . you must know that it's this way that you will go see whom you know, huh?! And then you get treatment quickly. Therefore many people . . . from among us from Giri come—I mean not whole Giri but the people from Regene and . . . some people from Giri 1. They come through to me and I generally say: "Okay, we go this way! This way we go quickly—go see the doctor, arrange medications, having a report written, depending on the sickness [having an] X-ray [photograph taken] or whatever." I usually tell them and they usually go . . . I know one or two doctors. I am here for a long time. I think I work here for twenty-three years now . . . work in the hospital. So, I know many people—the doctors. So, if I approach them [and] ask them, they will say, "Okay, just hurry up and we will deal with them [i.e., the Giri patients] . . . help them to get treatment."

Arthur paved a direct path to medical treatment that allowed Giri patients to bypass the institutionalized structures of the consultation process. They received faster medical treatment and thus returned more rapidly to the village. In chapter 3, I presented Rita's case and noted that Arthur had arranged for Rita to have an X-ray. He had also scheduled a consultation for Rita with the anesthetist Wendy from Giri 1. Rita would inform Arthur when she ran out of the asthma medications that she had been taking since 2007. Arthur would then approach a doctor he knew, who would write a prescription. When I was in Madang in 2009, I received a phone call from Rita's daughter, who—aware of the fact that I would be coming to Giri in two weeks' time—asked me to pick up medications from MGH for her mother. Arthur supplied me with the required medical prescription, which I was able to fill at the hospital's dispensary after I had made my payment at the cash counter. This way, it became unnecessary for Rita to come to Madang Town.

Aside from assisting outpatients, Arthur also helped his kin by accelerating the inpatient admission process to the hospital. His wife's younger sister's daughter, Anna, had been constantly sick since early childhood and was, at the age of nine, finally referred to MGH with suspected tuberculosis. Arthur and his wife accommodated Anna and her mother at their house, and Arthur helped them navigate Anna's ambulatory treatment and hospital admittance:

> When [Anna] and her mother came, they did not know how to move around, huh?! So, I brought them here and we went this way: We came to the TB clinic and then they took er... her sputum, [we received the] result, and then from there we went to... see doctor [doctor's surname deleted]. From there we went to the radiology, got an X-ray [image], and she admitted to ward four.

Aaron from Birap, a rural laboratory assistant and malaria micropist (employed by the Madang Provincial Health Office), helped Giri inpatients and outpatients, mostly from his village Birap, in the same manner:

> Sometimes... not sometimes, quite often people from the village, especially people from my community, they call[11] me when they come and say, "We will... come to see a doctor." Or, "The health worker at... Bunapas has seen us and sends us to go see a doctor." So, when they come here [i.e., to Madang Town], I wait for them at the outpatient [clinic] or I stay in my office and tell them thus, "Come straight to my office!" So, I help them go down to the outpatient [clinic], put them through to a medical specialist, or... bring them to the wards if they... stay at the outpatient [clinic] and spend the night at the outpatient [clinic], er... day clinic, so if they... are admitted to the ward, I use to bring them to the ward and admit them to the ward.

Arthur and his wife frequently accommodated patients who were unable to pay for inpatient treatment or who felt very uneasy about being admitted to the ward. A little more than a month before I interviewed Arthur, a middle-aged man from Giri 1 village who was suffering from peripheral edema had come to Arthur's house. Arthur brought him to MGH, where a doctor who was acquainted with Arthur examined him. The attending physician recommended that he be transferred to the general medical ward, but he expressed apprehension over the doctor's suggestion, whereupon Arthur cared for him at his own house:

I took him to see a doctor. Shortcut! We went to see a doctor at the outpatient [clinic] . . . They only treated him with medication . . . Thus, we took the medication to the house. He was supposed to sleep on the ward but the doctors know that if they hand out medication I will treat him at [my] house. Thus, we stayed at the house, he got the medications, [and] the swelling of his skin subsided.

Whether Giri hospital workers accommodate Giri patients depends much on their own housing situation. The proximity of Lisa's house (in the hospital compound) to the hospital buildings made the nursing officer's house an ideal place for Giri patients to stay. Giri patients also frequented Arthur and his family (living in the nearby Wagol Community Compound). But other hospital workers, like a Giri 1 nurse who worked for only a brief period at MGH's eye clinic (during which time she resided with other relatives) or Aaron (who lived on the outskirts of town), were less suitable hosts. Since Aaron took up work at the Provincial Health Office in 1999, he lived in various places in and near Madang. When I first met Aaron in 2006, he and a security guard were spending nights in the storage room of the Provincial Health Office. It is obvious that he could not take in any patients.

Patients who are accommodated by persons other than hospital workers still frequently approach the Giri employees of MGH for help mediating hospital services. Patients may not have seen their helpers for years or may be unable to identify their exact genealogical link with them, though they will have knowledge of a common ancestor in the more distant past. It also happens that Giri staff members support patients who they plainly know to be Giri. Often, they refer to these patients as wantok. Literally, wantok means "people of the same language group," but the concept is very flexible and, depending on the context, can be expanded to include people from a larger geographical area.

Even people who do not base their relationship on some notion of kinship or ethnic identity but on other forms of cooperation and trust may identify each other as wantok (Monsell-Davis 1993: 48–50). The people whom Giri health workers help include very distant relatives and people from neighboring, largely mutually intelligible, cultural-linguistic groups such as Mikarip, Seven, and Korak (see Repič 2011 on urban dwellers relying on their wantok for accommodation and, more generally, on the wantok system as a dynamic and urban system of social category).

The wantok system is a significant network on which Giri patients depend in order to access hospital services and receive care. Other scholars have mentioned the links between the wantok system and the Papua New Guinea health system. Street (2009) showed that MGH patients rely on their wantok for blood donations. Van Amstel and van der Geest (2004) discussed the role that medical reports issued by Mendi (Southern Highlands) hospital workers play in compensation claims of physical damage between wantok.

Obligations of "generalized reciprocity" (Sahlins 1972) characterize relationships between wantok: "long-term diffuse relationships, which imply mutual claims on each other's goods and services" (van Amstel & van der Geest 2004: 2090). When enquiring into Giri hospital workers' reasons for supporting people from the entire Giri area, responses echoed the notion of the wantok system. Aaron said:

> There is no real reason for this but, as I said before, we come from one area, huh?! From one area on the whole known as Giri . . . Therefore, I know that they are my wantok, huh?! If they come and need help . . . I just help and give whatever help they want . . .
>
> When . . . they come to ask me for my help, I know that . . . they acknowledge the kind of work I do. And they know that I am one man from their area who is here. Therefore, they directly come to me to ask for help. So, they genuinely need me to lead the way and tell whomever medical specialist . . . to give the right treatment to them. Therefore . . . I am very happy to help them when they approach me.

And Arthur explained:

> I must help them. I am not ill disposed or angry. I say, "Okay, you come to me, all right, I will help you, bring you to the hospital." I don't have an ulterior motive. Even if they stay at the hospital and die, I must also help to bring their body to the village, share this sorrow with [them] . . .
>
> The sick who come . . . who come to me . . . I am happy to put them up to take care of them [and] come with them to the hospital . . . They will look fit and go back again. I don't want them to come and then I say no to them and they go looking for . . . another poor place to sleep. I am [here]. So, they know that I am a Giri man who is here, huh?! So, when they come to me, I must accept them.

Both Aaron's and Arthur's statements reveal that helping wantok lends hospital workers prestige (see van Amstel & van der Geest 2004: 2090).

Hospital workers at MGH have elaborate social networks, which enable them to navigate patients to the most qualified doctors. Furthermore, hospital workers and their household members care for patients so that patients are visibly "fit" upon their return to the village. By doing this, hospital workers prove themselves to be highly sociable persons. As is true for the Lelet, a sociable Giri person embodies openness; she or he has "an 'open hand,' from which people receive things and from which 'many have eaten'" (Eves 1998: 269). The contributions that these hospital workers make to patients' convalescence through their aid and care should be reciprocated by Giri patients in the long run.

Furthermore, Monsell-Davis (1993: 54, 59) argued that the value of the wantok system in Papua New Guinea towns is charged with ambiguity. The wantok system provides a social safety net for urban dwellers, but it fails for other urban residents from households that are too poor to practice reciprocity and that then drop out of this rural-urban support system. Giri patients' continuous requests for assistance pose a significant economic burden on Giri MGH workers and their household members. Workers must constantly put up relatives at their homes, provide meals for them, and help them with money (e.g., for medical treatment, bus fare to get to the hospital and into town, or areca nuts and cigarettes). It was clear from conversations with Giri hospital workers that their fortnightly pay only rarely lasts for two weeks, and their households regularly confront serious food insecurity. However, hospital workers apparently possess intact social support networks, which they can draw on in times of trouble. Arthur stated:

> The money we earn is too little; it is not enough for two weeks, huh?! . . . We eat about twice a day. Sometimes we only eat once in the evening and we [go] sleep . . . [We] make breakfast for the children who go to school, huh?! We drink tea, they go to school, they come back in the afternoon . . . I have no idea how we survive, it is like a miracle! . . . Sometimes we do not have any food but somehow we will have . . . someone will provide us with some food or some money or . . . It is like this, huh?! . . . Often we are short of food.

Giri people think of Madang Town as a "place of hunger" (ples bilong hangre) and a "place of money" (ples bilong mani). Sometimes they (as do other town dwellers with salaries) feel battered by kin's "demands that they act relationally when they themselves want to act as individuals" (Wardlow 2006: 20). Yet, I did not hear Giri hosts complaining much about the pressure that their guests put on them, as Monsell-Davis (1993: 47) perpetually encountered. The Giri hospital workers acknowledged the difficulty of their economic situation in an urban place like Madang Town but portrayed Giri patients as understanding and considerate guests who brought food from the village and fended for themselves if the food situation was dire. As Arthur said, the struggle to survive in town was perceived as something mutually shared with one's guests:

> Sometimes we are short of food. So, we . . . struggle to find food to feed them, huh?! If we have some money when they return again [to the village] . . . we give [it] to them to pay the return PMV . . . Sometimes they bring food. We usually

share it with one another. Oh, life is . . . nowadays, this life is hard—very hard for us to survive in a place like this [i.e., an urban place]. Everything costs money, huh?! But . . . the villagers understand . . . how we live . . . Sometimes, they look after themselves for food and their bus fares to come [into town] and to return. But our house is always open to them. They can come sleep.

Giri hospital workers' support does not end with a patient's death. The Akan (Ghana) people regard the organization of the funeral as the most important aspect of caring for their elderly[12] (van der Geest 2002: 9). If they have become part of a patient's therapy managing group, Giri hospital staff members feel responsible for the patient until the patient returns to the village—be it dead or alive. Many times in the past, Arthur had arranged for deceased patients' corpses to be taken to the hospital morgue and shelved there until he could organize transportation to the village for burial (not an easy task, as the morgue is chronically overcrowded).

To summarize, reciprocity is a major factor in Giri caregiving relationships. It is important to note that caregiving (and also gift giving) does not require immediate return, but Giri people practice generalized reciprocity. For Giri people, relations are, in a way, always reciprocal, as reciprocity is the basis for enduring relationships. The principle of reciprocity applies to the relationship between the sufferer and all kinds of carers—be they professional carers or informal carers, such as close relatives, who cook meals.

I suggest that the reciprocal transactions that take place between Giri patients and professional carers at BHC and MGH are deeply rooted in Giri culture and have been transferred to these biomedical institutions by Giri[13] actors: patients, accompanying carers (wasman), and medical and paramedical staff. Giving and reciprocating is important for all sides, in order to pursue local ways of sociality. The importance of reciprocity in care relationships has also been highlighted by anthropologists studying care beyond Melanesia (e.g., Mageo 2001: 191, 195; van der Geest 2002), and we even find striking instances of the relevance of the return gift in Western biomedical environments.

M. Strathern (2012: 398, 401) wrote, in her topical article on organ and tissue donation, about the emotional upset that receptors of body parts experience if they are disabled from reciprocating the received organ gift and about the importance for receptors to create a relationship with the donor (400). M. Strathern's argument reminds us that reciprocity must not be seen in negative terms. For Giri, as I have argued above, it socially empowers both those who give and those who receive. Another example comes from Konrad, who argued that British ova donors are often very keen to know whether children have been born through their eggs. This knowledge takes, for the donors, the form of the return gift (2005: 95).

Synopsis

Using Janzen's (1978, 1987) concept of the therapy managing group, I have explored the importance of social support networks for Giri people accessing health services at BHC and MGH. Patients were shown to depend on a broad fabric of relations that is woven from relatives who are related to the patient in numerous ways, ranging from first-degree relatives to very distant kin and wantok connections. I argued that BHC and MGH are settings where sociality manifests in interactions between givers and recipients of care and among the various groups of carers. Acts of food giving are of pivotal significance here, as, for Giri, food is an inherently social substance, capable of producing and reproducing both the individual and the social body. For the Giri, what von Poser said for the Bosmun applies: "Foodways define . . . interpersonal sociality so notably" (2013: 30). Another significant finding to emerge from the chapter is that Giri people see care as something that should be reciprocated.

On a more general level, one can argue, "The obvious presence of relatives in the ward has both structural and cultural dimensions" (Zaman 2005: 120). Patients' social relations significantly shape the workings of these two biomedical institutions. Kin are indispensable actors in patients' care networks, responsible for meeting the bulk of care needs. With Papua New Guinea medical institutions suffering severe shortage in funds and workforce, hospital staff is able to run the medical side of BHC, but little else. From a cultural perspective, we know that the Giri person is largely constituted through social relationships. As theorized by M. Strathern (1988) and Wagner (1991), the Melanesian person is fundamentally (though not exclusively[14]) dividual/fractal. In the case of illness there is always family involvement, which is a vital aspect of the recovery process. Kin prove their good intentions by bestowing gifts of food upon patients and lending them social support, thus contributing to patients' bodily well-being and their reproduction as social persons.

In the next chapter, I resume the discussion of personhood with a special focus on the unborn and newborn. The present and following chapter connect in the sense that the well-becoming of the patient, as well as the becoming of the unborn and newborn, depend much on the contributions of others. "People are the products of the nurturing and feeding relationships of others. The person is seen in composite terms as the sum total of the contributions of those others who have provided things such as food, labour or knowledge to his or her upbringing" (Eves 1998: 37). This applies to every Giri person, but people in sickness, whose personhood is compromised, and the unborn and newborn, who have not yet attained full personhood, appear particularly dependent on the beneficial actions of others.

Notes

1. Men rarely cook; sometimes, they roast a yam or fish in the fire for themselves, but they do not cook meals that are exchanged in food-shifting routines.
2. The usage of food to construct and reaffirm relationships between people is not unique to Giri but is commonly found across Melanesia (e.g., see Anderson 2011: 47; Eves 1995: 213–14, 1998: 38; Fajans 1985: 372–73, 379–82, 1997: 22, 27, 70, 75, 78–79, 285; Hess 2009: 75–77; Kahn 1986: 151; Knauft 1989: 223; Munn 1986: chap. 3; Schieffelin 1976: 46–48, 50–52, 56, 63–64, 71–72; L. Stewart 1989: 113, 117–19, 124–29; A. Strathern & P. Stewart 2000: 25–26; Trompf 1994: 114; von Poser 2013; Whitehead 2000: 49–50).
3. Likewise, it was argued for other New Guinea societies that one must not eat the pigs that one has raised or hunted (e.g., Anderson 2011: 98; Goodale 1995: 85; Mead [1935] 2001: 78; Meigs 1997: 98; Rubel & Rosman 1978; Telban 1998: 60). Not uncommonly, domesticated pigs are considered family members (Rappaport 1968: 59). Meigs (1997: 98–99) argued that the pigs a person has raised or shot contain the person's vital essence ("nu"). Eating these pigs means reintroducing one's own "nu" into one's own body, which weakens and sickens the body. Similarly, Telban (1998: 60) explicated for the Ambonwari that, in hunting with a spear, pig and hunter come close together; the hunter, then, passes his strength to the pig. If the hunter consumes the meat of such a pig, he eats his own strength (i.e., himself). Compare Giri taboos on consumption of one's grandchildren's leftovers (see chap. 5). Interestingly, Anderson (2011: 99) suggested, drawing on M. Strathern's (1988) idea of food as a mediator for relations, that these food taboos (or, to be more specific, the conjoined prescription to give away certain food) enable relational flows.
4. Hard and dry, often chicken or beef flavored biscuits.
5. The same term is used for "contraception" (see chap. 5).
6. I understand friendship not in opposition to kinship but in terms of Strathern and Stewart's definition of friendship as "a state of mutual sociality predicated on goodwill and support that can exist either within or outside of the ambit of kinship and affinity" (2000: 22–23).
7. Typically, in cases of serious illness and death, men's and women's spaces are separate. Female relatives sit beside the sufferer, stroking them, caring for them, and keeping them company. In the case of death, the women gather around the corpse, holding it in turn and lamenting. The men come together on the clan platform or, if none is close by, on another nearby platform, veranda, or other shaded area, where they discuss the incident and further action. At Emma's house, the two outdoor kitchens served as separate women's and men's spaces.
8. This phenomenon has been described for other Papua New Guinea societies (see, e.g., Eves 1998: 39; Feld 1990: 27–28; Meigs 1997: 104; Schieffelin 1976: 50; Stewart 1989: 126; von Poser 2013: 115). Anthropologists have also provided us with accordant examples from other Oceanic cultures (e.g., see Lahn 2006: 305 for Warraber Island [Torres Strait]; Toren 2009: 134 for the Sawaieke of Fiji).
9. Out of the forty-one Regene men and women I interviewed, fifteen had never been to MGH.

10. Most Giri people dislike canned tuna and regard its consumption as a cause of boils and other ailments. Canned mackerel is not said to have any similarly detrimental effects on the body.
11. At the time of the interview in 2011, none of the Giri hospital workers had landlines, but all of them had mobile phones. The mobile network operator Digicel Papua New Guinea began to operate in rural areas of Papua New Guinea in July 2007 (Telban & Vávrová 2014: 225), and most Giri villagers had access to mobile phones in the village (although mobile phone network coverage was not complete) and when they stayed in Madang Town.
12. Van der Geest defines care as "doing things for people which they can no longer do for themselves" (2002: 17).
13. Similar reciprocity relationships seem to exist between MGH patients and carers of other cultural groups. However, at MGH, I limited my research to interactions between Giri patients and Giri personnel. As for BHC, I also briefly considered other Lower Ramu patients.
14. See LiPuma (1998), Strathern and Stewart (2000: chap. 4).

Chapter Five
Ingenious Women
Making Biomedical Reproductive Health Care Meaningful

Various authors have shown, through exploration of different aspects of Western reproductive health care, that the introduction of such reproductive services to Oceania has had both empowering and disempowering effects on women's lives. Their writings demonstrate that the particular outcome for women—whether advantageous or disadvantageous—has been heavily influenced by the specific processes that have been advanced by the medicalization of human procreation in the different cultures.

The concept of "medicalization" was introduced by the American sociologist Irving Zola, who argued that biomedicine has become an institution of social control, replacing "the more traditional institutions of religion and law" (1972: 487). Zola defined medicalization as "making medicine and the labels 'healthy' and 'ill' *relevant* to an ever increasing part of human existence" (ibid.). Medicalization is "the process of making something 'medical.' In other words, the extension of biomedicine into non-biomedical realms" (Ember & Ember 2004a: xxxv). Early feminist anthropologists deplored the medicalization of some aspects of women's normal life.

In their works, the disempowering effects of the medicalization of pregnancy and childbirth were emphasized, and women were portrayed as victims, deprived of the agency they were said to have in traditional childbirth. Proponents of this position argued that women had been stripped of the control over their bodies. Biomedical practices (in male-dominated technologized settings) were envisaged to have contributed to women's subordination, whereas indigenous birthing practices were extolled as having been empowering to women (see, for discussion, Ginsburg & Rapp 1991; Jolly 2002; Morton 2002).

These earlier theoretical constructs of feminist anthropology were not very helpful in explaining the particularities of situations in which Western biomedical knowledge and practice met Oceanic cultures. Today, the perspective that indigenous procreative knowledges and practices have undergone change, and that their contemporary forms were produced in interaction with introduced practices, is well established in Oceanic anthropology (Fiti-Sinclair

2002; Jolly 2002; Lukere 2002: 200; Salomon 2002). K. Sykes (2007) showed that, for the Lelet, as a consequence of the introduction of Western contraceptives, women have gradually lost their power to decide which social relations to keep or not to keep. This is a theme of extreme importance to Simbo (Western Solomon Islands) women, who explicitly deplore their loss of autonomic control over their fertility (Dureau 1998).

Similarly, Obrist van Eeuwijk (1998) argued that Kwanga (East Sepik Province) women's new understandings of menarche, menstruation, and childbirth—as altered by Christian creation theory and biomedical notions—have evoked the progressive abolition of female initiation rites since the 1980s. In this process, Kwanga women have "lost their control over their body and its reproductive capacity" (267). But other writers, such as Morton (2002), have claimed that, despite the flaws in the biomedical model of procreation, biomedically based educational programs on sexuality and reproduction are potentially empowering to Tongan women, as they may enable them to become more confident in their bodies. Tongan women pragmatically acknowledge the drop in maternal mortality rate and see biomedical care as expanding their range of options (51–52).

In this chapter, I contribute to the detailed analysis of outcomes that arise when biomedical reproductive health services meet Papua New Guinea people. As outlined above, reproductive health services form a large part of the biomedical services provided to the Giri. The Churches of Christ mission made maternal and infant health and family planning priority issues in the late 1950s and 1960s, and today these topics are given special emphasis at BHC and in Papua New Guinea more generally. At the local health center, provincial hospital, and other biomedical facilities from which Giri women seek health care, women are faced with new ways of dealing with procreation.

Yet Giri women are anything but passive recipients of these biomedical technologies and services. They make conscious decisions to draw on or dismiss biomedical care, informed by local notions of person and body and a conceptual model of birth that is rooted in Giri culture as well as pragmatism in each particular situation. Moreover, Giri women reinterpret the reproductive health care that they access during pregnancy, birthing, and the postpartum period in highly creative ways, making it suitable for their own culture. They interweave their local knowledge with novel ideas culled from an obstetric model of birthing.

With their clever strategies of negotiation and adaptation, Giri women become important actors in a process of cultural transformation. For instance, they acknowledge postnatal hospital stays and medical treatments as legitimate strategies for aiding the expulsion of *seva* (i.e., blood of parturition and postpartum discharge in this context). This enables women under adverse circumstances—such as in Madang Town, where they might not proceed into the customary month-long postpartum seclusion—to spend the postpartum phase in a culturally appropriate manner. By making biomedical options local to themselves, women expand their room for maneuvering.

To argue that the introduction of biomedical maternal health care services has only empowered Giri women would be naïve. In contrast, the medicalization and hospitalization of childbirth has fostered a focus on the dangerous aspects of *seva*—a substance that is traditionally believed to have both harmful and ritually beneficial properties. In compliance with the biomedical model, health workers generally view blood of parturition and postpartum discharge as waste fluids that must be discarded for hygienic reasons. Similarly, the afterbirth is defined as human waste matter and thrown away. Conversely, in indigenous terms, the placenta carries a dual quality: it is harmful *seva* but also part of the newborn and, as such, is viewed as a person. In Giri culture, women play a key role in children's identity formation by planting the afterbirth. With placentas increasingly handled by health workers, women are losing their central place in this sphere of the child's identity construction.

Considerations of Blood and Skin

As I demonstrated in previous chapters, the exploration of local thoughts about the body is requisite for the central objective of this book—to gain a deeper understanding of the ways in which Giri construct biomedicine. The individual body is a canvas upon which nature, society, and culture are displayed (MacQueen 2002: 62). Scheper-Hughes and Lock (1987: 7) argued that the human body is used to communicate social phenomena; it provides the imagery for the social world (Hsu 2003: 179).

Thus far, I have touched on various aspects of the human body, its parts, and its products. For example, in chapter 3, I focused on bodily substance (*fava ŋan*) and on the skin and its significance as body boundary. I first became aware of the concept of *fava ŋan* and its potential harmful effects through an encounter with Rita. Early in my fieldwork, I came up with the idea of hanging bananas and edible cane grass (*Saccharum edule*) inflorescences on my clothesline to protect them from being eaten by rats. I was rather pleased with my construction, which proved to be somewhat effective. One evening, making her way back from the garden, Rita took note of the comestibles dangling from my clothesline.

She hurried to my veranda and took me aside, explaining to me that I must not hang any foods on my clothesline if I wanted men and children to be able to safely consume the meals that I prepared. The *fava ŋan* from my underwear (which I dried, at other times, on the same clothesline) would spoil the comestibles. Rita further explained that food—cooked or uncooked—must not be carried underneath a clothesline. Also, men and children must not pass underneath a clothesline. Otherwise, children's growth could be impaired and men could develop respiratory troubles and dull skin. There is no reason other women should avoid passing underneath a clothesline, as their body eventually rids itself of *fava ŋan* by means of menstruation. Yet men struggle to rid themselves of *fava ŋan* and must do so by way of ritual cleansing. As Giri people say, "Men have to exert themselves for getting rid of the *fava ŋan*."

Blood and skin (as well as other bodily fluids and tissues) are key matters in Giri arguments about social relations (cf. Carsten 2011; P. Stewart & A. Strathern 2001a: 2). The Giri believe what P. Stewart and A. Strathern formulated for New Guinea in general: "The substances of human bodies define and delineate social relations, and are in turn given worth and significance through those relationships" (P. Stewart & A. Strathern 2001a: 1). From the foregoing, it is evident that we get closest to the Giri body by grasping it as the Giri people perceive and experience it.

In the present chapter, I shed light upon bodily substances, such as breast milk, semen, and menstrual and parturitional blood (which is different from the blood that runs in one's veins and arteries). For example, I show how the transfer of maternal substance enables relations (cf. Carsten 2011: 29) and then discuss the role of the afterbirth, which is seen as an extension of persons as relational entities (cf. P. Stewart & A. Strathern 2001a: 2), connecting the newborn with maternal and paternal kin. As a prelude to the chapter proper, I shall explore general Giri meanings of blood and skin more thoroughly.

In Giri, skin reflects a person's health. Skin that is shiny, smooth, and light in complexion, demonstrates health,[1] whereas Giri figuratively speak of papaya or banana peel—skin that is yellowish in color—when referring to the appearance of a sick person's skin. For the Giri, a person's strength is displayed on his or her skin. A popular Giri myth portrays Ngizuŋguma, a man who, when in his wives' company, would wear a second skin, which made him look old. Ngizuŋguma's second, old, dusty, fungal skin prompts associations with ill health and weakness. His two wives pitied him, and thereby Ngizuŋguma managed to escape from his daily duties. Ngizuŋguma's wives took over the heavy physical male tasks such as tree felling and fence building, while Ngizuŋguma comfortably rested near the hearth. Here, the German idiom "auf der faulen Haut liegen" (to laze around; literally: "to lie on the lazy skin") fits quite well.

The image of a second skin also appears in the myths, legends, and folktales of other Melanesian peoples (see A. Strathern 1996: 91–96 for an analysis of the theme of skin changing in various publications; see Hess 2009: 160–61 for Vanua Lava). In a Kwoma (Sepik) myth, the mythical figure Yondjesu has a dual skin very similar to Ngizuŋguma's. Yondjesu wears his second, rubbish skin like clothing and thus tricks his two wives (Holmes Williamson 2007: 202–4). Holmes Williamson (203) drew an association between

Yondjesu's blemished skin and his moral paucity (see O'Hanlon 1989: chap. 7; A. Strathern 1996: 89; M. Strathern 1979: 254 on the parallel between physical appearance and moral worth). We may apprehend Ngizuŋguma's physical appearance along the same lines: he not only is physically repulsive but stands out by his laziness and furtiveness.

The Kire language yields two terms for skin—*nder* and *fav* (also *fap*). *Nder* is a generic term that denotes not only human skin but also animal skin, tree bark, and vegetable and fruit peel. The Giri always employ the term *nder*, and never the term *fav*, if the skin of a distinctive body part is addressed; examples are *rima nder* (eyelid; literally: "skin of the eye") and *si nder* (foreskin; literally: "skin of the penis"). The word *fav* is utilized exclusively for human skin; it designates a person's bodily skin as a whole. The sole specific Kire term for the body is *karik*, which stands for trunk (namel nating). Apart from this, the Giri have no distinct term for the body as such (cf. Telban 1998: 62) and refer to it as *fav*; employing M. Strathern's words, "The term for 'skin' encompasses both epidermis and flesh, the body as well as its surface" (1979: 249).

What M. Strathern noted for Hageners applies equally well to certain other Melanesian peoples (cf. Read 1954/55: 266). Eves, who worked among the Lelet of New Ireland, similarly described the comprehensive nature of "skin," emphasizing that, although the Lelet speak of "skin" (and not "body"), this does not mean that the Lelet lack notions of body: "This is not to say that there is no conceptualisation of the body but merely that the skin comes to stand for the body as a whole" (1998: 26). If we focus on the utilization of the term *fav* in the Kire language, it appears that Eves's characterization also pertains to Giri notions of corporeality. For instance, when Giri speak of *fava kavgi*, they say "excite" or "arouse the skin" (i.e., sexually).[2]

"Skin" stands for the membrane between the outside world and the body as well as for the body, itself (Eves 1998: 28). A. Strathern (1975: 351–53) and O'Hanlon (1989: 66–67) have shown that enclosed inner emotional states, such as anger, may become exposed on the skin and become visible, for instance as sickness. A. Strathern (1975: 351) argued that Hageners feel "popokl" (anger) inside, and O'Hanlon stated likewise that for the Wahgi (Western Highlands Province), "popol" (anger) is "centered in the internal organs" (1989: 66). A. Strathern contrasted "popokl" with "pilpil" (shame). The latter does not come from the inside but is sparked by being seen or found out by others and hence solely "on the skin" (A. Strathern 1975: 348).

Shame lies on the skin as an embodiment of socially inept behavior, as Eves (1998: 28) explained for the Lelet. Giri share this thought as well as the Lelet view of a skin hevi (*fav simgi*) feeling when "weighed down by worries" (ibid.). Moreover, when Giri talk of slander—that is, of shame put wrongfully on the skin of someone else—they speak of *fava sigsigi* (literally: "deceive the skin"). Although the shame is put on the skin, it may become internalized and cause anger in the defamed person. This example clearly shows that skin is not merely an "inscribed canvas" (17) but, for Giri, a component of the body that experiences the world.

For Giri, dull, dry, dark skin (*fav singi*) displays failure to comply with moral obligations (cf. Bamford 2007b: 177; Eves 1998: 29; Jacka 2007: 49). Hence, beautiful shiny skin is an extremely desirable quality, as it shows not only physical health but also morality. As Eves reminds us: "Moral status is an embodied condition which is exhibited on the skin" (1998: 29). The Giri identify sorcerers, who are the epitome of evil and immorality (cf. Barker 1990: 147; Burridge 1960: 59–71), by their ashen, lackluster skin, snarled hair, and long, unkempt beards. The sorcerer's immorality is visible not only on his own body but also on his wife's and children's bodies. His wife is wasted and her skin dry, with sweat never glinting, and she looks like an old woman. His children show signs of malnourishment—swollen abdomens and bony bottoms.

For Giri men and women, as for many Melanesian cultures, it is of the utmost importance to observe taboos surrounding sexual behavior, menstruation, and parturition in order to maintain glowing, supple, and healthy skin (see, e.g., Biersack 1987; Jacka 2007: 49; O'Hanlon 1989: 41–42). These taboos, and their relevance in contemporary Giri society, are briefly touched upon below and find particular illumination later in this chapter. Another point worth mentioning is that the readability of the skin has been impaired in modern times. Formerly, it was almost certain that if a Giri man had dull skin, he must have had tabooed contact with a woman.

In a dialogue, a middle-aged Giri woman explained that the situation is now more complicated, and she specified four reasons for lackluster skin (often associated with weight loss) in men: (1) spatial proximity to a menstruating woman, (2) frequent sexual intercourse, (3) sexual intercourse with a new mother, and (4) marijuana smoking. She explained that, in former times, when a man had violated a taboo, the elders would instruct him on how to restore his skin. Nowadays, with marijuana consumption adding to the other three causes, it is much trickier for elders to tell why a man has dull skin (or is wasted) and hence to advise him on how to proceed. Traditional purification practices of penile incision and tongue brushing with thorny leaves (discussed further below) are not effective if the condition resulted from smoking marijuana.

Pregnancy is also written on the skin (I employ the term "skin" here to refer to both meanings of *fav:* the membrane between the body and the world and the body itself) and, hence, is another excellent example of how skin, and more generally the body, depicts social relations. Pregnancy is displayed on the woman's nipples, and their color changes from brown to black. The woman's neck becomes visibly elongated and her collarbones protrude. The biological father-to-be also shows the latter two signs, and paternity is often determined via his bodily changes, if otherwise uncertain. Further, if a pregnant woman has swollen legs and the biological father of the unborn child loses weight throughout the woman's pregnancy, this indicates to Giri people that the woman will give birth to a girl. The father is thought to give his weight away to his daughter in anticipation of the hard work that she will perform for him in the years to come (gardening, cooking, and so forth). If a woman is going to have a son, her body will feel light, and it will be easy for her to move her body.

A lightweight, agile, and virile body (*fav bigbigi*) is a male quality that is much aspired to. We find a similar conception among the Lelet. Allow me to use a quote from Fajans, as she appositely summarized the gendered division of lightness and heaviness in a review of Eves's *The Magical Body* (1998): "On the one hand, lightness, speed, and movement are highly desired and masculine qualities . . . On the other hand, heaviness and rootedness are important metaphors of social stability and fecundity. These qualities and their gendered opposition are widespread in Melanesia" (2000: 538; cf. Eves 1998: 45–47).[3]

Giri foods can be categorized according to those that are heavy on the skin (*fav simgi mbah*) and those that are light on the skin (*fav bigbigi mbah*). "Skin" stands here, again, as a metonym for the body. All kinds of *fav simgi mbah* make the body heavy, whereas *fav bigbigi mbah* leave the body lightweight and agile. Hence, strict food taboos need to be observed in order to achieve the desired lightweightness. A young woman from Giri 2 explained that it would be hard for a dancer who had consumed tabooed meat before a performance to move his legs fast and kneel down as the dance requires. However, if he observes the taboos, he will perform well. The consumption of tabooed meat may lead to illness in other contexts, as well; for example, a woman secluded after birth may feel stomachaches if she eats tabooed meat.

Food taboos always accompany phases of seclusion. Brian had to remove himself from society following his wife's death. In December 2006, his wife had passed away in childbirth with her fourth child on the way to BHC. During this phase of ritual seclusion, he had to observe dietary regulations directed at producing an ideal body. He spent three months in seclusion.

In seclusion, Brian was carefully supervised by two knowledgeable clan elders who put a taboo on certain heavy foods. The two men were in charge of preventing the widower from becoming too fat and heavy. Tabooed foods (*riru mbah*) are heavy foods such as pumpkin, the lesser yam (*Dioscorea esculenta*), and certain banana species. Brian was forbidden to eat the *phonu* banana. *Phonu* translates as "cassowary" and stands for a banana species that bears especially long and fleshy fruits. This banana is said to be "not right for the body," as it troubles the stomach and is hard to digest. But Brian was also given certain foods to give strength to his body. The most well-known of these are the young leaf buds of the wild fig (*Ficus* sp.), with which Brian's sago dishes were supplemented.

Brian's strength and bodily appearance depended not only on which foods he was given but also on who prepared the meals. A sexually active woman in her reproductive years would wreck Brian's body. Instead, a postmenopausal woman was appointed to be his cook. Given that she would only serve meals without coconut cream to Brian, as he was not allowed to consume greasy foods, I consider it a noteworthy coincidence that the woman's nickname was Drai Kaikai (which, in Tok Pisin, means "dry food," i.e., food without soup). Illustration 5.1 shows Drai Kaikai ascending the ladder to Brian's house. (He was secluded in the back of his own house.)

Illustration 5.1. Drai Kaikai serves *fav bigbigi mbah* to Brian (2007). Drai Kaikai is balancing Brian's dish of sago pudding, bamboo shoots, and a very few wild fig leaf buds on her head.

Brian, in his forties, was still a man in his prime, as the two elders who watched over him told me. They thought it likely that Brian would remarry, and, hence, it was crucial that he regain his strength, lightweightness, and virility. A pivotal purpose of the widower's spatial seclusion is his isolation from women, in order to restore these qualities. Throughout his wife's lifetime, the widower would have lost his bodily strength (*ngapngaŋ*) to her and their joint offspring. This parallels with the Yupno idea that adults lose energy (which they gain through knowledge, life experience, and social interaction) to their children (Keck & Wassmann 2010: 193).

Aging, as Meigs (1997: 99) argued for the Hua people of the Eastern Highlands, is not internal to the person but occurs because parents give their vital essence ("nu") to their children. Giri men, similarly, pass their *ngapngaŋ* to women during sexual intercourse (whether with their wife or another woman). If the woman conceives, the loss of *ngapngaŋ* is more significant, because the conceived child deprives his or her biological father of this essential strength. This is why the skin of a man who has frequent sexual intercourse (and many children) looks dull and "is loose," as the Giri would say.

The Giri use the term "loose skin" in reference to what we might call a haggard person. There is a strong taboo against Giri men eating their grandchildren's leftovers, as the strength that the grandfather has passed via his children to his grandchildren is said to return to him and destroy his eyesight, because the strength of it is "too much." Let me remark that, although Giri children take away their parents' strength, they themselves are not inherently strong. As I outline further below, relatives employ practices to amplify children's strength from early childhood onward. Later, adolescent men gain strength in the process of initiation.

That men feel lightweight, are able to move speedily, and appear in all their splendor is absolutely essential if they participate in dancing performances and fights. One Giri man formulated it as yu mas pilim yu man, yu lait, which translates as, "you have to feel that you are a man, that you are light." Lightness and speediness are not virtues only of Giri dancers. Munn (1986: 75) and Eves (1998: 50–51) also reported the significance of these qualities among Gawans (Massim) and Lelet.

Munn wrote about these valued properties: "Whereas slowness or heaviness is an undesirable spatiotemporal state of a person's bodily engagement with the external world, speedy activity . . . and buoyant lightness . . . are the opposed qualities conveying in different contexts the body's health, or youthfulness, and the feelings of joy . . . or well-being that go with these states" (1986: 76). Observation of the abovementioned taboos surrounding food and its preparation are not the only means to reach this state. Ritual bleeding of the tongue and penis is considered an even more effective strategy. Old, dark, and thick blood is thus removed and replaced with clean, light, and thin blood.

Adolescent Giri men are introduced to the practice of bloodletting during male initiation (*monigafoi*).

After the initiate's glans is incised with two cuts by his *kamavurfek* (ego's mother's brother, who is the fifth or sixth cousin of ego's mother[4]), a period of schooling follows, during which the young man also learns to purify his body of old blood (see Höltker 1962: 84–90; Panti 1991: 5 on incision during initiation). The proper method is carried out by the insertion of a thorny vine into the urethra. The vine is twirled between the hands, and the thorns gash the urethra. This procedure is extremely painful and feared by many men, who choose instead to cut around the urinary meatus with a razor blade or piece of broken glass.

Bloodletting is practiced in various ways among cultural groups throughout New Guinea.[5] Munn (1986: 191) mentioned the scratching of drum dance performers in order to let blood. Dancers are scratched at the opening of the performance to induce bodily lightness. In writing about medical practices of the Nekematigi, a Benabena-speaking people in the Eastern Highlands District, Johannes described that bleeding has a "therapeutic potential for men because of its association with male purificatory ritual which requires bleeding and is believed to result in improved strength and virility" (1980: 56).

Hogbin (1996) titled his ethnography about the people of Wogeo Island (part of the Schouten Island group), first published in 1970, *The Island of Menstruating Men*. Hogbin referred to male bloodletting practices as "artificial menstruation" (114), because it leads to the replacement of old blood equal to that of menstruating women. My two Lower Ramu colleagues, A. von Poser (2013: 146) and AT von Poser (2014: 134), reported the prevalence of strategies of penis cutting in Bosmun and Kayan. Höltker (1964: 50–51) wrote about Nubia and Awar bloodletting routines that resemble those of the Giri: sliding a vine into the urethra and rapidly pulling it out induces blood flow.

However, the brushing of the tongue with thorny leaves, which most Giri men practice with higher frequency (usually at least once a week) than bloodletting via the penis, is apparently not practiced in the Bosmun, Kayan, Nubia, and Awar villages. Moreover, Giri appears to stand out from these Lower Ramu cultural groups in that even women brush their tongue as a supplement to menstruation to make their skin especially shiny. Let me emphasize that, in the cultural logic of the Giri, the state of one's blood determines the visual appearance of one's skin: clean, light, and thin blood makes the skin appear lustrous and taut.

Hogbin ([1970] 1996: 114) surmised that the tongue is selected for bleeding because the absorption of dangerous substance has been—at least for adolescent men up to initiation—primarily oral, through breast milk. The belief that the mother's breast milk is not necessarily a mere nourishing substance but also threatening to the infant is deeply rooted in Giri society. If a woman does not abstain from sexual intercourse throughout the many months of breastfeeding, it is believed that the baby will ingest damaging substances (*seva*) through the milk (see below for more detailed information). Moreover, women must not conceive before weaning their previous child, lest the latter absorb the unborn's egesta, which would lead to illness.

In male initiation, the several months of social seclusion and tuition of the initiates end with a staggering dancing performance. This is the time when the bodies of the young men appear for the first time in all their virility. They are lightweight and move virtuously. As one man depicted, taim bilong singsing man bai speed i go (at the time of the dancing performance the man will hurtle). The Giri employ the phrase *vemkura hi* (to dance speedily) in reference to agile dancers.

Illustration 5.2. Virtuous Giri dancers (2007). The dancers' skin gleams in the sun. Their movements are fast and weightless.

With the male purificational ritual of bloodletting, I have touched on one theme pertaining to blood. I return to the topic of blood below, as there is much more about blood in Giri society to be examined. I then discuss its role in procreation and the ambiguous nature of menstrual blood and the blood of parturition. I hope to show that, for Giri, skin and blood are not purely physical components without any relation to other aspects of the person. I shall close this section by giving another example: as a potent form of love magic, Giri men and women mix their pubic or axillary hair and sweat in food that they serve the desired other, thus "binding the mind/inclinations" (P. Stewart & A. Strathern 2001a: 16; see for a similar example from Pangia in the Southern Highlands). Although this activity does not deal with blood or skin, but with sweat and hair, it is a good example of "embodied ideas of ... relationship" (9).

Seva—an Ambiguous Substance

In this section, I delve into the meanings of *seva* and sketch the traditional ways of managing the substance. *Seva* appears to be contextually marked; its careful handling is essential for receiving its benefits but, likewise, for avoiding its health-threatening effects. A detailed analysis of *seva* serves as preparation for a discussion of new ways of dealing with the substance in the context of biomedicine. As P. Stewart and A. Strathern wrote, "A better understanding of how people think about their bodies and the substances that constitute them should facilitate the conceptualization of developing arenas in which substances are transferred and transformed in new and unfamiliar ways" (2001a: 1). By drawing heavily on case studies and minimizing abstraction, I am less likely to commit what Akin criticized as "ahistorical symbolic or structural analyses of abstracted and otherwise simplified taboo systems" (2003: 382).

In his article on Kwaio (Malaita Island, Solomon Islands) menstrual taboos, Akin followed the example of Clark (1993), P. Stewart and A. Strathern (2002), and a few others by drawing attention to the ways in which menstrual taboos play out in practice. Akin (2003: 382) called for a case material-based approach that is centered upon the multifaceted change of ideas and practices surrounding menstrual taboos—an approach that extends far beyond marginal statements about a simple persistence, decline, or disappearance of taboos. In this chapter, I respond to Akin's challenge, albeit with a slightly different focus on parturitional blood and lochia.

Seva is blood, but it is not the blood that flows in one's veins (which, in contrast, is termed *vizin*[6]); it is the hot uterine blood of parturition and menstruation. *Seva* is a powerful substance and plays a vital role in magic. I first read about its powers in an article titled "The Women Have Power over Men"

(1991), authored by Vincent Rendap from Kɨmnɨng village. I learned that a man who seeks the magic for beating the slit-drum relies on the benevolence of a menstruating woman to provide him with her precious substance. The woman's menarche is essential, because her *seva* is most potent when she has just reached her reproductive age (cf. Anderson 2011: 81 on the difference between menstrual blood in general and menarcheal blood).

A woman in menarche who has agreed to help a man gain the magic for beating the slit-drum goes into the bush, where she scrapes the bark of a tree called *sankuargi*. When she climbs naked up the tree and slides down again, her menstrual blood clings to the roughened patch of bark. She collects bits of the bloody bark, covers them in a wild taro leaf, and walks to a prearranged spot at a stream. She undresses again and stands in the water with her legs apart. She then holds the leaf with the scrapings in her hands and blends the strands with water from the river. The man swims on his back through her legs (from behind) and the woman pours the fluid from the leaf into his mouth when his head appears in front of her.[7] The man swallows the mixture (Rendap 1991: 9). Rendap concluded, "She helps the young man with the gift of *tor*—beating the garamut [slit-drum]" (ibid.). In a later discussion, Vincent Rendap and other cultural experts from Kɨmnɨng emphasized that the man gains strength through the *seva,* a symbol of fecundity, the woman shares with him.

Menstrual blood of menarcheal women is used in slit-drum magic in a beneficial way, but *seva* is also potentially dangerous and may become health and even life threatening to those exposed to it if taboos are violated. As early as their ritual seclusion at menarche (*mon mbik*), Giri women learn to handle the substance carefully. However, the purpose of menarcheal seclusion is primarily to ensure the bodily flourishing of the young woman; a comprehensive set of regulations is directed at preserving her strength and good health through her reproductive years and up to an advanced age.

For instance, she must use bamboo sticks or a spoon for eating, to omit premature breaking or loosening of her teeth. Moreover, she must not immerse herself in a body of water but instead wash herself with wild cordyline (*piŋ*) leaves. She must keep the leaves until they are dry and then toss them into a stream. The purpose of this is to prevent a sorcerer from stealing her *fava ŋan* (egested body substance adhering to one's skin). In contemporary Giri society, however, menarcheal seclusion has become a rarity, due to its incompatibility with attending school.

Whereas most women of my mother Thiap's generation were secluded, I became aware of only one *mon mbik* (menarcheal woman) throughout my time in Giri—a young Tung woman who resided with her mother and paternal kin in a bush hamlet that her father's father had established. She was forced to leave the school in Giri 1 because of her father's involvement in a fight over customary land. I spent a weekend with her in April 2007, cooking for her. It is important that many female kin come and cook meals for the *mon mbik*, because the main purpose of this phase of seclusion (after the second menstruation) is to gain weight. Food during this seclusion phase should be plentiful and rich in protein.

This second phase is preceded by a time of extensive food taboos, which last from menarche to second menstruation, during which the young women typically lose weight. Visitors are also responsible for entertaining the *mon mbik*, because menarcheal seclusion should be a phase of joy. Other girls frequently keep her company, and her boyfriends may sneak up to her room. A dancing feast marks the end of seclusion. Beautifully decorated, the *mon mbik* is celebrated as she emerges from her enclosure and takes a slow walk through the village, admired by the community.

Illustration 5.3. Menarcheal woman washing her body with wild cordyline leaves (2007).

Note that menarcheal women typically have their hair dyed with red paint (*hip*) and wear old torn netbags or hand-fishing nets over their heads or shoulders for protection against illness. The menarcheal woman's flourishing is dependent on her body being sheltered by the netted material. Perhaps the broken netbag symbolizes the woman's detachment from her mother's womb (see below for the equation of netbag and womb). The red paint was possibly traditionally applied to indicate that the *mon mbik* was already promised to a man to be married (see Höltker 1962: 94) in exchange for a kinswoman of his own who had married a kinsman of the *mon mbik*. Nowadays, the red paint has become a general symbol of the *mon mbik*.

Anthropologists writing on Papua New Guinea Highlands societies have extensively discussed the powers of menstrual blood and other humors. Early anthropologists, such as Lewis Langness (1974) and Mervyn Meggitt (1964), pictured female substances as solely dangerous and polluting to men, whereas others (e.g., Meigs 1976, 1984; A. Strathern 1996: 65–76; A. Strathern & P. Stewart 1998a: 246; P. Stewart & A. Strathern 2002) recognized the twofold quality of female menstrual blood (and bodily fluids in general), showing that these substances are contextually marked (see Akin 2003: 382).

In understanding the characteristics of *seva,* I found P. Stewart and A. Strathern's interpretation particularly useful. They described a "concept of the varying values (negative and positive) associated with objects and substances that are placed outside of their properly prescribed context" (P. Stewart & A. Strathern 2002: 352), drawing on Douglas's notion of "dirt as matter out of place." In Douglas's interpretation, dirt is a relative idea, not an inherent quality of matter (1966: 35). Therefore, ideas of pathogenicity and hygiene should be discarded from analysis. One flaw inherent in this interpretation is what P. Stewart and A. Strathern called the "residual problem" (2002: 352). The term "dirt" appears to be inseparably tied to those very connotations of pathogenicity and hygiene that are deemed irrelevant.

I keep this in mind in the following analysis of a particular form of *seva:* the blood of parturition and lochia (i.e., the discharge of blood, cervical mucus, and cellular debris that weeps from the vagina for up to six weeks after delivery). Parturitional blood and lochia endanger the health of men and children. When taboos are violated, the *seva* dangerously crosses the boundary of its confines. After a woman has given birth, her body is tainted with the blood of parturition. The fluid evaporates from her vagina, and the airborne particles may then settle on objects and other persons. Therefore, the new mother must not hastily return to the dwelling house that she shares with her husband. She must stay spatially separated—on the back veranda or in another enclosure—until her *seva* has faded away. In Kire, this period is described as when "the new mother is on the platform" (*a mbirika ka-a ki*).

The term *mbirɨka* means "new mother." *Ka-a* refers to a split-palm platform on which the new mother traditionally rests.

A hole in the platform allows the lochia to flow through the platform onto a flower sheath of the *Kentiopsis archontophoenix* palm, which the new mother then discards. Throughout this time, she must observe certain taboos and follow specific rules to prevent illness in herself and her newborn child. Very strict rules also apply to persons and objects crossing the boundaries of post-partum seclusion. In February 2007, I visited Jessica, a young Giri 2 woman married to a Regene husband. A couple of days prior to my visit, Jessica had given birth to her first child and was passing time in a small ground-level room adjacent to her parents' dwelling house.[8] When her classificatory mother-in-law, Sarah, and I came to visit Jessica, she was absent. Jessica had left through an opening in the woven wall at the back of her room—an exit that was intended only for her. If her newborn son were to be carried through the same entrance, he would quickly develop respiratory illness. Jessica's baby was sleeping naked on a woven mat underneath a mosquito net.

Sarah explained that the number of items utilized by mother and child in seclusion is kept to a minimum. These items, such as clothes, bedding, and netbags, must not be reused outside or carried to a garden, and they are later either disposed of in the Ramu River or left behind in the room. This special care is taken because pigs may be attracted to the site by the scent of the *seva* and consequently ravage the garden. The netbag for carrying the infant, with which Jessica's mother-in-law, Rebecca, had presented her, was being kept in safe custody until Jessica left seclusion. Before entering Jessica's room, we hung our netbags on the branch of a shade tree, because comestibles such as tobacco, areca nuts, and mustard brought into the room must not be taken outside again. If they were to come in contact with men and children, they would cause respiratory illness. Women must decide whether they want to consume such tainted items, given that a small chance remains that they may also develop respiratory symptoms. Hence, female visitors usually avoid taking their netbags inside.

Sarah was acutely aware of the potential harmful effects of *seva* on a newborn. In 1999, she and her baby, Anna, had occupied a secluded room in the back of her marital house. Like Jessica, Sarah had her personal backdoor exit to relieve and wash herself. Once through the door, she would cross the back veranda, descend a ladder, and follow her private pathway to the bush and her own small pond in the swamps. New mothers either use a private pond or a bucket to wash themselves. They must not bathe in communally used waters, such as the Regene (an oxbow lake of the Ramu), because their *seva* will disperse and cause respiratory illness in those who come into contact with the water.

Sarah's family members left and entered the house via the front door and were mindful not to set foot on Sarah's trail. Shielding Anna from *seva* was also critical. Consequently, Sarah followed strict rules to safeguard her daughter's health. For example, she slept close to the back door and her baby slept near the opposite door, which opened to the other rooms in the house. Sarah was diligent in making sure that her baby never faced the back door and only slept on one side without turning the baby around. Sarah also positioned herself in such a way that her legs never pointed in the direction of her baby. She faced her baby to avoid turning her back toward Anna so that she would not waft air from her body to the baby.

Despite Sarah's conscientious efforts to keep herself (including her bodily fluids and scents) and Anna in their confined spaces, Anna was nevertheless exposed to Sarah's *seva*. After about the second week, Sarah's sister-in-law—a young woman thought to be *ŋaŋŋan* (mad/crazy) by the community—picked up Anna and carried her through the back door. Before long, Anna began to suffer from the consequences of the trespassing—from being struck by her mother's *seva*. She developed a chronic cough and a runny nose. Her mother Regina advised Sarah on how to intervene. To ease the baby's condition, Sarah took a bath in her private pond and, afterward, skimmed bubbly water from the surface. She carried the water in a coconut shell to her house, where she handed it to Regina. Regina held a dry leaf of the fishtail palm tree over Anna's head and shouted, while moving the shell in circles above the leaf: "Only you, [Sarah]! Your *seva* made her [sick]! You get out of her!" (*Ndu [Sarah] ra! Ndu seva aŋ mbui! Ndu aŋ ta ngiri!*)

Sarah explained that her daughter's health status improved after the performance of *nduigi,* the curing practice. However, symptoms persisted and Anna became a frequent patient at BHC. In 2009, a sputum sample was taken for *Mycobacterium tuberculosis* cultures and was found positive. Anna was referred to MGH, where the diagnosis was confirmed. In sum, this case demonstrates that, although her mother's *seva* had harmed Anna, it was, again, the mother's bodily fluids (concentrated in water bubbles) that momentarily ameliorated her symptoms.

A second brief episode illustrates this contextually determined value of the postpartum discharge and again emphasizes the fact that men depend upon women's courtesy. When dawn broke the morning after she had given birth to her first child, Rita, her husband, and her mother-in-law walked down to the pond that Rita used to bathe herself throughout her seclusion. Guided by her mother-in-law, Rita stepped into the shallow pond and squatted in the water. Her husband swam facedown through Rita's opened legs as his face plunged into the muddy water. When telling the story, Rita laughed at the image of her husband's dirty face. Rita's *seva* had flown into the water and engulfed her husband, who, she claimed, benefitted from this ritual action.

By exposing her husband deliberately to her *seva,* Rita had prevented him from aging prematurely; he would remain juvenescent, his skin firm to an advanced age.

Among the Paiela (Enga Province), women utilize their uterine blood to make their husbands' skin look beautiful. In contradistinction to Giri practices, Paiela women perform the magic in secrecy, and their husbands do not come into direct contact with the substance (Biersack 1982: 242). Men are highly dependent on the benevolence of women in both societies: "If the woman is angry with her husband, as Paiela women sometimes are, she may not bother to perform her magic, or she may perform it maliciously, to different and injurious specifications, so that her husband's skin will appear 'small' and 'bad'" (ibid.). In Giri, the situation becomes especially complicated if a man relies on the *seva* of a woman who is not his spouse—a woman who might be reluctant to engage in this intimate act of squatting over him and exposing her genitals. But if a man is seized by the *seva* of a woman, only that woman can help him restore his lost strength and vitality. Therefore, Giri men are eminently wary and cautious of provoking such dangerous situations.

For example, when a veranda post on which a woman was staying with her second newborn collapsed, none of the Regene men were willing to step underneath the veranda and replace the post, because all of them feared being left unaided if they subsequently developed respiratory illness. Generally, men and children must not pass underneath a seclusion building, because the woman's *seva* is said to seep through gaps in the split-palm floor.[9] Given that the veranda had to be fixed so the new mother and her infant's time in the enclosure would not be compromised, the male community members encouraged the woman's husband to undertake the repair. The point of argument was that if her husband were to become ill, his wife would surely assist him in recovery.

Thinking and Handling Seva in Altered Contexts

Having discussed both beneficial and dangerous aspects of the blood of parturition and lochia, in this section I delve deeper into contemporary Giri women's thoughts and handling of the substance in situations in which they find themselves facing new interventions in reproductive health. The focus of the analysis is on the ways in which Giri women incorporate local ideas and practices concerning birth with the notions and services that characterize biomedical prepartum, intrapartum, and postpartum health care. Two interconnected questions led my analysis: (1) In what ways do Giri women's thoughts on the effects that biomedicine has on *seva* contribute to the prominence of maternal health services? and (2) Has the employment of biomedical services transformed women's seclusion patterns to the extent that women remain for shorter periods inside the enclosure or even entirely abandon the practice? This second question is important, considering that postpartum seclusion and compliance with restrictions and taboos linked to it are, in the traditional context of Giri society, most central for controlling *seva*.

The data presented in the current and following section stem from thirty-five semistructured interviews with mothers from Regene, Kɨmnɨng, Niaŋ (a community of Giri 2 villagers), and Giri 1, which I carried out in 2009. A second series of combined structured and semistructured interviews was conducted in 2010 with twenty-eight Regene and Kɨmnɨng women (twenty-one of whom had already participated in the 2009 survey). Furthermore, much of the information provided was obtained over the years from various conversations with Regene, Kɨmnɨng, and other Giri women, a few men, and BHC and MGH medical personnel.

Controlling Seva with Biomedicine

Van der Geest founded the "anthropology of pharmaceuticals," which is concerned with the social and cultural meanings and uses of pharmaceuticals. In the late 1980s, he produced, together with his colleague, Whyte, a pioneering edited volume on the circulation and understanding of Western pharmaceuticals (van der Geest & Whyte 1988). In a subsequent publication,[10] Whyte et al. (2002) called attention to the social lives that medicines—as materia medica, "material *things* of therapy" (3)—have with regard to their uses and consequences. Western pharmaceuticals have voyaged to virtually all indigenous societies and taken on various cultural roles and lives:

> The medicines with the most active social lives in the world today are the commercially manufactured synthetic drugs produced by the pharmaceutical industry. They have vigorous commodity careers; their dissemination to every part of the globe has far-reaching implications for local medical systems. They have become part of the materia medica of every local society—an eminent example of globalization. (Whyte et al. 2002: 3)

In what follows, I expound on the acquired meaning of the pharmaceuticals that are administered to women throughout the prepartum, intrapartum, and postpartum periods within the Giri context. Following delivery at health centers and hospitals, women generally receive massages and a combination of medications. Immediately after delivery, the attending health worker massages the mother's fundus to make it firm, speed up expulsion of the placenta and blood lumps from the uterus, and stop postnatal bleeding. The health worker gives ergometrine (hastening the delivery of the placenta and thus preventing excessive postnatal bleeding) and oxytocin (a hormone that facilitates the clotting of the placental attachment point) injections. Sometimes paracetamol tablets are administered to prevent postnatal fundal pains.

Mothers receive a five-day course of iron folate tablets (Fefol) to reverse possible anemia. If the medical facility runs out of stock, women are advised to eat plenty of leafy green vegetables—especially *kui* (*Abelmoschus manihot;* aibika). A three-day dose of chloroquine should be routinely given, but BHC staff actually only administer the drug if a mother develops a fever. Mothers with no, or only limited, breast milk sometimes receive oral contraceptives to induce lactation. Moreover, these women are advised to hold their baby to their breast and let them suckle or to employ local herbal remedies like breadfruit or *bemge* sap to stimulate milk production. The actual range of medications given depends largely on availability and the attending health worker's subjective assessment, despite the fact that health workers have standardized treatment regimens.

Sandra delivered four of her five children at medical facilities—at MGH, at Paternoster Memorial Hospital (i.e., the old Bunapas hospital), and at BHC. In the course of our conversation it became obvious that Sandra's prime reason for delivering at medical facilities was access to postnatal services, which she believed to be helpful for cleansing her body from *seva*. At Paternoster Memorial Hospital, BHC, and MGH, Sandra received shots (most likely a combination of ergometrine and oxytocin, possibly also a booster dose of tetanus toxoid). Her sister-in-law elucidated: "There is an injection which they will give me. They give [it] to me to lower the heat of us women; it has to decrease." Giri women understand iron folate tablets to be further agents in this process. Termed "blood medication" (blut marasin), the tablets are perceived not only to lead to the production of new blood (*vizin*—blood that runs in one's veins) but also to purify the body by rejecting and replacing *seva* (old uterine blood).

Beyond that, Giri women interpret virtually any medication given postnatally to yield the faster ejection of *seva* and thus strengthen the mother's body. This includes the abovementioned painkillers but also antibiotics, which are often administered to women who deliver babies before arrival at the health facility—so-called BBA mothers. Giri women value the rapid ejection of *seva* and state that postnatal bleeding stops sooner when these medications are taken. In their opinion, new mothers who do not take the postpartum medications waste blood, because their lochia lasts much longer. In a similar way, women state that fundal massages promote a faster expulsion of *seva*. Massages have become, for Sandra and other Giri women, a vital part of the management of a safe delivery and a comfortable postnatal period.

It had been Sandra's wish to have all her births in medical environments, but her third child was born on the way to BHC. Sandra was relaxed when her labor began. She was well aware from her previous deliveries at BHC that the health personnel would likely refuse to admit her when contractions were still mild and far apart. Instead, the health workers would request that she take walks to speed up labor and return to the health center only when her contractions became closer—that is, for the actual act of delivery. In the village, the two World Vision–trained Regene village birth attendants palpated Sandra's abdomen and said that it was not yet time for her to give birth. Knowing that she would move into an enclosure after birth, unable to cook for her family, Sandra prepared a meal for her children and husband and tidied the house. Then she walked around the village. When intervals between the contractions became shorter, she set out for the fifteen-minute walk to BHC, accompanied by the two local birth attendants and her sister-in-law.

The village birth attendants suggested a detour, walking alongside the Ramu effluent that discharges into the Regene oxbow lake during the rainy season. This location was beside the actual pathway, in case Sandra gave birth before arrival at BHC, and for Sandra to take baths. After the first couple of baths, contractions became stronger, causing Sandra to kneel down. She wanted to lie on the ground, but the birth attendants summoned her to continue walking. Sandra alternated baths with walking. When the birth attendants examined her after her fourth bath, they knew that Sandra would not reach the facility in time for delivery. She laughed as she told me of how she gave birth to her son (with the help of her companions) by a row of coconut palms lining a stretch of the pathway. The oddness of the situation amused Sandra in retrospect; but, back then, although the delivery went smoothly and was unobstructed, she was in great pain the following night.

Having directly returned to Regene instead of proceeding to BHC, Sandra recalled how she cried out in pain because her womb had not been cleaned (i.e., inside the uterus) by a health worker. By this, she referred to the postpartum abdominal massages that health workers provide to ensure the removal of all placenta, which, as Sandra explained, help prevent fundal pains. Another of Sandra's sisters-in-law, who gave birth to her daughter at BHC, specified the advantages of a health center delivery: "The doctors [i.e., medical staff with various qualifications] will cleanse you properly . . . You will not suffer any bodily harm."

Even Giri women who give birth in the village or on the way to BHC often collect medications (mainly iron folate, paracetamol, antibiotics, and chloroquine) and maternity pads from BHC. Sometimes, the new mothers proceed to the health center (where they are then registered as BBA); at other times, relatives pick up the medications. Rita's husband fetched hospital supplies after she had delivered her first daughter:

> I went to Bunapas hospital [i.e., Paternoster Memorial Hospital]. But no, she was born halfway. And I did not go to the hospital. The mothers [i.e., Rita's mother-in-law and two other kin-related experienced mothers of her mother-in-law's age]

brought me back to the village. And thus I stayed in the birth hut [i.e., an enclosure, but which never is the actual birth place]. I remained in the village in the birth hut. But I still received medication against pain and for drying up the place where it [i.e., the placenta] had been [attached] . . . The mothers did not want me to go to the hospital. If I went to the hospital there would not be any . . . sizeable body of water for bathing. And how would I wash myself and remove the debris [i.e., blood clots, mucus, and placental tissue] from inside? And they told me thus: "We will not go to the hospital. We will go to the village. And you will bathe in a sizeable body of water."

Although Rita's birth attendants brought her back to the village, where conditions were better for washing the *seva* off her body (in her private pond and with aromatic ginger leaves, instead of at one of BHC's tanks), Rita still used biomedical drugs.

In addition to the postnatal care for women, services for newborns are very popular among women. Babies are weighed and checked for congenital abnormalities, and their overall health is assessed by the Apgar score (a score that evaluates the physical condition of the infant on the basis of five criteria: *a*ppearance, *p*ulse, *g*rimace, *a*ctivity, and *r*espiration). Their nose and mouth are suctioned and antibiotic eye ointment applied to stop possible neonatal conjunctivitis (which an infant may contract when passing through the birth canal of a mother infected with *Chlamydia trachomatis* or *Neisseria gonorrhoea*). The infant is injected with vitamin K (to stop umbilical bleeding in babies who suffer from vitamin K deficiency) and vaccinated against hepatitis B and tuberculosis. BBA babies are given antibiotic injections and, if they have developed a fever, amodiaquin (Camaquin) shots—a malaria treatment.

Giri women appreciate cleansing of the infant's skin, nose, and mouth from mucous and blood (*seva*), but the vitamin K, tuberculosis protection, and hepatitis B vaccine injections are far more popular. Mothers say that these strengthen the baby's body and free it from absorbed *seva*. Especially through breast milk, the baby imbibes its mother's *seva*. In Giri, as in much of Melanesia (see, for instance, Hogbin [1970] 1996: 114; Scaletta 1986: 45), babies are thought to absorb damaging substances via the mother's milk if the mother breaks certain postpartum taboos. A strong taboo is on sexual intercourse throughout the months or years during which the mother breast-feeds, because the baby will ingest the sexual secretions, and—if the mother conceives—the suckling child will also absorb the excretions of the unborn. Thus, the otherwise nourishing breast milk may become temporarily dangerous. Jolly (2001: 183) noted very similar rationales for prolonged postpartum sexual abstinence among the Sa speakers of South Pentecost.

Similar to them and the Ankave-Anga (northern Gulf Province; Bonnemère 2004: 62), the Giri take the opposite stance to the Sambia (Herdt [1981] 1994:

193, 234–35), among whom semen is viewed to promote growth, contribute to longevity, and activate breast milk production. Understandably, Giri women to whom health workers have suggested contraception through breastfeeding are somewhat bewildered by the inappropriateness of the underlying assumption that they might have sexual intercourse during the postpartum phase. Nowadays, however, Giri women appear to remain sexually abstinent for shorter periods than they did in the past. Frank and Ros Beale described the change brought about by missionary influence: "Mission teaching ... had the effect of breaking up the old taboos, eg [sic] ... no sex while breast feeding which usually was up to 2 years" (pers. comm. 2012). This is likely to have contributed to the prominence of the medications given to newborns.

The injections that the infant receives are perceived to have a positive long-term effect by preventing *seva*-related respiratory illness during childhood. Further vaccines given throughout infancy against measles and poliomyelitis as well as a combination diphtheria, tetanus, whooping cough, and *Haemophilus influenzae* type b vaccine and an orally administered vitamin A fluid (which comes in capsules, but BHC health workers prick the gelatin coating with a needle and directly squeeze the oily fluid into the infants' mouths) are interpreted along the same lines.

Prenatal care is extremely prominent among Giri women. The Churches of Christ mission put special emphasis on maternal health services and offered prenatal clinics from its early years in Tung in the late 1950s onward. The twenty-eight women participating in the 2010 survey had visited a prenatal clinic at least once before 90.4 percent of their deliveries. In an initiating conversation, the health worker asks the woman about the date of her last menstruation. The woman is weighed, fundal height measurements are taken, and the health worker feels the woman's belly and checks fetal heart sounds. These measures serve to determine whether the baby is alive, whether it lies in the right position, and whether multiple pregnancy is involved. Blood pressure and a urine sample are taken, as significant increases in blood pressure and high amounts of protein in the urine may indicate preeclampsia (pregnancy-induced hypertension). The first of two tetanus toxin injections (or a booster if the woman has already been vaccinated against tetanus) is given.

If the woman does not have a maternal clinic card, the health workers suggest that she buy one. She is given Fefol for one week and a month's supply of chloroquine (one tablet to be taken once a week as a malaria prophylactic). The expecting mother is then advised to proceed to MGH for a measurement of her hemoglobin and blood sugar levels to assess whether she suffers from pregnancy diabetes or anemia. Before the woman pays one kina for these prenatal services, she is given a brief health education session. In practice, however, BHC health workers rarely keep to this standard process accurately.

After I followed the visit of an eighteen-year-old first-time expecting mother from Garati, I asked the health worker attending to the woman to reflect on her own performance. She spelled out several deviations that had occurred. She had forgotten to measure the blood pressure. A urine sample had not been taken because the health center had run out of dipsticks. Moreover, the Fefol stock was nil, as was the stock of maternal clinic cards. The woman had not promptly paid the medical fee, but her mother was to bring in the outstanding amount in a few days, following a trip to Madang Town.

I was impressed by the high attendance rate for prenatal exams, given that the Giri women I interviewed voiced grave criticisms about the services they received: Consultations were usually short, without much explanation from the health worker. Examinations and treatments, including injections, were barely announced and were mainly performed in utter silence. Giri mothers also deplored that they were insufficiently informed, for example, about bodily changes that they would face throughout gestation and about how to cope with them. One woman told me that the female health worker did not give her any information on how the baby would develop in her body. According to her, women were forced to go to a family planning clinic in order to learn about conception and the baby's growth from a biomedical perspective.

Practical advice was limited to a few points of guidance pertaining to self-care, for example, the mother should eat plenty of leafy green vegetables, avoid strenuous work and the heat of the sun, and rest her body often. Audrey made a typical statement: "They only felt my belly and they only gave [me] medication. To give out information, they don't do it." Furthermore, palpation of the womb was contended among Giri women. Some women saw the examination as helpful. Alicia told me that her baby had moved more than usual when the female Giri nurse had palpated her womb, which had a positive effect on Alicia, who was happy to feel her baby and become aware of her pregnancy. Audrey was pleased, because the female health worker had straightened the baby's position in her womb. Generally, Giri women were not afraid of the examination, but they were concerned that a male health worker might perform the examination and touch their genitals.

Yet, Giri women were also pragmatists, weighing the advantages and disadvantages of prenatal clinic visits. Lock and Kaufert suggested that women are not just "passive vessels, simply acting in culturally determined ways with little possibility for reflection on their own condition" (1998: 2). Neither are women "inherently suspicious of and resistant to technological interventions. Rather . . . women's relationships with technology are usually grounded in existing habits of pragmatism" (ibid.). Women's key motivation to visit prenatal clinics appears to be access to the available medications (though it was not uncommon for BHC to run out of various medications).

Even those women who preferred to have their births in the village regularly resorted to medications. Rita, for example, utilized prenatal services for all of her five pregnancies but delivered only one child at a medical facility. Rita laid out her reasons:

> I usually get medication because I think of the time they are born. If you don't get medication . . . I don't get medication, I will find [it] hard. The medication helps us to deliver the child smoothly—fast . . . So when they gave me medication . . . they examined me, they gave me medication, they told me thus, "There is blood medication [that] you will take every day." Okay, there is a medication . . . I also don't know the name of this medication. When they gave it to me they told me thus, "Each Sunday . . . you have to take two and when finished you have to come back again" . . . The first time . . . so you go and . . . you go and say "I am pregnant," then they will give you an injection. They will only administer one injection. And that's it. And at your other times will . . . only getting medication. [It is] like this and the baby is born. When the baby is born, it is like this: you won't feel much pain . . . So, the medication helps you, and the medication also grows the baby inside [the womb].

Two points can be inferred from this quote: prenatally administered medications are perceived to be essential for the healthy growth of the fetus and a smooth delivery. Rita spoke about iron folate tablets, weekly doses of chloroquine, and tetanus toxin boosters.

The fact that Giri women generally understand these medications in a way similar to Rita may at least be partly provoked by health workers' attempts to threaten pregnant women into taking prenatal medications and attending prenatal clinics. A health worker told Megan that she would have a smooth delivery if she took the medications; otherwise she would suffer great pain during delivery. Sandra reasoned that if a woman had regularly attended prenatal clinics, there would be no immediate need for her to give birth at a health facility. Her body would have been prepared through the previously received medications for delivery, and there would be no need for her to deliver at a medical facility if a trained village birth attendant who knew how to cleanse the new mother's womb postpartum was available. Furthermore, prenatally taken iron folate tablets are envisaged to aid and accelerate the postnatal expulsion of *seva,* by replenishing the old blood with fresh blood, soon after delivery.

In sum, biomedicine has introduced new methods to deal with *seva*—a powerful substance that may affect mother, child, and others—and is, in this respect, extremely popular among Giri women. The most significant alteration that prenatal, natal, and postnatal health care has entailed is the capability to quicken the ejection of *seva.* As discussed below, this is of major importance in a changing world—namely, a world in which women are unable to continue exactly the same seclusion patterns as in the past.

No Female Space in the Health Center

The survey that I conducted in 2010 included information on whether women went into seclusion after child delivery. Let me begin with some numbers that will serve as a backbone for my discussion. An analysis of the 105 births of the 2010 sample shows that 58 births took place in nonbiomedical environments, of which 57 were in villages. The other 47 births were at biomedical facilities: 14 at MGH, 32 at health centers (of these 29 were at BHC[11]), and 1 in an examination room of a rural, non-Giri high school clinic. Women went into customary seclusion after 88 of the 105 deliveries.

Before exploring female seclusion patterns, I wish to explain another blatant point that arose from this survey: only a minority of babies is born at the local health center. Otherwise, women mostly deliver around the village in uncleared or cleared but uncultivated land, where the risk of other people accidentally dropping by is low. Sometimes they give birth alone; sometimes they are looked after by close kinswomen. Generally, the attending women have gained experienced through their own births or previously assisted births but do not hold any specialized knowledge in midwifery. (Nowadays, biomedically trained village birth attendants increasingly attend village births.) Men do not dare come close to birthing women for fear of being affected by the heat of their *seva*. For the same reason, children are prohibited from being present during deliveries. Not even the new mother and infant remain in the actual birth place. Thus, it would be extremely stressful for a birthing mother to deliver inside a dwelling house, because she would jeopardize her own and her baby's health and that of the other residents.

Some Giri mothers see it as advantageous to deliver at the health center to make sure that delivery does not inadvertently occur too close to garden plots and to prevent contact with accidental passersby. But, mostly, women go to the health center for the available medications and birth assistance (see above), and not because the health center is perceived to be a good and safe place for a delivery. BHC was rebuilt as a single building with two wards (one used as office space), a dispensary, and a tiny examination/emergency room; it has neither a labor nor a gynecological ward.

Actually, there is no exclusively female space. Women have to give birth in the examination room, which is used for all kinds of medical treatments and examinations, such as wound treatment and prenatal examinations. If an emergency patient arrives, the birthing woman may be rushed to leave the room. Usually, new mothers are urged to return to their homes on the same day of delivery. Only if they are notably weak or if other complications occur are they admitted to the ward—the general medical ward. This, in turn, is another stressful experience for most women, as they are in constant fear that their *seva* might affect adult male and pediatric inpatients in the room.

A look at BHC's obstetric record shows that it is anything but uncommon for males to attend deliveries. To my astonishment, 21 percent of the deliveries from February 2004 to November 2009 were attended by male health workers (none of them a kinsman to the birthing mother). Although the women I interviewed valued BHC's obstetric care, the shame of being exposed to and manually examined by men ranked among their prime reasons for denying maternal health services. A few male health workers were considered "honest," but others were known for touching women's genitals unnecessarily during prenatal check-ups and delivery. Sandra put it this way: "They [women in labor] will not like it if a male health worker goes to work; if a female health worker goes they will be content with her." Not uncommonly, this led to male non-Giri health workers being threatened out of the community.

Despite the health center's proximity (within minutes' walking distance), the male health workers' presence makes it unsurprising that the number of Regene women's deliveries at BHC is just about half of that of village births. Often, women make the decision to go to BHC only if they have been categorized as high-risk mothers[12] or after a long night in labor. As a nulliparous woman, BHC personnel classified Vivian as a high-risk mother and told her to give birth at a biomedical facility. The two Regene village birth attendants reinforced the request and brought Vivian to BHC. On their way, Vivian told the village birth attendants that she did not want any men to be present during delivery. But they just replied that it was also the male health workers' job to assist birthing women, and whoever was on duty would attend her delivery. At the health center, Vivian found one female and three male staff members working on her body. Although Vivian's female cousin was present to offer emotional support, Vivian was extremely unhappy and felt ashamed because of the men's presence, as she later told me.

With regard to *seva*, the women I interviewed felt more burdened in the presence of male health workers from Giri and neighboring villages than of non-Giri male staff members. They assumed that non-Giri medical staff or higher qualified personnel, possibly brought up in town and holding an overseas degree, would not believe in customary thoughts about *seva*. However, the women were uncertain whether male health workers might be impaired at all by *seva* in a biomedical environment and whether the medications administered to the women would also prevent health workers from being negatively affected.

I never encountered any woman who considered those brief, often stressful periods at the health center to be parallel to a customary phase of seclusion after birth. Per my survey, Regene woman usually proceeded into seclusion in the village after a BHC birth. Of course, the given medications led, in Giri women's opinion, to a faster expulsion of their *seva* and safeguarded against vigorous postpartum pains. Nevertheless, *seva* was said to have not entirely faded away in the hours or few days after the mother left the health center. That women had no decent washing facilities at BHC may have further contributed to this perception. Women had to fill up pails of water from one of the tanks and wash themselves from buckets.

I further suggest that, aside from the facility's premises and features, a second aspect shaped postinstitutional seclusion patterns: the location of BHC. The health center lies in the vicinity of the Giri villages, and it therefore seems that, for Giri women, moving into seclusion is a matter of course. If women return promptly to the village after birthing, other family members expect her to proceed into seclusion so as not to negatively affect their health. A woman who refuses to go into seclusion or who leaves seclusion before her *seva* has faded away is said to stap nating long ples. This phrase carries two meanings and may be translated as "to be in the village for no reason" and, more commonly, "to be without work in the village." Here, the phrase targets noncompliance with postpartum regulations and thus carries a bit of the weight of both purports: the new mother wrongly, "for no reason," takes part in everyday life, and this is also a realm in which she is superfluous, in which she has "no work," because she must not fulfill everyday tasks, such as cooking or gardening, at that special time.

However, my survey also shows that two BHC deliveries were not followed by customary seclusion. These births were at the former Paternoster Memorial Hospital and attributed to the same mother. Her parents came from other Madang villages. Newly wed, she moved with her husband, the son of a Churches of Christ long-term medical assistant, to her parents-in-law's dwelling house in the staff compound of Paternoster Memorial Hospital. After being discharged from the maternity ward (in distinction to BHC, Paternoster Memorial Hospital had a separate maternity ward), she moved back to her parents-in-law's dwelling house. Her father-in-law was genuinely convinced that the tenets of biomedicine were true.

He supplied her with medications, not deeming her seclusion necessary. This was in accord with his conviction that biomedical methods are the key to health. Due to her exceptionally good access to medical services throughout the prepartum, intrapartum, and postpartum periods and her father-in-law's belief in biomedicine, she returned to usual Giri village life in the postpartum phase. However, the situation was different after her next delivery. She and her husband had moved to a house in Giri 1, and she delivered her child in uncultivated lands in the vicinity of the village. As any other Giri 1 woman would do after a village delivery, she passed the common period of one month in seclusion.

The average length of time that women who proceeded into seclusion spent there did not differ much between those who had had their births in a biomedical versus a nonbiomedical environment. Women who had had village births stayed in seclusion for an average of 32.5 days, and women who had delivered at biomedical facilities stayed in seclusion for an average of 27.0 days. In theory, some women suggested that days spent in a health center or hospital ward should be subtracted from the one-month period. But others said that, independent of where a woman gives birth, she needs to pass at least one month in seclusion outside the biomedical facility. In practice, though, it appears that women pragmatically looked at their lochia and came outside when it had declined or, in some cases, when kinswomen had become tired of supplying meals. However, we find grave differences between seclusion patterns in the village and in Madang Town.

Postpartum Seclusion at the Hospital Ward?

My survey shows that all but one of the fifteen Giri women who gave birth in Madang Town did so at the provincial hospital. Among a range of factors in women's preference for birthing at biomedical institutions, the prevalent reason for choosing the biomedical environment over a family setting in the town context was that, in contrast to the retreat areas provided by untended lands around the village, there were no safe and protected spaces in Madang Town. One woman, who was employed in Madang Town and delivered in the hospital's labor ward, said that she could not think of any place in the settlement where she lived that would be appropriate for a delivery. MGH was a "safe" choice, as she put it. The hospital was a secure environment not only for the birthing process itself but also for the phase following confinement. This woman stayed with her infant in the gynecological ward for one week before returning to her townhouse, where she was promptly—without any further time in spatial seclusion—reintegrated into everyday life.

In chapter 4, I revealed Giri patients' fears about being admitted to the hospital's general ward, which is associated with death. The gynecological ward is not charged with such negative connotations. In fact, it is an all-female space, which made it a place where Giri mothers felt rather comfortable after delivery.

The one woman who had her baby in Madang Town and not at the hospital did so accidentally. In her younger years, Audrey had experienced a surgical miscarriage and had been referred to MGH for her first delivery after the miscarriage. A couple of days prior to her due date, she and her mother had boarded a PMV to Madang. The trip in the back of the jolting truck brought on the first contractions, so Audrey and her mother walked to MGH the next morning.

After an examination, the attending nurse told Audrey that she was many hours away from giving birth. Thus, the two women returned to their host's residential house. Audrey and her mother stayed with the older woman's second cousin, Arthur—the hospital porter. Late in the evening, Audrey went to sleep. She woke up to strong contractions at two o'clock in the morning. She rushed outside so as not to spoil the house with her *seva*. She gave birth soon after beneath areca palms and a *Gnetum gnemon* tree. It was raining heavily, and Audrey had to stand uncomfortably under the trees to give birth. Reflecting on the experience of giving birth near a residential townhouse, Audrey observed:

> I felt that it was a bit difficult for me. But this was really heavy rain coming down. So, there was no way that I . . . I would lie down and give birth to the baby. Hence, I was standing, and I gave birth to the baby . . . I was not especially content. You deliver the child comfortably if you lie down.
>
> Directly in the hospital would be alright. This was . . . at the house and I did not feel especially well because at the hospital would have been . . . a nurse would look after me or so.

One can also imagine that townhouses are anything but ideal places for a month-long seclusion. I know of only one woman who proceeded from the hospital ward to a private enclosure in town. All other Giri women who delivered at MGH returned to everyday town life after discharge, as practical reasons prevented them from going into seclusion. Townhouses often burst at the seams with household members and visitors, and questions arise regarding where a new mother can be secluded. Should one sacrifice a whole room? Moreover, a new mother must not make fire or cook food. She relies on other female relatives for meals—a circumstance that becomes a problem if all other adult household members pursue wage work and the younger ones go to school.

This problem is especially troublesome in situations in which the woman has other children for whom she has to care. Also, the woman has to discreetly dispose of the sanitary towels or self-made menstrual pads (made from pieces of cloth) she has utilized to soak up postpartum discharge. The same goes for the infant's excrements. Whereas women in Giri bury the waste in untended lands and bathe in their private ponds, women in Madang Town face a problem, with townhouses closely built together and often without sanitation.

The example of Sandra, the one woman to be secluded in Madang Town, illustrates the crucial importance of family support in facilitating seclusion in the town environment. Sandra delivered her first child at MGH. Two weeks prior to the actual delivery, she and her husband had come to Madang Town.

Sandra's parents considered the hospital a safer environment for a first delivery than the village, because medical aid would be available in the case of possible complications. Sandra's father had been involved in forestry work, and, after his resignation, Sandra's parents continued to live in Madang Town. They stayed with Sandra's older sister and suggested that Sandra reside with them during the final phase of her pregnancy. The evening her labor pains started, Sandra's husband and her parents walked her to MGH. She gave birth in the night and stayed for half a day in the obstetric ward until she was discharged. Her sister's husband, a carpenter, had skillfully fenced in the platform underneath their townhouse with sawn timber.

The "room" had a front door and a back door, in accordance with customary requirements. Sandra's brother-in-law had even built a bed for Sandra. She moved to the enclosure and spent a month on the platform until her *seva* had faded away. Sandra's relatives had provided an appropriate resting place—an exception in Madang. Sandra was content with her enclosure and considered herself fortunate to have such a place. She knew about the hardship other Giri women faced after giving birth in Madang Town:

> If you are a village woman and want to deliver in town, then you go and deliver. But where will you stay then after you have delivered and have been discharged [from the hospital]? This smell of the [newly] mother [i.e., *seva*] is still there; and she must stay in another house [or room]. This is difficult—difficult for the village women to go and deliver in town. Hence, when the village mothers deliver in the village they feel alright—so they hide their smell and they stay on their own until this smell has faded. [Only then] they come outside. And to deliver in town is difficult but some . . . they are aware of the kastom but don't have this area . . . such a place within this area, and so they just go and stay with their family [i.e., not in a separate enclosure].

Moreover, Sandra's mother and her sister supplied regular, ample meals. As extensively discussed in chapter 4, Giri people have strong networks in town, and hospital patients usually receive meals from various relatives. However, money in urban contexts does not always allow for provision of regular and sufficient meals over the period of several weeks, or even months, that a woman spends in seclusion: Sandra said:

> Food . . . is a bit difficult for them. Even also if they stay in the obstetric [or gynecological] ward in town—when the mother goes to deliver. How will you subsist in town? So, money dictates if you eat something, huh?! So, you [i.e., caring relatives] buy good food, cook, and go give it to the mother on the obstetric [or gynecological] ward. But, if not, then not.

I was interested in how Giri women explained their reincorporation into the everyday realm of living. When I asked them about what rendered seclusion superfluous after a few days in the gynecological ward, I always received the same answer: "The *seva* is finished." Giri women reasoned that the period of time at the gynecological ward was some kind of "speed seclusion" during which *seva* was quickly ejected with the help of biomedical drugs and treatments. In essence, these women believed that what is accomplished through arduous observance of taboos and regulations over a long period in customary seclusion can as well be achieved within a few days at the hospital, given that the new mother meticulously takes the provided medications and follows health personnel's instructions. Particularly striking is the fact that women who had given birth at MGH often stayed for a week, or even longer, in the ward.

That the effects of a week or so on an all-female ward and under constant medical care were interpreted analogously to customary seclusion is not surprising. Even my mother, Thiap, who I consider a strong adherent to kastom, shared this point of view. Having spent periods of up to three months in seclusion following village births, Thiap had, by far, surpassed the other women in my study, for whom the common length of seclusion was about one month.[13] Thiap heavily criticized younger women who violated seclusion taboos and regulations in the village, reasoning that their babies habitually suffered from respiratory symptoms and that these mothers and their children were hence frequent visitors to the health center. Yet Thiap, herself, did not spend any time in seclusion after her discharge from MGH.

Sandra's case highlights another point: alongside the actual place of birth, the specificities and possibilities of the environment in which the woman dwells in the weeks after confinement comprise a second critical factor in determining whether a new mother proceeds into seclusion after hospital discharge. Whereas all women who had a village delivery went into seclusion, the plain fact that a woman had her birth at the provincial hospital did not account for whether she subsequently passed any time in seclusion. Relatives' expectations and assistance played a critical part in determining the appropriate seclusion pattern in a particular situation. Let me return to Audrey's case, which may serve here as a second example. After delivering her infant in the pouring rain, Audrey woke her relatives. Arthur called the hospital to have the driver on duty pick her up. A nurse, who cut the umbilical cord, accompanied the driver. At MGH, Audrey had a perineal tear repaired. Moreover, her son had fallen onto a stone at birth, so the nurse suggested keeping him for a week under medical observation.

Audrey remained for a week in the hospital's gynecological ward. Her mother cared for her, but both women depended solely upon meals supplied by Arthur and his wife. Audrey expressed her discontent about the situation: "I did not feel particularly good. It would have been alright if I had kinspeople [caring for me]. [Arthur] himself, along with his wife, [looked after me] and I did not feel particularly good." That the opportunity to retreat into an enclosure in Madang Town did not arise for Audrey is obvious, and she returned to Regene village after her hospital discharge. Upon her arrival in the village, her older brother urged her to spend at least another two weeks in seclusion. Audrey chose instead to move into a room with her brother's two eldest daughters, as she was of the opinion that her *seva* had been ejected during her week in the gynecological ward. She shared a mosquito net with Phyllis, the younger of the two girls.

A couple of months later, Phyllis developed respiratory problems and her nose became constantly congested with a mucopurulent discharge. Audrey's brother attributed his daughter's illness to Audrey's violation of customary seclusion regulations and reasoned that her *seva* must have affected Phyllis. Enraged about his sister's noncompliance, he demanded that she perform a curing practice for Phyllis. Audrey agreed.

These two cases also exemplify women's different attitudes toward seclusion. Sandra was happy that her relatives had provided a safe enclosure to which she could move after hospital discharge. Audrey, on the contrary, felt excluded from her kin, as she told me. She wanted to spend time with her brother's daughters and decided not to follow her brother's request to remain in solitude.

Although women are highly influenced by relative's expectations and the particularities of the environment, with the new options that biomedical facilities and medications offer to them in dealing with their *seva,* women are able to create new models of seclusion. However, women's important role in handling their expelled matter has diminished with biomedicine's involvement in the birthing process. At biomedical facilities, the afterbirth is regarded as disposable human waste. In contrast, traditional notions of placenta and umbilical cord are much different, including beliefs that the newborn's growth and health depend on the placenta, as both are intimately connected.

If the placenta is not handled properly, the child's growth is believed to become disturbed. The thought that growth does not inhere in the child is already marked during the in utero phase. Therefore, I take a step back to explore Giri ideas of procreation and prenatal child development before proceeding to a discussion of the connection between child and placenta. This leads to an exploration of postnatal development and the role of the placenta therein. Another central concern of the two following sections, in which I engage in lengthy descriptions of Giri thoughts on procreation, fetal development, postnatal growth, and placental planting, is to shed light on Giri views of the person and its becoming. As will become apparent, kin undertake various practices that promote the child's prosperity.

Relationality 1: Procreation, Fetal Development, and Postnatal Growth

M. Strathern envisaged children as "the outcome of the interactions of multiple others" (1988: 316). She observed, in a section of *The Gender of the Gift* titled "Mothers Who Do Not Make Babies," "Women do not replicate raw material, babies in the form of unfashioned natural resources, but produce entities which stand in social relation to themselves" (ibid.). This brings us to the concept of the Melanesian relational person—of persons as composites, as fractal (in Wagner's [1991] terminology), or as dividuals—as enunciated by M. Strathern: "Far from being regarded as unique entities, Melanesian persons are as dividually as they are individually conceived. They contain a generalized sociality within. Indeed, persons are frequently constructed as the plural and composite site of the relationships that produced them. The singular person can be imagined as a social microcosm" (1988: 13). "The 'dividual' is always already social: born of others and dependent and interdependent rather than autonomous" as Biersack (1991: 147–48) said in a review of M. Strathern's book.

The Melanesian child does not achieve personhood at birth, or even before, but over time (Carrithers 2010: 533; Fajans 1985: 372; Keck & Wassmann 2010: 192; Wassmann & Keck 2007: 5). With the contributions kin make to the baby's physical growth, the infant's kinship identity forms (Lutkehaus 1995: 14). This also applies to the Giri person, who is a product of the contributions of others and, from conception onward, relational. Growing inheres neither in the fetus nor in the born child.

In LiPuma's words, Melanesian persons do not "mature biogenetically" (1998: 58), but they "grow transactionally as the beneficiary of other peoples's actions" (ibid.). The child, in utero and postnatally, is open to the influences of other people, who may contribute to but also inhibit its growth. The child is an amalgam of their influences. And, very importantly, through their involvement in this process, they give parts of themselves to the child. A child's mother plays the most crucial role. Lindstrom put it aptly in his exemplary description of M. Strathern's dividual, "I, as a person, include part of you—my mother—because of the direct impact your presence has had on me, and also because the food and other objects that you give me remain part of you as I take them into my body" (1999: 197).

First, the child is composed of gendered substances. According to Giri procreative theory, conception happens when father's blood (*ndia-a vizin*) and mother's blood (*niamu vizin*) mix. The father's blood is contained in his sperm (*nzip;* i kam long sperm), which enters the mother's body at sexual intercourse and mingles with the mother's blood in the womb.[14] The mother's blood, which is at work here, is not the mother's menstrual blood (*seva*) but her fresh and clean blood (*vizin*). Wagner (1983: 78–79) noted similar ideas for the Barok of New Ireland. There, the action of ample semen induces the flow of fresh blood in the woman's body, so repeated sexual intercourse is held necessary for conception.[15]

Nowadays, the Giri interweave biomedical conception theory with traditional knowledge and reason that the mother's blood comes through the ovum (*rer;* i kam long kiau).[16] Sex and the number of children depend on the texture of the father's and mother's blood. Under balanced conditions, the woman conceives a boy. If the mother's blood is "too strong," she has a girl (cf. Bamford 2007a: 66), and if her blood is weak and the father's blood strong, a multiple pregnancy is likely.

After about two months, the parents' blood congeals and forms a lump in the woman's breasts. The ancestors said, "the child is in the two breasts" (*tar tani aŋ ki*). During these initial months of pregnancy, the unborn is considered to be only made up of blood. Visible signs of the mother-to-be's pregnancy are the extremely dark coloring of her nipples and the tightness of her breasts; the latter, though, appears only in first-time mothers, I was told. In his *Guardians of the Flutes,* Herdt ([1981] 1994: 196) pointed, in an elaborate discussion of Sambia symbolism, to these two pregnancy markers of menstrual blood and conception. For the Sambia, the accumulation of semen brings about the bulging of the breasts; the black nipples are the result of coitus.

However, Giri women made very clear to me that the woman is not actually *with child* at this stage. Meat, bones, and muscles arise when the blood lump leaves the breasts and moves down to the mother's womb, after about three months; this is when the child forms.[17] From the fourth month onward, the mother may feel the child's movements. This is when body parts begin to form, from the bottom up: first the toes, then the feet, legs, trunk, arms, hands, and fingers. The head and hair develop in the eighth month. For the Lelet, the body parts form successively, as well, though from the top down, beginning with the eyes and the face and followed by the lower body parts (Eves 1998: 26–27).

As with the Giri and the Lelet, the Ankave-Anga perceive a certain formational order: the extremities form earliest and are later joined together as one (Bonnemère 1993: 163; also see Ayers Counts & Counts 1983: 49 for another example of successive body part formation). From some of the ethnographic studies of Papua New Guinea societies, we know about the different roles that male and female procreative substances play in the formation of flesh and blood (see, for instance, Bateson [1936] 1958: 42; Herdt [1981] 1994: 196; Jorgensen 1983: 61; Wagner 1983: 76; also see Kahn 1986: 100 and Wassmann 1987: 531 in which women contribute blood and men give bone; Silverman 2001a: 193 in which bones derive from semen and flesh from maternal blood; and Bamford 2007a: 60–61 in which skin and surface blood vessels form from the mother's fluids and bones, and internal organs from the father's semen).

On the other hand, there are equally numerous examples of Melanesian peoples who do not hold such theories about the becoming of different bodily components (e.g., Eves 1998: 27; Holmes Williamson 1983: 15; Jolly 2001: 181). The Ankave-Anga stand out somewhat as an exception, in that the blood of the fetus is said to stem from the mother alone, whereas the other parts of the fetus are not described as being formed by either exclusively male or female substances (Bonnemère 1993: 164, 2004: 60). Although Giri people do acknowledge the fetus' composition of male and female substances (i.e., blood), they are among those people who do not allocate certain bodily components of the fetus to either male or female substances.

The Giri are rather specific about fetal development. During the phase in which the body parts form, every day, week, and month is designated to the rise of a particular body component. However, if the mother's body gets perturbed in this phase, it may happen that a part of the body fails to develop or becomes misshapen. Hence, illness or disability is attributed to "failures of social nurturance in utero" (Morgan 1996: 57). This is most commonly due to the mother-to-be trespassing onto a bush spirit (masalai) site. I know a fair number of Giri people whose congenital physical ailments and infirmities have been attributed to encounters that their mothers had with bush spirits during pregnancy.

Prominent examples are deformed limbs and deafness. Pregnant women should avoid dangerous bush spirit sites at dawn and dusk—times when bush spirits are said to be active—to prevent dangerous situations. Illegitimate sexual intercourse between the mother-to-be and a man other than the unborn's biological father (or between the biological father and another woman) may also lead to deformities in the child.[18] Furthermore, the mother-to-be's mental imbalance (caused by worries or sadness) in the final phase of pregnancy may cause perpetual listlessness or madness in her infant.

At the end of the eighth month, the fetus is fully developed and referred to as *tar sangi* (*tar* is "child" and *sangi* means "strong," "firm," or "big"). It gains more strength and grows during the last phase of pregnancy. A brief digression to my interlocutor's thoughts on HIV transmission gives more clues on the perceived stages in the unborn child's development. My male and female conversational partners unequivocally stated that if a woman, her sexual partner, or both of them are afflicted with sik eds (HIV/AIDS) at the time a child is conceived, the virus (binatang) will be passed to the child.

If the father-to-be contracts sik eds after the child has been conceived and then has intercourse with the pregnant woman (or if she has intercourse with another infected man), the virus will certainly be transmitted to her. But whether the unborn is affected depends on the developmental stage: an unborn who is "only blood" will become infected, whereas a fetus that has already moved down into the mother's womb and formed its extremities will remain unaffected. This latter condition, pertaining to a late stage of fetal development, is often interchangeably described as "everything is readied" (olgeta samting i redi pinis), "the baby has formed out" (bebi i foam pinis), or "the baby has become a person" (bebi i kamap man pinis).

In utero, the fetus is nourished by the woman's blood (*vizin*), which flows through the umbilical cord (*beh*) from the woman to the unborn. To be more specific, ingested food enriches her blood: "The food that the mother eats passes into the mother's blood and in turn feeds the child." The Anganen of the Lai and Nembi valleys (Southern Highlands Province) have a word for this vital substance: "ip." "Ip" is a generic term for the "fertile substance which is located in the earth and food" (Merrett-Balkos 1998: 235). Aside from its nutritious value, "ip" also carries aspects of identity to the fetus. The mother-to-be ingests food that mainly stems from her husband's clan land. (The Anganen residential pattern is patrivirilocal.) She transforms the "ip" from this food and then passes it via her naval cord to the unborn child. A similar example comes from Hagen, where mothers are noted to impart grease (physical identity), which comes from the food they eat, to their unborn offspring:

> Through her own body the mother imparts a physical identity to her child that is compounded of her pre-existing paternal and maternal blood and of the food she has grown, prepared, and eaten on her husband's ground. The body of her child is made in this way, and so it acquires its kinship identity as a part of the whole cosmic process of fertility and reproduction of which human bodies are seen to be part. (P. Stewart & A. Strathern 2001a: 15)

While the Giri neither explicitly name the substance on which the unborn feeds nor state that it is of particular significance if the mother consumes food that originates from her own or her husband's clan land, they have a similar ideology of intrauterine nourishment and conveyance of physical identity. The umbilical cord is also, for the Giri, the "corporeal embodiment of the relationship between a child and his or her mother" (Merrett-Balkos 1998: 223). It connects woman and child, with the child's life entirely dependent upon it (221).

After delivery, its mother's breast milk (*taphoŋ*) nourishes the Giri newborn. Again, Giri and Anganen ideas align: breastfeeding is envisaged in both cultures as a continuation of the physical nourishment provided throughout gestation and the sharing that began during pregnancy (see Merrett-Balkos 1998: 222; see Kahn 1986: 101 for similar ideas among the matrilineal society of the Wamira of Milne Bay Province). Wet-nursing is rather uncommon in Giri.

When the baby is several months old, a kinswoman is allowed to breastfeed the child if, for example, the mother has gone to her garden and left the child behind. When the baby is only weeks or a couple of months old—still "red skinned" (skin ret) as Giri people would say—a mother should refrain from having her baby breastfed by another woman. This is because if the nursing woman is menstruating, the baby will sicken (throw up or develop diarrhea). Mothers, however, take this risk if they do not produce any or only insufficient amounts of breast milk or are seriously ill. In cases of maternal death, a relative usually wet-nurses the infant.

By refraining from certain foods and indulging in others, the mother ensures that she produces healthy breast milk. During postpartum seclusion, she primarily consumes sago pudding supplemented with large quantities of leafy vegetables—in particular the young leaves of *tiiŋ* (*Gnetum gnemon*) and *zori* (a type of tree similar to *Gnetum gnemon*). Moreover, she is ritually given a dish of gudgeon (*mbəgam pik*) and scrapings of the *phəh* tree. Both fish and tree are said to be bulky in growth, and when the baby imbibes the substances through the mother's milk, it is thought to assume the same quality.

The mother is restricted from eating bloody meat—mainly the meat of wild game such as cassowary, tree wallaby, bandicoot, lizard, crowned pigeon, and wild fowl. Pork is considered particularly bloody, possibly due to its sheer size. Violation of these food taboos causes the mother to show premature signs of aging—often chin or arm wattles. The newborn will possibly also inherit undesired features or traits of the respective animals (cf. Bonnemère 1993: 164 for taboos on eating marsupials during pregnancy to prevent the child from acquiring the animals' habits and traits). These food taboos also apply to the child. If disregarded, the spirit (*thum*) of the consumed animal may cause illness in the child. Most commonly, children will develop fever.

Food taboos for the new mother are complex, though not all women observe them with great strictness today. Tough and heavy foods like sago bread, red yam, and *khum* (sago cooked or reheated in a bamboo tube) as well as starchy roasted comestibles such as plantains, yam, and sweet potato must not be consumed. If the infant absorbs these foods via the mother's milk, its spleen is said to swell. Sago pudding and boiled white yam are good foods to be eaten in seclusion. Red foods (like aibika with red leafstalks, red yam, and red meat) are generally forbidden. This is possibly due to their association with *seva*. Moreover, betel chewing is prohibited until the mother has weaned her baby, as the lime is said to cut the child's intestines. I suggest, again, that the bright red juice produced by the chemical reaction between areca nut and lime resembles *seva* (cf. Silverman 2001b: 145). The mother forestalls the actual ingestion of *seva* (particles of which stick to her hands) by the usage of small bamboo sticks or, nowadays, cutlery.

Fetus and newborn rely on the maternal substance that comes via blood and milk for health and growth in addition to nourishment. The uterus, which protects the child during its early stages, finds its continuation in the netbag. The equation of netbag with womb is not exclusive to Giri but is found in other parts of Papua New Guinea. Merrett-Balkos (1998: 222) touched upon similar ideas among the Anganen. P. Stewart and A. Strathern described the netbag as a "marker of the female womb" (1997: 2) and gave the example of their own research among the Melpa. Furthermore, they referred to a good handful of other writings that stress the lexical link between netbag and womb (3).

MacKenzie pointed out for the Telefolmin,[19] "After a woman has given birth, the baby remains in close contact with the mother, nestled within the airy but secure space, *men am* (inside of the bilum [i.e., netbag], literally bilum house) which hangs constantly from the mother's head, providing the external equivalent of the *man am* (womb, literally child house) from which the infant originated" (1991: 130). In Kire, uterus and netbag are both *thar,* though the uterus may more specifically be called *tar thar* (literally: "child netbag"). The same term *tar thar* is used for "placenta," as in Giri traditional thought the placenta sheathes the unborn.

Netbags are traditionally made from the aerial roots of the pandanus palm or from *Asphodeloideae* fibers. Bags for carrying babies are usually constructed from the softer lepa (*Asphodeloideae* sp.), whereas the stronger karuka (*Pandanus* sp.) is favored for bigger netbags, in which heavy loads of yam, other garden produce, and sago-filled bamboo tubes are carried. The netbag for a baby may be manufactured by the mother. Often, though, the child's mother's mother or his father's mother, or sometimes another female relative, produces the netbag.

P. Stewart and A. Strathern argued that netbags are the "embodiments of the substances and powers" (1997: 5) of their manufacturer. The thread, twirled between the hand and thigh of the manufacturer, is invested with "hair, skin cells, body oils, and body odor" (4). A part of the manufacturer is incorporated into the netbag (5). One could say that the Giri infant who finds comfort in a netbag produced by a maternal or paternal relative other than its mother metaphorically dwells in this other woman's womb. For example, let us return to Rebecca, who presented her daughter-in-law, Jessica, with a netbag for her first child. Rebecca completed the netbag just a couple of days after Jessica gave birth to her son.

Without wasting any time, Rebecca promptly passed the netbag to Jessica. With this action, Rebecca ensured that the infant would further grow in her own "womb." I suggest that Rebecca's action established a strong bond between the newborn and his paternal clan. Rebecca produced a netbag

Illustration 5.4. Woman combing out the fiber from a pandanus aerial root with a knife to make thread (2007).

from traditional fiber. Yet, the less labor-intensive bags made from imported bright plastic string are becoming increasingly popular. These netbags are not imbued with personal substance from the combing of the fiber and twirling of the thread; rather, the producer incorporates herself into the netbag only through its actual fabrication.

The mother usually keeps the netbag with her baby in it under close watch and often by her body. Spirits of the dead (*thum*) can easily steal the baby's shadow soul (*ŋina*) if the baby is left crying. In Giri view, the shadow soul is only loosely attached to the body and may easily be dislodged. Describing corresponding notions for the Daribi, Wagner called childhood "a time of 'weak' soul" (1975: 98). P. Stewart and A. Strathern (1997: 12) expressed the thought that the netbag serves as home for the newborn's spirit in Melpa and Hagen cultures.

The Giri newborn should stay inside the netbag as much as possible. This also applies to the phase that the mother and infant pass in seclusion[20] and for the months following seclusion until the baby eats solid foods. When the mother breastfeeds her baby, she places the baby in the netbag across her lap. Frequent unbagging of the infant disturbs its growth. Ida and her husband adopted her husband's older brother's son, because its biological mother had

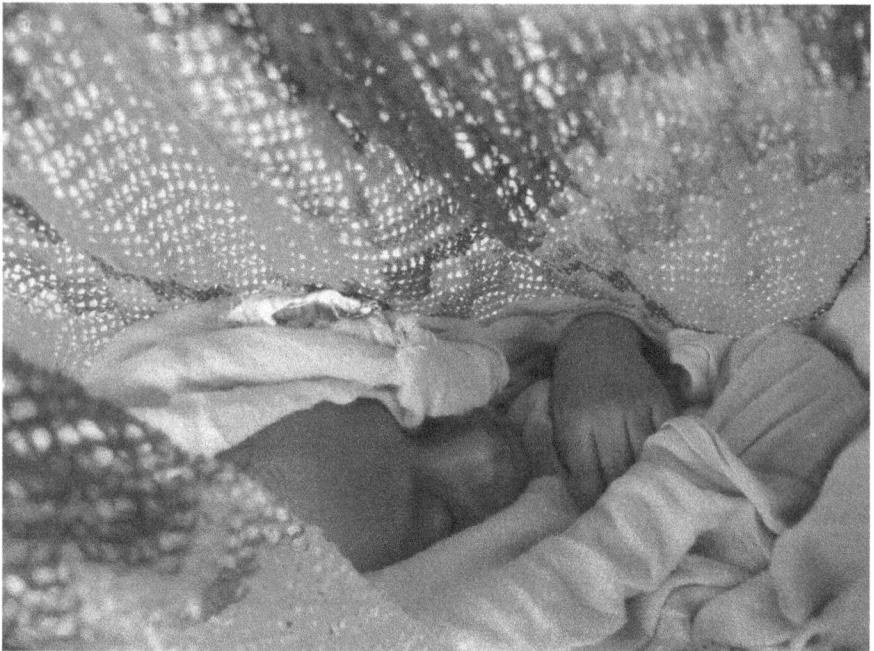

Illustration 5.5: My brother and sister-in-law's five-month-old son Mboruni nestling inside a netbag (2011). Note the cloth between the infant and the netbag protecting the baby's skin from being "eaten" (kaikai) by the rough plastic fabric from which this netbag is made.

died in childbirth. Ida noted that the baby was remarkably thinner than other babies of his age when he was three months old. The day he was delivered, he received an injection at BHC (preventing him from ingesting his deceased mother's *seva,* as Ida said). An abscess had formed at the injection site on his left upper leg. In an attempt to ease his pain, Ida took him out of the netbag and placed him on a pillow for several hours. This, she said, had perturbed his growth.

The association between netbags and notions of sheltering and protecting the baby becomes even more apparent in Giri burial practices. In the past, corpses of adults and children were cremated (see Höltker 1961); eventually, the Giri abandoned this practice due to governmental and missionary pressure.[21] Conversely, babies have always been buried—both in the past and in the present. They are said to be "not fit" to lie on the bare ground in the grave, with their bodies too fragile, weak, and small. Hence, a post is erected in the grave cut, and the corpse is accommodated in a netbag (usually the one that the mother used for the baby before its death), which is hung from the post. It appears that the small corpse is still in need of the protecting "womb." To my knowledge, Giri babies are today still exclusively buried in this way.

Another practice that traditionally makes an important contribution to the child's becoming is *girgirga* (to imitate, to mock). Nowadays, *girgirga* has been largely abandoned, a fact criticized by several village elders, who perceive today's youth to be less thriving than in the past. Right after the umbilical cord has been cut, the new mother's male affines enquire, *A nduiga virap min veergi? A mbi pufirigi thivin ndagi?* (Did she pull on a fishing net [and] go down to the water? Did he carry a spear [and] go onto the shore?) If a girl was born, the woman's female affines will respond, "She went down to the river." If a boy was born, the answer is, "He went onto the shore." These questions refer to two deeply gendered tasks: hunting with a spear and fishing with a netbag-like fishing net slipped over the lower arms. Although some women hunt bandicoots and lizards with dogs, it is only men who hunt with a spear for wild pigs and cassowaries. Giri men traditionally speared fish.

Although this practice has not been abandoned, nowadays Regene men cast fishing nets (imported nets made of synthetic fibers) daily. But fishing with hand-fishing nets remains a genuinely female task. A brief episode illustrates the perceived oddity of men performing this task. I vividly remember a day in 2007's late rainy season when water from the Regene oxbow lake flowed back into the Ramu. Women and girls ran with their bamboo hoop fishing nets (*mva-aŋ*) past my house down to the effluent to catch the fish that the water was pulling back into the Ramu. And then, to my surprise, my brother Konzari and another middle-aged man followed suit just as quickly. Bamboo hoops dangling from their heads, the strange sight did not remain uncommented on. I heard women ironically shouting, "Ah, the women now pull on fishing nets!" The phrase "go onto the shore" possibly also pointed to men's anchorage in the land (with patrilocal residency). Women's "floating away" to their husband's clan land is metaphorically represented by the phrase "go down to the river."

Let me return to the actual practice of *girgirga*. The new mother's birth attendants (often her female affines) will bring the newborn inside the house in which the mother is passing her time in seclusion. If a boy was born (and when this was made known by the phrase "go onto the shore"), a male affinal relative will come to see the child and mimic above the newborn the male everyday tasks with the respective tools. The items he brings are—apart from a spear for killing big game—a sago scraper, a basket for rinsing sago pith, an axe, a machete, a bow and arrow, and a multipronged fishing spear.

For a girl, a female affinal relative will pretend to perform female tasks with the two types of hand-fishing nets—*mva-aŋ* and *nduik*—a large netbag (for carrying heavy loads), a sago stirring stick, a coconut shell for serving sago, a pot, and a plate. *Girgirga* is said to enable the child to mature and swiftly learn the tasks associated with these tools and to prevent the child from injuries during the period of learning. Moreover, the ties between the newborn and its kin are buttressed through this practice. Bamford (1998: 166–67, 2007a: 69) described for the Kamea of Gulf and Morobe provinces a similar practice, through which the gendered productive spheres are inscribed on the newborn's body: a boy's umbilical cord must be cut with cane grass, which is typically used to make men's hunting arrows, whereas a girl's navel cord is severed with a type of bamboo that women use as water containers and cooking vessels. Should a boy's navel cord be cut with bamboo or a girl's with cane grass, they would, in later life, favor the other gender's tasks.[22]

Lastly, I shall mention the child's father's influence on the newborn. Throughout the first months of a child's life (even after the mother has left her enclosure), the father neither enters into direct bodily contact with the child nor otherwise displays affection for the child. In the past, this phase could even last until the child began to walk, as some of my elderly interlocutors explicated. This, however, does not mean that the father's actions do not bear upon the child's becoming. The father must take precautions to not jeopardize the newborn's health. For example, he must dig neither a grave cut nor a pit for a toilet nor any other deep hole. Violation of this taboo may cause respiratory problems and fever in his child.

Moreover, when the father washes sago starch out of the shredded pith (a genuinely male task in Giri), he must carefully disseminate the washed-out pith, or else extreme heat may build up in the mound of pith and cause fever in the child. Höltker (1964: 57–58) wrote about very similar taboos for the baby's father among the Nubia and Awar (see map 2.1). If a Nubia or Awar newborn dies, the father is soon blamed for the death, and he will mull over whether he has violated a taboo (58). According to Höltker (ibid.), these taboos persist for only the firstborn child. In contemporary Giri, these taboos are usually observed for all, not only firstborn, babies.

Relationality 2: Afterbirth

Immediately after birth, the Giri child becomes, as do children in much of Melanesia, more firmly anchored in its web of social relations. Placental planting on Giri land establishes the bond between the child and its ancestors. Anthropologists have described, for many parts of Oceania, the relevance that placental burial has for identity formation, linking the child with his or her birth place (e.g., Binder-Fritz 1995; De Coppet 1985; Merrett-Balkos 1998; Morton 2002; Saura 2002; P. Stewart & A. Strathern 2001b: 92–95).

An especially striking example is De Coppet's (1985) depiction of the planting of the afterbirth among the 'Are'Are of Malaita (Solomon Islands). Like the Giri and other Oceanic peoples, the 'Are'Are perceive a bond between child and afterbirth that transcends the cutting of the umbilical cord. Drawing on De Coppet's description, M. Strathern argued, "The placenta both remains part of the person and, in becoming detached at birth, is treated as another person. Detachment is conceptualized as a separation of (dividual) persons from one another" (1991: 588). The cutting of the navel cord separates baby and placenta after delivery, but it makes neither newborn nor placenta an autonomous entity. In 'Are'Are thought, placental burial enables the exchange of essential aspects of personhood between person and land—an exchange that is crucial for making these elements available again for the human life cycle.

'Are'Are women plant the afterbirth like "a dead taro which has lost its living stem (the new-born baby)" (De Coppet 1985: 86). Taro symbolizes "body," a central aspect of 'Are'Are personhood. Moreover, one may speak of the burial of a pig, as the 'Are'Are call the placenta "the child's pig" (ibid.). It should also be noted that pigs may dig the placenta up and feed on it, as it is only lightly covered over with earth. Pig denotes "breath," a second vital part. Yet the afterbirth is entirely lacking a third element—"image." The newborn "image" is still "tiny and fragile" (ibid.). Persons take on "image" when they die a natural death, that is, when their own ancestors kill them. De Coppet states:

> Nourishing the earth and feeding pigs[23] with someone's afterbirth gives a "body" element back to the taros and a "breath" element back to the pigs. This process not only assures the child's vitality, but also guarantees the necessary return of the two fundamental elements to the sacred species [i.e., taro and pig], which makes them available for the human life cycle. (1985: 87)

For the 'Are'Are, the living person is a composition of precisely those elements that constitute the land and that, again, nourish the edibles that the living person consumes—body and breath. In M. Strathern's words, "For the 'Are'Are person (land) thereby *enters into an exchange* with the land (person)" (1991: 589). The vital elements are in flux; they are exchanged between land and person and thus connect both. The Giri do not possess such differentiated ideas about circulating vital aspects (like the 'Are'Are body and breath), which are present in both newborn and placenta. Yet the 'Are'Are view of newborn and afterbirth as "dividual persons" appears to closely parallel Giri ideas. One Regene mother even compassionately said about her afterbirth, "She or he is a person" (em man).

Although the placenta is physically separated from the newborn at the moment the navel cord is cut, it continues to be vitally important to the Giri child. The child's health and growth depend on the afterbirth's safe positioning under the earth. The child's weight gain and navel healing depend on the afterbirth's uninterrupted continuance in the soil.[24] If the afterbirth is unearthed, the child will languish. Perhaps tearing the afterbirth out of the land symbolizes the uprooting of the child from its identity-generating land. The child sickens because the connection between child and land, and thus the connection between people (the child and its ancestors), is disrupted. Some Giri women place the placenta and umbilical cord in a coconut shell to deter pigs and dogs from digging them up.

The safekeeping of the afterbirth is vital to mother and child for another reason: protection against poison sorcery (*kuk*). As with any other excretable part of the mother's and child's body, egested body substance (*fava ŋan*) adheres to placenta and umbilical cord. Furthermore, *fava ŋan* of the woman is contained in the blood of parturition, which coats the afterbirth. If afterbirth and umbilical cord fall into the hands of someone who is ill-disposed toward the woman or who harbors animosity toward the child's paternal or maternal kin, the matter may be utilized for malevolent magic against the mother and child. The burial of both afterbirth and umbilical cord on clan land (and possibly in proximity to the mother's house so that she can keep an eye on it) is a measure that the mother takes to protect herself and her child. For the same reason, traditional places in cleared but uncultivated lands around the village are considered safer birth places than foreign land. Giving birth on alien land carries the risk of another person stealing bloodstained soil, leaves, or ground plant cover.

Among the Kabana of West New Britain Province and the Hageners, the dual relationship between the child and both the maternal and paternal clans is enforced through the burial of the navel cord (or both navel cord and placenta) together with a plant (Scaletta 1986; P. Stewart & A. Strathern 2001b). Hageners plant a cordyline or a banana tree with both placenta and navel cord. The sapling nourishes on the child's maternal substance and, at the same time, on the paternal soil and fastens maternal substance to paternal land (P. Stewart & A. Strathern 2001b: 92). The Kabana bury exactly that piece of umbilical cord that has been attached longest to the newborn (that is, the dried piece of navel cord that usually falls away in the first couple of weeks after delivery) at the base of a coconut palm, areca palm, banana tree, or the like (Scaletta 1986: 44).

Giri mothers do not immediately inter the umbilical cord stump (*behn thip*) after it has fallen off. Instead, it is wrapped up—today often with medical dressing material—and kept in the baby's netbag. Nombo and Leach (2010: 13) noted that, among the Reite of Madang Province's Rai Coast, the navel cord is tied to the mouth of the baby's netbag. This is in order to mark the netbag as belonging to the baby and to prevent it from being used for other purposes. In Giri, the *behn thip*'s safekeeping ensures that the baby's shadow soul (*ɲina*) remains in the netbag. Mothers continue to safeguard the *behn thip* several years after the child has outgrown the netbag. Most women then tuck the navel cord piece into the sago palm leaf thatched roof of their house. Only when the child is approximately five years old and his or her shadow soul is tightly bound to his body does the mother slip the cord piece between the upper sago palm fronds of an immature sago palm.

Giri women are also familiar with practice of planting a new tree together with maternal substance. Yet this is done for a different purpose: contraception. The location has to be carefully chosen and is ideally in proximity to the woman's house so that she can watch over the placenta and umbilical cord. Among the trees most commonly chosen are sago palms, coconut palms, and mango trees. Often a fence is erected to keep pigs away from the strong-smelling matter. When a shoot becomes visible, the roots are said to have clasped the afterbirth. Although the roots tangibly anchor the placenta in the land, what is emphasized is the roots' fastening of the placenta and—in more figurative terms—the locking of the womb.[25] Giri people sometimes use the phrase "sewing up the womb" (samapim bel) when referring to this procedure. The method is perceived to be a highly effective form of contraception and is impossible to undo once a shoot has sprouted.

It is also available to nonparous women and to women who have not recently given birth; they may plant their used menstrual pads (some women utilize factory-made pads and others use self-made plant fiber ones). New mothers may bury maternity pads soaked with lochia, as well. In Giri, as in much of Melanesia, the placenta is conceptualized as part of the child, rather than the mother. Merrett-Balkos called the placenta the "base-place" (1998) of the Anganen fetus. As its life-giving "base-place," the placenta is regarded as part of the fetus, rather than the mother (225).

Thus, it appears that it is not the placenta itself that needs to be locked by the tree roots but the Giri woman's uterine blood (the maternal substance that coproduces children together with male blood), which is present in and adherent to the placenta and comes in highly concentrated form as menstrual blood or lochia. Another prominent method for locking womb blood is the burial of soaked menstrual or maternity pads in the reeds on the bank of the Ramu River. This is done only during the dry season, when river levels are low. The woman picks an area that is likely to be flooded during the rainy season so that silt will then cover up the pads. The hole she digs for planting the pads needs to be deep to prevent the pads from being washed away.

These two methods are still highly prominent in Giri. In Regene, at least four elderly women possessed special knowledge in the field of traditional contraception. Furthermore, their popularity may be explained by the absence of any equivalent biomedical permanent contraceptive method. Whereas traditional practices are painless for the woman, the only permanent method that biomedicine offers to women—tubal ligation—involves surgery. Women who undergo this procedure are severely impaired for months, or even years. When recovering from the surgery, they must not carry heavy loads or perform other physically arduous tasks. This poses a major problem for Giri women, and Sandra rhetorically asked, "Who is gonna do my job?" This is why Sandra repeatedly decided to employ traditional methods of locking her womb.

In 1999, after she had given birth to her third child, Sandra decided to stop conception. She buried her used cloth maternity pads beside her house. As she had not erected a fence, the pads were dug out by an animal—presumably a dog. Hence, the method lost its potency and she conceived again, delivering her fourth child in 2003. Sandra made a second attempt to stop further conception and asked the old woman Teresa for help. Teresa and her daughter planted Sandra's maternity pads on the Ramu riverbank in the reeds. Despite this, Sandra became pregnant again and her fifth child was born in 2009.

Other women surmised that the pads must have become loose and suggested that Sandra carefully wrap the maternity pads in plastic bags. Throughout her time in seclusion, Sandra collected her maternity pads and wrapped them as recommended. After leaving seclusion, she went to the swamps and dug a hole in which she planted her pads and a sago seedling on top. At the time of our last conversation, Sandra had not become pregnant again, but her husband had been imprisoned for fourteen months and had only just returned to Regene village four months prior to our last encounter; this would have allowed a short period for possible conception with her husband.

Afterbirth Planting Today and New Ways of Afterbirth Disposal

The afterbirth is charged with ambivalence. On the one hand, it causes the child to grow and is central to its identity formation; on the other, ideas and practices surrounding *seva* extend to it. It is the materialization of the woman's nourishing blood, *vizin* (cf. Bonnemère 1993: 163), but it also becomes, after the cutting of the umbilical cord, associated with parturitional blood and lochia and is thus potentially dangerous to others (cf. Merrett-Balkos 1998: 225; Saura 2002: 136–37). Hence, placental planting aims at a twofold purpose: alongside the anchorage of the child in ancestral land, it further serves to dispose of the placenta so that other people will be prevented from coming into contact with the *seva*.

The majority of Giri women still carry out today the kastom of planting the placenta. But it has undergone changes, primarily concerning burial place. As we will see, afterbirths are now also planted at the back of the health center or on hospital grounds. Moreover, new ways of dealing with the afterbirth have been introduced at the medical institutions to which Giri women resort.

These methods range from incineration to disposal in hospital waste pits and pit toilets. In this section, I discuss Giri women's employment of these old and new modi operandi, focusing on women's changing roles in placental disposal.

Once more, I should like to resort to the 2010 survey that I conducted among twenty-eight women and to the ways in which placentas were disposed in relation to the location in which the birth occurred. Among the most notable points is that all of the women who had village births—be they in Giri or outside—planted their afterbirths in and around the village (either near the mother's residential house, in cleared but uncultivated bushland, or in uncleared bushland). Women who gave birth outside of Giri villages planted their placentas on this foreign land. None of the women who delivered at biomedical facilities took their placenta home to plant it in proximity to their residential house. Instead, placentas were either buried close to the medical institution, disposed of in the facility's pit toilets and waste pits, or destroyed through incineration. Further, it appears that the whereabouts of a large number of placentas among women who delivered at MGH are unknown.

When women were asked about the place of placental burial after village births, they often offered one of two rationales for the choice they had made. It was either stressed that the chosen location was close to the residential house, which allowed the women to watch over their placenta, or, contrastingly, it was emphasized that the placenta was planted, although on Giri land, at an ample distance to inhabited village grounds, so as not to jeopardize others' health through the *seva*. The rationales women provided for the choice of placental burial place following BHC deliveries were based on similar considerations relating to providing a safe spot, ensuring that others were not affected by the *seva* and guarding the placenta from being excavated. Allow me to illustrate this with a few examples.

Polly bore all three of her children not far from her parents' house. (Polly resided with her parents because she was unmarried.) She selected spots equally close to the house, where her mother planted her placentas and navel cords. Polly explained for one of her afterbirths, "She [i.e., her mother] planted him next to the house; but it was not in the bush because he is a person." That the afterbirth—as part of her son—was buried within everyday living space where interpersonal encounters occurred and where Polly could keep an eye on the afterbirth while carrying out various everyday activities was of great concern to her.

To deliver in uncultivated lands and bury the afterbirth out of sight would harbor dangers, as untended lands are where sorcerers roam. The thought of throwing the afterbirth in a pit toilet seemed absolutely inhuman to Polly, although this would have ensured that sorcerers could not get hold of it. Another important point that emerges from this example is the fact that the birthing woman not necessarily plants the afterbirth. Trustworthy female relatives, often those who have assisted the woman in birth, may take on this task (also see discussion further below).

Rita's logic was somewhat different from that of Polly. Taking her first two deliveries into consideration, it would appear reasonable to argue that, like Polly, Rita gave prime importance to the spatial closeness of her afterbirths. After delivering her first child on the pathway to the health center, she brought her placenta back home and planted it beside her marital house. After bearing her second child in bushland, she carried her placenta back to the village and buried it underneath her dwelling house. But then it came as a surprise to me to find that, following her third delivery, which was at Paternoster Memorial Hospital, Rita left her afterbirth with a related nurse, who disposed of it in the waste pit. Rita explained to me that it was most crucial for her to ensure that the placenta was in a safe location, inaccessible to others. According to her reasoning, this could be at her house under her watch but also in the hospital waste pit.

Alicia was among the women who considered it important to leave a certain distance between inhabited village space and the burial place of the afterbirth. She was caught off guard by strong contractions and barely managed to take herself to the dense patches of sword grass (kunai; *Imperata cylindrica*) around her house, where she delivered her daughter. Her mother-in-law reckoned that the actual place of birthing was too close to the residential area, and Alicia thus planted the afterbirth deeper in uncleared lands, "leaving a fair distance to the house," as Alicia said.

Eva bore her fourth child at BHC. She interred her afterbirth in a hole that her sister-in-law had excavated behind the health center. She buried the placenta, the navel cord, and the disposable blood-spattered medical materials (gauze, tubes, etc.) the health worker had used during or after the birthing process on Eva and her infant. The spot was off the pathways that patients and carers followed to and from the health center and were frequented by other villagers heading to their gardens, the Ramu, the primary school, and other places. Her sister-in-law specified two reasons for choosing that location off the beaten track: (1) to reduce the likelihood that another would come into contact with Eva's *seva* and have her or his health negatively affected, and (2) to prevent a sorcerer from easily stumbling upon the afterbirth.

We learn from the above examples that, although the afterbirth is ideally planted on paternal clan land, in practice, it may be planted or disposed of on other land. From Polly's case, we know that a factor contributing to this is the place of residency. In principle, the pattern of Giri residence is patrivirilocal, and traditional burial places are located on the paternal clan land of the newborn. But, in practice, one often comes across alternative residential patterns. This affects women's choices of burial sites.

Considering that the afterbirth is *seva,* most women were reluctant to carry it around much. Rita's firstborn daughter, Gloria, delivered her first baby in January 2011. Gloria had the afterbirth planted by Rita and her father's younger sister in the swamps on her father's clan land. The child's biological father resided in his home village in the Dreikikir area of East Sepik Province. When I asked Gloria if she had considered burying the child's afterbirth on the child's paternal clan land, Rita burst out laughing and ironically asked me if I would consider taking my afterbirth home on a plane to Germany. She made an important point: women are also pragmatists (here certainly more so than the anthropologist) who handle the afterbirth as seems most appropriate in the individual situation. In this light, it appears that planting the placenta on Giri land at the back of the health center, be it clan land of the newborn's kin or not, was no great departure from contemporary women's pragmatic proceedings with placentas delivered in the village.

In her writing of the Anganen, Merrett-Balkos (1998: 220) emphasized that women had already abandoned placental planting (and birthing in traditional mothers' houses) at the time she undertook research in the late 1980s. As I identified in my survey, for Giri, placental planting is still a very common practice of placental disposal, with 77 percent of the 105 mothers' placentas planted. Now we have seen that placental burial may occur on maternal clan land or other Giri land, there remains the question of the actors involved in the burial process. It actually appears that, in the village, only fourteen afterbirths were planted by the new mother herself, whereas forty-three afterbirths were buried by relatives. The involved female relatives were mostly close kin and members of the group of women who assisted the mother in childbirth. They were the woman's kinswomen but also often female affinal kin. No preference for kin of either side was expressed.

From what Giri women said, I surmise that it was less common for kinswomen to take care of placentas in the past. This matches women's statement that, traditionally, births were less likely to be attended. (These days, some, especially elderly women, are still reluctant to assist anyone other than close female kin in birthing and placental burial, because they fear the women's *seva,* although women are said to be generally less severely affected by it than men.) Despite the perceived health risks, women are often ready to assist their near relatives. My interviewees mostly explained this willingness with feelings of compassion and concern (wari) for the birthing woman. Alicia, for instance, delivered her first infant in the intact caul. Her attending female relatives (including an experienced local village birth attendant) ran away in horror at the sight because they had never before seen a baby delivered in an unbroken amniotic membrane. Alicia's mother was as shocked as the other women were, yet she assisted her daughter in her distress.

Although Alicia's example tells us differently, village birth attendants are often more nonchalant about the effects of *seva* and see the aid they provide from a biomedical perspective. Not surprisingly, in more than a third of the cases surveyed, the female relative who took charge of the placenta was a village birth attendant. If more distant female relatives (not biomedically trained) were involved, this was mostly because they were neighbors or happened to be around at the time of birthing.

Eva unexpectedly went into labor with her third child while picking cocoa pods. Shortly after, she gave birth in adjacent bushlands. Ashley, to whom she was only distantly related but who was her neighbor and close friend, assisted Eva readily and also planted Eva's placenta. After only one of the village births, a woman who did not stand in any kinship relation to the birthing mother planted the placenta. This was because, at the time she gave birth, Paula lived with her husband in a village at the Keram, a river that flows into the Sepik River, where he attended Bible training. Paula bore her sixth child in a classroom assisted by the principal's wife. Subsequently, the principal's wife buried the placenta beside her own house.

Almost two thirds of the placentas delivered at BHC were also planted. The situation at BHC was different from that of village births, in that female Giri and non-Giri health workers were involved in placental burial in equally high numbers, as were female relatives. Not uncommonly, health workers and relatives cooperated in this task. Only one woman planted her afterbirth all by herself. Sarah was accompanied to the health center by her father's brother's wife. Sarah knew of her companion's fear of *seva* and swiftly buried the afterbirth to take the burden of handling the dangerous matter off her relative's shoulders.

BHC staff disposed of the remaining placentas in various ways. Similarly, MGH health workers engaged in a range of placental disposing methods. Women would leave their placentas to the health workers, who would discard them in disused pit toilets, rubbish pits, the hospital's incinerator, or whatever they thought proper. Sarah said, about the afterbirth she expelled after her first delivery at MGH, "It's the nurses' business"; and about her afterbirths delivered at BHC: "I don't know. [Name of Giri nurse deleted] must have taken care of it." Vanessa, who delivered seven of her eight children at MGH, asserted, "I can't know. The female nurses took [them]." Other women anticipated what must have happened to their afterbirths. Statements like the following were typical: "They disposed of it in . . . I don't know . . . the toilet, I suppose"; "They wrapped it up, and they must have thrown [it] in the Ramu or planted [it]. I don't know"; "The female nurse, who is my friend, put it in a bucket and carried it away. She put it in a plastic bag and threw it into the sea, I suppose."

At first glance, it may seem odd that women relinquished the responsibility of disposing of their afterbirths to health workers, some of whom were strangers. What motivated Giri women to leave their afterbirths to foreign medical personnel and let them manage the disposal? The women who had their births at MGH, in particular, appear to have been barely inclined to learn the whereabouts of their afterbirths. Most of them were outright uninformed about what had happened to their afterbirths. As I discussed above, women who reside in town generally adjourn to MGH for birthing, because townhouses only rarely provide secure spaces where they can properly handle their *seva*. MGH's ways of handling the afterbirth are aimed at destroying the placenta as septic organic waste. In recent years, placentas were incinerated.[26]

This was the case until about three years ago, when the incinerator broke down. Since then, women have been asked to take their placentas home. The placenta is wrapped in one or two plastic dispensing bags and passed to the new mother. However, women who refuse to take the placenta may leave it for disposal in an organic waste pit. Giri women generally prefer placental disposal to the uncertainty of its burial in another's front or backyard in Madang Town. Yards do not make appropriate burial places due to numerous passersby and a high chance of enemies getting hold of the placenta. A woman's decision to leave the afterbirth with a nurse for destruction may secure her own and her baby's well-being. Women leaving their placenta to BHC personnel for destruction also highlighted this benefit. The health risk that women perceived for the child and themselves was lower when the placenta was "destroyed" at the hospital than when it was found by others.

Although MGH personnel generally use hygienic regulations to explain the necessity of disposing of the afterbirth, Giri women's familiarity with the management of the placenta as a dangerous substance makes the health workers' actions intelligible to them. However, it appears that the placenta becomes plainly negatively loaded in the biomedical contexts of BHC and MGH: as septic substance. The growth-promoting benefit and identity-forming aspect that customary placental burial had for the child disappears when the afterbirth is tossed away or incinerated.

I did not hear of any woman who had given her placenta away to health workers for disposal later deploring the health workers' way of dealing with the placenta. That women entrusted their afterbirth to health personnel may, to some degree, have its roots in history. In the early years of medical missionary work in Tung, villagers certainly wondered about what the mission nurses did with the afterbirths. They suspected that the women's umbilical cords must have helped the missionaries gain access to refrigerators, tables, chairs, bedsheets, blankets, and so forth. The navel cord as a road through which nutritious substance flows to the unborn could possibly have been the means to make cargo flow to the missionaries from their gods—a secret that Tung villagers hoped to discover.

The nurses liked to decorate their houses with flowers, a phenomenon that Tung villagers closely observed and that made them suspect that the nurses kept the umbilical cords in their vases. Soon, the missionaries found Tung visitors lifting the flowers from the vases to catch a glimpse of what it was that the flowers covered (Beresford, pers. comm. 2009). That the vases were empty, apart from a few inches of water, perhaps averted a protest such as that at the Anganen Aid Post that Merrett-Balkos (1998: 213–14, 232–33) reported. In the 1970s, conflict arose between Anganen women and missionary sisters due to mission staff withholding the women's placentas, and several hundred women reclaimed their placentas from the mission sisters. In further distinction to the situation at the Anganen Aid Post, it had also been up to the women to decide about the disposal of their placenta. Since the early years of missionary medical work, the Churches of Christ mission's medical staff permitted women to take their afterbirths home.

Having written about the new mothers, their female kin, and female health workers handling placentas, I shall mention that placental planting has remained in the female domain—though one exception needs mentioning. Melinda, who, in contradistinction to my other interlocutors, did not proceed into seclusion after a delivery at Paternoster Memorial Hospital (see above), had three of her five placentas planted by her husband near Paternoster Memorial Hospital and BHC. Her husband is the glaring exception here, and I never heard of any other Giri man considering coming close to his wife's placenta. We need to keep in mind, though, that Melinda's husband was, as his father was, intrigued by biomedicine. He volunteered at BHC and his view on birthing was filtered through a biomedical lens.

Synopsis

I have described biomedicine's impact on two practices surrounding childbirth: postpartum seclusion and placental burial. In Giri, the arrival of biomedicine further diversified the variety of beliefs, attitudes, and practices relating to these. However, to a large extent, women have preserved both seclusion and placental burial as separate female spheres, which they share nowadays with female health workers. Giri women have accepted the services offered at medical facilities, so these services have become helpful in fulfilling traditional birthing requirements (e.g., to protect the baby and other kin from the mother's *seva*).

Indigenous ideas regarding bodily fluids (particularly the power of *seva*), bodily growth (particularly that of the unborn/newborn), and the maintenance of health (of mother, child, and others) have informed women's responses to the pharmaceuticals that they receive throughout pregnancy, birth, and the postpartum period. Women have created spaces in which they can draw on biomedical reproductive care without having to counterpose traditional practices connected to birthing. On the other hand, biomedical notions of hygiene have altered Giri women's thoughts about bodily substances and led to a devaluation of the afterbirth.

At several points in this chapter we came up against blatant instances of the medicalization of pregnancy and birth: women are advised to take iron folate tablets, oral contraceptives to induce lactation, and so forth. There are also more obvious examples of the infringement on women's autonomous control of their bodies in procreation: women are manually examined (sometimes even by male health workers), forced to give birth in a supine (on the back) position, reprimanded by health personnel, and threatened into attending prenatal clinics and giving birth at biomedical institutions.

But, in line with recent accounts of women's roles in Papua New Guinea societies (e.g., Jolly 2005; Knauft 2004; Lepani 2008; Rumsey 2000; Wardlow 2004, 2006; Zimmer-Tamakoshi 2012), I have focused more on exploring whether and how women have been able to exert agency in reproductive health rather than portraying them as victims of modernity. It appears that biomedicine has offered women new ways to consolidate their autonomy. The intake of biomedication and stays in the maternity ward have given women scope for action in determining postpartum seclusion patterns.

In sum, it is impressive that Giri women have created gateways to the new forms of reproductive medicine for themselves, making these services accessible without sacrificing much personal power in birthing. Mostly, Giri women do not appear to perceive biomedical notions and practice as contradictory to their own; rather, they integrate both—they make the best use of the different practices available to them. Still, Giri women are aware of areas of conflict between their own and biomedical thought and practice, which sometimes makes it difficult for them to resort to biomedicine. This particularly applies to the actual process of birthing (which was only briefly referred to in this chapter). During village births, Giri women make sure that the infant does not pass underneath their lower body, as, according to indigenous thought, the mother's *seva* will trickle down on the newborn and make it ill.

Giri women perceive the supine birthing position as disadvantageous for accomplishing this goal. They criticize the fact that health workers do not pay attention to this important kastom and do not properly coach women through the birthing process. But, as Sandra accentuated, "Our birthing kastom is powerful." Rita described the tension between obstetric and traditional practice:

> It [i.e., the infant] must not go to the back and they cut . . . its navel. It must go forward. It must only go forward [and] they cut its navel. If they pull it to the

back, cut [it], it will sicken. [At] the hospital they comply with the teachings of the doctors, medicine. Therefore they work arbitrarily. Uh-huh. The local kastom is alright. Uh-huh.

Indeed, it is surprising how little effort the medical authorities have made to offer culturally sensitive reproductive health services and how much interpretative skill has been demanded from Giri women. To begin with a simple proposition, the most urgent priority that Giri women have articulated for BHC is the construction of separate labor and gynecological wards. The conclusion of this book provides further suggestions on how health care services can be tailored to local needs.

Notes

1. Other Papua New Guinea cultural groups—for instance the Kwoma, a Sepik people—cherish dark (but also shiny) skin (Holmes Williamson 2007: 202).
2. Telban even went so far as to say that "not only Cartesian dualism of Western philosophical tradition but the concepts of 'mind' and 'body' themselves are Western inventions" (1998: 65), suggesting that the Ambonwari of East Sepik Province do not have a "concept of 'body' as such" (1998: 65) but rather place emphasis on being.
3. Other examples of notions of bodily lightness in Melanesian cultures are provided by Munn (1986: chap. 4) and Roscoe (2001: 291).
4. Ego has a joking relationship with him, which is more sensitive and less exceedingly disrespectful than that of the first, second, third, and fourth mother's cousins.
5. Traditional practices of bloodletting find their continuation in blood donation, which is interpreted, along the same lines, as a strategy to cleanse one's blood (see Street 2009: 203 for blood donation at MGH).
6. See Schneider (2011: 267) for a similar distinction among the Gawigl.
7. The passage through the woman's legs also symbolizes rebirth to a new state. This behavior becomes more explicit when we study male initiation (*monigafoi*), wherein, prior to penile incision, the boys dive not through the legs of any women but through their biological mothers' legs. The direction is strictly defined from back to front, so that the head of the initiate emerges first in front of his mother. Likewise, the position of the baby in actual childbirth is crucial, such that the infant appears in front of its mother and not by passing underneath her and emerging at her back.
8. Giri marital residency is patrivirilocal, but Jessica came from a politically powerful Giri 2 family who had tried to obviate Jessica's move away from the village, so her own and her husband's kin were still negotiating at that time about the residency of the newly married couple.
9. This could further explain why Regene women often stay in small, ground-level buildings during seclusion, and not in regular stilt houses. Among the Kabana of West New Britain Province, women prefer to give birth on the ground so as not to endanger those who pass under the house (Scaletta 1986: 38).
10. Van der Geest and others have produced a substantial body of literature on pharmaceuticals as rendered through local paradigms (e.g., Etkin 1992; Gartin et al. 2010;

Haak & Hardon 1988; Jenkins 2010; van der Geest & Whyte 1989; van Staa & Hardon 1996).
11. In the statistical analyses of this chapter, births at the former Paternoster Memorial Hospital are included with those at BHC. As outlined in chapter 2, the facilities of the Paternoster Memorial Hospital were those of a well-equipped health center, but certain technologies, such as X-ray machines, were not present, and the facility was not permanently staffed with a medical doctor.
12. Whether a woman is identified as a "high-risk mother" depends on her obstetric history. She is considered such if one or more of the following conditions apply: she has had a miscarriage; she has been in labor for more than twenty-four hours; she has had a vacuum extraction; she has had a stillbirth or a baby that died within seven days of birth; she has had a cesarean section, a symphysiotomy, or forceps delivery; she has had a retained placenta; she has suffered from postpartum hemorrhage; she has tried for more than five years to conceive; she has had multiple pregnancies or breech deliveries. Other risk factors are if the woman is in her first pregnancy or if she has had more than four pregnancies; if the woman is aged under eighteen or over thirty-five; and if her last child is younger than three years of age. At prenatal clinics, health workers are meant to advise high-risk mothers to deliver at a hospital.
13. Women were said to have stayed up to six months in seclusion in the past, a length of time not met by any of my interlocutors. Some cultural experts informed me that the mother was not meant to leave seclusion until her baby was able to turn itself around.
14. We must be cautious, as Bamford wrote, not to make overhasty equations with "Western ideas concerning the inheritance of biogenetic substance" (2007a: 61). Bamford demonstrated, thereby providing an innovative look at social kinship, that, although the Kamea (Gulf and Morobe provinces) child is made with the contribution of both parents' substances, sociality is disjointed from the body and its ability to procreate (Bamford 2007a: 56). For the Kamea, the mother-child bond is conceived through "an image of 'containment' (i.e., being enclosed within a particular womb)" (Bamford 2007a: 58). This image finds its manifestation in what Bamford called the "one-blood relationship" (2007a: 60–63, passim): a child is one-blood with its siblings, who have been nurtured in the same woman's womb. This is irrespective of who the father is. Hence, two children born to the same woman are one-blood with one another, whereas two children with the same father but different mothers are not. Also, a mother is not one-blood with her children but, instead, with her own siblings, with whom she has "originated from the same maternal container" (Bamford 2007a: 61).
15. Like others, Bamford (2007a: 60), Eves (1998: 27), Herdt ([1981] 1994: 195), and Jolly (2001: 181) have reported the necessity of repeated sexual acts for conception among Melanesian societies. The Ankave-Anga see a single act of sexual intercourse as sufficient to induce pregnancy (Bonnemère 1993: 163). The Giri share this belief with the Ankave-Anga.
16. *Rer*—a term that was used in the past exclusively in reference to animals' eggs—has been transposed into local conception theory.
17. Not surprisingly, Giri women generally start to visit prenatal clinics when they are in their fourth or fifth month of pregnancy, when they feel their baby's movements, and when they believe that a child grows in their womb. Giri women do not see the point of having their abdomen palpated if the child is still "in the breasts." This is

despite continuous efforts of the BHC health workers to persuade women to come in as soon as they note that they have stopped menstruating. Marshall (1985: 347) and her female assistant asked a sample of forty-eight women at Port Moresby General Hospital in 1981 for reasons for the timing of their first prenatal visit. Two of the interviewees stated that a blood clot had turned into a baby at the time of their first visit, which was in the fourth month of pregnancy.

18. Among the Gawigl, women are expected to completely suspend sexual intercourse when the unborn begins to move. Failure to observe this prohibition may cause deformations or disabilities in the child (Schneider 2011: 265, n. 18).
19. Also see Mimica (2008: 171) for the Anganen.
20. Not all mothers place their babies in netbags throughout seclusion because the very same netbag may not be utilized outside the enclosure, as I outlined above.
21. The practice was abolished in all Giri villages between the mid- to late 1970s. In Regene, the last cremation took place in either 1978 or in 1979. After corporeal death, the spirits of the cremated were said to travel to the coastal village Awar. The spirits would then sit down on a knoll and lament their own family, garden, and so forth. They would be visible to the Awar people as shooting stars. After a few seconds of rest, they would proceed to Kamdoŋ, an elevation where they would dive into the sea and take a bath. They would then journey to Manam Island, where they would linger and be visible as stars. Giri people see mainly disadvantages in inhumation. The corpse's ashes cannot be searched to ascertain whether a person has died from assault sorcery. (If the spleen does not burn up, one may assume death from sorcery.) Moreover, two Giri 1 village elders emphasized how emotional relief had been brought on by cremation—unlike inhumation: "To cremate a person is good because we can forget [the deceased]. Today, the body remains at the graveyard and we [continue to] mourn. In the past, we used to cry once [i.e., during the death wake until the corpse had been cremated] and then forgot him or her." Also see Bamford's (2007a: 131–34) discussion on the meaningfulness of the traditional smoking of corpses for the Kamea. Like the situation in Giri, this practice was abolished under missionary influence.
22. Further, see Mimica (2008), who provided an ethnographic exploration of a transgendered person, the disappearance of whose umbilicus (metaphoric for his penis) foreboded his womanliness. The umbilical cord went missing shortly after birth, instead of being disposed of by the infant's mother in the forest (Mimica 2008: 169–71).
23. The 'Are'Are allow—or even embrace—the consumption of the afterbirth by pigs to make breath available again to the 'Are'Are human life cycle. This is in contrast to Giri practice, in which the placenta is buried in such a way that it is unlikely to be dug up. This is in order to secure the bond between the Giri newborn and the land.
24. Schneider (2011: 279, n. 52) argued, for the Gawigl, that careless discarding of the afterbirth is tantamount to a refusal of the child, as the mother thereby compromises the child's life.
25. The Tok Pisin term *pasim bel*, which stands for any method of stopping conception, including female sterilization, literally translates as "to fasten the belly."
26. In the early to mid-1990s, placentas from first-time mothers were sent to the Papua New Guinea Institute of Medical Research for research purposes, as a Giri health worker who was employed at the hospital at that time remembered.

Conclusion

I set out to study biomedicine in its local entanglements. The aim of this book was to explore how Giri people reinterpret—and construct through their reinterpretations—biomedicine against the backdrop of local conceptualizations of the person in health and illness or, put another way, to analyze Giri people's responses to biomedicine using Giri—and more broadly Melanesian—conceptions of personhood as analytical tools.

A central intention motivating this work was to push forward biomedicine as an anthropological subject. Anthropologists have only recently begun to research biomedical settings in Papua New Guinea. With this monograph, which conjoins the ethnographic data of two biomedical settings with detailed case study material about an ethnographically underrepresented area of Papua New Guinea, I seek to advance the relatively scant existing literature on the forms that biomedicine takes in Papua New Guinea.

I opened this book with a presentation of anthropological engagements with biomedicine. The notion that biomedicine is a sociocultural system and, hence, practiced and consumed differently under diverse social and cultural conditions informed my study (see, e.g., Gaines & Davis-Floyd 2004; Gaines & Hahn 1982; Hahn & Kleinman 1983; Lock & Gordon 1988: 15). Today, biomedical knowledge, technologies, and treatments constitute a substantial portion of the local Giri medical system. When writing about biomedicine, it is impossible to separate it from other aspects of the plural Giri medical system, with which biomedicine is tightly intertwined. In Giri, biomedical knowledge and practice are closely tied to indigenous medical tradition (and also to Christian religious and shamanic healing practices), and these two medical systems mutually impact one another.

Biomedicine interacts and hybridizes with indigenous medical tradition in multiple ways. In Giri, patients simultaneously use and blend elements from different medical traditions; biomedical technologies, such as the X-ray, or pharmaceuticals, such as iron folate tablets, are appropriated to fit into local ways of thinking and reasoning about health and illness. Rita took biomedical drugs as well as local herbal remedies, and, for diagnosis, she depended on shamans (glasman) as well as biomedical practitioners. This multiplicity generates diversification within biomedicine; biomedicine itself is plural, shaped by the beliefs and inventive responses of the members of the cultures in which it is practiced. Therapy managing groups often play a central role in choices of diagnostic and therapeutic options.

Whereas Western biomedicine is rooted in a Cartesian ontology and has eclipsed the mind of clinical theory, entailing "a failure to conceptualize a 'mindful' causation of somatic states" (Scheper-Hughes & Lock 1987: 9), Giri people do not entertain the idea of a dualistic separation of mind and body. Instead, they acknowledge the mindful causation of bodily states (Scheper-Hughes & Lock 1987). I delved deeper into a discussion of Giri ideas of the body. Two aspects of the body—skin and blood—were portrayed as irreducible to the merely physical; instead, they were shown to be interwoven with other dimensions of the Giri person. Moreover, and very significantly, social relations affect individual bodies and the ways in which individuals experience their bodies in health and illness.

The Giri believe "that unbalanced or otherwise unsettled social relations can make them sick. Social discord (which we would see as external) leads to imbalance, or illness, in the body" (Lindstrom 1999: 197). To substantiate this point, I devoted a significant portion of the introduction to an outline of landmark theories of personhood and sociality in Melanesia that theorize Melanesian persons as predominantly constituted through their relations (see, in particular, M. Strathern 1988; Wagner 1991) as "nodes in a matrix of social relations" (Foster 1995a: 19).

My view that Giri people actively shape the biomedical realities in which they live is strongly informed by a dynamic view of culture as lived through practice in everyday life (see Ingold 1993, 1994, 1996; Wagner 1975). The thought that Giri people are anything but passive recipients of biomedicine was furthered in chapters 3 to 5, in which I portrayed Giri people as active and creative agents in dealing with biomedicine. I investigated the ways in which Giri people make the X-ray and other Western biomedical (and nonmedical) technologies available to themselves by recontextualizing them according to indigenous knowledge of the body, health, and illness.

Furthermore, I dealt with women's encounters with biomedical reproductive health services and their ingenious strategies for making these services suitable for their own culture. For example, I showed that pharmaceuticals that women receive throughout pregnancy, birth, and the postpartum period are interpreted to quicken the ejection of blood of parturition and postpartum discharge (*seva*). I highlighted the active roles that Giri receptors of biomedicine play in the process of cultural transformation. Moreover, we learned how biomedicine is embraced in a changing world in which Giri women are no longer able to sustain traditional practices surrounding birth (i.e., postpartum seclusion and placental burial) in exactly the same ways as in the past and in which novel sicknesses (tuberculosis) and novel illness-causing agents (marijuana) impinge upon health.

A central thread that has run through the chapters is the argument that Giri people are enmeshed in their social relations. I argued that the Giri person is essentially relational, only able to become through engagement with others (cf. Keck & Wassmann 2010: 192). In illness, health, and healing, the individual body is linked to the social body (Scheper-Hughes & Lock 1987: 7, 20). The body is "a microcosm of the universe" (Scheper-Hughes & Lock 1987: 21) amenable to the feelings, wishes, and actions of other humans (alive or dead) and nonhuman beings. We learned how conflict or violation of social bans, norms, and taboos may cause illnesses. Likewise, the course of an illness may be impacted, beneficially or adversely, by others. Patients suffering from illnesses grounded in disrupted social relations (*gun rimrim*) can only recover if the social body is healed.

Sufferers were revealed to be highly social agents who draw on extensive webs of relatives and wantok during episodes of illness. Moreover, Giri patients, their caring relatives, and health center/hospital personnel constitute themselves relationally through their interactions. Of particular importance is the giving and sharing of food, which offers a significant opportunity for the actualization of social relationships; in Schieffelin's words: "The giving and sharing of food does not merely express a social relationship; it validates and develops it. Kinship connections may be viewed as avenues of potential personal relationships—always open, perhaps, but not necessarily actualized. It is through giving and sharing food that the relationship becomes socially real" (1976: 63).

Consumption of food that others have grown and prepared produces the patient's body by adding substance to it in two respects: first, and most basically, the nutritional value of the food strengthens the patient's body; second, personal aspects of the food producer augment the food and thereby build up the receiver's body. I corroborated the idea that the Giri person's body "grow[s] transactionally" (LiPuma 1998: 58). Placing particular emphasis on the unborn and newborn, I demonstrated how the child becomes through maternal substance (which is said to flow through the umbilical cord from woman to unborn and comes, after delivery, through breast milk) and thrives in the protecting womb and the netbag—its continuation.

Placental planting and safekeeping of the umbilical cord stump are further practices that ensure the child's prosperity. Other actions of the child's relatives that impact the child's well-being and flourishing are *girgirga* (i.e., mimicry of gendered tasks above the newborn), the mother's observance of food taboos, and the father's avoidance of prohibited actions, such as digging a hole or heaping up washed-out sago pith.

It is largely through this predominantly relational, "dividual" (M. Strathern 1988), or "fractal" (Wagner 1991) lens of the person that Giri people view biomedicine. Biomedical institutions and the services they offer have taken new forms, as Giri people have imbued them with their "social thinking" (Robbins 2006: 172). A relational understanding of personhood informs their decisions to draw on or dismiss certain biomedical services. I showed a biomedical technology (the X-ray), a Western entertainment technology (the television), a U.S. parlor game (Ouija board), and an Australian-introduced drug (marijuana) to all be invested with social meaning: the X-ray is imbued with the capacity to relay information on the disruption of the social body; the spirit (Ouija) board and television screen unexpectedly enable contact with the ancestors; the television screen is a medical diagnostic tool; and marijuana is not simply viewed as an object but is said to have a spirit similar to that of a bush spirit or ancestor. Then, I focused on two biomedical institutions: BHC and MGH.

I envisioned these places to be inwrought with networks of Giri (and other) relations, where sociality is made manifest between givers and recipients of care. I argued that the care given to Giri patients by family members and health workers is with reciprocity expectations/obligations. Moreover, I suggested that the reciprocal transactions that take place between Giri patients and professional carers at BHC and MGH were brought to these institutions by Giri (and other) actors. I also demonstrated that, in contrast, the adoption of biomedical practices sometimes entails a loss of traditional practices, which, in former times, were crucial to the creation of relations.

We learned of the practice of discarding the placenta as medical waste at biomedical institutions. Whereas I described how, with the arrival of biomedicine, more diverse medical options have become available to Giri people, in this we find an example of how biomedicine has severely impinged on the traditional practice of placental planting, challenging its relevance. From a traditional perspective, burial of the placenta on Giri land is said to anchor the child in its web of social relations. Furthermore, the safe positioning in the earth is believed to be conditional to the child's health and growth. Today, the "disposal" aspect comes to the fore. For Giri mothers, it appears to be more important for the placenta to be destroyed (so that no enemy can get hold of it) rather than planted on Giri land.

Implications for Public Health Interventions

Ethnographic research can tell us much about the health care needs of Giri people. In this book, I offered Giri perspectives on different types of health care services and revealed some of these services' limitations. We learned about the absence of psychiatric health services within the province. We discovered that, due to a lack of nursing manpower, patients' relatives deliver the bulk of nursing care. We read about reproductive health services that could certainly be more culturally sensitive. Apparently, medical authorities have made only minimal—if any—effort to offer culturally sensitive reproductive health care, and Giri women need considerable interpretative skills to integrate these biomedical services with local notions of reproduction.

However, instances of cultural sensitivity in health care have occurred during the early days of biomedicine in Giri. For example, Frank Beale of the Churches of Christ mission incorporated residents' wishes into the design of the first maternity ward in Rumogo (Tung) and erected a building (with no windows, five-feet-high opaque external walls, and an overhanging roof) that could not be seen into. Also, he complied with Tung villagers' requests to clear the Bunapas area of a bush spirit who lived in a whirlpool washing around a rock in the Ramu River, to enable safe relocation of the mission to Bunapas and to prepare the land for the Paternoster Memorial Hospital. (Beale gave one shilling to the presumed landowner and bought food to offer to the bush spirit.) Both examples show that an appreciation of indigenous beliefs does not necessarily inhibit health care delivery but, quite the contrary, can facilitate service delivery.

Indeed, Giri people have a lot to say on and to contribute to the improvement of health care services, but their voices have not been given fair time. It is important not to disregard the fact that Giri people exercise creative agency in their dealings with biomedicine, whereas the health services offered to them are generally not culturally sensitive and accommodating to Giri culture. I presented recipients' perspectives on BHC and suggestions for improvement of the health care services rendered there. At different points in this book, I presented my Giri interlocutors' further wants and needs. Predominantly, they articulated problems related to well-known weaknesses of Papua New Guinea's public health system.

Allow me to recapitulate a few key concerns. As to BHC, washing and kitchen facilities were said to need maintenance. Critique was furthermore levied on the poverty of diagnostic aids. Another issue (which has received attention in the national press) was the insufficient supply of medications. We also heard the voices of BHC staff problematizing workload issues. But, aside from these more practical matters, other issues were closely related to the problem of cultural insensitivity. Frequently, my interlocutors expressed the need for expanding the clinic buildings to include delivery, maternal, and other special wards in order to spatially separate inpatient and outpatient clinics. (This request relates to indigenous notions of sickness transmission, particularly of the potential danger presented by birthing women, as discussed in chapter 5.)

Furthermore, many women identified the issue of health care staff gender as important. They clearly stated their need to have female health workers for their care, particularly in gynecological examinations and births. Also, women felt inadequately coached through pregnancy and the birthing process.

Some of my conversational partners expressed their preference for local staff, with whom they could communicate in the vernacular and whom they perceived to be more empathetic. This theme was also a major concern regarding the provincial hospital, because Giri patients felt subjected to and disciplined by the non-Giri personnel there.

In order to offer health care services tailored to the local needs, it would certainly be reasonable to involve Giri and other communities as partners in the process of knowledge creation for and implementation of culturally sensitive health services, embracing a bottom-up approach (cf. Lock & Nguyen 2010: 10). In this, however, still lies a major weakness of public health programs, as Hahn and Inhorn elaborated, "Anthropologists have noted that public health programs in the past were often based on the assumption that the communities for which programs were planned were 'empty vessels,' lacking the relevant knowledge of how to improve some facet of their lives; it was assumed that the problem would be solved by introducing the Western 'expert's' knowledge and techniques" (2009: 10).

Allow me to buttress this argument with a case study from Ecuador (Fassin 2001: 302–6), to which Lock and Nguyen (2010: 8) alluded: The Ecuadorian Ministry of Public Health had commissioned a team of physicians and anthropologists to conduct a cross-country survey, with the aim of explaining high rates of maternal mortality and low levels of utilization of maternal health services. Notably, the study population was predominantly composed of indigenous women living in rural areas. The researchers' bottom-line conclusion was that women underutilize maternal health services because they hold cultural beliefs that run against biomedical rationales and practices. Consequently, programs were set up to "educate" these women. Fassin (2001: 305; see Lock & Nguyen 2010: 8), in contrast, argued that, rather than cultural obstruction, other obstacles have more significant explanatory power to illuminate the women's nonuse of maternal health services.

These include geographic and economic constraints on the accessibility of maternity clinics, poor treatment offered, and attitudes and behaviors of the medical staff. Fassin accused health authorities of using "culturalism," that is, "commonsense knowledge, implicitly or explicitly applied, when describing the behaviour of others or when justifying actions that are intended for them" (Fassin 2001: 301), to obfuscate their own responsibilities for creating and running programs. Instead, the target group was blamed for the difficulties faced in trying to implement programs (Fassin 2001: 306; see Helman 2007: 4–5; Lock & Nguyen 2010: 8). Also, Fassin deplored that a culturalistic attitude deprives people of their right to think in different ways about their bodies, in terms of health and illness (Lock & Nguyen 2010: 8). Particularly in chapters 3 and 5, I showed that the various ways in which Giri people understand their bodies indeed do differ from Western biomedical constructs but are not "intrinsically opposed" (Fassin 2001: 305) to the use of biomedical services.

Hahn and Inhorn noted that anthropology differs from other disciplines that study humans, in that anthropologists commonly assume that "expertise resides in others" (2009: 10). The benefit of fostering dialogue with local communities and including recipients' voices in health planning is increasingly recognized in public health literature and research. In public health, participatory (action) research acknowledges the importance of the involvement of those for whom the programs are designed, so that they may take ownership of the research (Cargo & Mercer 2008: 326–27).[1] In this regard, public health can gain a lot from anthropology, as anthropology can help to contextualize public health issues.

A major challenge that global health faces is, according to Hahn and Inhorn, "the failure of some public health agencies to reflect on their own cultural assumptions or to base programs on misleading concepts and erroneous theories and information" (2009: 5). Anthropology can strengthen public health by providing detailed and in-depth information on indigenous knowledge and practices regarding health. Importantly, this encompasses local thought on the causes of health problems, but also indigenous solutions to these problems (Hahn & Inhorn 2009: 6). Hahn and Inhorn further argued that the systematic application of anthropological theory and methods can assist in tackling public health challenges, as it provides public health with "nuanced social and cultural assessment" (2009: 5).

Let me return to the key question that guided my work. It is interesting to reflect upon the benefit that we can derive from knowing that the Giri understand and construct biomedicine differently from Western persons. For that purpose, I draw on an approach taken by Bamford. Bamford used Kamea views of the world as a foil against which to explore Euro-American biological understandings of kinship and society (Bamford 2007a: 171–72). Likewise, Giri provide a useful mirror against which we might reflect on the Western biomedical model of health, illness, and the body.

With their startlingly different views of biomedical technologies and practices, Giri people vividly remind us that biomedicine is socially and culturally constructed and that it can be very different across geographical and cultural spaces. From a public health perspective, it must be considered that biomedical technologies and services take on their own lives in different cultural-historical contexts. Giri base biomedicine on the social, rather than the biological, body, as they essentially understand the body to be generated and reproduced through social relations and not as a biological object. Similarly, they have a social, rather than a biological, model of health and illness, with the belief that many health problems have social origins grounded in social disruption.

Biomedical diagnostic and therapeutic devices and procedures are reinterpreted accordingly. If we take the example of the X-ray machine, we see that, for Giri people, an X-ray image can do a lot more than provide an image of the inside of the physical human body: X-ray photographs have the ability to disclose information on disruptions in the social body. Hence, and not surprisingly, the X-ray is one of, or perhaps the most, desired biomedical technology that my Giri interlocutors hope to have at BHC in the future. Without background knowledge on indigenous concepts of the body and illness causation, it would hardly be possible to understand the enormous popularity that radiological imaging enjoys among Giri people.[2]

However, it is not conducive to the goal of raising awareness of health issues, disease transmission, and disease prevention to portray the indigenous population as irrational or superstitious or to negate or ridicule indigenous knowledge by comparing it with Western "scientific fact." In what follows, I provide an example of health awareness promotion gone awry—at least in the Giri context. I discuss a poster that was used in the DOTS (Directly Observed Treatment, Short-Course) campaign to disseminate information on tuberculosis.

The poster combines biomedical and allegedly "indigenous" medical knowledge.[3] The slogan reads as follows: "Assault sorcery does not cause tuberculosis." (Pasin sanguma i no save kamapim sik TB.) To my Giri interlocutors, this slogan was thought to state the obvious. Clearly intended to "enlighten" the viewers about their misconceptions of causes for tuberculosis and to correct their delusions, the poster did not have the desired effect on Giri people. Instead, they read the slogan with bewilderment—why would anyone formulate a slogan that is self-evident without contributing any new information?

Concepts of sorcery vary widely across Papua New Guinea and have been subject to historic change. In order to understand Giri people's reactions to this poster, we must consider their contemporary concept of assault sorcery (sanguma). In Giri thought, assault sorcery does not cause tuberculosis. Rita, whom health workers had suspected to be sick with tuberculosis and whose case I presented in chapter 3, explained to me that tuberculosis is a foreign illness. Causes for foreign illnesses are to be found in foreign illness agents, but not in sorcery (which is local). A second problem with the poster, if viewed from a Giri perspective, lies in its blurring of the difference between assault sorcery (sanguma) and poison sorcery (poisin). As my Giri interlocutors emphasized, assault sorcery causes few if any symptoms in the victim, however soon it brings on death.[4]

But symptoms caused by tuberculosis may indeed resemble those originating from poison sorcery. One such symptom is wasting. An X-ray image can provide clarification in order to establish a diagnosis, as Rita said (see discussion in chap. 3 of her thorax X-ray image). To summarize, there are

Conclusion

Illustration 6.1. National Department of Health poster: "Pasin sanguma i no save kamapim sik TB" (2010).

two conceptual problems with the message content of the poster in Giri. First, assault sorcery is unlikely to cause symptoms resembling those caused by tuberculosis. However, symptoms produced by poison sorcery may indeed be similar to those brought on by tuberculosis. But, second, if the diagnosis "tuberculosis" is established and accepted by the patient, this also means that the patient acknowledges a foreign agent (such as a virus or bacteria), and not sorcery, to be the cause of the illness.

Of course, it would be absurd to suggest that, when designing awareness posters, one should take into account concepts of body, health, and illness causation of each of Papua New Guinea's more than 850 cultural-linguistic groups. However, a starting point could be—rather than accusing the target audience of being superstitious—acknowledging that, from indigenous perspectives, illnesses can have social causes that must be treated by addressing the social body. If a patient is convinced that his or her illness is attributable to a social cause (such as a dispute), she or he will not be healed by simply taking medications for tuberculosis. This, however, is the only treatment provided at biomedical institutions such as BHC and MGH, which focus their efforts on curing the disease rather than healing the illness.

Social illnesses fall outside the scope of biomedical health care, which only accepts biomedical explanatory models of health and illness (see Greifeld 2013: 30). But, in order to significantly improve public health, people "must 'buy into' program efforts" (Hahn & Inhorn 2009: 5). This can be achieved only by acknowledging indigenous explanatory models for health and illness—and these models are focused on the social causes of illness. If medical personnel (or awareness posters) ridicule patients because their explanatory models involve spirits (or sorcerers), this will, in all likelihood, discourage them from seeking biomedical care (see Greifeld 2013: 30). Effective awareness-raising campaigns should build on, rather than negate, indigenous knowledge and points of view.

Allow me to dwell a little longer on the poster and, specifically, the illustration. The graphic language of the poster makes reference to the rod-shaped *Mycobacterium tuberculosis*. Yet the graphic realization is anything but clear, and one needs a great deal of imagination to draw a link between something that could as well be a cucumber or a bean, rather than the bacterium (if this is what it is actually meant to be). It is even more surprising that the target audience, which, on the one hand, is portrayed as superstitious and unknowledgeable when it comes to biomedical "facts," is, on the other hand, expected to recognize a tuberculosis bacterium in the picture on the poster.

In fact, few Giri people have ever seen the enlargement of a tuberculosis bacterium (whereas they are quite familiar with cucumbers and beans). The leaves in the creature's hand are possibly meant to depict leaves used as a divination tool for communication with the spirits of the dead (cf. Telban & Vávrová 2014). However, according to Giri knowledge, assault sorcerers do not work with charmed plants (only poison sorcerers do), but their tools are surgical instruments made from bamboo and flying fox bones. Let me move on to the explanatory text at the bottom of the poster. It reads:

> Wanpela kain binatang i save kamapim sik TB. Sik TB i ken kalap long manmeri na pikinini i gat sik na ino stap long marasin o DOTS. Sik TB save kalap i go long narapela taim sik man i kus, snez na spet.
>
> Sapos yu laik save more long TB, go long klinik klostu long yu.

(A certain bacterium causes tuberculosis. Tuberculosis can be transmitted by adults and children who have the sickness but are not on medication or DOTS. Tuberculosis is transmitted to others when a sick person coughs, sneezes, and spits. If you want to know more about tuberculosis, go to your nearest clinic.)

These lines were far more intelligible to my Giri interlocutors than were the poster's slogan and image.

As mentioned above, tuberculosis is, in Giri thought, caused by a foreign agent, which, on the poster, is specified as binatang. The Tok Pisin term binatang has a broad range of meanings, most often "virus," "bacterium," "insect," "bug," "grub," or "germ." Microscopically small parasites and other organisms visible under a microscope are also binatang. Furthermore—and I now refer to the mentioned transmission via coughing, sneezing, and spitting—Giri people are highly familiar with the potency of bodily substances and the role they can play in illness causation. It even appears that Rita assumed the language of the poster when talking about poison sorcery and the similarity of symptoms caused by poison sorcery and tuberculosis. She said, "The virus/bacteria/germs of the poison will eat away the skin and she or he will be emaciated just as with tuberculosis."

Another difficulty with the poster is the underlying assumption that biomedical and indigenous medical knowledge—deeply entwined in the Giri medical landscape—are reseparable. As I hope to have shown in this book, biomedicine in Giri does not just speak to the biological body but takes its own form, building on the idea of social and relational bodies.

More Technologies—Possibilities for Future Research

A major change that occurred after my first fieldwork in Giri (2006–7) was that Giri villagers gained substantially greater access to communication technology. The Giri area still was without electricity, television, landline telephone service, and internet access. However, whereas Giri had no mobile phone connection in 2007, in 2009, villagers showed me three locations around Giri 1 and 2 villages (two on elevations, one up on a tree) that had network coverage. A considerable number of villagers had mobile phones and used them. In 2011, network coverage was much more extensive. Regene villagers, for example, could reach a spot with mobile phone reception within, at most, a few minutes of walking. They used their phones extensively to communicate with relatives in Madang Town and elsewhere. In chapter 4, I noted that Rita's daughter had asked me in a phone call to bring medications for her mother to Giri. By 2011, it had become commonplace for Giri villagers to call their relatives at the provincial hospital to see if they were in need of any more comestibles.

In future research, it would be interesting to explore how Giri patients use mobile phones to navigate their way through biomedical institutions. Moreover, research on the ways in which Giri patients use mobile phones to access health care services and secure caregiving by relatives would surely add to the findings on therapy management presented in chapter 4. In chapter 4, I noted that Giri hospital staff arrange for dead bodies to be brought back to the village. It is, I suggest, well worth exploring the role of mobile phones in the transportation of sick villagers and corpses (see Telban & Vávrová 2014). Furthermore, particularly participatory research could contribute to exploring the potential of mobiles phones in enhancing villagers' and health workers' access to medical knowledge and services. In Milne Bay Province, for instance, rural health workers seeking advice on obstetric cases can use their mobile phones to call a toll-free (available twenty-four hours) phone number, which gets them through to the labor ward of Alotau Provincial Hospital (Watson et al. 2015).

Provision of emotional support over the mobile phone to and from relatives living outside Giri in case of sickness and death is another topic that merits further research. In August 2011, when on a holiday on the Papua New Guinea island of New Ireland, I received a text message (addressing me by my Giri nickname) on my mobile phone: "Cassowary, [Anna] died on Wednesday and the body came to the village, buried on Friday afternoon." The brother of my close interlocutor Sarah informed me in this message of her only daughter Anna's death in the pediatric ward of MGH and the repatriation of her remains. In the weeks following her daughter's death, I tried to lend Sarah emotional support on the mobile phone and via text messages.

In addition to the exploration of the use of communication technology in medical contexts, research on further biomedical technologies (beyond the X-ray) would also likely produce useful information. Studies on the repurposing of biomedical technologies would very likely yield some valuable insights regarding Giri conceptions of the person, and possible redefinitions thereof. As Janzen wrote, novel technologies and other innovations in biomedicine challenge the boundaries of what is defined as a person: "Most of the received theories of personhood of the world's cultures are, however, challenged by global medical techniques and innovations such as invasive surgery, blood transfusions, organ and tissue transplants, fetal monitoring and amniocentesis, reproductive technologies such as in vitro fertilization, and surrogate parenting" (2002: 141).

Giri people's creative use of the X-ray spurred my interest in the local appropriation of another biomedical imaging technology—the ultrasound. As with the X-ray, this prenatal diagnostic technology allows one to gaze into the living human body. Hence, I hoped to undertake research on Giri women's use of ultrasonography in pregnancy, their experiences with the ultrasound machine, and their understandings of ultrasound scan images. It would have been interesting to study how ultrasonography affects women's reproductive experiences and to what use they put ultrasounds. In this, I was also inspired by Müller-Rockstroh's (2009, 2010, 2012) work on the appropriation of ultrasound by different user groups in Northwest Tanzania.

However, fetal ultrasound was not part of the package of routine prenatal care offered at Madang's provincial hospital, where only a small number of Giri women would attend prenatal care services anyway. In fact, none of the women I spoke with had ever undergone ultrasound screening during pregnancy. Yet, should ultrasound scans become more readily available to pregnant Giri women in the future, research on this issue would certainly be fruitful. In chapter 5, I presented Giri ideas on the development of the unborn. Given that Giri notions of the development of the unborn differ from the Western biomedical model (though contemporary women's views are influenced by it), it would no doubt be intriguing to see how Giri women interpret ultrasound scans showing their fetus in the womb.

Furthermore, I outlined that Giri personhood is gained (and can be lost) over time. The Giri unborn and the newborn do not yet possess full personhood. It has been shown that ultrasonography has altered local concepts of the person in U.S. society. Rapp (1997) demonstrated that ultrasounds help construct fetal personhood. The fetus is personified during ultrasound screening; it becomes a "baby." Individualization of the fetus is furthered by the separation of the fetus from the pregnant woman, as it is the sole focus of the ultrasound screen (Rapp 1997: 32, 39).

The fetus is further personified in U.S. culture by the ascertainment of its sex (Rapp 1997: 40) and, thereupon, possibly even by the conferral of a personal name by the parents, which establishes it as a family member (Morgan 1997: 325–26). Whether ultrasonography would alter Giri concepts of the person in a similar way and make the unborn more of a person would have to be seen. An example from Ecuador, though, offers grounds for arguing that ultrasound screening does not necessarily lead women to take the unborn as a person. Morgan showed that women in northern highland Ecuador do not accord unborn children full personhood but imagine them to be ambiguous, "liminal, unripe, and unfinished creatures" (1997: 329). Also, newborns' bodies are still "unfinished and malleable," and their spirits and souls are "not yet firmly tethered to the social world" (1997: 343).

The notion that newborns are "still in the process of becoming" (Morgan 1997: 330) matches Giri views. Remember, for example, that Giri newborns dwell in netbags (the continuation of the womb), and frequent unbagging is said to disturb their growth and possibly entail illness. Another example was described in chapter 3: a bush spirit could have snatched Rita's infant son's *vuŋ khom* (literally: "his or her good face or nose"), as he winced when Rita abruptly vaulted over a snake that was lying on the pathway. Although adults may lose their *vuŋ khom* in the same way, this usually only happens if their body is already otherwise weakened. Even ultrasound screening did not lead women in highland Ecuador to personify or individualize fetuses, as was described for people in the United States (Morgan 1997: 324).

Postlude

I shall close this book with an episode that once more tellingly illustrates the subject of the appropriation of biomedicine. To be more specific, the episode is about a biomedical artifact that was put to uses other than those it had been intended for. It is also a description of a joyous gathering that happened toward the end of my first fieldwork trip. I fondly remember this occasion, as it represents the many intimate moments I experienced with my close female interlocutors.

It was after sunset on an evening in late August 2007 that my sister and two of my sisters-in-law came to my veranda. The occasion for their visit was to inspect a female condom. They had brought up the topic of female condoms in an earlier discussion of biomedical methods of contraception. However, none of them had ever seen a female condom (which they imagined to be some kind of rubber underpants). They approached me with their request to pick up, from BHC, a female condom, which they described as a tool to enable them to actively protect themselves from unwanted pregnancies and HIV/AIDS (sik eds). They were afraid of asking for condoms, as they were afraid of being labeled promiscuous by Bunapas health workers.

Our gathering started with us examining a female condom and discussing its usage, its advantages and disadvantages, and the possibilities of safe disposal (a topic of particular concern to my interlocutors, as bodily substances of its users would cling to the worn condom). Then the conversation shifted to alternative ways in which condoms can be used. One of the women rubbing the moist condom on the tinea-affected skin of her inner thighs sparked this thematic change. Multiple times she had treated her tinea with lubricants and moist male condoms that one of her brothers, with whom she had a particularly close relationship, had brought from BHC.

BHC personnel promote lubricants as a less painful alternative to some of the severely skin irritating and caustic tinea lotions. As other interlocutors had, the three women further mentioned that male condoms are popular fish bait used by Madang coastal people. Finally, one of the women tried on the transparent flexible inner ring of the female condom as a bracelet, as it reminded her of the sealing rings of oil drums worn by many Papua New Guinea women as attire. The ring, though, was very tight, and she realized that other villagers might notice that her "jewelry" was part of a female condom. Hastily, she stripped the ring off again. We all had to laugh.

Notes

1. A topical example of a participatory action research project from Papua New Guinea is Vaughan's (2011) study in which she used photovoice (a conventional participatory action research strategy) to learn about youths' priorities related to health and HIV and to explore how participation can facilitate young people's ability to actively engage in their health priorities.
2. It must be mentioned that none of my interlocutors ever mentioned the health hazards that radiation exposure can pose. Public health programs should inform the public about X-ray examinations and their associated risks.
3. See Hammar (2008: 70) for the examples of an HIV/AIDS awareness poster that combines biomedical knowledge and local metaphor more successfully.
4. In Giri, victims of assault sorcery are thought to be inevitably doomed to death. Assault sorcerers attack their victims when they are alone in the bush or garden. (For this reason, Giri people rarely go alone to the bush or to gardens.) In chapter 3, I explained that assault sorcerers remove the victim's strength. Also, they mark a day for the victim to actually pass away by saying to the victim, for example, "Next Wednesday, a snake will bite you and you will die." At that point, they let the victim return to the village. The victim is already dead (i.e., without any strength), although this is not noticeable to others. The victim is said to be unable to tell others that she or he has been killed by assault sorcerers. Often, sorcery victims die in accidents. It is not uncommon for them to pass away showing few, if any, symptoms of illness. Attribution of death to assault sorcery is done in retrospect and is based on a postmortem examination and knowledge of interpersonal conflict between the deceased and others. Sometimes, sorcery victims indirectly announce their death and bid good-bye to their relatives by talking about an upcoming journey, saying, "I will not see you again. I will go to Port Moresby." If this relative passes away only shortly afterwards, you will remember the statement and realize that the idea of the relative going to Port Moresby is nonsense and that she or he must have been talking about having been killed by an assault sorcerer.

Glossary

aŋ	1. him, her, it; 2. his, hers, its.
beh	umbilical cord.
behn thip	umbilical cord stump.
bemge	type of tree.
bibi tivi	respiratory illness; lit. "short breath".
dam	pig.
fav	1. skin; 2. body.
fava kavgi	to excite or arouse the skin (i.e., sexually).
fava ŋan	1. various substances that have evaporated from one's skin or emerged from one's body; 2. female sexual secretions.
fava sigsigi	put shame on the skin of someone else; lit. "deceive the skin".
fav bigbigi	lightweight body.
fav bigbigi mbah	food that is light on the skin/body.
fav simgi	weighed down by worries; lit. "skin heavy" (skin hevi).
fav simgi mbah	food that is heavy on the skin/body.
fav singi	dull/dry/darkish skin.
fiaŋ	dog.
fiaŋ guma	1. death / assault sorcerer; lit. "dog man"; 2. death / assault sorcery.
girgirga	1. to imitate, to mock; 2. mimicry of gendered everyday tasks with respectively gendered tools above the newborn (this practice traditionally makes an important contribution to the child's becoming).
guma-a vuŋ	1. good man (i.e., a man who acts in accordance with kastom); 2. healthy man.
guma gu mbik vur	"overaged" people; lit. "old man and woman".
gun rimrim	local illness; lit. "illness of the place/village".
hip	1. the color red; 2. red paint.
hui-in	saliva.

ka-a	1. clan; 2. platform / bed / stool / table.
ka-a bisane	1. subclan; 2. small platform / bed / stool / table.
kamavurfek	maternal fifth / sixth cousin one generation up.
kamfarkhem	type of plant.
karɨk	torso, trunk.
khos	1. dish of mushy yam and taro mixed with grated coconut; 2. machete; 3. coconut grater.
khum/ber khum	1. stirred sago conserved in a bamboo tube; 2. sago cooked or reheated in a bamboo tube.
kui	*Abelmoschus manihot* (aibika).
kuk	poison sorcery.
kurkum	friend with inherited friendship ties from one's father.
mba-atɨk	bad / dangerous / malevolent / evil.
mbathar	small decorative netbag.
mbəgam	fish.
mbəgam pɨk	gudgeon; lit. "black fish".
mbik vuŋ	1. good woman (i.e., a woman who acts in accordance with kastom) 2. healthy woman.
mbirɨka	new mother.
monigafoi	male initiation ritual.
mon mbik	1. ritual seclusion at menarche; 2. menarcheal woman; lit. "new woman".
mva-aŋ	bamboo hoop fishing net.
mvɨgvɨgi	boils (pl.) (sg. *mvɨg*).
ŋama rimgi	unconscious; lit. "dead, yet still alive".
ŋaŋŋan	1. mad / crazy / deranged; 2. drunk / "high" / disoriented; 3. naughty / unreasonable / inconsiderate; 4. ignorant/untaught; 5. deep and sound asleep; 6. delirious.
nder	1. skin (i.e., human skin and animal skin); 2. tree bark; 3. vegetable peel, fruit peel.
ndia-a vɨzɨn	father's blood (*ndia-a vɨzɨn* is the paternal contribution to procreation).
ndɨgndɨgi	grief / worries; lit. "to think much".
ndo	bush fowl.

nduigi	indigenous curing practice.
nduik	netbag-like fishing net slipped over the lower arms.
ngapngaŋ	bodily strength.
nguar hip	red yam.
niamu	ego's biological and classificatory mother.
niamu vɨzɨn	mother's blood (*niamu vɨzɨn* is the maternal contribution to procreation).
nɨmsɨk	bandicoot.
ŋina	1. shadow soul; 2. vision.
nzɨp	sperm.
phəh	type of tree.
phonu	1. cassowary; 2. name of a subclan; 3. type of banana.
pi	to eat.
piŋ	wild cordyline sp.
puk	areca nut.
rai bavira	subclan; lit. "one line".
rer	1. egg; 2. ovum.
rɨma nder	eyelid; lit. "skin of the eye".
rɨi gari guma	shaman; lit. "man who sees the illness" (*rɨi gari guma* is the Kire translation of the Tok Pisin term glasman).
rɨmrɨm	1. illness; 2. trivial illness; 3. illness responsive to biomedical treatment in order to distinguish it from a local illness.
rɨmrɨm ba-akeri	fatal illness attributable to a social cause; lit. "big / large / great / major illness".
rɨmrɨm do-ogi	nonlethal disorder ascribable to a natural cause; lit. "small / little / minor illness".
rɨngi	to shiver.
riri	shadow soul, "worry spirit".
riru mbah	tabooed food.
sangi	strong / firm / big.
sankuargi	type of tree.
seva	1. blood of menstruation; 2. blood of parturition; 3. lochia / postpartum discharge.

sɨk	urine.
sɨm bisane	small knife.
si nder	foreskin; lit. "skin of the penis".
sum	wound.
taphoŋ	breast / mother's milk.
tar	child, also used for the unborn (dual *tarani*; pl. *tari*).
tar sangi	fetus from about the eighth month of pregnancy up until delivery.
tar thar	1. uterus (*tar thar* is more specific than the broader term, *thar*); 2. placenta; lit.: "child netbag".
thar	1. netbag; 2. uterus.
thor	bush spirit.
thori bisarire	small holes (pl.) (sg. *thoŋ bisane*).
thor mba-atɨk	malevolent / dangerous bush spirit; lit. "bad bush spirit".
thor vuŋ	benevolent/helpful bush spirit; lit. "good bush spirit".
thum	1. vital/life energy; 2. ancestral spirit / spirit of the dead.
tiiŋ	*Gnetum gnemon* (tulip; a tree with evergreen edible leaves and large edible seeds).
tor	slit-drum beating.
vemkura hi	to dance speedily.
vɨzin	the blood that flows in one's veins.
vove	white cockatoo.
vuŋ khom	intellect / knowledge / thought / ability to reason; lit. "good face or nose".
vurfek	1. mother's biological and classificatory brother; 2. maternal second / third / fourth cousin one generation up.
zori	type of tree similar to *Gnetum gnemon*.
zoruk	sweat

References

Akin, David. 2003. "Concealment, Confession, and Innovation in Kwaio Women's Taboos," *American Ethnologist* 30(3): 381–400.
Albaniel-Evara, Rosalyn. 2012a. "BSP Madang Helps Hospital," *Papua New Guinea Post-Courier,* 20 December, 5.
———. 2012b. "Hospital Fees Go Up," *Papua New Guinea Post-Courier,* 7 May, 3.
———. 2012c. "Mentally Handicapped Persons on an Increase," *Papua New Guinea Post-Courier,* 1 March, 14.
Allan, Bryant J. 1989. "Infection, Innovation and Residence. Illness and Misfortune in the Torricelli Foothills from 1800." In *A Continuing Trial of Treatment. Medical Pluralism in Papua New Guinea,* edited by Stephen Frankel and Gilbert Lewis (Culture, Illness, and Healing). Dordrecht: Kluwer Academic, 35–68.
Amarasingham Rhodes, Lorna. 1996. "Studying Biomedicine as a Cultural System." In *Medical Anthropology. Contemporary Theory and Method,* edited by Carolyn F. Sargent and Thomas M. Johnson. Rev. ed. Westport, CT: Praeger, 165–80.
Anderson, Astrid. 2011. *Landscapes of Relations and Belonging. Body, Place and Politics in Wogeo, Papua New Guinea* (Person, Space and Memory in the Contemporary Pacific, vol. 3). New York: Berghahn Books.
Anonymous. 1960. "Missionary News. Tragedy of Sickness," *The Australian Christian* 63, 4 October, 613–14.
———. (1992) 1997. *Kire Kaman Mparmpare Arfabet Ŋkeran Khivi Gap (Teacher's Guide for the Tok Ples Prep School). Kiren Kam, Fhuvara Sure Gap.* Madang: Pioneer Bible Translators Association of Papua New Guinea.
———. 2011. "Pharmaceutical Society Calls for Govt Intervention," *Papua New Guinea Post-Courier,* 11 April, 12.
Aura, Siru. 2008. *Women and Marital Breakdown in South India. Reconstructing Homes, Bonds and Persons.* Dissertation, University of Helsinki.
Ayers Counts, Dorothy. 1991. "Aging, Health and Women in West New Britain," *Journal of Cross-Cultural Gerontology* 6(3): 277–85.
Ayers Counts, Dorothy and David R. Counts. 1983. "Father's Water Equals Mother's Milk. The Conception of Parentage in Kaliai, West New Guinea," *Mankind* 14(1): 46–56.
Baer, Hans A., Merrill Singer, and Ida Susser. 1997. *Medical Anthropology and the World System. A Critical Perspective.* Westport, CT: Bergin & Garvey.
Baing, Susan, Brian Deutrom, Russell Jackson, and Craig A. Volker. 2008. *Papua New Guinea Tok Pisin English Dictionary. The Perfect Dictionary for Learners of English and Tok Pisin.* Oxford: Oxford University Press in association with Wantok Niuspepa.
Bamford, Sandra. 1998. "To Eat for Another. Taboo and Elicitation of Bodily Form among the Kamea of Papua New Guinea." In *Bodies and Persons. Comparative Perspectives from Africa and Melanesia,* edited by Michael L. Lambek and Andrew Strathern. Cambridge, UK: Cambridge University Press, 158–71.

Bamford, Sandra. 2007a. *Biology Unmoored. Melanesian Reflections on Life and Biotechnology.* Berkeley: University of California Press.
———. 2007b. "Unholy Noses." In *Embodying Modernity and Post-Modernity. Ritual, Praxis, and Social Change in Melanesia,* edited by Sandra Bamford (Ritual Studies Monographs). Durham: Carolina Academic Press, 161–84.
Banks, Cyndi. 1993. *Women in Transition. Social Control in Papua New Guinea* (Australian Studies in Law, Crime and Justice). Canberra: Australian Institute of Criminology. Retrieved 22 August 2015 from http://www.aic.gov.au/media_library/publications/lcj/women/women_full_report.pdf.
Barker, John. 1990. "Encounters with Evil. Christianity and the Response to Sorcery among the Maisin of Papua New Guinea," *Oceania* 61(2): 139–55.
Bateson, Gregory. (1936) 1958. *Naven. A Survey of the Problems Suggested by a Composite Picture of the Culture of a New Guinea Tribe Drawn from Three Points of View.* Stanford: Stanford University Press.
Battaglia, Debbora. 1983. "Projecting Personhood in Melanesia. The Dialectics of Artefact Symbolism on Sabarl Island," *Man, n.s.* 18(2): 289–304.
———. 1990. *On the Bones of the Serpent. Person, Memory, and Mortality in Sabarl Island Society.* Chicago: University of Chicago Press.
———. 1992. "The Body in the Gift. Memory and Forgetting in Sabarl Mortuary Exchange," *American Ethnologist* 19(1): 3–18.
Bauze, Anna, Chris Morgan, and Russel Kitau. 2009. *Developing an Investment Case for Financing Equitable Progress towards MDGs 4 and 5 in the Asia Pacific Region. Papua New Guinea. Phase 1: Mapping Report.* Retrieved 22 August 2015 from http://www.burnet.edu.au/system/asset/file/273/ICMappingReport-PNG.pdf.
Bernard, Harvey R. 2006. *Research Methods in Anthropology. Qualitative and Quantitative Approaches,* 4th ed. Lanham: Altamira.
Biersack, Aletta. 1982. "Ginger Gardens for the Ginger Woman. Rites and Passages in a Melanesian Society," *Man* 17(2): 239–58.
———. 1987. "Moonlight. Negative Images of Transcendence in Paiela Pollution," *Oceania* 57(3): 178–94.
———. 1991. "Thinking Difference. A Review of Marilyn Strathern's 'The Gender of the Gift,'" *Oceania* 62(2): 147–54.
Binder-Fritz, Christine. 1995. "Der Wandel der Geburtshilfe bei den Maori in Neuseeland." In *Gebären—Ethnomedizinische Perspektiven und neue Wege,* edited by Wulf Schiefenhövel, Dorothea Sich, and Christine E. Gottschalk-Batschkus (Curare Special Volume, vol. 8). Berlin: VWB, 93–126.
Boddy, Janice. 1994. "Spirit Possession Revisited. Beyond Instrumentality," *Annual Review of Anthropology* 23: 407–34.
Bonnemère, Pascale. 1993. "Maternal Nurturing Substance and Paternal Spirit. The Making of a Southern Anga Sociality," *Oceania* 64(2): 159–86.
———. 2004. "When Women Enter the Picture. Looking at Anga Initiations from the Mothers' Angle." In *Women as Unseen Characters. Male Ritual in Papua New Guinea,* edited by Pascale Bonnemère (Social Anthropology in Oceania). Philadelphia: University of Pennsylvania Press, 57–74.
Bourdieu, Pierre. (1972) 2002. *Outline of a Theory of Practice,* translated by Richard Nice 1977 (Cambridge Studies in Social and Cultural Anthropology, vol. 16). Cambridge: University of Cambridge Press.

Brown, Michael F. 1997. *The Channeling Zone. American Spirituality in an Anxious Age.* Cambridge, MA: Harvard University Press.

Buchanan-Aruwafu, Holly and Angelyn Amos. 2010. *HIV Prevention in Rural Economic Enclaves. A Health Workers Baseline Survey* (Special Publication, no. 60). Boroko, Papua New Guinea: National Research Institute.

Burridge, Kenelm. 1960. *Mambu. A Melanesian Millennium.* London: Methuen.

Cargo, Margaret and Shawna L. Mercer. 2008. "The Value and Challenges of Participatory Research. Strengthening Its Practice," *Annual Review of Public Health* 29: 325–50.

Carrithers, Michael. 2010. "Person." In *The Routledge Encyclopedia of Social and Cultural Anthropology*, 2nd ed., edited by Alan Barnard and Jonathan Spencer. Adingdon, UK: Routledge, 532–35.

Carsten, Janet. 2011. "Substance and Relationality. Blood in Contexts," *Annual Review of Anthropology* 40: 19–35.

Caudill, William. 1958. *The Psychiatric Hospital as a Small Society.* Cambridge, MA: Harvard University Press.

Chowning, Ann. 1987. "Sorcery and the Social Order in Kove." In *Sorcerer and Witch in Melanesia,* edited by Michele Stephen. Melbourne: Melbourne University Press in association with La Trobe University Research Centre for South-West Pacific Studies, 149–82.

Clark, Jeffrey. 1993. "Gold, Sex, and Pollution. Male Illness and Myth at Mt. Kare, Papua New Guinea," *American Ethnologist* 20(4): 742–57.

Clifford, James. 1983. "On Ethnographic Authority," *Representations* 1(2): 118–46.

———. 2003. *On the Edges of Anthropology (Interviews).* Chicago: Prickly Paradigm.

Coffey, Amanda. 1999. *The Ethnographic Self. Fieldwork and the Representation of Identity.* London: Sage.

Coreil, Jeannine, Carol A. Bryant, and Joseph N. Henderson. 2001. *Social and Behavioral Foundations of Public Health.* Thousand Oaks, CA: Sage.

Counts, David R. and Dorothy Ayers Counts. 1989. "Complementarity in Medical Treatment in a West New Britain Society." In *A Continuing Trial of Treatment. Medical Pluralism in Papua New Guinea,* edited by Stephen Frankel and Gilbert Lewis (Culture, Illness, and Healing). Dordrecht: Kluwer Academic, 277–94.

Courtens, Ien. 2008. *Restoring the Balance. Performing Healing in West Papua.* (Verhandelingen van het Koninklijk Instituut voor Taal-, Land- en Volkenkunde, vol. 241). Leiden: KITLV.

Csordas, Thomas J. 1990. "Embodiment as a Paradigm for Anthropology," *Ethos* 18(1): 5–47.

Csordas, Thomas J. and Arthur Kleinman. 1996. "The Therapeutic Process." In *Medical Anthropology. Contemporary Theory and Method,* rev. ed., edited by Carolyn F. Sargent and Thomas M. Johnson. Westport, CT: Praeger, 3–20.

Danziger, Eve. 2006. "The Thought That Counts. Interactional Consequences of Variation in Cultural Theories of Meaning." In *Roots of Human Sociality. Culture, Cognition and Interaction,* edited by Nicholas J. Enfield and Stephen C. Levinson (Wenner-Gren International Symposium Series). Oxford: Berg, 259–78.

———. 2010. "On Trying and Lying. Cultural Configurations of Grice's Maxim of Quality," *Intercultural Pragmatics* 7(2): 199–219.

Daston, Lorraine and Peter Galison. 1992. "The Image of Objectivity," *Representations* 40(special issue "Seeing Science"): 81–128.
———. 2007. *Objectivity.* New York: Zone Books.
Davy, Carol. 2007. "Contributing to the Wellbeing of Primary Health Care Workers in PNG," *Journal of Health Organization and Management* 21(3): 229–45.
Dawson, Angela, Tara Howes, Natalie Gray, and Elissa Kennedy. 2011. *Human Resources for Health in Maternal, Neonatal and Reproductive Health at Community Level. A Profile of Papua New Guinea.* Sydney: Human Resources for Health Knowledge Hub & Burnet Institute. Retrieved August 22, 2015 from https://sphcm.med.unsw.edu.au/sites/default/files/sphcm/Centres_and_Units/MNRH_PNG_report.pdf.
De Coppet, Daniel. 1985. ". . . Land Owns People." In *Contexts and Levels. Anthropological Essays on Hierarchy,* edited by Robert H. Barnes, Daniel De Coppet, and Robert J. Parkin (JASO Occasional Papers, vol. 4). Oxford: JASO, 78–90.
DelVecchio Good, Mary-Jo. 1995. "Cultural Studies of Biomedicine. An Agenda for Research," *Social Science & Medicine* 41(4): 461–73.
Denoon, Donald. (1989) 2002. *Public Health in Papua New Guinea. Medical Possibility and Social Constraint, 1884–1984* (Cambridge History of Medicine). Cambridge: Cambridge University Press.
Diliberto, Gioia. 2010. "Ghost Writer," *Smithsonian* 41(5): 84–101.
Douglas, Mary. 1966. *Purity and Danger. An Analysis of Concepts of Pollution and Taboo.* London: Routledge & Kegan Paul.
Downs, Ian. 1980. *The Australian Trusteeship. Papua New Guinea 1945–75.* Canberra: Australian Government Publishing Service.
Dureau, Christine. 1998. "From Sisters to Wives. Changing Contexts of Maternity on Simbo, Western Solomon Islands." In *Maternities and Modernities. Colonial and Postcolonial Experiences in Asia and the Pacific,* edited by Kalpana Ram and Margaret Jolly. Cambridge: Cambridge University Press, 239–74.
Ember, Carol R. and Melvin Ember. 2004a. "Glossary." In *Encyclopedia of Medical Anthropology. Health and Illness in the World's Cultures. Volume I. Topics,* edited by Carol R. Ember and Melvin Ember. New York: Springer, xxiii–xliv.
———. 2004b. "Preface." In *Encyclopedia of Medical Anthropology. Health and Illness in the World's Cultures. Volume I. Topics,* edited by Carol R. Ember and Melvin Ember. New York: Springer, xiii–xvi.
Errington, Frederick and Deborah Gewertz. 1996. "The Individuation of Tradition in a Papua New Guinean Modernity," *American Anthropologist, n.s.* 98(1): 114–26.
Etkin, Nina L. 1992. "'Side Effects.' Cultural Constructions and Reinterpretations of Western Pharmaceuticals," *Medical Anthropology Quarterly, n.s.* 6(2): 99–113.
Evara, Rosalyn. 2011a. "Call to Erect Mental Care Centres," *Papua New Guinea Post-Courier,* 6 June, 9.
———. 2011b. "Madang Faces Health Crisis," *Papua New Guinea Post-Courier,* 21 January, 8.
———. 2011c. "Medical Supplies Held up," *Papua New Guinea Post-Courier,* 4 February, 5.
———. 2011d. "Mentally Disturbed Worry Police," *Papua New Guinea Post-Courier,* 16 May, 6
Eves, Richard. 1995. "Shamanism, Sorcery and Cannibalism. The Incorporation of Power in the Magical Cult of 'Buai,'" *Oceania* 65(3): 212–33.
———. 1998. *The Magical Body. Power, Fame and Meaning in a Melanesian Society* (Studies in Anthropology and History, vol. 23). Amsterdam: Harwood Academic Publishers.

Fabrega, Horacio. 1975. "The Need for an Ethnomedical Science," *Science* 189(4207): 969–75.
Fajans, Jane. 1985. "The Person in Social Context. The Social Character of Baining 'Psychology.'" In *Person, Self, and Experience. Exploring Pacific Ethnopsychologies*, edited by Geoffrey M. White and John Kirkpatrick. Berkeley: University of California Press, 367–97.
———. 1997. *They Make Themselves. Work and Play among the Baining of Papua*. Chicago: The University of Chicago Press.
———. 2000. "Review of The Magical Body. Power, Fame and Meaning in a Melanesian Society, by Richard Eves," *The Contemporary Pacific* 12(2): 538–40.
Fassin, Didier. 2001. "Culturalism as Ideology." In *Cultural Perspectives on Reproductive Health*, edited by Carla Makhlouf Obermeyer (International Studies in Demography). Oxford: Oxford University Press, 300–17.
Feld, Steven. 1990. *Sound and Sentiment. Birds, Weeping, Poetics, and Song in Kaluli Expression*, 2nd ed. (Conduct and Communication). Philadelphia: University of Pennsylvania Press.
Finkler, Kaja. 2004. "Biomedicine Globalized and Localized. Western Medical Practices in an Outpatient Clinic of a Mexican Hospital," *Social Science & Medicine* 59(10, special issue "Hospital Ethnography"): 2037–51.
Fiti-Sinclair, Ruta. 2002. "Childbirth in Papua New Guinean Villages and in Port Moresby General Hospital." In *Birthing in the Pacific. Beyond Tradition and Modernity?* edited by Vicky Lukere and Margaret Jolly. Honolulu: University of Hawai'i Press, 56–78.
Fortune, Reo F. (1932) 1989. *Sorcerers of Dobu. The Social Anthropology of the Dobu Islanders of the Western Pacific*. Prospect Heights: Waveland Press.
Foster, Robert J. 1990. "Nurture and Force-Feeding. Mortuary Feasting and the Construction of Collective Individuals in a New Ireland Society," *American Ethnologist* 17(3): 431–48.
———. 1995a. "Introduction. The Work of Nation Making." In *Nation Making. Emergent Identities in Postcolonial Melanesia*, edited by Robert J. Foster. Ann Arbor: University of Michigan Press, 1–30.
———. 1995b. *Social Reproduction and History in Melanesia. Mortuary Ritual, Gift Exchange, and Custom in the Tanga Islands* (Cambridge Studies in Social and Cultural Anthropology, vol. 96). Cambridge: Cambridge University Press.
———. 2002. "Bargains with Modernity in Papua New Guinea and Elsewhere," *Anthropological Theory* 2(2): 233–51.
Foucault, Michel. (1975) 1995. *Discipline and Punish. The Birth of the Prison*, 2nd ed., translated by Alan Sheridan 1977. New York: Vintage.
Fox, Renée C. 1959. *Experiment Perilous. Physicians and Patients Facing the Unknown*. Glencoe, IL: Free Press.
Frankel, Stephen. 1986. *The Huli Response to Illness* (Cambridge Studies in Social Anthropology, vol. 62). Cambridge: Cambridge University Press.
Frankel, Stephen and Gilbert Lewis, eds. 1989. *A Continuing Trial of Treatment. Medical Pluralism in Papua New Guinea* (Culture, Illness, and Healing). Dordrecht: Kluwer Academic.
Gaines, Atwood D. and Robbie Davis-Floyd. 2004. "Biomedicine." In *Encyclopedia of Medical Anthropology. Health and Illness in the World's Cultures. Volume I. Topics*, edited by Carol R. Ember and Melvin Ember. New York: Springer, 95–109.

Gaines, Atwood D. and Robert A. Hahn, eds. 1982. "Physicians of Western Medicine. Five Cultural Studies," *Culture, Medicine and Psychiatry* 6 (3, special issue): 215–324.
Gartin, Meredith, Alexandra A. Brewis, and Norah A. Schwartz. 2010. "Nonprescription Antibiotic Therapy. Cultural Models on Both Sides of the Counter and Both Sides of the Border," *Medical Anthropology Quarterly, n.s.* 24(1): 85–107.
Geertz, Clifford. 1988. *Works and Lives. The Anthropologist as Author.* Cambridge: Polity.
Gewertz, Deborah and Frederick Errington. 2004. "Toward an Ethnographically Grounded Study of Modernity in Papua New Guinea." In *Globalization and Culture Change in the Pacific Islands,* edited by Victoria S. Lockwood (Exploring Cultures). Upper Saddle River, NJ: Pearson Prentice-Hall, 273–84.
Ginsburg, Faye and Rayna Rapp. 1991. "The Politics of Reproduction," *Annual Review of Anthropology* 20: 311–43.
Glick, Leonard B. 1998. "Medicine as an Ethnographic Category. The Gimi of the New Guinea Highlands." In *The Art of Medical Anthropology. Readings,* edited by Sjaak van der Geest and Adri Rienks. Amsterdam: Het Spinhuis Publishers, 23–37.
Goddard, Michael. 1992. "Bedlam in Paradise. A Critical History of Psychiatry in Papua New Guinea," *The Journal of Pacific History* 27(1): 55–72.
———. 1998. "What Makes Hari Run? The Social Construction of Madness in a Highland Papua New Guinea Society," *Critique of Anthropology* 18(1): 61–81.
———. 2011. *Out of Place. Madness in the Highlands of Papua New Guinea* (Social Identities, vol. 6). New York: Berghahn Books.
Goldman, Laurence. 1993. *The Culture of Coincidence. Accident and Absolute Liability in Huli* (Oxford Studies in Social and Cultural Anthropology). Oxford: Clarendon Press.
Goodale, Jane C. 1995. *To Sing with Pigs Is Human. The Concept of Person in Papua New Guinea.* Seattle: University of Washington Press.
GoPNG. 2010a. *National Health Plan 2011–2020. Volume 1 Policies and Strategies.* Waigani: GoPNG.
———. 2010b. *National Health Plan 2011–2020. Volume 2 (Part B) Reference Data and National Health Profile.* Waigani: GoPNG.
Greifeld, Katarina. 2013. "Einführung in die Medizinethnologie." In *Medizinethnologie. Eine Einführung,* edited by Katarina Greifeld. Berlin: Reimer, 13–37.
Griffiths, Anne. 2001. "Gendering Culture. Towards a Plural Perspective on Kwena Women's Rights." In *Culture and Rights. Anthropological Perspectives,* edited by Jane K. Cowan, Marie-Bénédicte Dembour, and Richard A. Wilson. Cambridge: Cambridge University Press, 102–26.
Haak, Hilbrand and Anita P. Hardon. 1988. "Indigenised Pharmaceuticals in Developing Countries. Widely Used, Widely Neglected," *The Lancet* 332(8611): 620–21.
Hahn, Robert A. 1984. "Rethinking 'Illness' and 'Disease,'" *Contributions to Asian Studies* 18: 1–23.
Hahn, Robert A. and Marcia C. Inhorn. 2009. "Introduction." In *Anthropology and Public Health. Bridging Differences in Culture and Society,* 2nd ed., edited by Robert A. Hahn and Marcia C. Inhorn. Oxford: Oxford University Press, 1–31.
Hahn, Robert A. and Arthur Kleinman. 1983. "Biomedical Practice and Anthropological Theory. Frameworks and Directions," *Annual Review of Anthropology* 12: 305–33.
Haiveta, Chris. 1990. "Health Care Alternatives in Maindroin." In *Sepik Heritage. Tradition and Change in Papua New Guinea,* edited by Nancy Lutkehaus, Christian

Kaufmann, William E. Mitchell, Douglas Newton, Lita Osmundsen, and Meinhard Schuster. Durham: Carolina Academic Press, 439–46.
Halvaksz, Jamon and David Lipset. 2006. "Another Kind of Gold. An Introduction to Marijuana in Papua New Guinea," *Oceania* 76(3): 209–19.
Hammar, Lawrence J. 2008. "Fear and Loathing in Papua New Guinea. Sexual Health in a Nation under Siege." In *Making Sense of AIDS. Culture, Sexuality, and Power in Melanesia*, edited by Leslie Butt and Richard Eves. Honolulu: University of Hawai'i Press, 60–79.
Hamnett, Michael P. and John Connell. 1981. "Diagnosis and Cure. The Resort to Traditional and Modern Medical Practitioners in the North Solomons, Papua New Guinea," *Social Science & Medicine, Part B: Medical Anthropology* 15(4): 489–98.
Harris, Grace G. 1989. "Concepts of Individual, Self, and Person in Description and Analysis," *American Anthropologist, n.s.* 91(3): 599–612.
Hartmann, Betsy. 1997. "Women, Population and the Environment. Whose Consensus, Whose Empowerment?" In *The Women, Gender and Development Reader*, edited by Nalini Visvanathan, Lynn Duggan, Laurie Nisonoff, and Nan Wiegersma. Dhaka: University Press, 293–302.
Helman, Cecil G. 2007. *Culture, Health and Illness*, 5th ed. London: Hodder Arnold.
Herbst, Franziska A. 2013. *Multiplicity, Ingenuity, and Creativity. Relational Encounters with Biomedicine in a Papua New Guinea Society*. Doctoral Thesis, University of Heidelberg.
Herdt, Gilbert H. 1989. "Doktas and Shamans among the Sambia of Papua New Guinea." In *A Continuing Trial of Treatment. Medical Pluralism in Papua New Guinea*, edited by Stephen Frankel and Gilbert Lewis (Culture, Illness, and Healing). Dordrecht: Kluwer Academic, 95–114.
———. (1981) 1994. *Guardians of the Flutes*. Chicago: University of Chicago Press.
Hess, Sabine C. 2009. *Person and Place. Ideas, Ideals and the Practice of Sociality on Vanua Lava, Vanuatu* (Person, Space and Memory in the Contemporary Pacific, vol. 2). New York: Berghahn Books.
Hirsch, Eric. 2001. "When Was Modernity in Melanesia?" *Social Anthropology* 9(2): 131–46.
Hogbin, Herbert I. 1935/36. "Sorcery and Administration," *Oceania* 6(1): 1–32, plates i–iv.
———. (1970) 1996. *The Island of Menstruating Men. Religion in Wogeo, New Guinea*. Long Grove, IL: Waveland Press.
Höltker, Georg. 1961. "Leichenbrand und Anderes vom Unteren Ramu (Neuguinea)." In *Beiträge zur Völkerforschung. Hans Damm zum 65. Geburtstag*, edited by Museum für Völkerkunde Leipzig (Veröffentlichungen des Museums für Völkerkunde zu Leipzig, vol. 11). Berlin: Akademie-Verlag, 285–301, plates 61–64.
———. 1962. "Aus dem Kulturleben der Kire-Puir am Unteren Ramu (Neuguinea)," *Jahrbuch des Museums für Völkerkunde zu Leipzig* 19: 76–107, plates vi–viii.
Höltker, Georg. 1964. "Die Nubia-Awar an der Hansa-Bucht in Nordost-Neuguinea," *Jahrbuch des Museums für Völkerkunde zu Leipzig* 20: 33–70, plates ix–xvi.
Holmes Williamson, Margaret. 1983. "Sex Relations and Gender Relations. Understanding Kwoma Conception," *Mankind* 14(1): 13–23.
———. 2007. "The Thickness of Blood. Kwoma Definitions of 'Us' and 'You.'" In *Embodying Modernity and Post-Modernity. Ritual, Praxis, and Social Change in Melanesia*, edited by Sandra Bamford (Ritual Studies Monographs). Durham: Carolina Academic Press, 185–210.

Hsu, Elisabeth. 2003. "Die drei Körper—oder sind es vier? Medizinethnologische Perspektiven auf den Körper." In *Kulturelle Dimensionen der Medizin. Ethnomedizin—Medizinethnologie—Medical Anthropology,* edited by Thomas Lux. Berlin: Reimer, 177–89.

Independent State of Papua New Guinea. 1971. "Sorcery Act," *Papua New Guinea Consolidated Legislation* (Chapter no. 274).

Ingold, Tim. 1993. "The Art of Translation in a Continuous World." In *Beyond Boundaries. Understanding, Translation and Anthropological Discourse,* edited by Gísli Pálsson (Elaborations in Anthropology). Oxford: Berg, 210–30.

———. 1994. "Introduction to Culture." In *Companion Encyclopedia of Anthropology,* edited by Tim Ingold. London: Routledge, 329–49.

———. 1996. "Culture, Perception and Cognition." In *Psychological Research. Innovative Methods and Strategies,* edited by John Haworth. London: Routledge, 99–119.

Izard, John and Maryse Dugue. 2003. *Moving Toward a Sector-Wide Approach. Papua New Guinea. The Health Sector Development Program Experience.* Manila: Asian Development Bank. Retrieved 22 August 2015 from http://www.adb.org/sites/default/files/pub/2003/health-sector-development-program-png.pdf.

Jacka, Jerry. 2007. "'Our Skins Are Weak.' Ipili Modernity and the Demise of Discipline." In *Embodying Modernity and Post-Modernity. Ritual, Praxis, and Social Change in Melanesia,* edited by Sandra Bamford (Ritual Studies Monographs). Durham: Carolina Academic Press, 39–67.

Janzen, John M. 1978. *The Quest for Therapy in Lower Zaire* (Comparative Studies in Health Systems and Medical Care, vol. 1). Berkeley: University of California Press.

———. 1987. "Therapy Management. Concept, Reality, Process," *Medical Anthropology Quarterly, n.s.* 1(1): 68–84.

———. 2002. *The Social Fabric of Health. An Introduction to Medical Anthropology.* New York: McGraw-Hill.

Jenkins, Janis H., ed. 2010. *Pharmaceutical Self. The Global Shaping of Experience in an Age of Psychopharmacology* (School for Advanced Research Advanced Seminar Series). Santa Fe: School for Advanced Research Press.

Johannes, Adell. 1980. "Many Medicines in One. Curing in the Eastern Highlands of Papua New Guinea," *Culture, Medicine and Psychiatry* 4(1): 43–70.

Jolly, Margaret. 2001. "Damming the Rivers of Milk? Fertility, Sexuality, and Modernity in Melanesia and Amazonia." In *Gender in Amazonia and Melanesia. An Exploration of the Comparative Method,* edited by Thomas A. Gregor and Donald Tuzin. Berkeley: University of California Press, 175–206.

———. 2002. "Introduction. Birthing beyond the Confinements of Tradition and Modernity?" In *Birthing in the Pacific. Beyond Tradition and Modernity?* edited by Vicky Lukere and Margaret Jolly. Honolulu: University of Hawai'i Press, 1–30.

———. 2005. "Beyond the Horizon? Nationalisms, Feminisms, and Globalization in the Pacific," *Ethnohistory* 52(1): 137–66.

Jorgensen, Dan. 1983. "Mirroring Nature? Men's and Women's Models of Conception in Telefolmin," *Mankind* 14(1): 57–65.

———. 2007. "Changing Minds. Hysteria and the History of Spirit Mediumship in Telefolmin." In *The Anthropology of Morality in Melanesia and Beyond,* edited by John Barker (Anthropology and Cultural History in Asia and the Indo-Pacific). Aldershot: Ashgate, 113–30.

Josephides, Lisette. 1991. "Metaphors, Metathemes, and the Construction of Sociality. A Critique of the New Melanesian Ethnography," *Man, n.s.* 26(1): 145–61.
Kahn, Miriam. 1986. *Always Hungry, Never Greedy. Food and the Expression of Gender in a Melanesian Society.* Cambridge: Cambridge University Press.
Keck, Verena. 1992. *Falsch gehandelt—schwer erkrankt. Kranksein bei den Yupno in Papua New Guinea aus ethnologischer und biomedizinischer Sicht* (Basler Beiträge zur Ethnologie, vol. 35). Basel: Wepf.
———. 1993a. "Talk about a Changing World. Young Yupno Men in Papua New Guinea Debate Their Future," *Canberra Anthropology* 16(2): 67–96.
———. 1993b. "Two Ways of Explaining Reality. The Sickness of a Small Boy of Papua New Guinea from Anthropological and Biomedical Perspectives," *Oceania* 63(4): 294–312.
———. 2005. *Social Discord and Bodily Disorders. Healing among the Yupno of Papua New Guinea* (Medical Anthropology Series). Durham: Carolina Academic Press.
Keck, Verena and Jürg Wassmann. 2010. "Das Älterwerden, der Tod und die Erinnerung—ein Beispiel aus Melanesien." In *Potenziale im Altern. Chancen und Aufgaben für Individuum und Gesellschaft*, edited by Andreas Kruse. Heidelberg: Akademische Verlagsgesellschaft, 185–201.
Kleinman, Arthur. 1980. *Patients and Healers in the Context of Culture. An Exploration of the Borderland between Anthropology, Medicine, and Psychiatry* (Comparative Studies of Health Systems and Medical Care, vol. 3). Berkeley: University of California Press.
———. 1982. "Neurasthenia and Depression. A Study of Somatization and Culture in China," *Culture, Medicine and Psychiatry* 6(2): 117–90.
———. 1995. *Writing at the Margin. Discourse between Anthropology and Medicine.* Berkeley: University of California Press.
Knauft, Bruce M. 1989. "Bodily Images in Melanesia. Cultural Substances and Natural Metaphors." In *Fragments for a History of the Human Body*, edited by Michel Feher (Part 3, Zone 5). New York: Zone, 198–279.
———. 2004. "Relating to Women. Female Presence in Melanesian 'Male Cults.'" In *Women as Unseen Characters. Male Ritual in Papua New Guinea*, edited by Pascale Bonnemère (Social Anthropology in Oceania). Philadelphia: University of Pennsylvania Press, 179–200.
Knibbe, Kim and Peter Versteeg. 2008. "Assessing Phenomenology in Anthropology. Lessons from the Study of Religion and Experience," *Critique of Anthropology* 28(1): 47–62.
Koczberski, Gina and George N. Curry. 1999. "'Sik Bilong Ples.' An Exploration of Meanings of Illness and Well-Being amongst the Wosera Abelam of Papua New Guinea," *Australian Geographical Studies* 37(3): 230–47.
Kolo, Pearson. 2007. "Marijuana Cause of Mental Ills," *Papua New Guinea Post-Courier*, 14 September, weekend edition, 3.
Konrad, Monica. 2005. *Nameless Relations. Anonymity, Melanesia and Reproductive Gift Exchange between British Ova Donors and Recipients* (Fertility, Reproduction and Sexuality, vol. 7). New York: Berghahn Books.
Kulick, Don. 1992. *Language Shift and Cultural Reproduction. Socialization, Self, and Syncretism in a Papua New Guinean Village* (Studies in the Social and Cultural Foundations of Language, vol. 14). Cambridge: Cambridge University Press.

Lahn, Julie. 2006. "Women's Gift-Fish and Sociality in the Torres Strait, Australia," *Oceania* 76(3): 297–309.
Langness, Lewis L. 1974. "Ritual, Power, and Male Dominance," *Ethos* 2(3): 189–212.
Lattas, Andrew. 2000. "Telephones, Cameras and Technology in West New Britain Cargo Cults," *Oceania* 70(4): 325–44.
———. 2006. "Technologies of Visibility. The Utopian Politics of Cameras, Televisions, Videos and Dreams in New Britain," *Australian Journal of Anthropology* 17(1): 15–31.
———. 2010. *Dreams, Madness, and Fairy Tales in New Britain* (Ritual Studies Monograph Series). Durham: Carolina Academic Press.
Laub Coser, Rose. 1962. *Life in the Ward*. East Lansing: Michigan State University Press.
LeCompte, Margaret D. and Jean J. Schensul. 1999. *Designing and Conducting Ethnographic Research* (Ethnographer's Toolkit, vol. 1). Walnut Creek: AltaMira.
Lepani, Katherine. 2008. "Fitting Condoms on Culture. Rethinking Approaches to HIV Prevention in the Trobriand Islands, Papua New Guinea." In *Making Sense of AIDS. Culture, Sexuality, and Power in Melanesia*, edited by Leslie Butt and Richard Eves. Honolulu: University of Hawai'i Press, 246–66.
Lepowsky, Maria. 1990. "Sorcery and Penicillin. Treating Illness on a Papua New Guinea Island," *Social Science & Medicine* 30(10): 1049–63.
Lewis, Gilbert. 1975. *Knowledge of Illness in a Sepik Society. A Study of the Gnau, New Guinea* (London School of Economics Monographs on Social Anthropology, vol. 52). London: Athlone Press.
———. 2000. *A Failure of Treatment* (Oxford Studies in Social and Cultural Anthropology). Oxford: Oxford University Press.
Lindenbaum, Shirley. 1979. *Kuru Sorcery. Disease and Danger in the New Guinea Highlands* (Explorations in World Ethnology). Mountain View: Mayfield.
Lindstrom, Lamont. 1999. "Social Relations." In *The Pacific Islands. Environment & Society*, edited by Moshe Rapaport. Honolulu: Bess Press, 195–207.
Lindstrom, Lamont and Geoffrey M. White. 1994. "Cultural Policy. An Introduction." In *Culture, Kastom, Tradition. Developing Cultural Policy in Melanesia*, edited by Lamont Lindstrom and Geoffrey M. White. Suva: Institute of Pacific Studies, University of the South Pacific, 1–18.
Lipset, David. 2004. "Modernity without Romance? Masculinity and Desire in Courtship Stories Told by Young Papua New Guinean Men," *American Ethnologist* 31(2): 205–24.
LiPuma, Edward. 1989. "Modernity and Medicine among the Maring." In *A Continuing Trial of Treatment. Medical Pluralism in Papua New Guinea*, edited by Stephen Frankel and Gilbert Lewis (Culture, Illness, and Healing). Dordrecht: Kluwer Academic, 295–310.
———. 1998. "Modernity and Forms of Personhood in Melanesia." In *Bodies and Persons. Comparative Perspectives from Africa and Melanesia*, edited by Michael L. Lambek and Andrew Strathern. Cambridge: Cambridge University Press, 53–79.
———. 2000. *Encompassing Others. The Magic of Modernity in Melanesia*. Ann Arbor: University of Michigan Press.
Lock, Margaret. 2004. "Biomedical Technologies. Anthropological Approaches." In *Encyclopedia of Medical Anthropology. Health and Illness in the World's Cultures.*

Volume I. Topics, edited by Carol R. Ember and Melvin Ember. New York: Springer, 86–95.

Lock, Margaret and Deborah R. Gordon. 1988. "Relationships between Society, Culture, and Biomedicine. Introduction to the Essays." In *Biomedicine Examined,* edited by Margaret Lock and Allan Young (Culture, Illness, and Healing). Dordrecht: Kluwer Academic, 11–16.

Lock, Margaret and Patricia A. Kaufert. 1998. "Introduction." In *Pragmatic Women and Body Politics,* edited by Margaret Lock and Patricia A. Kaufert (Cambridge Studies in Medical Anthropology, vol. 5). London: Routledge, 1–27.

Lock, Margaret and Vinh-Kim Nguyen. 2010. *An Anthropology of Biomedicine.* Chichester: Wiley-Blackwell.

Lohmann, Roger I. 2003. "Glass Men and Spirit Women in Papua New Guinea," *Cultural Survival Quarterly* 27(2, special issue "Shamanisms and Survival"): 52–54.

Long, Debbi, Cynthia L. Hunter, and Sjaak van der Geest. 2008. "Introduction. When the Field Is a Ward or a Clinic. Hospital Ethnography," *Anthropology & Medicine* 15(2, special issue "When the Field Is a Ward or a Clinic. Hospital Ethnography"): 71–78.

Lukere, Vicky. 2002. "Conclusion. Wider Reflections and a Survey of Literature." In *Birthing in the Pacific. Beyond Tradition and Modernity?* edited by Vicky Lukere and Margaret Jolly. Honolulu: University of Hawai'i Press, 178–202.

Lutkehaus, Nancy C. 1995. "Feminist Anthropology and Female Initiation in Melanesia." In *Gender Rituals. Female Initiation in Melanesia,* edited by Nancy C. Lutkehaus and Paul B. Roscoe. New York: Routledge, 3–29.

Lutz, Catherine A. 1988. *Unnatural Emotions. Everyday Sentiments on a Micronesian Atoll and Their Challenge to Western Theory.* Chicago: University of Chicago Press.

Macfarlane, Joan. 2009. "Common Themes in the Literature on Traditional Medicine in Papua New Guinea," *Papua New Guinea Medical Journal* 52(1–2): 44–53.

Macintyre, Martha, Simon Foale, Nicholas Bainton, and Brigid Moktel. 2005. "Medical Pluralism and the Maintenance of a Traditional Healing Technique on Lihir, Papua New Guinea," *Pimatisiwin. A Journal of Aboriginal and Indigenous Community Health* 3(1): 87–99.

MacKenzie, Maureen A. 1991. *Androgynous Objects. String Bags and Gender in Central New Guinea* (Studies in Anthropology and History, vol. 2). Chur: Harwood Academic Publishers.

Macpherson, Cluny and Laavasa Macpherson. 1990. *Samoan Medical Belief and Practice.* Auckland: Auckland University Press.

MacQueen, Kathleen M. 2002. "Anthropology in Public Health." In *Encyclopedia of Public Health. Volume 1. A–C,* edited by Lester Breslow. New York: Macmillan Reference USA, 61–63.

Madang Provincial Administration, Division of Corporate and Technical Services, Health Branch. 2008. *Provincial and District Annual Activity Plan.* Madang: unpublished.

Madden, Raymond. 2010. *Being Ethnographic. A Guide to the Theory and Practice of Ethnography.* London: Sage.

Mageo, Jeannette M. 2001. "Dream Play and Discovering Cultural Psychology," *Ethos* 29(2): 187–217.

Maher, Patrick. 1999. "A Review of 'Traditional' Aboriginal Health Beliefs," *Australian Journal of Rural Health* 7(4): 229–36.

Mallett, Shelley. 2002. "Colonial Impregnations. Reconceptions of Maternal Health Practice on Nua'ata, Papua New Guinea." In *Birthing in the Pacific. Beyond Tradition and Modernity?* edited by Vicky Lukere and Margaret Jolly. Honolulu: University of Hawai'i Press, 125–47.

Marcus, George E. 1995. "Ethnography in/of the World System. The Emergence of Multi-Sited Ethnography," *Annual Review of Anthropology* 24: 95–117.

Marcus, George E. and Dick Cushman. 1982. "Ethnographies as Texts," *Annual Review of Anthropology* 11: 25–69.

Marriott, McKim. 1976. "Hindu Transactions. Diversity without Dualism." In *Transaction and Meaning. Directions in the Anthropology of Exchange and Symbolic Behavior*, edited by Bruce Kapferer (ASA Essays in Social Anthropology, vol. 1). Philadelphia: Institute for the Study of Human Issues, 109–42.

Marshall, Leslie B. 1985. "Influences on the Antenatal Clinic Attendance of Central Province Women in Port Moresby, PNG," *Social Science and Medicine* 21(3): 341–50.

Marshall, Mac. 1987. "An Overview of Drugs in Oceania." In *Drugs in Western Pacific Societies. Relations of Substance*, edited by Lamont Lindstrom (ASAO Monograph, vol. 11). Lanham, MD: University Press of America, 13–49.

———. 2004. "Market Highs. Alcohol, Drugs, and the Global Economy in Oceania." In *Globalization and Culture Change in the Pacific Islands*, edited by Victoria S. Lockwood (Exploring Cultures). Upper Saddle River, NJ: Pearson Prentice-Hall, 200–221.

Mattingly, Cheryl and Linda C. Garro, eds. 2000. *Narrative and the Cultural Construction of Illness and Healing.* Berkeley: University of California Press.

Mauss, Marcel. (1938) 1985. "A Category of the Human Mind. The Notion of Person; The Notion of Self." In *The Category of the Person. Anthropology, Philosophy, History*, translated by Wilfred D. Halls, edited by Michael Carrithers, Steven Collins, and Steven Lukes. Cambridge: Cambridge University Press, 1–25.

McDonald, David. 2004. "Cannabis in Papua New Guinea," *Pacific Health Dialog* 11(1): 96–101.

———. 2005. "A Rapid Situation Assessment of Drug Use in Papua New Guinea," *Drug and Alcohol Review* 24(1): 79–82.

McGrath, Barbara B. 1999. "Swimming from Island to Island. Healing Practice in Tonga," *Medical Anthropology Quarterly, n.s.* 13(4): 483–505.

Mead, Margaret. (1935) 2001. *Sex and Temperament in Three Primitive Societies.* New York: Perennial.

Meggitt, Mervyn J. 1964. "Male-Female Relationships in the Highlands of Australian New Guinea," *American Anthropologist* 66(4, Part 2: "New Guinea. The Central Highlands"): 204–24.

Meigs, Anna S. 1976. "Male Pregnancy and the Reduction of Sexual Opposition in a New Guinea Highlands Society," *Ethnology* 15(4): 393–407.

———. 1984. *Food, Sex, and Pollution. A New Guinea Religion.* New Brunswick: Rutgers University Press.

———. 1997. "Food as a Cultural Construction." In *Food and Culture. A Reader*, edited by Carole Counihan and Penny van Esterik. New York: Routledge, 95–106.

Merrett-Balkos, Leanne. 1998. "Just Add Water. Remaking Women through Childbirth, Anganen, Southern Highlands, Papua New Guinea." In *Maternities and Modernities. Colonial and Postcolonial Experiences in Asia and the Pacific*, edited by Kalpana Ram and Margaret Jolly. Cambridge: Cambridge University Press, 213–38.

Mihalic, Frank. (1971) 1986. *The Jacaranda Dictionary and Grammar of Melanesian Pidgin.* Papua New Guinea: Web Books.
Miles, John AR. 1984. "Public Health Progress in Melanesia." In *Public Health Progress in the Pacific. Geographical Background and Regional Development,* edited by John AR Miles. Helmstedt: GeoWissenschaftliche Gesellschaft, 125–44.
Mimica, Jadran. 2008. "Mother's Umbilicus and Father's Spirit. The Dialectics of Selfhood of a Yagwoia Transgendered Person," *Oceania* 78(2): 168–98.
Mitchell, Timothy. 2000. "Introduction." In *Questions of Modernity,* edited by Timothy Mitchell (Contradictions of Modernity, vol. 11). Minneapolis: University of Minnesota Press, xi–xxvii.
Mitchell, William E. 1990. "Therapeutic Systems of the Taute Wape." In *Sepik Heritage. Tradition and Change in Papua New Guinea,* edited by Nancy Lutkehaus, Christian Kaufmann, William E. Mitchell, Douglas Newton, Lita Osmundsen, and Meinhard Schuster. Durham: Carolina Academic Press, 428–38.
Mol, Annemarie. 2002. *The Body Multiple: Ontology in Medical Practice* (Science and Cultural Theory). Durham: Duke University Press.
Monsell-Davis, Michael. 1993. "Urban Exchange. Safety-Net or Disincentive? 'Wantoks' and Relatives in the Urban Pacific," *Canberra Anthropology* 16(2): 45–66.
Morgan, Lynn M. 1996. "Fetal Relationality in Feminist Philosophy. An Anthropological Critique," *Hypatia* 11(3): 47–70.
———. 1997. "Imagining the Unborn in the Ecuadoran Andes," *Feminist Studies* 23(2, special issue "Feminists and Fetuses"): 322–50.
Morris, Brian. 1994. *Anthropology of the Self. The Individual in Cultural Perspective* (Anthropology, Culture and Society). London: Pluto Press.
Morton, Helen. 2002. "From Māʻuli to Motivator. Transformations in Reproductive Health Care in Tonga?" In *Birthing in the Pacific. Beyond Tradition and Modernity?* edited by Vicky Lukere and Margaret Jolly. Honolulu: University of Hawai'i Press, 31–55.
Mosko, Mark S. 2000. "Inalienable Ethnography. Keeping-While-Giving and the Trobriand Case," *Journal of the Royal Anthropological Institute* 6(3): 377–96.
———. 2010. "Partible Penitents. Dividual Personhood and Christian Practice in Melanesia and the West," *Journal of the Royal Anthropological Institute* 16(2): 215–40.
Mulemi, Benson A. 2008. "Patients' Perspectives on Hospitalisation. Experiences from a Cancer Ward in Kenya," *Anthropology & Medicine* 15(2, special issue "When the Field Is a Ward or a Clinic. Hospital Ethnography"): 117–31.
———. 2010. *Coping with Cancer and Adversity. Hospital Ethnography in Kenya* (African Studies Collection, vol. 22). Leiden: African Studies Centre.
Müller-Rockstroh, Babette. 2009. "Imagin(in)g Pregnancy in Northwest Tanzania. Networks, Experiences, and Translations." In *The Body Within. Art, Medicine and Visualization,* edited by Renée van de Vall and Robert Zwijnenberg (Brill's Studies in Intellectual History, vol. 176; Brill's Studies on Art, Art History, and Intellectual History, vol. 3). Leiden: Brill, 139–56.
———. 2010. "Ultraschall in Tansania. Ethnographische Explorationen in den Transfer von Medizintechnologie." In *Medizin im Kontext. Krankheit und Gesundheit in einer vernetzten Welt,* edited by Hansjörg Dilger and Bernhard Hadolt. Frankfurt am Main: Peter Lang, 35–52.

Müller-Rockstroh, Babette. 2012. "Appropriate and Appropriated Technology. Lessons Learned from Ultrasound in Tanzania," *Medical Anthropology: Cross-Cultural Studies in Health and Illness* 31(3): 196–212.

Munn, Nancy D. 1986. *The Fame of Gawa. A Symbolic Study of Value Transformation in a Massim (Papua New Guinea) Society* (Lewis Henry Morgan Lecture Series). Cambridge: Cambridge University Press.

Murchison, Julian M. 2010. *Ethnography Essentials. Designing, Conducting, and Presenting Your Research* (The Lewis Henry Morgan Lecture Series). San Francisco: Jossey-Bass.

Newman, Philip L. 1964. "'Wild Man' Behavior in a New Guinea Highlands Community," *American Anthropologist* 66(1): 1–19.

Nichter, Mark. 2002. "The Social Relations of Therapy Management." In *New Horizons in Medical Anthropology. Essays in Honour of Charles Leslie,* edited by Mark Nichter and Margaret Lock (Theory and Practice in Medical Anthropology and International Health, vol. 8). London: Routledge, 81–110.

Noho, Bola. 2011. "Malau. Dept to Re-Supply," *Papua New Guinea Post-Courier,* 21 April, 5.

Nombo, Porer and James Leach. 2010. *Reite Plants. An Ethnobotanical Study in Tok Pisin and English* (Asia-Pacific Environment Monograph, vol. 4). Canberra: ANU E Press. Retrieved 22 August 2015 from http://press.anu.edu.au/wp-content/uploads/2011/05/whole_book15.pdf.

Obrist van Eeuwijk, Brigit. 1998. "Intrusions into the Female Realm. The Medicalization of Human Procreation among the Kwanga in Papua New Guinea." In *Common Worlds and Single Lives. Constituting Knowledge in Pacific Societies,* edited by Verena Keck (Explorations in Anthropology). Oxford: Berg, 251–72.

O'Hanlon, Michael. 1989. *Reading the Skin. Adornment, Display and Society among the Wahgi.* Bathurst: Crawford House Press.

Ortner, Sherry B. 1984. "Theory in Anthropology since the Sixties," *Comparative Studies in Society and History* 26(1): 126–66.

Osella, Caroline and Filippo Osella. 2006. *Men and Masculinities in South India* (Anthem South Asian Studies). London: Anthem Press.

Otto, Ton. 2007. "Rethinking Tradition. Invention, Cultural Continuity and Agency." In *Experiencing New Worlds,* edited by Jürg Wassmann and Katharina Stockhaus (Person, Space and Memory in the Contemporary Pacific, vol. 1). New York: Berghahn Books, 36–57.

Panti, Andrew P. 1991. "Initiation or 'Monigafoi,'" *Grassroots Research Bulletin* 1(1): 3–8.

———. 1992. "Growing Yams in Kumanung," *Grassroots Research Bulletin* 2(2): 17–21.

Patterson, Mary. 1974. "Sorcery and Witchcraft in Melanesia," *Oceania* 45(2): 132–60.

Pendene, Jessy. 2009. "Health Workers Call for Better Facilities," *Papua New Guinea Post-Courier,* 4 November, 13.

Rannells, Jackson. 1995. *PNG. A Fact Book on Modern Papua New Guinea,* 2nd ed. Melbourne: Oxford University Press.

Rapp, Rayna. 1997. "Real-Time Fetus. The Role of the Sonogram in the Age of Monitored Reproduction." In *Cyborgs and Citadels. Anthropological Interventions in Emerging Sciences and Technologies,* edited by Gary L. Downey and Joseph Dumit (School of American Research Advanced Seminar Series). Santa Fe, NM: School of American Research Press, 31–48.

Rappaport, Roy A. 1968. *Pigs for the Ancestors. Ritual in the Ecology of a New Guinea People.* New Haven: Yale University Press.
Read, Kenneth E. 1954/55. "Morality and the Concept of the Person among the Gahuku-Gama," *Oceania* 25(4): 233–82.
Rendap, Vincent. 1991. "The Women Have Power over Men," *Grassroots Research Bulletin* 1(1): 9–10.
Repič, Jaka. 2011. "Appropriation of Space and Water in Informal Urban Settlements of Port Moresby, Papua New Guinea," *Anthropological Notebooks* 17(3), 73–87.
Rio, Knut. 2010. "Handling Sorcery in a State System of Law. Magic, Violence and Kastom in Vanuatu," *Oceania* 80(2): 182–97.
Rio, Knut M. and Olaf H. Smedal. 2008. "Totalization and Detotalization. Alternatives to Hierarchy and Individualism," *Anthropological Theory* 8(3): 233–54.
Risse, Guenter B. 1993. "History of Western Medicine from Hippocrates to Germ Theory." In *The Cambridge World History of Human Disease,* edited by Kenneth F. Kiple. Cambridge: Cambridge University Press, 11–19.
Robbins, Joel. 2006. "Creative Land. Place and Procreation on the Rai Coast of Papua New Guinea, and: Papua New Guinea's Last Place. Experiences of Constraint in a Postcolonial Prison (Review)," *Contemporary Pacific* 18(1): 171–75.
Robbins, Joel and Alan Rumsey. 2008. "Introduction. Cultural and Linguistic Anthropology and the Opacity of Other Minds," *Anthropological Quarterly* 81(2): 407–20.
Robertson, Roland. 1992. *Globalization. Social Theory and Global Culture* (Theory, Culture & Society). London: Sage.
———. 1995. "Glocalization. Time—Space and Homogeneity—Heterogeneity." In *Global Modernities,* edited by Mike Featherstone, Scott Lash, and Roland Robertson (Theory, Culture & Society). London: Sage, 25–44.
Roscoe, Paul. 1989. "Medical Pluralism among the Yangoru Boiken." In *A Continuing Trial of Treatment. Medical Pluralism in Papua New Guinea,* edited by Stephen Frankel and Gilbert Lewis (Culture, Illness, and Healing). Dordrecht: Kluwer Academic, 199–215.
———. 2001. "'Strength' and Sexuality. Sexual Avoidance and Masculinity in New Guinea and Amazonia." In *Gender in Amazonia and Melanesia. An Exploration of the Comparative Method,* edited by Thomas A. Gregor and Donald Tuzin. Berkeley: University of California Press, 279–308.
Roth, Julius A. 1963. *Timetables. Structuring the Passage of Time in Tuberculosis Treatment and Other Careers.* Indianapolis: Bobbs-Merrill.
Rubel, Paula G. and Abraham Rosman. 1978. *Your Own Pigs You May Not Eat. A Comparative Study of New Guinea Societies.* Chicago: University of Chicago Press.
Rumsey, Alan. 2000. "Women as Peacemakers—a Case from the Nebilyer Valley, Western Highlands, Papua New Guinea." In *Reflections on Violence in Melanesia,* edited by Sinclair Dinnen and Allison Ley. Leichhardt/Canberra: Hawkins Press/Asia Pacific Press, 139–55.
Russell, Andrew. 1999. "Taking Care? The Depo-Provera Debate." In *Extending the Boundaries of Care. Medical Ethics and Caring Practices,* edited by Tamara Kohn and Rosemary McKechnie (Cross-Cultural Perspectives on Women, vol. 21). Oxford: Berg, 65–88.
Saethre, Eirik J. 2007. "Conflicting Traditions, Concurrent Treatment. Medical Pluralism in Remote Aboriginal Australia," *Oceania* 77(1): 95–110.

Sahlins, Marshall. 1972. *Stone Age Economics.* Chicago: Aldine Atherton.
Saillant, Francine and Serge Genest. 2007. "Introduction." In *Medical Anthropology. Regional Perspectives and Shared Concerns,* edited by Francine Saillant and Serge Genest. Malden, MA: Blackwell, xviii–xxxiii.
Salisbury, Richard F. 1968. "Possession in the New Guinea Highlands," *International Journal of Social Psychiatry* 14(2): 85–94.
Salomon, Christine. 2002. "Obligatory Maternity and Diminished Reproductive Autonomy in A'jië and Paicî Kanak Societies. A Female Perspective." In *Birthing in the Pacific. Beyond Tradition and Modernity?* edited by Vicky Lukere and Margaret Jolly. Honolulu: University of Hawai'i Press, 79–99.
Saura, Bruno. 2002. "Continuity of Bodies. The Infant's Placenta and the Island's Navel in Eastern Polynesia," *Journal of the Polynesian Society* 111(2): 127–46.
Scaletta, Naomi M. 1986. "Childbirth. A Case History from West New Britain, Papua New Guinea," *Oceania* 57(1): 33–52.
Schensul, Stephen L., Jean J. Schensul, and Margaret D. LeCompte. 1999. *Essential Ethnographic Methods. Observations, Interviews, and Questionnaires* (Ethnographer's Toolkit, vol. 2). Walnut Creek: AltaMira.
Scheper-Hughes, Nancy and Margaret M. Lock. 1987. "The Mindful Body. A Prolegomenon to Future Work in Medical Anthropology," *Medical Anthropology Quarterly, n.s.* 1(1): 6–41.
Schieffelin, Edward L. 1976. *The Sorrow of the Lonely and the Burning of the Dancers.* New York: St. Martin's.
———. 1996. "Evil Spirit Sickness, the Christian Disease. The Innovation of a New Syndrome of Mental Derangement and Redemption in Papua New Guinea," *Culture, Medicine & Psychiatry* 20(1): 1–39.
Schinzel, Britta. 2006. "The Body in Medical Imaging Between Reality and Construction," *Poiesis & Praxis* 4(3): 185–98.
Schneider, Almut. 2011. *La Vie qui vient d'ailleurs. Mouvement, échanges et rituel dans les Hautes-Terres de la Papouasie-Nouvelle-Guinée.* Doctoral Thesis, École des Hautes Études en Sciences Sociales.
Schwartz, Lola R. 1969. "The Hierarchy of Resort in Curative Practices. The Admiralty Islands, Melanesia," *Journal of Health & Social Behavior* 10(3): 201–9.
Setepano, Nellie. 2011. "Mental Health, a Problem in PNG," *Papua New Guinea Post-Courier,* 11 October, 5.
Siegel, Matt. 2013. "Nation Acts to Repeal Sorcery Law after Strife," *New York Times,* 30 May, A10.
Silverman, Eric K. 2001a. "From Totemic Space to Cyberspace. Transformations in Sepik River and Aboriginal Australian Myth, Knowledge, and Art." In *Emplaced Myth. Space, Narrative, and Knowledge in Aboriginal Australia and Papua New Guinea,* edited by Alan Rumsey and James Weiner. Honolulu: University of Hawai'i Press, 189–214.
———. 2001b. *Masculinity, Motherhood, and Mockery. Psychoanalyzing Culture and the Iatmul Naven Rite in New Guinea.* Ann Arbor: University of Michigan Press.
Sobo, Elisa J. 2011. "Medical Anthropology in Disciplinary Context. Definitional Struggles and Key Debates (or Answering the Cri Du Coeur)." In *A Companion to Medical Anthropology,* edited by Merrill Singer and Pamela I. Erickson (Blackwell Companions to Anthropology). Malden, MA: Wiley-Blackwell, 9–28.

Spitz, Herman H. 1997. *Nonconscious Movements. From Mystical Messages to Facilitated Communication.* Mahwah, NJ: Erlbaum.
Stanhope, John M. 1968. "Competing Systems of Medicine among the Rao-Breri, Lower Ramu River, New Guinea," *Oceania* 39(2): 137–45.
———. 1972. "The Language of the Kire People, Bogia, Madang District, New Guinea," *Anthropos* 67: 49–71.
Stanton, Alfred H. and Morris S. Schwartz. 1954. *The Mental Hospital. A Study of Institutional Participation in Psychiatric Illness and Treatment.* New York: Basic Books.
Stephen, Michele. 1996. "The Mekeo 'Man of Sorrow.' Sorcery and the Individuation of the Self," *American Ethnologist* 23(1): 83–101.
Stewart, Lynn L. 1989. *"Our People Are Like Gardens." Music, Performance and Aesthetics among the Lolo. West New Britain Province, Papua New Guinea.* PhD Thesis, University of British Columbia.
Stewart, Pamela J. and Andrew J. Strathern. 1997. "Netbags Revisited. Cultural Narratives from Papua New Guinea," *Pacific Studies* 20(2): 1–29.
———. 2000. "Introduction. Narratives Speak." In *Identity Work. Constructing Pacific Lives,* edited by Pamela J. Stewart and Andrew Strathern (ASAO Monograph Series, vol. 18). Pittsburgh, PA: University of Pittsburgh Press, 1–26.
———. 2001a. "Introduction. Gathering the Threads of the Flow of Life." In *Humors and Substances. Ideas of the Body in New Guinea,* edited by Pamela J. Stewart and Andrew Strathern. Westport, CT: Bergin & Garvey, 1–21.
———. 2001b. "Substance Transfer. Conception, Growth, and Nurturance in Highlands Papua New Guinea." In *Humors and Substances. Ideas of the Body in New Guinea,* edited by Pamela J. Stewart and Andrew Strathern. Westport, CT: Bergin & Garvey, 83–97.
———. 2002. "Power and Placement in Blood Practices," *Ethnology* 41(4, special issue "Blood Mysteries. Beyond Menstruation as Pollution"): 349–63.
———. 2004. *Witchcraft, Sorcery, Rumors, and Gossip* (New Departures in Anthropology). Cambridge: Cambridge University Press.
Strathern, Andrew J. 1975. "Why Is Shame on the Skin?" *Ethnology* 14(4): 347–56.
———. 1989. "Health Care and Medical Pluralism. Cases from Mount Hagen." In *A Continuing Trial of Treatment. Medical Pluralism in Papua New Guinea,* edited by Stephen Frankel and Gilbert Lewis (Culture, Illness, and Healing). Dordrecht: Kluwer Academic, 141–54.
———. 1996. *Body Thoughts.* Ann Arbor: University of Michigan Press.
Strathern, Andrew J. and Pamela J. Stewart. 1998a. "Embodiment and Communication. Two Frames for the Analysis of Ritual," *Social Anthropology* 6(2): 237–51.
———. 1998b. "Melpa and Nuer Ideas of Life and Death. The Rebirth of Comparison." In *Bodies and Persons. Comparative Perspectives from Africa and Melanesia,* edited by Michael L. Lambek and Andrew Strathern. Cambridge: Cambridge University Press, 232–51.
———. "Seeking Personhood. Anthropological Accounts and Local Concepts in Mount Hagen, Papua New Guinea," *Oceania* 68(3): 170–88.
———. 1999. *Curing and Healing. Medical Anthropology in Global Perspective.* Durham: Carolina Academic Press.
———. 2000. *Arrow Talk. Transaction, Transition, and Contradiction in New Guinea Highlands History.* Kent, OH: Kent State University Press.

Strathern, Marilyn. 1979. "The Self in Self-Decoration," *Oceania* 49(4): 241–57.
———. 1988. *The Gender of the Gift. Problems with Women and Problems with Society in Melanesia* (Studies in Melanesian Anthropology, vol. 6). Berkeley: University of California Press.
———. 1991. "Partners and Consumers. Making Relations Visible," *New Literary History* 22(3): 581–601.
———. 2012. "Gifts Money Cannot Buy," *Social Anthropology* 20(4): 397–410.
Street, Alice. 2009. "Failed Recipients. Extracting Blood in a Papua New Guinean Hospital," *Body & Society* 15(2): 193–215.
———. 2011. "Artefacts of Not-Knowing. The Medical Record, the Diagnosis and the Production of Uncertainty in Papua New Guinean Biomedicine," *Social Studies of Science* 41(6): 815–34.
———. 2012. "Affective Infrastructure. Hospital Landscapes of Hope and Failure," *Space and Culture* 15(1): 44–56.
———. 2014. *Biomedicine in an Unstable Place. Infrastructure and Personhood in a Papua New Guinean Hospital* (Experimental Futures. Technological Lives, Scientific Arts, Anthropological Voices). Durham: Duke University Press.
Sullivan, Noelle. 2011. *Negotiating Abundance and Scarcity. Health Sector Reform, Development Aid, and Biomedical Practice in a Tanzanian Hospital.* PhD Thesis, University of Florida.
———. 2012. "Enacting Spaces of Inequality. Placing Global/State Governance within a Tanzanian Hospital," *Space and Culture* 15(1): 57–67.
Sykes, Gresham M. 1958. *The Society of Captives. A Study of a Maximum Security Prison.* Princeton: Princeton University Press.
Sykes, Karen. 2007. "'Family Planning.' The Politics of Reproduction in Central New Ireland." In *Embodying Modernity and Post-Modernity. Ritual, Praxis, and Social Change in Melanesia,* edited by Sandra Bamford (Ritual Studies Monographs). Durham: Carolina Academic Press, 211–38.
Telban, Borut. 1998. "Body, Being and Identity in Ambonwari, Papua New Guinea." In *Common Worlds and Single Lives. Constituting Knowledge in Pacific Societies,* edited by Verena Keck (Explorations in Anthropology). Oxford: Berg, 55–70.
———. 2001. "Temporality of Post-mortem Divination and Divination of Post-mortem Temporality," *The Australian Journal of Anthropology* 12(1): 67–79.
Telban, Borut and Daniela Vávrová. 2014. "Ringing the Living and the Dead. Mobile Phones in a Sepik Society," *The Australian Journal of Anthropology* 25(2): 223–38.
Thomason, Jane A. and Riitta-Liisa Kolehmainen-Aitken. 1991. "Distribution and Performance of Rural Health Workers in Papua New Guinea," *Social Science & Medicine* 32(2): 159–65.
Toren, Christina. 2009. "Intersubjectivity as Epistemology," *Social Analysis* 53(2): 130–46.
Trompf, Garry W. 1994. *Payback. The Logic of Retribution in Melanesian Religions.* Cambridge: Cambridge University Press.
Tuzin, Donald F. 1980. *The Voice of the Tambaran. Truth and Illusion in Ilahita Arapesh Religion.* Berkeley: University of California Press.
———. 1992. "Sago Subsistence and Symbolism among the Ilahita Arapesh," *Ethnology* 31(2): 103–14.
Umau, Poreni. 2011. "Medical Store Closed," *Papua New Guinea Post-Courier,* 18 January, 14.

van Amstel, Hans and Sjaak van der Geest. 2004. "Doctors and Retribution. The Hospitalisation of Compensation Claims in the Highlands of Papua New Guinea," *Social Science & Medicine* 59(10, special issue "Hospital Ethnography"): 2087–94.
van der Geest, Sjaak. 1984. "Anthropology and Pharmaceuticals in Developing Countries," *Medical Anthropology Quarterly* 15(3): 59–62.
―――. 2002. "Respect and Reciprocity. Care of Elderly People in Rural Ghana," *Journal of Cross-Cultural Gerontology* 17(1): 3–31.
van der Geest, Sjaak and Kaja Finkler. 2004. "Hospital Ethnography. Introduction," *Social Science & Medicine* 59(10, special issue "Hospital Ethnography"): 1995–2001.
van der Geest, Sjaak and Samuel Sarkodie. 1998. "The Fake Patient. A Research Experiment in a Ghanaian Hospital," *Social Science & Medicine* 47(9): 1373–81.
van der Geest, Sjaak and Susan R. Whyte, eds. 1988. *The Context of Medicines in Developing Countries: Studies in Pharmaceutical Anthropology* (Culture, Illness, and Healing, vol. 12). Dordrecht: Kluwer Academic.
―――. 1989. "The Charm of Medicines. Metaphors and Metonyms," *Medical Anthropology Quarterly, n.s.* 3(4): 345–67.
van Staa, AnneLoes and Anita Hardon. 1996. *Injection Practices in the Developing World. Results and Recommendations from Field Studies in Uganda and Indonesia.* Prepared for WHO-DAP (EDM Research Series, no. 20). Retrieved 22 August 2015 from http://apps.who.int/medicinedocs/pdf/s2232e/s2232e.pdf.
Vaughan, Catherine M. 2011. *A Picture of Health. Participation, Photovoice and Preventing HIV among Papua New Guinean Youth.* PhD Thesis, The London School of Economics and Political Science.
von Poser, Alexis T. 2014. *The Accounts of Jong. A Discussion of Time, Space, and Person in Kayan, Papua New Guinea* (Heidelberg Studies in Pacific Anthropology, vol. 2). Heidelberg: Winter.
von Poser, Anita. 2013. *Foodways and Empathy. Relatedness in a Ramu River Society, Papua New Guinea* (Person, Space and Memory in the Contemporary Pacific, vol. 4). New York: Berghahn Books.
Wagner, Roy. 1975. *The Invention of Culture.* Englewood Cliffs, NJ: Prentice-Hall.
―――. 1983. "The Ends of Innocence. Conception and Seduction among the Daribi of Karimui and the Barok of New Ireland," *Mankind* 14(1): 75–83.
―――. 1991. "The Fractal Person." In *Big Men and Great Men. Personifications of Power in Melanesia,* edited by Maurice Godelier and Marilyn Strathern. Cambridge: Cambridge University Press, 159–73.
Wallis, Robert J. 2003. *Shamans/Neo-Shamans. Ecstasy, Alternative Archaeologies and Contemporary Pagans.* London: Routledge.
Wardlow, Holly. 2004. "Anger, Economy, and Female Agency. Problematizing 'Prostitution' and 'Sex Work' among the Huli of Papua New Guinea," *Signs* 29(4): 1017–40.
Wardlow, Holly. 2006. *Wayward Women. Sexuality and Agency in a New Guinea Society.* Berkeley: University of California Press.
Wassmann, Jürg. 1987. "Der Biß des Krokodils. Die ordnungsstiftende Funktion der Namen in der Beziehung zwischen Mensch und Umwelt am Beispiel der Initiation, Nyaura, Mittel-Sepik." In *Neuguinea. Nutzung und Deutung der Umwelt, Band 2,* edited by Mark Münzel (Roter Faden zu Ausstellung, vol. 13). Frankfurt am Main: Museum für Völkerkunde, 511–57.

Wassmann, Jürg and Verena Keck. 2007. "Introduction." In *Experiencing New Worlds*, edited by Jürg Wassmann and Katharina Stockhaus Books (Person, Space and Memory in the Contemporary Pacific, vol. 1). New York: Berghahn, 1–18.

Wassmann, Jürg and Katharina Stockhaus, eds. 2007. *Experiencing New Worlds* (Person, Space and Memory in the Contemporary Pacific, vol. 1). New York: Berghahn Books.

Wassmann, Jürg, Birgit Träuble, and Joachim Funke, eds. 2013. *Theory of Mind in the Pacific. Reasoning across Cultures* (Heidelberg Studies in Pacific Anthropology, vol. 1). Heidelberg: Universitätsverlag Winter.

Watson, Amanda HA, Gaius Sabumei, Glen Mola, and Rick Iedema. 2015. "Maternal Health Phone Line. Saving Women in Papua New Guinea," *Journal of Personalized Medicine* 5(2): 120–39.

Weiner, Annette B. 1992. *Inalienable Possessions. The Paradox of Keeping-While-Giving*. Berkeley: University of California Press.

Whitehead, Harriet. 2000. *Food Rules. Hunting, Sharing, and Tabooing Game in Papua New Guinea*. Ann Arbor: University of Michigan Press.

Whyte, Susan R., Sjaak van der Geest, and Anita Hardon. 2002. *Social Lives of Medicines* (Cambridge Studies in Medical Anthropology, vol. 10). Cambridge: Cambridge University Press.

Wind, Gitte. 2008. "Negotiated Interactive Observation. Doing Fieldwork in Hospital Settings," *Anthropology & Medicine* 15(2): 79–89.

World Health Organization (WHO). 1978. "Declaration of Alma-Ata." In *International Conference on Primary Health Care, Alma-Ata, USSR, 6–12 September 1978*. Retrieved 22 August 2015 from http://www.who.int/publications/almaata_declaration_en.pdf.

———. 2005. *The World Health Report 2005. Make Every Mother and Child Count*. Geneva: WHO Press. Retrieved 22 August 2015 from http://www.who.int/whr/2005/whr2005_en.pdf.

———. 2011. *Western Pacific Country Health Information Profiles. 2011 Revision*. Geneva: WHO Press. Retrieved 22 August 2015 from http://www.wpro.who.int/health_information_evidence/documents/CHIPS2011.pdf.

Young, Allan. 1982. "The Anthropologies of Illness and Sickness," *Annual Review of Anthropology* 11: 257–85.

Zaman, Shahaduz. 2005. *Broken Limbs, Broken Lives. Ethnography of a Hospital Ward in Bangladesh* (Health, Culture and Society. Studies in Medical Anthropology and Sociology). Amsterdam: Het Spinhuis.

Zimmer-Tamakoshi, Laura. 2012. "Troubled Masculinities and Gender Violence in Melanesia." In *Engendering Violence in Papua New Guinea*, edited by Margaret Jolly, Christine Stewart, and Carolyn Brewer. Canberra: ANU E Press, 73–105. Retrieved 22 August 2015 from http://epress.anu.edu.au/wp-content/uploads/2012/07/whole.pdf.

Zola, Irving K. 1972. "Medicine as an Institution of Social Control," *The Sociological Review* 20(4): 487–504.

Index

abortion, 33, 34
accommodation of patients at health personnel's homes, 9, 101, 116, 126, 127
admission (to medical institution), 23, 32–33, 44, 45, 47n10, 60, 93, 101, 102–3, 104, 111, 116, 117, 118–19, 120, 121, 126, 153–54, 159–60, 162
adoption, 68, 101, 104, 114, 173
adolescence/adolescents, 44, 68, 75, 78, 84, 106, 142, 143
afterbirth, 136, 137, 166, 176–78, 179, 180–86, 187, 190n23–24. *See also* placenta
age, 17, 18, 37, 58, 126, 174, 189n12
  advanced, 146, 151
  at death, 83
  marital age, 97n18
  reproductive, 146
agency, 7, 11, 12n1, 95, 100, 106, 134, 187, 192, 193, 195
aging, 142, 151, 171
aid post, 29, 30, 31, 38, 42, 56
  in Akurai, 29
  in Anganen, 186
  in Bivi, 29
  in Bosmun, 29
  in Bulivar, 29
  in Giri, 17, 29
  and mission, 17, 27, 51, 103
  "orderlies", 37
  in Seven, 29
Aiome, 58
Akikim, 63, 107
Akin, David, 145
Akurai. *See* aid post: in Akurai
Albaniel-Evara, Rosalyn, 47n10
Allan, Bryant J., 57, 60
Amarong, 110
Ambai'ati, 58

Ambonwari, 80, 132n3, 188n2
ambulance, 33, 76, 115
Anderson, Astrid, 16, 104, 106–7, 132n3
ancestors/ancestral spirits, 26n4, 48, 50–51, 72, 73, 78–82, 83, 85–88, 90, 127, 168, 176, 177, 194
Anganen, 170, 172, 179, 183, 186, 190n19
Ankave-Anga, 155, 168–69, 189n15
Annaberg, 58
"anthropology of pharmaceuticals", 152
anxiety, 44, 76, 121
'Are'Are, 176–77, 190n23
areca nut, 2, 41, 44, 60, 74, 84, 85, 113, 115, 123, 129, 149, 171
Australian Agency for International Development, 38
Awar, 29, 143, 176, 190n21
awareness campaigns, 31, 32, 198–201, 205n3. *See also* health education
Ayers Counts, Dorothy, 168

Baining, 7–8, 106
Bamford, Sandra, 176, 189n14–15, 190n21, 197
Barok, 168
Base Camp, 41, 44, 45
Battaglia, Debbora, 7, 106
becoming of person, 131, 166, 175–76, 203
Begesin, 59, 61
betel. *See* areca nut
Biersack, Aletta, 167
biomedical artifacts, 10, 204
biomedical care, 1, 10, 11, 38, 94, 96n3, 135, 200
biomedical drugs, 88
  administering, 117, 153
  combination of, 62, 66
  commercially manufactured synthetic, 152
  dispense of, 37

effectiveness and ineffectiveness of, 67, 88
intake of, 1, 69, 70, 155, 191
meaning of, 66–67
potential of, 165, 187
promotion of, 96n3
response to, 1, 56, 83
shortage of supplies, 35, 36, 40, 41–42, 195
treatment with, 60
biomedical practices
anchorage of in pluralistic medical system, 94
appropriation/change/reinterpretation of, 10,11, 96, 134, 197
change through, 194
underutilization of, 196
and women's subordination, 134
biomedical realities, 25, 192
Birap, 14, 18, 57, 65, 78, 83, 90, 126
birth, 11, 17, 33, 140, 148, 154, 172, 176, 179, 180, 187
before arrival (BBA), 34, 153, 154, 155
assistance/attendants/supervision, 38, 96n3, 154, 155, 158, 159, 160, 175, 182, 183–84; (see also midwifery/midwives)
in biomedical facilities, 34, 41, 121, 152, 153, 154, 158–62, 162, 164, 165, 181, 184–86, 187, 189n11
control, 30, 34, 35, 46n6; (see also contraception/contraceptives)
in dwelling house, 159, 188n9
medicalization of, 134, 136, 187
models/understandings of, 135, 151
and pharmaceuticals, 152–57, 158, 159, 187, 191
process of, 162, 166, 182, 187, 188n7, 195
supervision of, 38
in town, 162–64, 185
traditional, 134, 186–88, 192
in/around village, 154, 158, 159, 160, 162–63, 165, 178, 181, 184, 187
birthing position, 163, 187
Bivi, 29

blood
count, sample and tests, 23, 53, 54, 59, 65, 121
father's and mother's 167–69, 170, 179, 180; (see also maternal substance)
"medication", 153, 158; (see also birth: and pharmaceuticals)
menarcheal/menstrual, 137, 145, 146, 148, 167–68, 179
of parturition, 135, 136 , 137, 145, 148, 151, 178, 180, 192
postpartum/lochia, 135, 136, 145, 148–49, 151, 153, 155, 162, 179, 180, 192; (see also postpartum discharge)
pressure and sugar levels, 156–57
renewal, 78
running in veins and arteries, 137, 153, 167–68
and social relations, 137
unborn made up of, 168, 170, 190n17
uterine, 145, 151, 152, 153, 179
bodily disorder, 1, 50–51, 56, 62, 63, 66, 70, 95
body
boundaries, 52, 80, 138, 139
gaze into, 57, 60, 65–66, 81, 92, 198, 202
heaviness and lightweightness of, 140, 142
intrusion into, 54–56
knowledge/notions/understanding of, 10, 95, 107, 135, 136, 138, 188n2, 192, 197, 198,199
"mindful", 71
as "organic recording device", 22, 25
parts, 57, 130, 138, 168–69
social, 51, 131, 193, 194, 198, 199
strength of, 71, 78, 107, 108, 112–13, 132n3, 137,141–42, 143, 146, 151, 153, 155, 169,193, 205n4
Bogia District, 30
Bogia Health Center, 30–31, 33, 39, 46n3, 115
Bogia Town, 27, 118
Bonnemère, Pascale, 171

Index 233

Bosmun, 7, 77, 107, 131, 143. *See also* aid post: in Bosmun
Bourdieu, Pierre, 24
breastfeeding, 35, 144, 155–56, 170–71, 173
breast milk, 137, 143–44, 153, 155–56, 170–71, 172, 193
Breri, 58–59
Bulivar, 29. *See also* aid post: in Bulivar
burial, 15, 86, 87, 130, 174
   of menstrual and maternity pads, 179
   of placenta and umbilical cord, 11, 136, 166, 176–86, 192, 193, 194; (*see also* placenta)

catchment area of health center, 28–29, 31, 38, 43, 101, 109
childbirth. *See* birth
child health care, 35, 46. *See also* public health: services
Chungrebu, 29
clan, 14, 17, 20, 58, 85, 86, 88, 91–92, 100, 104, 132n7, 178
   land, 19, 20, 83, 170, 172, 175, 178, 182–83; (*see also* ancestral land)
   names, 71, 97n15
   platform, 20, 74, 97n17, 104, 132n7
Clark, Jeffrey, 145
Clifford, James, 21
clinic cards, 1–2, 13, 36, 56, 57, 61–62, 65, 69, 156, 157
closure of health center, 9, 32, 39, 114–18
colonization and colonizers, 27, 46n2, 93
compensation, 84, 91, 128
conflict, 20, 21, 26n1, 32, 33, 39, 44, 45, 63, 74, 77, 84, 90, 92, 118, 146–47
   and illness, 51, 52, 59, 61, 67–68, 70, 71, 83, 90, 91, 93, 95–96, 178, 192–93, 194, 197,198, 199, 200
   between local and introduced biomedical thought and practice, 187
   and sorcery, 60, 91–92, 205n4
construction of biomedicine, 3, 25, 136, 192, 197
contraception/contraceptives, 35–36, 46n6, 117, 135, 153, 156, 179–80, 187, 204
cordyline, 60, 146, 147, 178

corpse, 22, 64, 130, 132n7, 174–75, 190n21, 202
Counts, David R., 168
court
   Bine (Giri) village, 67
   provincial, 91
Courtens, Ien, 87
cremation, 87, 190n21
crimes, 43–44, 114, 117
Csordas, Thomas J., 72
"culturalism", 196
cultural transformation, 135, 192
culture
   dynamic view of, 23–26, 192
   hospital, 5
   as practice, 24–25, 192
custom, 24, 25, 26n4, 70, 72, 74, 86, 89, 97n17, 135–36, 146–47, 159, 160, 161, 164, 165, 166, 185. *See also* kastom

dancers/dancing, 17, 140, 142, 143, 144, 147
Daribi, 173
data collection, 21–22, 25, 30, 73
death, 22, 68, 80, 132n7, 202
   corporeal, 64, 190n21
   attributed to grief, 55, 71
   at health center, 33
   on hospital ward, 119–20, 122, 124, 130, 162, 202
   maternal, 34, 46n5, 135, 140, 171, 173–74, 196
   natural/unnatural, 55, 177
   neonatal, 34, 37, 174, 175
   prediction of, 64
   and sorcery, 15, 52, 55, 59, 63, 190n21, 198, 205n4
Declaration of Alma-Ata, 96n3
De Coppet, Daniel, 176–77
delivery. *See* birth
DelVecchio Good, Mary-Jo, 4
Descartes, René, 4
diagnosis, 2, 6, 10, 18, 23, 31, 33, 38, 42, 50, 53–54, 55, 57, 58, 60, 61–62, 66–67, 69, 72, 81, 84, 91, 92, 94, 95, 103, 115, 118, 150, 191, 194, 195, 198–99, 202

disability, 55, 58, 71, 82, 83, 96n5, 103, 169, 190n18
discharges from medical institutions, 33, 111, 114, 161, 163, 164, 165, 166
dispensary, 30, 126, 159
"dividual", 8, 9, 12n7, 106, 107, 131, 167, 177, 193
divination, 57, 80, 81, 88, 200
"docile bodies", 121
donation
    of blood, 127, 188n5, 202
    of organs, 130, 202
    of ova, 130
    of tissue, 130, 202
Douglas, Mary, 148
dreaming/dreams, 57, 68, 83, 97n6
Dreikikir, 57, 183
drinking, 44. See also homebrew

Ecuador, 196, 203
Ember, Carol R., 3
Ember, Melvin, 3
embodiment, 22, 26, 64, 71, 128, 138–39, 145, 170, 172
empowerment, 108, 130, 134–36
Enlightenment, 4, 54
entrance into adulthood, 52
Errington, Frederick, 12n8
ethnography. See also fieldwork
    doing and writing of, 10, 13, 21–23, 25, 26
    medical, 5–6, 23, 99
    "mobile", 21
    "multi-sited", 21
ethnomedicine, 4
Eves, Richard, 104, 107, 138, 139, 142, 189n15
examination room, 30, 41, 159

Fabrega, Horacio, 12n2
Fajans, Jane, 7–8, 106, 140
family planning. See birth: control
Fassin, Didier, 196
fava ŋan, 2, 52, 59, 136–37, 146, 178
fear of admission to hospital, 119–22, 162
feminist anthropology, 134
fertility, 35, 135, 170

fetus, 156, 202
    composition of, 169
    development/growth/nourishment of, 156, 158, 166, 167, 169–70, 172; (*see also* growth of child)
    identity of, 170, 179
    personification of, 203
fieldwork, 8, 10, 13, 15, 16, 18, 21–23, 25, 26, 70, 97n15, 98n22, 136, 201, 204
Finkler, Kaja, 5, 113
fishing, 16, 19, 20, 105, 106–7, 148, 175, 204
food
    acceptance of, 113
    accumulation of, 103
    denying of, 52, 119–17
    eating of, 107
    giving and sharing of, 11, 16, 33, 76, 87, 98n23, 104, 105, 106, 109, 111, 112, 113, 114,116, 117, 118, 124, 131, 193; (*see also* gift: of food)
    harmful, 123
    hospital, 123, 124
    and identity, 106, 108
    and illness, 16, 22, 102, 136–37
    imported and purchased, 108, 112, 123, 124
    as inalienable exchange objects, 106–7
    incorporation of place through, 106, 107, 170
    incorporation of relations through, 101, 106–7, 108–9, 113, 116, 117, 131, 132n2–3, 167,193
    insecurity, 33, 103, 129–30, 164; (*see also* hunger)
    local, 11, 16, 22, 108, 109, 124, 129
    longing for a change of, 110
    poisoning, 33
    preparation, 16, 22, 102, 103, 104, 109, 123–24
    production, 19, 103, 106, 109
    provision, 11, 23, 101, 102, 103, 113, 117, 124
    refusal of, 113
    remains, 2
    serving of, 16, 87, 111–12

Index 235

shifting routines, 63, 102, 109–11, 113–14, 132n1
supplies for patients, 112
taking of, 106
taste of/tasting, 16, 22
valued, 108
Foster, Robert J., 106
Foucault, Michel, 95, 121
"fractal person", 8–9, 131, 167, 193
Frankel, Stephen, 50, 96n4, 100
friendship, 16–17, 26n2, 67, 71, 89, 100, 115, 132n6, 184

Gaines, Atwood D., 4
Garati, 20, 68, 75, 78, 92, 98n22, 102–3, 157
garden/gardening/garden produce, 15, 16, 19, 20, 43, 51, 67, 76, 83, 91, 97n15, 103, 105, 107, 110, 113, 124, 136, 140, 149, 159, 161, 171, 172, 182, 190n21, 205n4
Gawans, 142
gendered tasks, 16, 175–76, 193
Gewertz, Deborah, 12n8
gift
    of care, 110, 130
    of food, 25, 74, 85, 106–7, 108, 112, 114, 116–17, 131
    of organs, 130
glasman. *See* shaman/shamanic medicine
Glick, Leonard B., 96n4
Goddard, Michael, 72, 93, 96n4
Government of Papua New Guinea (GoPNG), 34, 96n3
growth of child, 137, 157, 166, 167, 171, 172, 173, 174, 177–78, 185, 186, 194, 203

"habitus", 21, 24
Hagen, 8, 170, 173
Hahn, Robert A., 4, 49, 196, 197
Haiveta, Chris, 59
Hammar, Lawrence J., 205n3
Hansa Bay, 14, 18
Harris, Grace G., 7
harvest, 19, 107, 108
Hatzfeldthafen Health Center, 46n3, 60
healing, 51, 68–69, 99–100, 200

(Christian) faith, 59, 72, 73, 87, 88, 96n3, 191
    inhibition of, 61, 67, 90, 193
    practice/technique, 25, 50, 55, 72, 73, 87, 191
health delivery system, 40, 96n3
health education, 4, 31, 34, 37, 135, 156, 196
herbalist, 2–3, 96n3
herbal remedies, 1, 3, 22, 50, 51, 56, 61, 63, 70, 96n3, 153, 191
Herbst, Franziska A., 27
Herdt, Gilbert H., 97n9, 168, 189n15
Hess, Sabine C., 106
high-risk mothers, 160, 189n12
history
    of biomedical services in Giri, 13, 27
    of biomedical technologies in Giri, 53
    oral, 20
    patient's medical, 56, 58
    of shamanic medicine, 58–59
HIV/AIDS, 169, 204, 205n1, 205n3
Hogbin, Herbert I., 143
Holmes Williamson, Margaret, 137–38
Höltker, Georg, 143, 176
homebrew, 70, 75, 78, 82, 84
hospitalization, 111, 118, 136
Hua, 142
Huli, 93, 100
hunger, 33, 103, 108, 113, 129
hunting, 19, 20, 132n3, 175, 176
hygiene, 31, 83, 109, 115, 149, 187

identity. *See also* kinship: identity
    ethnic, 127
    formation, 136, 167, 170, 176, 178, 180, 185
    male, 17
    sense of, 26n4
Igos Health Sub-Center, 41, 46n3
illness
    categories, 2, 50–52, 55, 56–57, 69, 71
    episode, 50, 55, 56, 69, 72, 73, 74, 78, 80–81, 88, 90, 92, 93, 94, 100, 193
    foreign, 3, 51, 55, 62, 69, 70, 88, 198–99, 201

local, 2, 3, 50–52, 55, 57, 62, 66, 67, 69, 72, 88, 92, 198
onset of, 1,56, 60, 74, 76, 89
respiratory, 1, 2, 56, 149, 151, 156
social, 50–51, 92, 200
immunization, 31, 36–37. *See also* vaccination/vaccines
improvement of health services, 32, 40, 72, 195–96, 200
individual/individuality/individualization, 7–9, 73, 97n15, 129, 131, 136, 167, 192, 193, 203
individual names and nicknames, 71, 92, 97n15, 141, 202, 203
informal carers 109, 115, 130
Ingold, Tim, 23–24
Inhorn, Marcia C., 196, 197
initiation, 52, 135, 142, 143–44, 188n7
inpatient, 18, 32, 41, 44, 101, 102, 103, 109–114, 118, 119, 124, 126, 160, 195
  services, 31, 34, 39, 41, 46, 116, 119, 126
intersubjectivity, 23
interviews and interviewees, 17, 18, 20, 30, 40–41, 45, 56, 73, 126, 132n9, 133n11, 152, 157, 160, 183, 190n17

Janzen, John M., 99–100, 131, 202
Johannes, Adell, 143
joking relationship, 188n4
Jolly, Margaret, 155, 189n15
Jorgensen, Dan, 73
Josephides, Lisette, 12n3

Kabana, 178, 188n9
Kahn, Miriam, 168, 170–71
Kakoli, 72, 95
Kaliai, 73, 81–82, 97n12
Kamdoŋ, 190n21
Kamea, 176, 189n14, 190n21, 197
kastom, 25, 26n4, 74, 104, 164, 165, 180, 187–88
Kaufert, Patricia A., 157
Kayan, 143
Kayoma, 61, 67
Kayoma Health Sub-Center, 29, 46n3

Keck, Verena, 6–7, 26n4, 48, 49, 51, 56, 71, 96n4, 100
Kenya, 6
Keram (river), 184
Kimning, 14, 17, 18, 20, 43, 44, 63, 146, 152
kinship, 2, 100, 101, 113, 116, 117, 124–25, 132n6, 184, 193, 197
  identity, 127, 167, 170
  social, 189n14
  system, 108
  terms, 92
Kire (language), 50, 51, 57, 138, 148, 172
Kleinman, Arthur, 48–49, 72
Knauft, Bruce M., 106
Knibbe, Kim, 23, 25
knowledge, 64, 127, 142, 159, 196, 205n4
  biomedical, 4, 10, 25, 134, 191, 201, 202, 205n3
  construction and production, 10, 23, 26, 196
  cultural, 24
  indigenous/indigenous medical/indigenous procreative, 10, 58, 96, 96n3, 134, 135, 168, 179, 192, 197, 198, 200, 201
  and intellect, 71, 82–84, 203
  secret and sensitive, 13, 82
  of shamanic medicine, 58, 84
Kolo, Pearson, 93, 94
Konrad, Monica, 130
Korak, 29, 76, 127
Kukum, 104–5
Kwaio, 145
Kwanga, 135

land
  ancestral, 180
  ownership, 18
Langness, Lewis L., 148
Lattas, Andrew, 57, 73, 81–82, 93, 97n12
Laub Coser, Rose, 118
Leach, James, 178
Lelet, 104, 128, 135, 138, 140, 142, 168
Lepowsky, Maria, 100
Lewis, Gilbert, 50, 96n4

life cycle, 52, 177, 190n23
Lindstrom, Lamont, 26n4, 167
Lipset, David, 9
LiPuma, Edward, 9, 97n7, 167
Lock, Margaret, 24, 53, 136, 157, 196
Lohmann, Roger I., 57, 60
Lolo, 109, 116
Lutz, Catherine A., 71

Macfarlane, Joan, 96n2, 97n7
MacKenzie, Maureen, 172
Madang, 18, 26n1, 28, 39, 42, 58, 68, 93, 101, 161, 204
   area medical store, 42
   Provincial Health Office, 18, 34, 98n25, 118, 126, 127
   Town, 13–14, 17, 18, 33, 60, 61, 64–65, 70, 73, 74, 79, 80, 82, 83, 85, 88, 93, 97n20,98n25, 119, 122, 123, 124–26, 127, 129, 133n11, 135, 157, 162–64, 166, 185, 201
madness, 64, 70–72, 73, 75, 78, 80–81, 82, 87–92, 93, 94–95, 97n12, 150, 169
magic, 60, 78, 145–46, 151, 178
Maindroin, 58–59
Malala, 46n3, 60
malaria, 18, 31, 33, 51, 53–54, 121, 126, 155, 156
Manam Island, 14, 190n21
Marangis, 29
Marcus, George E., 21
marriage, 9, 19, 20, 78, 85, 97n18, 104, 119, 142
Marriott, McKim, 12n7
Marshall, Leslie B., 190n17
maternal health care services, 34–35, 36, 46, 136, 151, 156, 160, 196; (see also public health: services; reproductive health services)
maternal mortality. *See* death: maternal
maternal substance, 106, 137, 172, 178, 179, 193
Mauss, Marcel, 7
mediators between patients and hospital services, 11,118, 124–27, 128
medical fee, 35, 41, 47n10, 65, 70, 156–57
medicalization, 134, 136, 187

medical patrols, 27, 29, 31. *See also* mobile clinics
medical pluralism, 50, 69, 72, 94, 96n2, 99
medical records and reports, 13, 21, 31–33, 34, 35, 38, 46n5, 56, 125, 127–28, 154, 160
medical system, 4,12
   Giri, 10, 11, 48, 50, 57, 191
   imported, 58
   indigenous, 3
   local, 53, 152
   pluralistic, 94
   single, 3, 50
medical traditions, 4, 10, 48, 49, 50, 54, 191
medical training, 23, 37–38, 58, 72, 93
medicinal plant. *See* herbal remedies
Meggitt, Mervyn J., 148
Meigs, Anna S., 132n3, 142
Melpa, 7, 82, 93, 104, 172, 173
menarche, 52, 98n21, 135, 146–48. *See also* menstruation
Mendi, 128
men's house/clan platform, 17, 20, 26n3, 74, 75, 76, 91, 97n17, 104, 132n7
menstruation, 135, 137, 139, 143, 145, 146, 147, 156, 171, 190n17
Merrett-Balkos, Leanne, 172, 179, 183, 186
midwifery/midwives, 38, 96n3, 159
Mihalic, Frank, 57
Mikarip, 41, 127
millenarian movements, 81–82
Mimica, Jadran, 190n22
mind, 7, 24, 71, 145
   mind/body dichotomy, 4, 49, 71, 188n2, 192
Minung, 18, 41, 103
miscarriage, 162, 189n12
mission/missionaries, 36, 39, 46n1, 46n3, 53, 83, 87, 97n10, 98n22, 103, 135, 156, 174, 185–86, 190n21, 195
Mitchell, William E., 57
mobile clinics, 17, 18, 29, 30, 31, 32, 34, 35, 36–37, 46
mobile phones, 82, 133n11, 201–2

modernity, 9, 12n8, 73, 187
Mol, Annemarie, 49
mon mbik, 52, 146–48
Monsell-Davis, Michael, 129
Morgan, Lynn M., 203
Morris, Brian, 7
Morton, Helen, 135
Mosko, Mark S., 106
mother's brother, 61, 80, 100, 110, 143
mourning ceremony, 22
Mulemi, Benson A., 6
Müller-Rockstroh, Babette, 202
Munn, Nancy D., 142, 143, 188n3
Murik Lakes, 9
mythical ancestry, 20

natal and prenatal care, 31, 34, 37, 153, 155, 156, 158, 203
national health plan, 34, 37, 96n3
native hospital in Bogia, 103
"negotiated interactive observation", 23, 26
Nekematigi, 143
netbags, 16, 83, 102, 111, 149, 175, 178–79, 190n20
    equation with womb, 148, 172–75, 193, 203
    manufacturing of, 172–73, 174
New Melanesian Ethnography, 6, 12n3, 101
Nguyen, Vinh-Kim, 24, 53, 196
Nichter, Mark, 95, 99
"noman", 7, 82
Nombo, Porer, 178
North Coast Road, 14, 18
Nubia, 2–3, 143, 176

objectivity, 3, 23–24, 49, 54
Obrist van Eeuwijk, Brigit, 135
obstetric care, 37, 160, 187, 202
O'Hanlon, Michael, 138
"one-blood relationship", 189n14
"opacity of other minds", 8
"ordinary ailments", 51
Otto, Ton, 12n1
Ouija, 79, 95, 97n19, 194
outpatient, 18, 31, 118, 119, 126
    clinic, 29, 31, 44, 62, 125, 126–27, 195
    services, 34, 41, 46, 47n10, 119

outreach clinics. *See* mobile clinics
outreach patrols. *See* mobile clinics

Pacific War, 27, 58
Panti, Andrew P., 107
paramedical personnel, 6, 11, 45, 65, 99, 100, 101, 118, 124, 125, 130, 163, 165
partibility, 12n6, 64, 106
participant observation, 21, 22, 26
participatory (action) research, 197, 202, 205n1. *See also* public health: and anthropology
Paternoster Memorial Hospital, 27, 29–30, 51, 153, 154, 161, 182, 186, 189n11, 195
patient figures, 30, 31
permeability and impermeability, 12n6, 52, 55, 106, 107
perspectivalism, 49
phenomenology, 25
physical disorder. *See* bodily disorder
physician-patient relationship, 5, 6
pigs, 19, 68, 132n3, 149, 175, 177, 178, 179, 190n23
placenta
    discarding and incineration of, 181, 182, 184–85, 186, 194
    expulsion of/removal of/retained, 33, 152–53, 154–55, 189n12
    and growth/health/protection of child, 166, 172, 177–78, 185
    handling of, 136, 185, 186
    notions of, 166, 177, 179, 181
    terminology, 136, 172
police, 72, 80, 93–94, 117–18
population growth, 20, 35, 46n6
postmortem examinations, 55, 205n4
postpartum abdominal massages, 152, 153, 154
postpartum discharge, 135–36, 150, 163, 192
postpartum period, 11, 135, 148–49, 152, 153, 161–62, 187, 192
pragmatism, 25, 50, 59, 94, 135, 157, 162, 183
prayer/praying, 25, 50, 63, 72, 73, 87, 88–89, 90, 116, 117

pregnancy
    and body/skin, 139–40, 168
    and diabetes/anemia, 153, 156
    -induced hypertension, 156
    multiple, 156, 168, 189n12
prison, 15, 26n1, 70, 91, 104, 123, 180
procreation, 134–35, 145, 166, 167–68, 187, 189n14
pseudopatient, 23
psychiatric services, 93, 95, 194
psychiatric unit, 72, 93, 98n25
public health
    and anthropology, 197
    improvement of, 200
    interventions/measures/programs, 11, 27, 196, 205n2
    Ministry of, 196
    perspective, 197
    services, 46
    system, 96n3, 195
Puir, 18, 41
purification practices, 139, 142–43, 145, 153, 188n5, 188n7

Ramu River, 13, 17, 18, 20, 27, 41, 61, 78, 84, 97n10, 104, 105, 112–13, 149, 154, 175, 179, 180, 182, 184, 195
Rao, 58–59, 97n10
Rapp, Rayna, 203
reciprocity, 105
    of care, 11, 110, 122, 129, 130, 131, 194; (*see also* gift: of care)
    of food, 16, 105, 109, 110, 112, 133n13; (*see also* gift: of food)
    and friendship, 17
    "generalized", 128, 130
    of organs; (*see* gift: of organs)
    and wantok system, 129, 130
referral (to medical institution), 18, 30–31, 33, 54, 60, 62, 64–65, 115, 119–20, 126, 150, 162
Reite, 178
"relational-individual", 9
relationality, 6, 8–9, 10, 11, 12n6, 24, 52, 92, 95, 99, 101, 108, 109, 129, 132n3, 137, 167, 192–94, 201
"relational technologies", 95

relocation of hospital and health center, 29, 195
Rendap, Vincent, 146
Repič, Jaka, 127
reproductive health services, 11, 134, 135, 188, 192, 194–95
Rio, Knut M., 8, 70
Röntgen, Wilhelm C., 54
Roscoe, Paul, 188n3
Rumogo, 17, 195

Sabarl, 7, 106
Saethre, Eirik J., 69, 72
sago
    bamboo tubes filled with, 51–52, 56, 74, 172
    basket for rinsing pith of, 175
    bread, 77–78, 171
    coconut shell for serving, 175–76
    cooked or reheated in bamboo tube, 171
    cultural value of, 108
    grubs, 77
    harvest, 19
    leafstalks, 63, 77, 85, 89
    leaves/thatching, 56, 63, 179
    palm/seedling, 179, 180
    planting of, 107
    porridge/pudding, 63, 74, 77, 85, 101, 102, 107, 110, 112, 113, 115, 141, 171
    processing, 19
    scraper, 175
    as source of bodily strength, 107, 112–13
    stirring of, 101, 104, 110, 124
    stirring stick, 175
    swamps, 14, 18, 20, 91, 107
    work, 20, 76, 176, 193
saliva, 2, 60, 64
Schensul, Stephen L., 21
Scheper-Hughes, Nancy, 71, 136
Schieffelin, Edward L., 73, 193
Schinzel, Britta, 54–55
Schneider, Almut, 190n24
seclusion
    at male initiation, 144

menarcheal, 52, 146–47
postpartum, 11, 135–36, 140, 148–50, 151–52, 154, 155, 159, 160–64, 165–66, 171, 173,175, 176, 180, 186, 187, 188n9, 189n13, 190n20, 192
  following relative's burial, 15, 140–42
self, 7, 51, 71, 112
semen. *See* sperm
Seven, 127. *See also* aid post: in Seven
sexuality, 34, 135
sexually transmitted diseases, 31, 47n7
shadow soul, 52, 71, 97n6, 97n14, 173, 178–79
shaman/shamanic medicine, 50, 55, 57–59, 60–61, 66, 67, 70, 79, 81, 84, 92, 96n3, 100, 191
Silverman, Eric K., 168
Simbo,135
Sissano, 58
skin
  appearance of, 68, 137–39, 142, 143, 144, 151, 188n1, 204
  and food, 140–41
  meaning of, 55, 137–39
  and social relations, 137; (*see also* pregnancy: and body/skin)
  terminology, 138
Smedal, Olaf H., 8
Sobo, Elisa J., 49
sociality, 8, 12n7, 74, 98n23, 101, 104, 128, 130, 131, 132n6, 167, 189n14, 192, 194
social organization, 10, 19
social support networks, 97n20, 121, 129, 131
sorcery. *See* death: and sorcery; conflict: and sorcery
Sorcery Act, 70, 97n13
sperm, 2, 137, 155–56, 167, 168–69
spirit
  ancestral/of the dead, 48, 50, 64, 72, 73, 75, 78–80, 81, 82, 83, 85, 86, 87, 88, 90, 98n21,120, 171, 173, 190n21, 194
  bush, 25, 50, 51, 52, 69, 70, 72, 73, 75–76, 82–84, 85, 86, 87, 88, 90, 96n5, 100, 169,194, 195, 200, 203

  guardian of, 84, 85, 86
  malevolent, 63, 89
  of marijuana, 48, 87–88, 89, 91
  mediumship, 73, 84, 200
  offerings to, 83, 84, 85, 86, 87
  pacification of, 84, 85, 86, 87, 89, 90, 94, 100
  possession, 73, 76, 78, 82, 83, 85–86, 89
Spitz, Herman H., 79
sputum/sputum sample, 1, 53, 61, 62, 64, 126, 150
Stanhope, John M., 58
Stephen, Michele, 107
Stewart, Lynn L., 109, 117
Stewart, Pamela J., 7, 9, 49, 52, 64, 82, 93, 104, 132n6, 137, 145, 148, 172, 173
stillbirths, 34, 189n12
Strathern, Andrew J., 7, 9, 49, 52, 64, 71, 82, 93, 104, 132n6, 137, 138, 145, 148, 172, 173
Strathern, Marilyn, 6, 8–9, 12n7, 106, 130, 131, 132n3, 138, 167, 177
Street, Alice, 66, 95, 127
subclan. *See* clan
Sullivan, Noelle, 6
surgery, 30, 33, 36, 117, 179–80, 202
Sykes, Gresham M., 5
Sykes, Karen, 56, 135

taboo
  during breastfeeding, 143–44
  food, 52, 132n3, 140–42, 147, 163, 171, 193
  menstrual, 139, 145
  postpartum, 139, 149, 152, 155, 156, 165
  place, 51
  systems, 145
  violation, 50, 139, 146, 148, 155, 165, 171, 176, 193
Tanga, 106
Tanzania, 6, 202
technology
  biomedical, 3, 10, 11, 17, 25, 33, 48, 53–55, 57, 59, 62, 64–67, 81, 92–93, 94, 95–96,119, 125–26,

134, 135, 157, 189n11, 191, 192, 194, 197–98, 201, 202–3, 205n2
communication, 201–202; (*see also* mobile phones)
entertainment, 48, 81–82, 92–93, 95–96, 194, 201
Telban, Borut, 80, 82, 132n3, 188n2
Telefolmin, 73, 172
television. *See* technology: entertainment
Temning, 18, 29, 41
Teptep Health Center, 119
theory of practice, 24
therapy managing group, 22, 73, 95, 99–100, 101, 114, 124, 130, 131, 191, 201
tobacco/cigarettes, 2, 60, 84, 102, 129, 149
Tok Pisin, 27, 57, 97n16, 141, 190n25, 201
Tsumba, 29, 97n10
tuberculosis (TB), 33, 37, 53, 61–62, 66, 114, 126, 150, 155, 192, 198–201
Tung, 14, 17, 18, 20, 27, 91, 146, 156, 185–86, 195
Tung Aid Post, 51, 103

ultrasound. *See* technology: biomedical
umbilical cord, 165, 166, 170, 175, 176, 177, 178–79, 180, 185–86, 190n22, 193
United States, 38, 46n1, 46n6, 79, 203
urine/urine sample, 2, 156, 157
Urinebu, 58
uterus, 62, 152, 154, 172

vaccination/vaccines, 30, 34–35, 37, 155, 156
van Amstel, Hans, 127–28
Vanatinai, 100
van der Geest, Sjaak, 3, 5–6, 23, 113, 127–28, 133n12, 152, 188n10
Vanua Lava/Vanua Lavans, 106, 137
Varaning, 14, 18, 63, 75, 83, 97n17, 114, 115, 116, 117, 119
Vaughan, Catherine M., 205n1
Vávrová, Daniela, 82
Versteeg, Peter, 23, 25
village settlement, 10
vital energy, 64, 71

von Poser, Alexis T., 143
von Poser, Anita, 7, 107, 131, 143
vulnerability, 78, 100

Wagner, Roy, 6, 7, 8–9, 23–24, 26n2, 131, 167, 168, 173
Wahgi, 138
wantok, 101, 127–29, 131, 193
ward
  delivery/obstetric/labor, 41, 120, 159, 162, 164, 188, 202
  eye, 120
  general medical, 30, 32, 41, 93, 119, 122, 126, 160, 162
  gynecological, 120, 159, 162, 165–66, 187, 188
  maternity, 30, 41, 161, 195
  orthopedic, 6
  pediatric, 22, 30, 47n10, 120, 123, 202
  surgical, 120
Warlpiri, 69
Wassmann, Jürg, 71, 168
White, Geoffrey M., 26n4
Whyte, Susan R., 152
Wind, Gitte, 23
Wogeo, 16, 104, 106–7, 143
Wokam, 29
womanhood, 17
World Health Organization (WHO), 34, 62, 46n6, 96n3
World Vision, 38, 154
worship practice, 25, 85
"writing culture" debate, 23

X-ray. *See* technology: biomedical

yam, 103, 107, 112, 124, 132n1, 172
  cultural value of, 108
  dish, 14, 83, 87, 107
  gardens, 19, 67, 107
  harvest, 107
  tabooed, 140, 171; (*see also* taboo: food)
Yupno, 26n4, 97n6, 119, 142

Zaman, Shahaduz, 6, 109, 113, 118–19
Zola, Irving K., 134

www.ingramcontent.com/pod-product-compliance
Lightning Source LLC
Chambersburg PA
CBHW070917030426
42336CB00014BA/2454